Table of Contents

Introduction

Learning Web Page Design with Dreamweaver CS3 works alongside you to help build the exciting, changing, and interactive Web sites that today's information-driven world demands from businesses, governments, schools, and virtually every organization that needs to communicate.

WHAT THIS BOOK IS ABOUT

Learning Web Page Design with Dreamweaver CS3 is written for beginning Web page designers. The book assumes the reader has a working knowledge of the Internet, basic design elements, and common Windows navigation.

WHO SHOULD READ THIS BOOK?

This book is for everyone who needs to know how to add solid design and interactivity to his or her Web site. You can use this book as an exercise-by-exercise tutorial on many Dreamweaver features or refer to it on an as-needed topical basis.

You should read this book if you need to design, manage, and modify a Web site and want to learn how to add interactive and advanced elements to its pages.

WHAT YOU NEED

To gain the most from this book, you will need:

- Knowledge of fundamental Windows navigation and terminology.

- Intel® Pentium® 4, Intel Centrino®, Intel Xeon®, or Intel Core™ Duo (or compatible) processor.

- Microsoft® Windows® XP with Service Pack 2 or Windows Vista™ Home Premium, Business, Ultimate, or Enterprise (certified for 32-bit editions).

- 512MB of RAM.

- 1GB of available hard-disk space (additional free space required during installation).

- 1,024 x 768 monitor resolution with 16-bit video card.

- Dreamweaver CS3 (and other Creative Suite applications if available such as Photoshop and Fireworks).

- An Internet browser such as Microsoft Internet Explorer, Netscape, Mozilla, or Mozilla Firefox that supports multimedia, animation, and advanced interactive features.

- For the best results, Microsoft Internet Explorer 6.0 or 7.0 should be used.

HOW THIS BOOK IS ORGANIZED

This book is organized into seven lessons that begin with Web site basics and then move to advanced features.

- **Lesson 1—Get Started with Dreamweaver.** This lesson introduces the program and its workspace. You learn how to start and exit the program and create a new site using the Site Definition wizard. You also learn how to create and save Web pages and view site files. Finally, you are introduced to HTML structure and syntax and the importance of adding keywords to a site. You learn how to add text to a Web page and view page content in both Design and Code views, as well as how to switch from one Dreamweaver site to another.

- **Lesson 2—Work with Web Page Text and Links.** This lesson focuses on creating Web page text content. It discusses how to enter text and import text from Microsoft Office documents, as well as how to find and replace text, check spelling, and insert special characters. You learn how to format text in many ways: change text fonts, sizes, styles, and colors; change text alignment; and create lists. You explore the Dreamweaver Code view and other options for viewing and modifying HTML and other kinds of Web page code. You also learn how to use the History panel to repeat or undo tasks. This lesson introduces links, the means by which visitors navigate a Web site. You learn how to create relative links within a site, absolute links to other sites, links to named anchors on a page, and links to e-mail addresses. You preview your site files in a browser, explore the new Device Central interface for viewing files in mobile devices, learn more about the Files panel's expanded window, and learn how to view and modify the site map.

- **Lesson 3—Work with Graphic Elements and Templates.** This lesson explores Dreamweaver's graphic capabilities. You are introduced to Adobe Bridge, an application that makes it easy to organize graphic files. You add horizontal rules, apply background colors and images, and insert images on Web pages using accessibility options. You also learn how to modify image size, position an image so text wraps around it, and edit a graphic from within Dreamweaver. You insert a Photoshop image directly on a page and explore options for optimizing the image. You learn how to create rollover images that change when the mouse pointer rolls over the graphic or navigation bar. You create image maps that contain hotspots to link pages in a site. You create and use a template to give pages a consistent look. After you store items in the Library, you insert them throughout the Web site. You also learn how to create design notes for pages in the site.

- **Lesson 4—Work with Tables and Forms.** This lesson introduces you to tables, which can be used to organize information or an entire Web page. You create and format a table to hold data on a page and structure a Web page using Dreamweaver's Layout mode features. You also learn how to import tabular data into a table, sort table content, and insert table-related tags. This lesson introduces forms, and you have the opportunity to create an accessible form by inserting various types of form fields: text boxes, radio buttons, checkboxes, list-menu boxes, and buttons. Then you learn how to connect to a database to store form results and create a recordset to display dynamic data from a database.

- **Lesson 5—Work with AP Elements, Frames, and Styles.** Dreamweaver AP elements include absolutely positioned objects and AP divs that can hold any HTML content. You learn how to create, resize, position, and format AP divs to add visual impact to a page. This lesson shows you how to create frames on a Web page to open specific Web page content. You learn how to set up and modify frames in a frameset and how to specify target frames for links. Finally, you explore styles and style sheets, used to apply consistent formats throughout a Web site. You learn how to create internal styles and an external style sheet that can be applied to all pages in a site.

- **Lesson 6—Create Dynamic and Interactive Pages.** You begin this lesson by exploring the new Spry framework that allows you to insert interactive elements on Web pages. Spry Validation widgets, menu bars, and collapsible panels enhance Web pages and make them more useful as well. Behaviors are actions that occur when visitors interact with a Web page. In this lesson, you learn how to apply some of Dreamweaver's commonly used behaviors to specific events. This lesson also introduces the multimedia capabilities of Dreamweaver and shows you how to insert, modify, and view Flash movies. You also learn how to create Flash buttons and Flash text right in the Dreamweaver workspace.

■ **Lesson 7—Manage and Publish a Web Site.** This lesson explores some regular site maintenance operations, such as testing a site using one or more target browsers, checking and modifying links, and running various kinds of reports that can help you make your site more accessible and locate problems such as untitled documents. You explore Dreamweaver's Validator feature, which helps you locate tag and syntax errors in your HTML code. You also learn how to put (publish) files on an FTP, WebDAV, or local server and how to use the Check In/Out feature to control access to sites maintained by a team.

■ **Capstone Project.** This comprehensive final project takes students through the process of creating a new Web site for a country inn, providing content for the pages, formatting content, and completing the process by running reports and publishing the site.

■ **Appendix A—Dreamweaver Preferences.** Dreamweaver enables you to customize the environment in a number of ways using the Preferences dialog box. This appendix explores the many user settings and provides guidance on changing them.

Learning Web Page Design with Dreamweaver CS3 is designed to make your learning experience easy and enjoyable. Lessons are comprised of short exercises designed to help you learn how to use Dreamweaver CS3 in real-life business settings. Every application exercise is made up of seven key elements:

■ **Software Skills.** Each exercise starts with a brief description of how you would use the features of that exercise in the workplace.

■ **Application Skills.** A scenario is set to put the Dreamweaver features into context.

■ **Terms.** Key terms are included and defined at the start of each exercise, so you can quickly refer back to them. The terms are then highlighted in the text.

■ **Notes.** Concise notes aid in learning the computer concepts.

■ **Procedures.** Hands-on mouse and keyboard procedures teach all necessary skills.

■ **Application Exercise.** Step-by-step instructions put your skills to work.

■ **On Your Own.** Each exercise concludes with a critical thinking activity that you can work through on your own. You are frequently challenged to provide your own Web page content. The "On Your Own" sections can be used as additional reinforcement, for practice, or to test skill proficiency.

Enhanced End-of-Lesson material puts skills to the test:

■ **Summary Exercise.** Comprehensive exercises that touch on most skills covered in the lesson. Step-by-step directions guide you through the exercises.

■ **Application Exercise.** The level of difficulty starts to ramp up with the application exercises. These summary exercises do not contain detailed steps.

■ **Curriculum Integration Exercise.** Integrate other subject areas into the computer course with the curriculum integration exercises. Topics include math, English, social studies, and science.

■ **Critical Thinking Exercise.** These challenging exercises are scenario-based—no specific steps are given.

In addition, **E-Commerce Connections** throughout the book encourage students to learn about the electronic marketplace, and **Dreamweaver IN DEPTH** activities introduce students to more-advanced skills and activities.

WORKING WITH DATA AND SOLUTION FILES

As you work through the exercises in this book, you'll be creating, opening, and saving files. You should keep the following instructions in mind:

■ You will create much of the content of your Web sites on your own, but a number of data files are included to provide specific types of Web site content, such as images, multimedia objects, and page text that would be time consuming to type.

■ When the application or On Your Own exercise includes a file name and a CD icon ⊙, you can open the file provided on the CD that accompanies this book.

■ The Directory of Files lists the exercise file (from the CD-ROM) you need to complete each exercise. Unless the book instructs otherwise, use the default settings when creating a file.

■ Make sure you save all new materials to the Web site you are currently working on.

COPY DATA FILES

You can copy data files from the CD-ROM to a hard drive.

1. Open Windows Explorer. (Right-click the ![start] button and click Explore.)

2. Be sure that the CD is in your CD-ROM drive. Select the CD-ROM drive letter from the All Folders pane of the Explorer window.

3. Click to select the Data folder in the Contents of (CD-ROM drive letter) pane of the Explorer window.

4. Drag the folder onto the letter of the drive to which you wish to copy the data files (usually C:) in the All Folders pane of the Explorer window.

USE THE WINDOWS IIS WEB SERVER

If you are running the Windows 2000, XP Professional, or Vista operating system, you can publish your Web sites to the IIS personal Web server available on those operating systems.

For more information on installing the personal Web server, consult Help (Start>Help). Search for IIS and click the topic IIS Installation. You use the Add/Remove Windows Programs feature to install IIS components. You may need your Windows CD to install this feature.

DIRECTORY OF DATA FILES ON CD

EXERCISE NUMBER	FILE NAME
Exercise 1	01/garden/index.html
Exercise 8	newtext.doc testimonials.html indextext.doc location.html
Exercise 10	services.html DID_write.html DID_read.html
Exercise 11	events.html
Exercise 13	membership.html memberform.doc
Exercise 17	people.html
Exercise 18	CinciTorial_logo.gif JHorner.jpg CPreston.psd TMeadows.jpg daylily.jpg daffodils.jpg DID_mountain.psd DID_lake.psd

EXERCISE NUMBER	FILE NAME
Exercise 39	index.html products.html
Exercise 41	shadow.jpg
Exercise 42	locationover.gif locationup.gif showover.gif showup.gif findover.gif findup.gif
Exercise 45	faqs.html forums.html news.html support.html DID45.xml
Exercise 46	expopub.html bertha_richards.jpg
Exercise 47	divback.gif
Exercise 48	cinci_flash.swf intro.html gardenmovie.swf DID48.html vinferno.class
Exercise 50	grandmovie.swf
Capstone Project	butterfly.psd deepanimation.swf deer.jpg driving.html flower.jpg gorge.jpg lake.jpg map.jpg waterfall.jpg welcome.doc

Lesson | 1

Get Started with Dreamweaver

Exercise | 1

Skills Covered

- About Adobe Dreamweaver CS3
- Start Dreamweaver
- Open a Web Page
- Dreamweaver Workspace
- Work with Panels and Panes
- Close and Exit Dreamweaver

Software Skills Dreamweaver has many innovative features to make designing, creating, editing, managing, and publishing your new Web site easier and more intuitive.

Application Skills In this exercise, you will learn how to open a site and then explore the Dreamweaver workspace to become familiar with menus, toolbars, and panels.

TERMS

Expander arrow The small arrow icon at the bottom right of the Property inspector that, when clicked, enlarges the panel to reveal additional properties.

Floating panel Dreamweaver container for tools and properties that is undocked and can be repositioned anywhere in the workspace or closed if desired.

Insert bar A toolbar in the Dreamweaver window that shows tabs or categories from which to insert objects into a Web page, including graphics, text features, tables, multimedia objects, etc.

Object Element such as a form, image, or multimedia file added to a Web page.

Panel Dreamweaver container for tools and properties that is integrated into the Dreamweaver window either alone or as part of a panel group. Panels can be undocked and repositioned anywhere in the workspace or closed if desired.

Property Object characteristic that defines the value, appearance, and state.

Property inspector Dreamweaver panel that displays properties for the currently selected object.

Web page A single file in a collection of files that make up a Web site.

Web site A collection of Web pages and other objects such as images that are linked to create a resource dedicated to a particular subject.

Workspace In Dreamweaver, the desktop area in which the Document window and panels appear.

NOTES

About Adobe Dreamweaver CS3

- Adobe Dreamweaver has been one of the most widely used Web site design programs for many years. Combining sophisticated design tools with an easy-to-use interface, Dreamweaver makes it simple for anyone to create and manage many types of Web sites.

- Dreamweaver offers design environments friendly to both new and experienced designers. A new user does not have to be HTML literate to create a Web site in Dreamweaver. Dreamweaver's Design view and Code and Design view interfaces allow a user to create pages using familiar word processing–type tools to format text and insert images.

- For designers who customarily work directly in HTML, Dreamweaver's Code view and many code features speed the process of inserting and troubleshooting HTML code.

- For designers who are familiar with cascading style sheet (CSS) formatting, Dreamweaver's integrated CSS panel enables them to create, apply, and manage CSS styles almost effortlessly. The new Spry framework combines HTML, CSS, and JavaScript to create a number of interactive and dynamic features that can really spark up a Web page.

- Using Dreamweaver, it is easier than ever to construct a Web site and manage files. For example, a designer can now modify image files right in Dreamweaver rather than have to work in an outside graphics program. Integration with Adobe Photoshop allows a designer to insert Photoshop images directly onto a Web page and then edit the image if desired in Photoshop. Improved and expanded templates allow a designer to create many types of pages and apply cascading style sheets at the same time.

- Dreamweaver CS3 also allows a designer to preview files not only in a number of browsers but in simulated mobile devices.

- You will learn about these features and many more as you work through this course.

Start Dreamweaver

- Start Dreamweaver by clicking the **start** button on the Windows taskbar, clicking All Programs, and navigating to the folder that contains Dreamweaver CS3.

Dreamweaver Welcome Screen

Dw
ADOBE® DREAMWEAVER® CS3

Open a Recent Item
- Open...

Create New
- HTML
- ColdFusion
- PHP
- ASP VBScript
- XSLT (Entire page)
- CSS
- JavaScript
- XML
- Dreamweaver Site...
- More...

Create from Samples
- CSS Style Sheet
- Frameset
- Starter Page (Theme)
- Starter Page (Basic)
- More...

Extend
- Dreamweaver Exchange »

- **Getting Started »**
- New Features »
- Resources »

Dw **Get the most out of Dreamweaver**
Find the latest tips, podcasts, and more in Adobe Bridge.

- Don't show again

✔ *The folder name will depend on whether Dreamweaver is installed as a standalone product or as part of the Creative Suite 3 Web Standard or Premium set of applications.*

▪ Click the folder and then Adobe Dreamweaver CS3 on the pop-out submenu to open the Dreamweaver workspace.

▪ Dreamweaver opens the Welcome Screen shown in the illustration on the previous page. In this screen, you can choose to open an item you have recently worked on; create a new page or site from scratch; or create a new page from sample style sheets, framesets, or page designs. For Dreamweaver novices, the Starter pages offer simple, attractive designs that can be customized to create a wide variety of Web sites.

▪ Click the Dreamweaver Exchange option to jump to a site where you can buy or download programs designed to extend Dreamweaver's usefulness. This is the place to go to find customized navigation buttons, table layouts, and scripts that perform various functions.

▪ If you are new to Dreamweaver, you may want to use the options at the lower left of the dialog box to take a tour or run a tutorial to help you get up to speed.

Open a Web Page

▪ When Dreamweaver starts, it automatically opens the **Web site** that was active the last time the program was used. For each Web site you intend to create or work with in Dreamweaver, you must define the Web site so that Dreamweaver knows where to locate the site files.

✔ *You will learn how to create a site in the next exercise.*

▪ You can open any Web page in Dreamweaver, even if you have not created a site related to the page. A **Web page** is a single file in a Web site, usually devoted to one part of the Web site's topic.

▪ To open a Web page from the Start page, click 📁 Open... . Or, at any time during a Dreamweaver session, use the File>Open command to display the Open dialog box, shown in the illustration above.

▪ This dialog box will look familiar to anyone who has worked with Windows programs. Navigate to the location of the Web page to open, select it, and click [Open] to display the page in Dreamweaver.

▪ The [Site Root] button in the lower-left corner of the Open dialog box allows you to open the root folder of the current Dreamweaver site without having to navigate through a number of folders.

Default Dreamweaver CS3 workspace

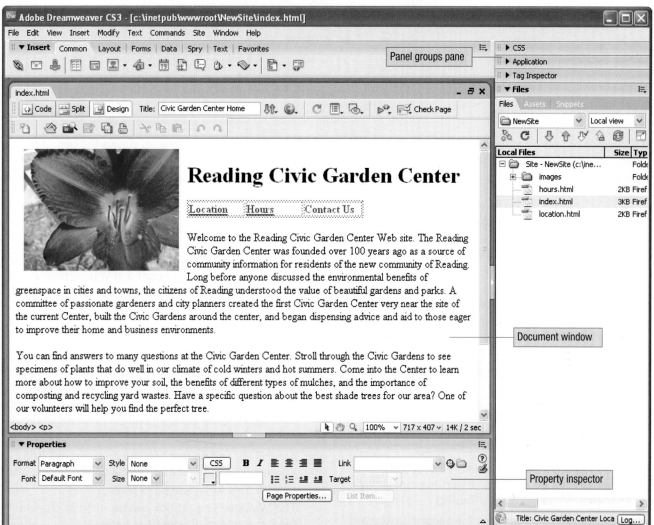

Dreamweaver Workspace

- Dreamweaver files are created and saved from the **workspace**. The Dreamweaver workspace is divided into several sections, as shown in the illustration above.

- The largest area in the workspace is the Document window. Use the Document window to create page content.

- The **panel** at the bottom of the screen named Properties is known as the **Property inspector** because it allows the user to look at the settings, or properties, for the currently selected object. You will use this panel constantly in the course of creating and modifying Web pages.

- The pane at the right side of the screen contains a number of other panel groups. By default, only the Files panel group is open, as shown in the previous illustration.

- The workspace also contains a menu bar, a status bar, and two toolbars that provide easy access to commonly used tools: the Insert bar and the Document toolbar. You will learn more about parts of the workspace in the following sections.

Property Inspector

- The Property inspector displays the properties of the element you select. Dreamweaver considers a **property** to be an HTML or other Web code characteristic, such as alignment or size, that you can assign to an element—such as a text paragraph or a picture—in your project.

- Use the Property inspector to select formats and position items precisely to ensure a consistent look on all pages in a Web site.

- Properties displayed in the Property inspector depend on what item is currently selected in the document. The following illustration shows HTML properties for a heading.

Property inspector showing properties for a heading

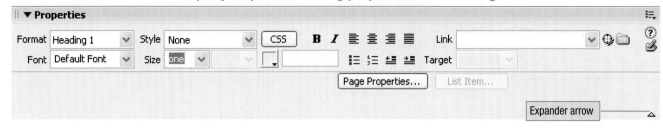

The most common properties are displayed in the panel's fields. If your monitor is large enough, you will see all available fields, as shown in the previous illustration. On a smaller monitor, you may need to click the **expander arrow** at the lower-right corner of the inspector to display additional fields.

Insert Bar and Document Toolbar

- The **Insert bar** (see the first illustration below) is a toolbar divided into tabs or categories that contain buttons for creating Web page objects. **Objects** are elements added to a Web page. Forms, images, animation files, sound files, and so on are objects.

- The Insert bar displays the Common tab's buttons by default. To display buttons for other tabs, click the tab name.

  ✔ *The Insert bar's tabs can also be displayed as a menu by clicking the Options menu at the far right of the toolbar and selecting Show as Menu.*

- To identify a button on the Insert bar, rest the mouse pointer on the tool. Dreamweaver displays the name of the button in a ToolTip.

- The Document toolbar (see the second illustration below) displays in the Document window directly above the window's contents. The toolbar displays Code, Split, and Design buttons that you can use to toggle between Code view, Code and Design view, and Design view. You will learn more about these and other view options later in the course.

- The Document toolbar also shows the title of the current page and gives easy access to tools that allow the user to check browser compatibility, preview the page, and modify how page content displays.

- Dreamweaver also offers a Standard toolbar with tools for creating new pages; saving; and cutting, copying, and pasting. This toolbar does not display by default, but it is very useful. If your screen is large enough, you may want to display this toolbar all the time.

Status Bar

- Every Web page document features a status bar underneath it (see the third illustration below) that displays information about the Web page, such as the type of coding it contains, the window size, and how long it takes to download on different kinds of modem and broadband connections.

- The HTML coding symbols such as <body> and <p> are also buttons that can be used to select the objects they are associated with.

- The Window Size list box can be used to change the window size of your Web page.

- The default connection speed at which your Web pages are downloaded by users is 56kbps. You can change the connection speed shown in the status bar by clicking Edit>Preferences>Status Bar and selecting the desired connection speed in the Connection speed list box.

Insert bar showing Common tab

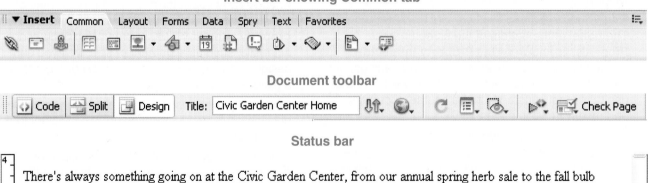

Document toolbar

Status bar

Work with Panels and Panes

- Dreamweaver opens with the panel groups you need to begin creating a Web page. (The panels that you see depend on what panels were open during Dreamweaver's last session and any changes made to the default Preference settings.)

- A *panel group* contains several related panels. For example, the Files panel group contains the Files panel, the Assets panel, and the Snippets panel. To switch from one panel to another in a group, simply click the panel's tab.

- Panel groups can be opened and closed as you require. To open a panel group, click the expander arrow (the small black triangle to the left of the panel name) so that it points downward. To close a panel group, click the expander arrow so that it points to the right.

- You can drag a panel group away from its default location by clicking on the ⣿ gripper in the panel group's title bar. The mouse pointer becomes a four-headed arrow. Hold down the mouse button to drag the panel group to a new location. If you leave the panel group undocked in the workspace, you have created a **floating panel** group.

  ✔ *Floating panel groups are helpful when you want to view the contents of several panels at the same time.*

- You can return the panel group to its previous position in a pane by dragging it by the gripper until a heavy black bar or outline displays. When you release the mouse button, the panel group docks at the location of the black bar or outline.

- To access additional options for an open panel group, click its ▤ Options menu to display a drop-down menu. Commands on the Options menu always include an option to close the panel group.

- The panes that contain panel groups—the pane at the bottom of the screen that contains the Property inspector and the pane at the right of the screen that contains the CSS, Tag Inspector, and other panel groups—can be hidden to allow more room on the screen for the Document window. To show or hide these panes, use the Collapse/Expand button attached to the pane. This button can be horizontal, such as this one ⃞▼⃞ that is attached to the Property inspector, or vertical, such as the one for the right panel group pane.

- Floating panel groups and the Document window can be closed by clicking the ⊠ or ✖ Close button.

- Dreamweaver "remembers" the workspace setup from its last session. If you close panels, they will not display when you next start Dreamweaver. To open a panel that has been closed, select the name of the panel from the Window menu.

- If you work frequently with the same panels and want an easy way to display them, you can save a workspace layout. Open and position the panels where you want them and then issue the Window>Workspace Layout>Save Current command. Provide a name for the layout. It will then appear at the top of the list of default layouts on the Workspace Layout submenu.

Close and Exit Dreamweaver

- After completing work on a Web page or site, close all open documents and then exit Dreamweaver. You can use File menu commands to close documents and exit the program or use the ⊠ Close button in the program's title bar.

E-Commerce Connection

About E-Commerce
E-commerce is the process of buying or selling products or services online. E-commerce has come a long way from its origin in banner ads on fledgling Web sites

Investigate E-Commerce
Use the Internet to search for information on the origins and development of e-commerce. Write a report in which you summarize the evolution, characteristics, and purpose of e-commerce.

PROCEDURES

Start Dreamweaver

1. Click **start** on the Windows taskbar.
2. Click **All Programs** . . . . . . Ⓟ
3. Click the folder that contains Dreamweaver.
4. Click **Adobe Dreamweaver CS3**.

Open a Web Page (Ctrl + O)

1. Click 📁 Open... on the Welcome Screen.

   OR

   a. Click **File** . . . . Alt)+Ⓕ
   b. Click **Open** . . . . Ⓞ, ↵Enter)
2. Click the **Look in** arrow . . . . Alt)+Ⓘ, →)
3. Select the drive or folder.

   ✔ *If necessary, double-click folder name.*

4. Click a file name to select it.
5. Click [**Open**].

Open a Panel

▪ Click the expander arrow to the left of the panel group name to point downward.

Close a Panel

▪ Click the expander arrow to the left of the panel group name to point to the right.

   OR

▪ Click the panel group's 🗏 Options menu and click **Close panel group**.

   OR

▪ Click **Close** button ☒ in the panel group or inspector.

Move Panels

1. Click the ⠿ grabber in the panel title bar.
2. While holding down the mouse button, drag the panel (or panel group) to new location.

Hide/Show All Panels (F4)

1. Click **View** . . . . Alt)+Ⓥ
2. Click **Hide/Show Panels** . . Ⓟ

Close a Document (Ctrl + W)

1. Click **File** . . . . Alt)+Ⓕ
2. Click **Close**. . . . . Ⓒ

   ✔ *Click Yes or No as desired if asked to save the document.*

Exit Dreamweaver (Ctrl + Q)

1. Click **File** . . . . Alt)+Ⓕ
2. Click **Exit** . . . . Ⓧ

   OR

▪ Click **Close** button ☒ in the Dreamweaver title bar.

EXERCISE DIRECTIONS

1. Start Dreamweaver.
2. Open a Web page as follows:
   ▪ Issue a command to open a file in Dreamweaver.
   ▪ Navigate to the location of the Data files for this course.
   ▪ Open the **Lesson01** folder.
   ▪ Open the **01garden** folder.
   ▪ Select and open the **index.html** file.

   ✔ *This Web page is the home page for a Web site under construction. Note that, depending on your computer's settings, you may not see the .html extension.*

3. Locate the following items in the workspace:
   ▪ Document window
   ▪ Menu bar
   ▪ Insert bar
   ▪ Document toolbar
   ▪ Property inspector

   ✔ *If some of these items are not displayed in the workspace, open them from the Window or View menu.*

4. Click in the *Reading Civic Garden Center* heading and view the properties shown for this heading in the Property inspector. Also notice the HTML tags for the heading in the status bar.
5. Collapse the Property inspector and all panels at the right side of the screen.
6. Use the Window menu to open the Property inspector. Use the Collapse/Expand button to redisplay the panels at the right side of the screen.
7. Rearrange the workspace by dragging the Property inspector into the Document window and docking the Files panel at the bottom of the Property inspector.
8. Drag and redock both the Property inspector and Files panel in their original positions.
9. Close the current document without saving it and exit Dreamweaver.

ON YOUR OWN

1. Start Dreamweaver.

2. In the Welcome Screen, locate the file you opened in the Exercise Directions, 01garden/index.html.

3. Explore this simple Web site as follows:

   - On the Document toolbar, locate the button that allows you to preview/debug the current page in the browser.

   - Select your browser from the list.

   - Use the links below the heading to navigate from page to page in the site. (The Contact Us link has not yet been set up, so don't try that one.)

   - Close the browser when you have finished testing the site.

4. View the different tabs of buttons available for the Insert bar.

5. Click in the *Location* link below the main heading and view the properties for this object in the Property inspector and the status bar.

   ✔ *Note that this and the other links are inserted in table cells. You will learn how to use tables to organize Web page objects in Lesson 4.*

6. Open each of the panel groups in the right pane to see what kind of information displays in each.

7. Close the current document and exit Dreamweaver.

Exercise | 2

Skills Covered

- **Create a New Site**
- **Create Web Pages**
- **View Site Files**
- **Web Design Guidelines**

Software Skills Correctly setting up your Web site is crucial in Dreamweaver. You might be tempted to skip this step and begin building your pages right away. But you should take time to set up a Web site folder and the Web site itself so that later in the development process you can use the site management features effectively.

Application Skills In this exercise, you will set up a site for CinciTorial, an editorial services company. You will define the site, create several new Web pages for the site, and then view the site files using the Files panel.

TERMS

Browser A program that works with an Internet connection to display pages located on the World Wide Web. Internet Explorer, Firefox, Netscape, Opera, and Safari are examples of popular Web browsers.

Home page The first page displayed when a Web site is accessed.

Remote server A server, such as an FTP or WebDAV server, on which you put or publish your Web site; it is typically the server from which your Web site's visitors see and interact with your finished Web site.

NOTES

Create a New Site

- Setting up a new Web site in Dreamweaver is an automated multistep process in which you name your site and its folder, choose an application server, and specify a location in which to store the site folder for your Web site. It is important that all materials you create for the Web site reside together in the site folder so that the pages will display properly in the browser.

- If you know the settings required to publish the Web site, you can configure the site as you create it.

- You will find it helpful to plan your Web site before you begin the process of creating its pages. Take the time to prepare your site *mentally* and consider how the site will grow.

  ✔ *You can start small, with only a single page in your Web site. Dreamweaver makes it easy to expand an existing site.*

However, anticipating such items as growth factors, layout changes, and merging company images and ideals will result in the most efficient and professional use of the Dreamweaver tools.

- The quickest way to define your Web site is to open Dreamweaver and click the ⚏ Dreamweaver Site... option in the Welcome Screen. If you are already working in Dreamweaver, click the Site>New Site menu command.

- Either action opens the Site Definition dialog box shown in the following illustration. By default, the Basic tab is selected. Following the Basic steps is the most streamlined way to set up a site. If you know more about site settings and server setup, you may want to switch to the Advanced tab to supply that information.

Site Definition wizard—naming the site

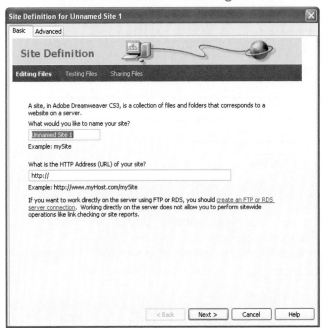

- The Editing Files screen is the first step in the process of defining the site. Here you give your site a name in the *What would you like to name your site?* text box. If you know the URL of your site, you can supply it in this dialog box. Then click Next to move to the next screen as you complete your entries.

  ✔ *At any point as you work your way through the Site Definition wizard, you can click the Back button to return to a previous wizard screen.*

- As you choose a name for your Web site, consider where you intend to publish the Web site. Most Web servers use UNIX-based operating systems and have specific limitations for file names.

- If you have verified that your ISP or Web server is UNIX-based, remember these file-naming rules for the site names, page names, and the names used for other objects that the server stores:

  - The underscore (_) is the only special character allowed.
  - No spaces are allowed.
  - UNIX file names are case sensitive. As a general rule, use lowercase for page and other object files.

- Recognizing these rules before designing your site will save you hours of frustration that can result if you use names your server will not recognize.

Select a Server Technology

- In the Editing Files, Part 2 screen, you have the option of selecting a server technology. If your site will feature a Web application such as a form for entering data, you can select the desired server

technology to support different kinds of dynamic (interactive) content.

- If you are not sure, you can select No. You can change this option at any time later by editing your site definition.

- If you know the server technology that you will use, select Yes and then select the desired server technology from the drop-down list (see the following illustration).

Selecting a server technology

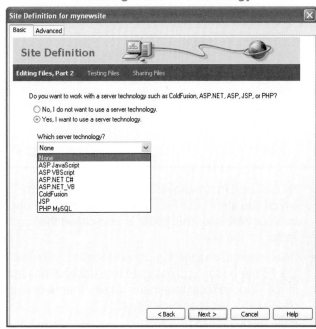

✔ *Ask your teacher, Web server administrator, or ISP what server technology you should choose for a new site.*

Where to Store Your Web Site

- In the third screen, Editing Files, Part 3, you can select how you want to work with your files. You can choose to store your Web folder and files locally on your hard drive.

- You can also choose to create and edit your Web site on a remote server.

- As suggested in the introduction to this book, you will probably want to create your Web site locally, taking advantage of the IIS Web server software that can be installed in operating systems such as Windows XP and Windows Vista.

- Dreamweaver detects the presence of this software on your hard drive and may automatically select it in the *Where on your computer do you want to store your files?* text box (see the following illustration).

Selecting a storage location

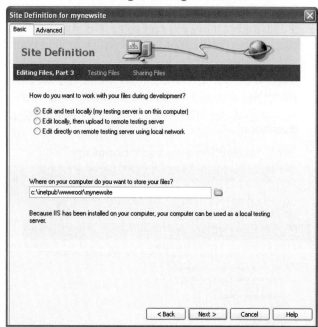

Setting a root URL

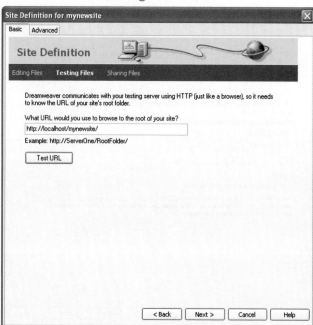

- By default, Dreamweaver will name the folder in which you store your files with the name you chose for your Web site. This folder is also called the *root folder* for the site.

- If you want to change the default location, click the 📁 Folder button and navigate to a desired location in the Choose local root folder for site [name of site] dialog box, and then click Select.

- If you select an FTP or RDS server, you will need additional information from your network administrator, ISP, or other site provider to set up the FTP host, host directory, login, and password.

  ✔ *FTP techniques and requirements are discussed in Lesson 7.*

Test Your Web Site

- If you selected a server technology, you will also see the Testing Files screen of the Site Definition wizard. You can select the URL (the Web address your browser uses) to open the Web site for testing purposes.

- The default choice for the URL is the name of the local or remote host and the root folder in which you have stored your files (see the following illustration).

- Typically, you will want to keep the URL provided by Dreamweaver. You should also take this opportunity to test it.

- Click the [Test URL] button. If the test is successful, a message box will appear. If it is unsuccessful, you will need to consult with your teacher, network administrator, or ISP to obtain the correct URL, which you can enter in the *What URL would you use to browse to the root of your site?* text box.

  ✔ *If you did not enter an HTTP address for the site in the first Site Definition window, you may receive a warning message that the URL you specify in the Testing Files window does not match the HTTP address. You can ignore this warning while defining the site.*

Select a Remote Server

- In the next screen of the Site Definition wizard, you can select the option for setting up your **remote server** site (see the following illustration). This is the server where your published Web will be accessed by the production team working collaboratively on your Web site—or the actual server where Internet (or intranet) users access the site with their Web browsers.

**A remote server is where
users will browse your site**

In the Sharing Files, Part 2 screen, click the *How do you connect to your remote server?* list box arrow and select the type of remote server that you will use to put ("publish") your Web site (see the following illustration).

Select your remote server

Many Internet Web sites are stored on FTP servers. Choosing the FTP option displays the screen shown in the previous illustration.

After you enter the appropriate information for an FTP remote site—including any login name and password—you can test the connection by clicking the [Test Connection] button.

For a Local/Network remote site, you can enter the file path or click the 📁 Folder button and navigate to the desired location in the Choose remote root folder for site [name of site] dialog box.

For a Local/Network remote site, click the checkbox next to *Refresh remote file list automatically* if you want an automatic file update every time you copy files into your Web site. This feature requires only a small amount of resources and is a valuable tool for keeping your site up to date.

These are the common remote connection types that are covered in this course. Consult Dreamweaver Help to learn about the other types of remote connections.

✔ *You will learn more about making a remote server connection in Lesson 7.*

Check In/Check Out Feature

In the Sharing Files, Part 3 screen, the check in/out option allows you to set up procedures so that no member of a Web design team can edit a file at the same time as another member. When you select the *Yes, enable check in and check out* option, all team members can see files that are checked out by a team member (and also see who is working on the file).

When you open a file, you can have Dreamweaver check it out (the default option) or enter the name you want to display when the file is checked out in the *What is your name?* text box (see the following illustration). You can also add your e-mail address so that other members of the team can communicate with you when a file is checked out.

Enabling the check in/out feature

Finish the Site Setup

- The Summary screen in the Site Definition wizard lists the local and remote information about your Web site as well as other options that you have selected (see the following illustration). Review these options and change any if necessary by clicking the Back button to return to the desired tab. If you are finished defining your site, click [Done].

Summary of a newly created Web site

- The new site—shown as a green folder—is listed in the Files panel in the panel group on the right side of the screen by default (see the following illustration). This panel's window is the hub of file management, and you will use it many times as you design your site.

Files panel for new Web site

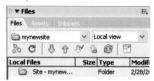

Create Web Pages

- Your Web site content appears on documents stored within the site. These documents become the Web pages that visitors open when the Web site is put (or published) on a Web server.

- You can create new Web pages from the Welcome Screen if you have no other pages open in a site. Select a type of page from the Create New section. You will probably choose the HTML option most often to open a blank page that uses XHTML coding to display page elements. Some types of Web content, such as dynamic page content, require other page options.

- You can also choose to create a new page based on samples. Samples are like templates in a word processing program. You can create a new page already formatted with a cascading style sheet (CSS), create a frames page, or create a page based on a page design.

  ✔ You will learn more about cascading style sheets and frames pages later in this course.

- If you have a page open in a site, you can create a new page using the File>New command, or you can click the 🗋 New button on the Standard toolbar. The New Document dialog box opens, as shown in the following illustration.

New Document dialog box

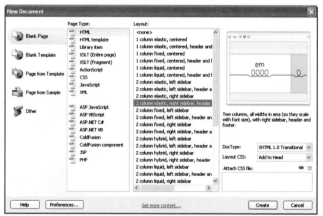

- Select an option in the first column and then select the desired page type in the second column. The third column allows you to select a default CSS layout that can help you quickly set up a page with regions to which you can add your own content.

- Before you begin adding content to a new page, you should save it. Use the File>Save (or Save As) command to save a new document.

- You can also right-click the untitled document's tab in the upper-left corner of the Document window and select Save or Save As from the shortcut menu.

- The process of saving a document in Dreamweaver is very similar to saving files in any Windows program: Give the new file a name and specify the location where it will be stored and the file type (see the following illustration).

Save new document in site folder

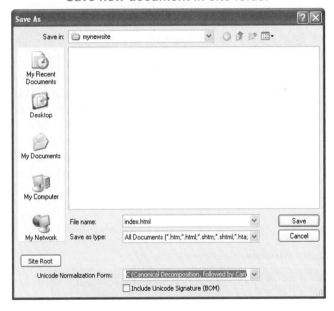

- The [Site Root] button in the Save As dialog box makes it easy to jump right to the folder that contains your site files. This is especially handy when you are opening an existing file from a location outside your site and saving it to your root folder.

- Note in the previous illustration that Dreamweaver supplies the *.html* extension by default. You can, if desired, change the default extension to *.htm* or to another extension based on the types of pages you create most often.

  ✔ *You change the default extension in the Edit>Preferences dialog box in the New Document category. You can learn about how to choose preferences in Appendix A.*

- After you save a page, the title bar shows the file folder and file name in parentheses.

- As you add pages or open existing pages, they display with tabs in the Document window. Click a page tab to activate the page so you can work with it.

- Many servers expect the home page of a Web site to be named *index.htm* or *index.html.* The Microsoft IIS server can use either *default* or *index* as the file name for the home page. To make sure your Web pages are published without error, use the appropriate name for your home pages.

- The **home page** is the first page that opens in a Web site. This page usually gives general information about the site and has links to other pages in the site.

- You can designate one of the site's pages as the home page by right-clicking the page in the Files panel and selecting the Set as Home Page command on the shortcut menu.

- As part of the page creation process, you should also give each page a title. A page's title appears in the title bar of the **browser** when the page is opened.

- Use the Modify>Page Properties menu command or the [Page Properties...] button in the Properties inspector to open the Page Properties dialog box. You can type the page's title in the Title text box (see the following illustration). Or, type the page title right in the Document toolbar's Title box.

  ✔ *Both page names and page titles can be changed later from the Files panel or the Document window.*

Add a page title to a saved document

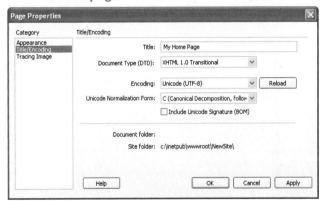

- To create additional pages for a Web site, use the File>New command to select and create a new, blank document in the New Document dialog box.

  ✔ *You can also use the New button on the Standard toolbar if you have it displayed.*

- If you select Close before you have saved a new page, you will be prompted to save if any changes have been made to the current Web page.

View Site Files

- The Files panel gives you easy access to your Web site and its files and folders. The Files panel group also includes the Assets panel, which allows you to track colors, images, and objects used in a site, and the Snippets panel, which provides a variety of small coded programs you can insert in your Web pages.

  ✔ *You will learn more about the Assets and Snippets panels later in this course.*

- As you add pages and other files to a Web site, you may need to see a more detailed and expanded view of your site than the Files panel's small window.

- Click the ⊞ Expand/Collapse button in the Files panel's toolbar. The expanded, window-sized Files panel in Site Files view shows the Local Files in the right pane and the server information in the Remote Site pane at the left (see the illustration below).

- To collapse the Files panel window, click the ⊞ Expand/Collapse button in the window's toolbar.

Web Design Guidelines

- Dreamweaver is an application that encourages creativity, and it provides considerable support and assistance in realizing a designer's ideas. Before jumping in with your site design, however, consider some design guidelines that can help you turn out professional-quality pages.

  ✔ *This book assumes that you are using Dreamweaver for business and informational sites, but the following design rules apply equally well to less formal content or to personal Web sites.*

- **Be consistent.** Consistency in color, graphics, and placement helps your visitor understand your site.

- **Make your site easy to navigate.** When visitors come to your Web site, they should be able to tell from your home page how to get around your site and find the features they need.

- **Pay attention to connection speed.** If it takes too long to download your Web site, your visitors will not return. Time is valuable, both theirs *and* yours.

- **Keep it simple.** Clean lines and clear, easy-to-read content are features you always should keep in mind when building your site.

- **Be unique.** When you copy another designer's site ideas, you are not only plagiarizing but also limiting your own ideas and site potential.

- **Respect your visitors.** Make sure your site looks professional from the very first moment it is online. Don't fall into the habit of posting a "construction guy" graphic or similar icon to notify your visitors that your site is under construction. If your visitors are visiting your site for information, they likely will look elsewhere.

Expanded Files panel window

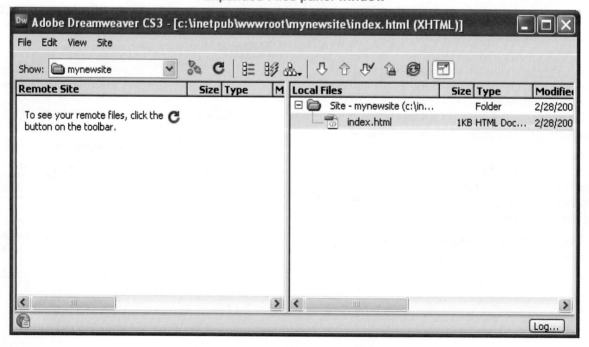

E-Commerce Connection

The Importance of Design

An e-commerce Web site's design can make or break the business. A well-designed site encourages visitors to stay in the site and use the site's services. A poorly designed site can drive visitors away, resulting in loss of potential sales.

Evaluate Web Page Design

Use the Internet to search for Web page design guidelines and develop a rubric covering the most important guidelines. Visit a number of e-commerce Web sites and evaluate Web page design in each site according to your rubric.

PROCEDURES

Create a Web Site

✔ *Note that the options available in the Site Definition dialog box depend on your system setup and the choices you make as to server technology and remote server option.*

1. Click ⊞ Dreamweaver Site... on the Welcome Screen.

   OR

   a. Click **Site** . . . . . . Alt+S
   b. Click **New Site** . . . . . . N

2. Click the **Basic** tab if necessary.

3. Type the site name in the *What would you like to name your site?* text box.

4. Type the HTTP address (URL) of the site if you know it.

5. Click Next>.

6. Select the desired server technology option:

   No, I do not want to use a server technology . . . . . . Alt+O

   OR

   Yes, I want to use a server technology . . . . . . Alt+Y

   Which server technology? . . . . . Alt+W

   Select the desired server technology from the drop-down list.

7. Click Next>.

8. Select the desired option for *How do you want to work with your files during development?*

✔ *Depending on the option you choose, you may, after clicking Next, skip some or all of the screens used in steps 10–14.*

9. Type the path to the root folder in the *Where on your computer do you want to store your files?* text box.

   ✔ *The server software on your computer may already be recognized (such as Microsoft IIS Web server software), in which case the path will be entered by default and the name of your Web site will be the name of its storage folder.*

   OR

   Click 🗀 to browse to the Web site folder, and click Select.

10. Click Next>.

11. Type the URL of your site in the **What URL would you use to browse to the root of your site?** text box . . . . . . Alt+W

    ✔ *If you are using the Microsoft IIS Web server, the URL will be entered by default.*

12. Click Test URL to test the URL.

13. Click Next>.

14. Select the desired remote server option:

    Yes, I want to use a remote server . . . . Alt+Y

    OR

    No . . . . Alt+N

15. Click Next>.

✔ *If No is selected, skip to step 18.*

16. Select, configure, and test the desired remote server type if you have that option. Consult Dreamweaver Help for additional information using the remote server type as the index or search keyword(s).

17. Click Next>.

18. Select the desired check in and check out option:

    Yes, enable check in and check out . . . . Alt+Y

    OR

    No, do not enable check in and check out . . . . . Alt+N

    ✔ *If Yes is selected, click the desired option for who should check out files and type a name and e-mail address (optional).*

19. Click Next>.

20. Review the information in the Summary tab and click Done.

Add a New Web Page (Ctrl + N)

▪ Click the page type on the Dreamweaver Welcome Screen.

   OR

1. Click **File** . . . . Alt+F
2. Click **New** . . . . N
3. Click a page type in the first column.

4. Click a page option in the Page Type list.

5. Click [Create].

Save a Web Page (Ctrl + S)

1. Click **File** . . . . [Alt]+[F]

2. Click **Save** . . . . [Alt]+[S]

   OR

   Click **Save As** . . . . [A]

   OR

   a. Right-click the Web document tab.

   b. Click **Save** or **Save As**.

3. Type the file name in the **File name** text box . . . . . [Alt]+[N]

4. Click [Site Root] if necessary to go to the current Web site's root folder.

5. Click [Save].

Set a Page Title (Ctrl + J)

■ Click in the **Title** box in the Document toolbar and type the page title.

   OR

1. Click **Modify**. . . . . . [Alt]+[M]

2. Click **Page Properties** . . . . [P]

   OR

   Click [Page Properties...] in the expanded Property inspector.

3. Click **Title/Encoding** in the list at the left side of the dialog box.

4. Type the page title in the **Title** text box . . . . [Alt]+[T]

5. Click [OK].

Select an Open Web Document

1. Click **Window** . . . . . [Alt]+[W]

2. Select the Web document's file name.

   OR

■ Click the desired Web document tab in the Document window.

View the Files Panel (F8)

1. Click **Window** . . . . . [Alt]+[W]

2. Click **Files** . . . . [F]

Expand/Collapse the Files Panel Window

■ Click ⬚ in the Files panel toolbar.

Set a Home Page

1. Display the Files panel, if necessary.

2. Right-click the file name and select **Set as Home Page**.

EXERCISE DIRECTIONS

✔ *Instructions in this and subsequent exercises assume you will be using the IIS local Web server available for Windows 2000, XP, and Vista. If you are using a different server type, your instructor will supply the necessary instructions for setting up the site.*

1. Start Dreamweaver.

2. Create a new Web site and name it cincitorial using the Site Definition wizard, as follows:

   ■ Verify that the Web site's local root folder is also named cincitorial.

   ■ Choose not to use a server technology.

   ■ Choose to edit local copies on your machine and then upload when ready. You should see a path similar to C:\Inetpub\wwwroot\cincitorial\ in the Where on your computer do you want to store your files? box.

   ■ Choose to connect by Local/Network, and store files on the server in the C:\Inetpub\wwwroot\cincitorial\ folder.

   ■ Do not enable check in and check out.

3. Use the Start page to create a new HTML page. Save it as index.html in the cincitorial folder.

   ✔ *Make sure that your Web page is saved as an HTML document with an .html extension.*

4. Give the page the title Home Page.

5. Create a new blank page of HTML type and name it history.html. Give it the page title CinciTorial History.

6. Create a new blank HTML page and name it contactus.html. Give it the page title Contact Us.

7. Close the history.html and contactus.html documents and click Yes when prompted to save.

8. View the Web site's files in the Files panel. If you do not see any files in the site, choose Local view from the drop-down list to the right of the site name.

9. Expand the Files panel.

10. Set the index.html file as the site's home page.

11. Collapse the expanded Files panel window.

12. Close the index.html page, saving changes if prompted, and exit Dreamweaver.

13. Optional. Read the Web Design Guidelines in the Notes section again.

   ■ Either on your own or with other classmates, use a search engine to locate Web design criteria used by Web design firms.

   ■ Use appropriate keywords and search engine techniques such as Boolean search strategies to narrow your search.

- Use the design criteria document that you create for creating your Web sites.

- Share your results with others via your network or as an e-mail attachment.

ON YOUR OWN

✔ *You will create a new Web site for the Reading Civic Garden Center similar to the example pages you reviewed in Exercise 1.*

1. Start Dreamweaver.
2. Create a new site and name it gardencenter using the Site Definition wizard. Use the same settings you used to set up the cincitorial site.
3. Create a new blank page of HTML type and save it as index.html with the page title Civic Garden Center Home.
4. Create another new blank HTML page and save it as contact.html with the page title Contact Information.
5. View the files in the Files panel.
6. Make the index.html page the site's home page.
7. Save changes to all pages and close them.
8. Exit Dreamweaver.

Exercise | 3

Skills Covered

- **About HTML and XHTML**
- **HTML Document Structure**
- **HTML Tags**
- **Add Keywords to a Web Site**

- **Enter Text on a Web Page**
- **Use Paragraph and Heading Tags**
- **Use Code and Design Views**
- **Open a Different Web Site**

Software Skills Dreamweaver's Web design tools make it unnecessary for users to work directly in HTML and other Web page–programming code if they prefer not to. However, it can be helpful to know some HTML basics. Add keywords to a site to make it easy for searchers to locate it. Text can be entered on a Web page in any Dreamweaver view, and standard HTML styles make it easy to format paragraphs and headings.

Application Skills In this exercise, you will enter text in several pages in the CinciTorial site, add keywords to the site, view HTML content, and switch among Dreamweaver's views.

TERMS

Attribute An HTML specification that modifies tag behavior.

Closing switch The / character used in a closing tag.

Closing tag An HTML tag used to indicate the end of a defined section. For example, </body> is the closing tag for the Body section.

Code view In Dreamweaver, the view that shows HTML code. Dreamweaver can show an entire page of code or show both Code view and Design view on a split page.

Design view In Dreamweaver, the default Document window view that shows page content similar to how it will appear in the browser.

Element Name of an HTML tag.

Head An important section of Web page code that contains information that browsers need to display the document, such as the page title and the character set used to create the page.

HTML (Hypertext Markup Language) The code used to create all Web pages.

HTML tag Formal name for an HTML markup element. HTML tags appear inside angle brackets (<tag>).

Insertion point Blinking vertical line that indicates where text will appear when typed or an object will appear when created or inserted.

Keywords Words or phrases relating to the site that search engines index.

Line break A <br> tag that starts a new line but not a new paragraph.

Nest To place one object inside another. HTML tags are often nested.

One-sided tag HTML tag that does not require a closing tag. A <br> line break tag is a one-sided tag.

Opening tag Identifier in HTML of the start element. The opening tag for a paragraph is <p>.

Syntax Rules that govern the use of HTML code and are a connected, orderly system.

Value In HTML code, precise instruction for a particular attribute.

Wicket In HTML coding, the angle brackets (< >) that surround the HTML tag.

XHTML (Extensible Hypertext Markup Language) The current version of HTML that combines HTML structure with XML power and flexibility.

NOTES

About HTML and XHTML

- **HTML (Hypertext Markup Language)** is a scripting language—or code—used to create text that can be viewed with a Web browser. Nearly every item on a Web page—including text, formatting, pictures, and other page elements—is controlled by HTML coding.

  ✔ *In addition to HTML coding, Web pages may also incorporate Java scripts, ColdFusion's CFML code, ActiveX, and other specialized Web page coding designed for different kinds of dynamic or interactive application and content. These codes, too, can be applied and edited in Dreamweaver.*

- Dreamweaver CS3 supports **XHTML (Extensible Hypertext Markup Language)**. XHTML is a reformulation of the most current version of HTML (HTML 4.0) using *XML (Extensible Markup Language)*. XML is a language that uses tags to structure information, similar to HTML. Unlike HTML, however, XML allows you to create your own tags to fit your information more specifically.

- XHTML was developed to answer a need for a stricter version of HTML that could be used to deliver content across a wide variety of devices: not merely computer browsers, but also mobile phones, laptops, PDAs, and so on. XHTML combines the standard HTML structure with the power and flexibility of XML.

- By default, Dreamweaver saves new Web pages as XHTML Transitional documents and applies code necessary to meet XHTML requirements, such as including an XHTML DOCTYPE declaration in the Head section of the document. You can convert HTML documents to XHTML documents if desired using the File>Convert menu command. Converting HTML documents to XHTML Transitional format ensures that the document meets current Dreamweaver coding standards.

  ✔ *If you are interested in learning more about how Dreamweaver supports XHTML standards, consult the Dreamweaver Help files.*

- The value of using a program such as Dreamweaver is that you do not have to worry about HTML, XHTML, or XML to create Web content. Dreamweaver automatically applies the correct markup as you select features from its menus and panels.

- However, as you become more proficient with Dreamweaver you may find that you need to "tweak" the code for a specific page element. Knowing the basics of HTML coding can help you to troubleshoot page display problems and easily modify page elements. The following information gives you a brief tutorial in HTML basics.

HTML Document Structure

- HTML documents have a standard structure that consists of two sections: a Head section and a Body section.

- The **Head** section contains information that browsers need to display the Web page, such as the page title and the character set used to create the page (see the following illustration). None of the information in the Head section appears in the browser except the page title, which displays in the browser's title bar.

Head and Body sections in Dreamweaver Code view

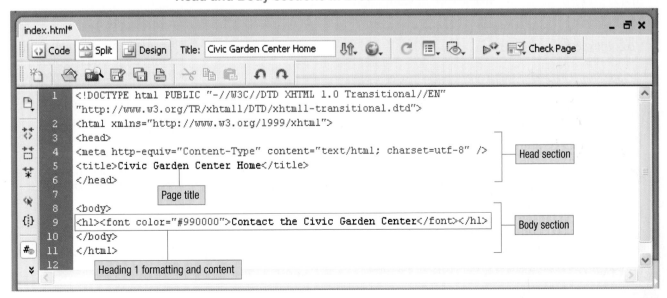

21

- The Body section contains the actual Web page content, such as the page's headings (see the previous illustration), paragraphs, and pictures.

HTML Tags

- HTML coding instructions are delivered to the browser by means of **HTML tags**. As you can see in the preceding illustration, HTML tags have a specific structure, or **syntax**:
  - The first part of an HTML tag is the left **wicket** (<).
  - Next is the tag **element**, or name, such as title or h2.
  - Tag **attributes** may follow the tag element. For example, the color="#990000" information that follows the font tag in the preceding illustration is the attribute that controls text color.
  - Last is the right wicket (>).

  ✔ *HTML tags may be written with all capital letters or all lowercase letters. Dreamweaver's tags are all lowercase, so that convention will be used in this book.*

- Most HTML codes require both an **opening tag** and a **closing tag**. The opening tag instructs the browser to begin displaying a format or feature. For example: <title>.

- The closing tag usually has the same syntax as an opening tag, but also contains a **closing switch** (/) before the tag element. For example: </title>.

- Text that appears between an opening tag and a closing tag is affected by that tag. For example, in the following HTML code, the (Heading 2) formatting is applied to a heading:

  ```
  <h2>Welcome to CinciTorial</h2>
  ```

- Tags may be **nested** to supply additional formatting to text. For example, in the following HTML code, the word *also* will appear in italics in the paragraph:

  ```
  <p>We <i>also</i> offer three kinds
  of chocolate truffles.</p>
  ```

  ✔ *Don't forget the closing switch when nesting tags, or applied formats will not be "turned off."*

- Some HTML tags are **one-sided tags** (also called *standalone* or *empty tags*). One-sided tags do not require a closing tag. The
 (line break) tag is a one-sided tag.

- XHTML coding handles one-sided tags in a special way, by adding the closing switch after the element in the opening tag. To make sure the tag will not cause problems in older browsers that are not XML compliant, a space is inserted before the closing switch. If you create a line break in your text and

view the code in Code view, the break tag looks like this: <br />.

Attributes and Values

- Tag attributes modify a tag element by supplying additional instructions to the browser about how to display an element.

- Attributes appear within HTML tags, usually between the tag element and the right wicket. Attributes often include **values** to supply the specific instructions to the browser. Attribute values are usually enclosed in quotation marks.

- Typically, attributes are not repeated in the closing tag.

- In the following HTML code, for example, the tag element is font. The size attribute tells the browser to display a specific size. "4" is the value, the exact size the browser should display.

  ```
  <font size="4">
  ```

Common HTML Tags

- There are dozens of HTML tags and attributes that can be used to create sophisticated effects on Web pages. The following table lists a few of the most common tags.

Tag(s)	Result
<html> </html>	Sets the page as an HTML document so that its code can be interpreted by the browser software.
<head> </head>	Begins and ends the section that contains information on content, language, and keywords for the page.
<title> </title>	Encloses the Web page's page title. In a browser, the page's title appears in the browser's title bar.
<meta>	Records information about the current page and supplies information such as keywords that search engines use to identify your page. (Does not require a closing tag and appears in XHTML coding as <meta />.)
<body> </body>	Defines the section of the Web page that displays in a browser.
<p> </p>	Begins and ends a paragraph on the Web page.

Tag(s)	Result
` `	Inserts a line break. (Does not require a closing tag and appears in XHTML coding as ` `.)
`<h1>` `</h1>`	Defines the first heading level (Heading 1). Use the same syntax for other heading levels, such as `<h2>` `</h2>`, `<h3>` `</h3>`, etc.
`<b>` `</b>`	Turns on and off bold formatting. Use the same syntax for font styles such as italics: `<i>` `</i>`, etc. You may also use the `<strong>` `</strong>` tag to apply bold formatting.
`<font>` `</font>`	Changes the font of text between the tags; requires an attribute to identify the new font.
`<align>` `</align>`	Changes the alignment of text between the tags; requires an attribute such as right to specify exact alignment.
`<ol>` `</ol>`	Begins and ends an ordered (numbered) list.
`<ul>` `</ul>`	Begins and ends an unordered (bulleted) list.
`<li>` `</li>`	Identifies each item in an ordered or unordered list.
`<dl>` `</dl>`	Begins and ends a definition list.
`<a>` `</a>`	Identifies a hyperlink; requires the href attribute and a value to specify target of link.
`<img>` `</img>`	Indicates location of a picture in a Web page.

HTML vs. CSS

- In recent years, the emphasis on using cascading style sheets (CSS) as the standard for formatting Web pages has greatly increased. Using CSS, a designer can format a page precisely using styles. Styles can be used to format text and headings, tables, blocks of type on a page, and images, and even change the default formats of HTML tags.

- As a result of the widespread use of CSS, many standard HTML tags have been *deprecated* in recent versions of HTML. This means that, although they are still supported by most browsers, they may not be supported for much longer. The `<font>` tag is a case in point. In later exercises, when you learn how to validate the markup language in your site, you may be warned that `<font>`

is deprecated and you should instead consider using CSS styles to format text.

- By default, Dreamweaver is set up to create CSS styles for you when you apply formats to text. This means that if you check the code after applying formats to a page, you will not see HTML tags, attributes, and values such as those discussed in previous sections of this exercise. You will instead see CSS style definitions.

- You can change this default setting in the Preferences dialog box so that Dreamweaver will display HTML tags rather than create CSS styles.

- Because it is important for new Dreamweaver users to gain an understanding of HTML tags, you will be directed in Lesson 2 to change the default to display HTML tags rather than CSS styles. You will restore the default setting in Lesson 5, once you are a bit more familiar with Dreamweaver, so you can create and apply CSS styles.

Add Keywords to a Web Site

- To make sure many visitors locate your site, you can supply **keywords** that search engines use to index a site in their databases. You add keywords to the Head section of a site using a `<meta>` tag.

- To add a `<meta>` tag containing keywords to your home page, use the Insert>HTML>Head Tags>Keywords menu command to open the Keywords dialog box (see the following illustration). Here you can type the keywords that summarize your site's subject.

Keywords dialog box

- ✔ *You can also display this dialog box by displaying the Common tab on the Insert bar, clicking the Head button's list arrow, and then selecting Keywords.*

- Separate groups of keywords with commas, and use care when selecting them. Some search engines accept only a specific number of keywords and ignore keywords altogether if too many are supplied.

- Clicking the OK button in the Keywords dialog box inserts the keywords as a value for a new `<meta>` tag in the Head section of the Web page.

Enter Text on a Web Page

- After you have set up your site and created pages, you are ready to add content. Your pages should contain a balance of text and graphics to make the pages both informative and attractive. You can if desired display rulers on pages (see the following illustration) to show you the position of content on the page.

- A newly opened Dreamweaver document displays a blinking **insertion point** at the top left of the Document window. To enter text on a page, simply begin typing at the location of the insertion point (see the following illustration).

Type text at the insertion point

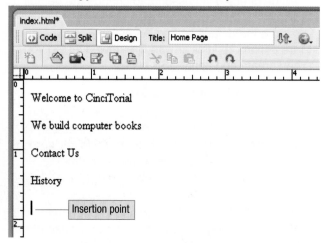

- As in a word processing document, you do not need to press the Enter key at the end of each line. Dreamweaver wraps text automatically at the right side of the page. Press the Enter key only to start a new paragraph.

   ✔ *As a general rule, Web page paragraphs do not have a first-line indent. Dreamweaver does not recognize tabs or spaces at the beginnings of paragraphs.*

- Dreamweaver automatically inserts space after a paragraph, so you do not have to double-space between paragraphs as you might be used to doing in a word processing document.

- If you do not want the default space after a paragraph, insert a **line break** rather than a paragraph break.

- For easy access to the break tag (and other special characters), display the Text tab on the Insert bar. Clicking the ▣ ▾ button on the Text tab inserts the HTML
 (Break) tag, which creates a new line but not a new paragraph. You can also insert this tag as you type by pressing the Shift + Enter key combination.

Use Paragraph and Heading Tags

- Text in a Dreamweaver document can be formatted with standard HTML paragraph and heading tags that control font style and size.

- By default, all new text is formatted with the Paragraph format. This format equates to the HTML <p> (Paragraph) tag.

- You can use the Property inspector or the Text tab on the Insert bar to apply other formats, including six levels of headings and the preformatted font that can be used to display program code (see the following illustration).

Apply text formats with the Property inspector

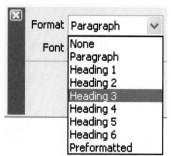

- Click anywhere in the paragraph to format and click the Format list arrow on the Property inspector to display the list of paragraph and heading formats. Or, choose the format and then begin typing to apply the format to new text.

- Heading levels are ordered from largest (Heading 1) to smallest (Heading 6) (see the following illustration).

HTML heading levels

Heading 1

Heading 2

Heading 3

Heading 4

Heading 5

Heading 6

■ The Property inspector will not show font sizes or styles for headings because these formats are specified by the HTML tag for that heading.

Use Code and Design Views

■ By default, the Document window displays page content in **Design view**. In Design view, content looks almost identical to the way it will display in a browser.

■ When you switch to **Code view**, the page content's HTML coding displays (see the illustration below). Code view allows you to write or edit HTML code in the full Document window.

Page shown in Code view

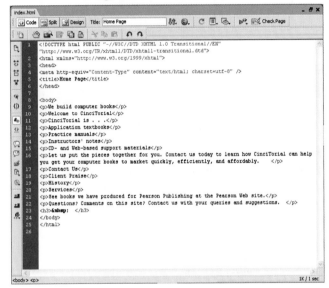

Display both Code and Design views

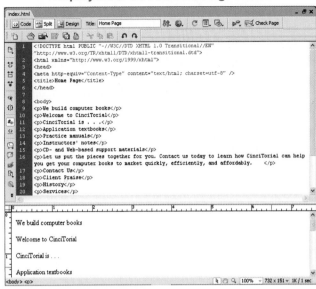

Open a Different Web Site

■ As you work with Dreamweaver, you will probably create a number of Web sites in various folders on your local drive. When you start Dreamweaver, the program opens the last Web site you worked on.

■ You can open a different Web site from the Files panel. Click the drop-down list in the Files panel's toolbar—either in its expanded window or collapsed panel form—and select the desired Web site (see the following illustration).

Click a Web site in Files panel toolbar to open it

■ Switch to Code view using the View>Code menu command, or simply click the [Code] Show Code view button at the far left of the Document toolbar. (The button is labeled Code, but if you hover the mouse pointer over it, you will see a ToolTip identifying the button as Show Code view.)

■ When you have finished working in Code view, use the View>Design menu command or the [Design] Show Design view button to restore Design view. (The Show Design view button is labeled Design.)

■ Dreamweaver also allows you to display both views in the Document window at the same time so you can see immediately the results of your coding. Use the View>Code and Design menu command or the [Split] Show Code and Design views button to turn on a display like the one shown in the following illustration. (The Show Code and Design views button is labeled Split.)

■ By default, Code view appears at the top of the window. You can move Design view to the top by clicking the [icon] View options button on the right side of the Document toolbar and selecting Design View on Top.

- When you open a Web site using this method, the Files window's contents change to the selected site. You can then open pages or other objects directly from the Files panel.
- You can also use the Manage Sites dialog box, shown in the following illustration, to switch from one site to another. Display this dialog box using the Site>Manage Sites menu command or Manage Sites at the bottom of the Files panel menu.
- You can also use this dialog box to create a new site, edit a site, duplicate a site, remove a site, or export or import a site. Duplicate a site to create a backup or to save effort when creating a site with similar layout or text.

Choose site to work with

E-Commerce Connection

Use the Right Keywords

One of the most important aspects of creating a new Web site is to identify keywords that will help potential visitors locate the site using a search engine. Keyword research is one important strategy for promoting a new Web site.

Promotion Techniques

Use the Internet to search for information about how to expose and promote a Web site. Write a report that lists the most common techniques and strategies a new site designer can use to get his or her site noticed.

PROCEDURES

Add Keywords to a Web Site

1. Click **Insert** . . . . Alt+I
2. Click **HTML** . . . . H
3. Point to **Head Tags** . . . . . . H
4. Click **Keywords** . . . . K
5. Type keywords in the Keywords dialog box, separating keywords with commas.

   OR

1. Display the Common tab on the Insert bar.
2. Click the **Head** button ⬚ ▾ list arrow and click **Keywords**.
3. Type keywords in the Keywords dialog box, separating keywords with commas.

Insert a Line Break

- Press Shift + Enter at end of line of text.

  OR

- Click 🔳 ▾ on the Text tab of the Insert bar.

Apply a Paragraph or Heading Tag

Click in paragraph to format or position insertion point where new format should begin:

1. Click the **Format** list arrow in the Property inspector.
2. Select a heading level or paragraph format.

   OR

1. Click **Text** . . . . Alt+T
2. Point to **Paragraph Format** F
3. Select a heading level or paragraph format on the submenu.

OR

1. Display the Text tab on the Insert bar.
2. Click buttons for desired heading level or paragraph format.

Display Code and Design Views (Ctrl+`)

To display Code view:

1. Click **View** . . . . Alt+V
2. Click **Code** C

   OR

   Click **Show Code view** button 🔳 Code on the Document toolbar.

To display Design view:

1. Click **View** . . . . Alt+V
2. Click **Design** . . . . D

   OR

Click **Show Design view** button [Design] on the Document toolbar.

To display both Code and Design view:

1. Click **View** . . . . Alt+V
2. Click **Code and Design** . . . A

   OR

Click **Show Code and Design views** button [Split] on the Document toolbar.

Open Different Web Sites

In Files panel toolbar:

- Click the drop-down list in the Files panel toolbar and select a site to open.

OR

1. Click **Site** . . . . Alt+S
2. Click **Manage Sites** . . . . . . M
3. Select a site to open.
4. Click [Done].

EXERCISE DIRECTIONS

1. Start Dreamweaver.
2. Switch to the cincitorial site if necessary.
3. Open index.html.
4. Add the following keywords for this site: editorial services, book production.
5. Display Code view and locate the new <meta> tag in the page's Head section. Also take this opportunity to locate the DOCTYPE declaration at the top of the page that identifies this document as an XHTML 1.0 transitional document.
6. Switch back to Design view and enter the text shown in Illustration A. After you type *Application textbooks*, insert a line break rather than a new paragraph, and repeat this process after the next two items in the list.
7. Display Code and Design view. (Click the Split button.)

8. Apply heading and paragraph formats as follows:

   - On the Property inspector, click the Style list arrow and select None. (This prevents Dreamweaver from creating CSS styles as you format the text.)

   ✔ *You will learn about creating CSS styles later in this course.*

   - Apply the Heading 4 tag to *We build computer books*.
   - Apply the Heading 1 tag to *Welcome to CinciTorial*.

9. In the Code view region of the split document, locate the HTML tags that have been applied to the text you just formatted.
10. Open contactus.html and type Contact CinciTorial at the top of the page.
11. Apply the Heading 2 tag to the new text.
12. Switch to Design view.
13. Save and close all open pages and exit Dreamweaver.

We build computer books

Welcome to CinciTorial

CinciTorial is . . .

Application textbooks
Practice manuals
Instructors' notes
CD- and Web-based support materials

Let us put the pieces together for you. Contact us today to learn how CinciTorial can help you get your computer books to market quickly, efficiently, and affordably.

Contact Us

Client Praise

History

Services

See books we have produced for Pearson Publishing at the Pearson Web site.

Questions? Comments on this site? Contact us with your queries and suggestions.

ON YOUR OWN

1. Start Dreamweaver.
2. Open the gardencenter site.
3. Open index.html and type the heading Reading Civic Garden Center.
4. Apply the Heading 1 tag to the heading.
5. Open contact.html and type the heading Contact Us.
6. Apply the Heading 2 tag to the heading.
7. Insert the following text below the heading. Use line breaks when typing the first two lines of the mailing address.

Our mailing address is:

Reading Civic Garden Center
10456 Reading Road
Reading, OH 45215

Reach us by phone at (513) 555-4445 (voice) or (513) 555-4446 (fax).

Leave a message for us at contactus@readinggarden.net.

Would you like to receive information about Civic Garden Center events? Join our mailing list and let us know how to contact you.

8. Add the following keywords on the index.html page: Reading Civic Garden Center, Reading Civic Gardens
9. Use Code view or Code and Design view to locate the new keywords in the Head section of the page.
10. Save and close all pages and exit Dreamweaver.

Exercise | 4

Summary Exercise

Application Skills   High Ridge Swim & Tennis Club is interested in creating a Web site to provide information on the club for prospective members as well as news for current members. The Board has asked you to design a site. In this exercise, you will begin the process by creating the site and the home page.

DIRECTIONS

1. Start Dreamweaver.
2. Use the Site Definition wizard to create a site using the following settings:
   - Name the site highridge.
   - Choose not to use a server technology.
   - Choose to edit and test the site locally using the Windows IIS, if available. Make sure the folder in which to store files is the same as the site name.
   - Test the URL if you are storing your site on the http://localhost site. If you receive a warning about the site URL not matching the HTTP address, you can click OK to dismiss the warning.
   - Choose not to use a remote server.

3. Create a new Web page and save it as index.html. Give the page the title High Ridge Swim & Tennis Club.
4. Make this page the site's home page.
5. Insert the text shown in Illustration A on the page. Use line breaks when creating the list of club features.
6. Format the first heading with the Heading 1 format. Format the heading *Club Features* with the Heading 2 tag.
7. Add the following keywords to the site: High Ridge, High Ridge Swim Club
8. Check in Code view to make sure you entered the keywords correctly.
9. Save your changes to index.html.
10. Close the document and exit Dreamweaver.

High Ridge Swim & Tennis Club

Welcome to High Ridge! The High Ridge Swim & Tennis Club has been a part of the High Ridge community for more than 50 years and is one of the oldest clubs in the city. Our heritage is evident in the many mature trees scattered on the club grounds, but our facilities are completely contemporary.

Club Features

Members enjoy the following amenities:

New clubhouse and changing facilities
Eight-lane heated lap pool
Separate diving/family pool
Children's pool
Six lighted tennis courts (available for year-round play)
Sand volleyball court
Basketball courts
Shaded picnic area
Children's playground and plenty of open space for running and jumping

In addition, the club offers free swimming lessons and tennis lessons. High Ridge has a silver-medal swim team that competes in weekly meets with other neighborhood clubs, as well as a highly competitive tennis team. Add to this mix a busy social schedule for both children and adults, and you have a great summer resource for family fun.

For more information on joining High Ridge, visit our membership page.

Exercise | 5

Application Exercise

Application Skills   The Village Council in your neighborhood is currently renovating its historic movie theatre. You have been asked to create a Web site for the theatre. In this exercise, you will define a new site for the Grand Theatre and create content for its home page and location page.

DIRECTIONS

1. Start Dreamweaver
2. Define a new site for the theatre. Use the site name grand and use your own judgment about site settings.
3. Create a home page for the site and save it as index.html. Give the page the title Welcome to the Grand Theatre.
4. Enter the following text on the index.html page.

   Now Showing at the Grand

   Click here to see show times for our current releases.

   How to Find Us

   The Grand Theatre is located in the historic Madison Village area of Jefferson. Click here to see a selection of maps that will guide you to the general region and show you our exact location and parking options.

   Grand Theatre Special Features
   Four screens
   Dolby surround sound
   Concession stand specialties
   All matinees $6.00
   Bargain Tuesday $5.50 any show
   Senior citizen discounts on all evening shows

5. Format the three headings (*Now Showing at the Grand, How to Find Us,* and *Grand Theatre Special Features*) with the Heading 2 tag.

6. Create another new blank HTML page and save it as location.html. Give it the page title Grand Theatre Location.
7. Enter the following text on the location.html page:

   You Can't Miss Us!

   The Grand Theatre is located at 2750 Madison Road, the main street through Madison Village. If you are unfamiliar with the Madison Village historic region, you can find it by traveling north on Madison Road. The Grand has occupied this location since 1932 and is distinguished by its gorgeous neon-highlighted marquee. Click here if you would like to see a map of Jefferson with Madison Village clearly marked. Click here if you would like to see a street map of Madison Village showing the location of the theatre.

   Grand Parking

   You have several parking options when you visit the Grand. You can park anywhere on the nearby residential streets. You can park in the Grand's free lot, though parking spaces are limited so come early! Or you can park in the Madison Village Merchants' Lot for a nominal charge.

8. Format the headings with the Heading 3 format.
9. Add keywords to the index.html page. Use your own judgment about what kinds of keywords would help a visitor find this site. (pg 23)
10. Save and close all open pages.
11. Exit Dreamweaver.

Exercise | 6

Curriculum Integration

Application Skills The Math Department at your school is developing a Web site containing pages that students can refer to for basic math information. You have been asked to create a page listing and defining common geometry terms. Before you begin this exercise, refresh your memory about these terms:

- Point

- Line

- Plane

- Line segment

- Ray

- Angle

DIRECTIONS

You can define a new site if desired, or simply create the page in any site and then save it in a solutions folder named Exercise06.

If you create a site, use your own judgment about what to name the site and what settings to apply to it. Name the page geomterms.html and give it an appropriate page title.

Type the terms listed above on the page. Then add a definition for each term below the term.

Format the terms with a heading of your choice to make them stand out on the page. View the page in Code view to see the HTML tags applied for the term headings.

Save changes to the page and close it. Exit Dreamweaver.

Critical Thinking

Application Skills   In this exercise, you will create a Web site for a club, a team, or other organization of which you are a member or would like to be a member. After defining the site, you will add several pages to the site and rough in some site content.

DIRECTIONS

- First determine the subject of the new Web site. You might want to create a site for a school club, the local library's book club or ESL group, an organization at your place of worship, your running or walking group, a neighborhood watch committee, or an employee wellness program at your place of work, to name a few ideas.

- Next, create a rough outline showing the material you need to include in your site and the pages that will be required to present that information.

- Before you begin the process of site creation, trade your outline with a classmate and ask him or her to critique your Web page design using the guidelines for effective page design you developed in Exercise 1. Incorporate any suggestions you think important in your outline.

- Create the new site with an appropriate site name and site settings.

- Create a basic HTML page that will be the home page of the site. Name it index.html and give the page an appropriate page title.

- Add keywords to the site.

- Enter text on the index.html page that introduces the organization and gives some information about it. Insert headings as necessary to separate areas of text and format them with appropriate heading tags. Illustration A shows an example of a club home page.

- Add another page to the site from your site diagram and save it with an appropriate name and title.

- Enter text on the new page and format any headings with heading tags.

- Save all open documents and close them.

- Exit Dreamweaver.

Clifton Drama Club

Welcome to the Drama Club!

The Clifton Drama Club is a group of people who love everything about the theater, including:

Acting in dramas
Writing drama
Production design
Costume design
Makeup design
Stage management
Lighting and other technical support

If you're interested in any of these areas, the Drama Club is for you.

What We Do

The Clifton Drama Club sponsors four plays a year and contributes expertise and support for the school's musical production. When we're not working on school dramatics, we schedule visits to local and regional theater productions to see how the pros do it. The Drama Club also arranges for seminars and workshops with local theater groups to learn the nuts and bolts of production design, costumes and makeup, and the behind-the-scenes technical skills without which the show would never be able to go on.

For more information on the Drama Club, contact studentname@website.net.

Lesson | 2

Work with Web Page Text and Links

Exercise | 8

Skills Covered

- Insert Text from Office Documents
- Modify Font Formats
- Insert Special Characters
- Check Spelling
- Find and Replace Text
- Save Edits

Software Skills Text is the most important aspect of your Web page content. Besides typing your site content, you can import or copy text from other documents. Use formatting to ensure that your text is both easy to read and attractive. Special characters can help to communicate more precisely. Use the spelling checker and find and replace features to make sure text is correct and accurate.

Application Skills In this exercise, you will continue working on the CinciTorial site. You will add site content by importing and copying text, modify font formats on several pages, insert special characters, check spelling, and use Find and Replace to locate and change text on a page.

TERMS

Font A design of type. Also called a *typeface*.

Font combination A collection of fonts that can be applied to text on a Web page. The browser will display the first font in the collection, or other fonts in order if it does not support the first.

Font style Format applied to a font to change its appearance, such as **bold** or *italic*.

Points Measurement used for fonts. There are 72 points in one inch.

NOTES

Insert Text from Office Documents

- Although you can type all the text you need for your Web site's pages, you have another option for adding text to pages: You can insert text from Microsoft Word or Excel.

- The Word or Excel document can be in its native format—.doc or .docx for Word, .xls or .xlsx for Excel—or saved in HTML format.

- The method you use to insert the text depends on what format the document is saved in, as discussed in the following sections.

Importing or Copying Office Text

- The easiest way to insert Office text in a Dreamweaver page is to use the File>Import>Word Document or File>Import>Excel Document command. This command displays the Import Word Document or Import Excel Document dialog box,

where you can navigate to the location of the Word or Excel document you want to insert.

- Word text inserted this way is imported into the current page, and its text is converted to HTML text indistinguishable from other HTML text on the page.

- Excel spreadsheet text inserted this way displays on the Dreamweaver page in tabular format that can be edited just like any other tabular material you might create using Dreamweaver's table tools.

- You can also insert Office document text using the Copy and Paste commands. Copy the Word text or Excel spreadsheet data and then use one of the following Paste options:

  - Use Edit>Paste to convert the pasted text to HTML format, the same as when importing a Word or Excel file.

■ Use Edit>Paste Special to open the Paste Special dialog box shown in the following illustration.

Paste Special dialog box

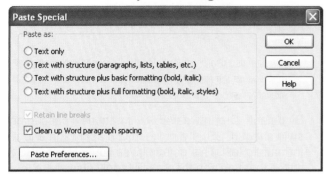

Insert Document dialog box

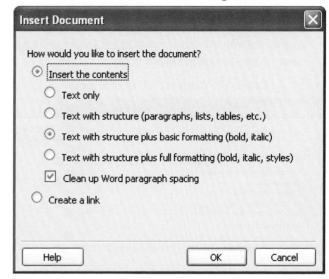

■ Use the options in this dialog box as follows:

■ *Text only* pastes the copied material as basic text. Excel data pastes as a block of text without any tabular organization.

■ *Text with structure* pastes the copied material with its basic paragraph or spreadsheet structure in place.

■ *Text with structure plus basic formatting* pastes the copied material with structure plus any bold or italic formatting that has been applied.

■ *Text with structure plus full formatting* pastes the copied material with structure and all applied formatting, such as font color or cell fill color.

■ If both the Office document and the Dreamweaver page are displayed on the screen at the same time, a user can simply drag content from the Office document onto the Dreamweaver page. This gives the same result as using the *Text with structure plus full formatting* option.

✔ *Hold down Ctrl while dragging to copy the Word or Excel information, or simply drag to move the information from the Office document into the Dreamweaver page.*

Create a Link to an Office Document

■ Another method of inserting Office information into a Dreamweaver page is to drag the file itself from an application such as Windows Explorer or the Dreamweaver Files panel onto the Dreamweaver page.

■ After the file icon is dragged and released on the page, Dreamweaver displays the Insert Document dialog box shown in the following illustration.

■ You can choose to insert the contents of the file and select a paste option, as in the Paste Special dialog box.

■ You can choose instead to create a link to the Office document. This choice places a link on the page where you "dropped" the file. The link text is the same as the file name.

■ If the Office document is not already stored in the site folder along with the other site files, Dreamweaver will prompt you to store it there so that it will be available to display when someone clicks the link.

■ This linking feature makes it easy to include information in formats other than HTML in a Web site. For example, a designer could include a Word or PDF version of a form for persons who prefer to print and mail the form rather than complete it online.

Opening Office HTML Files

■ All Microsoft Office applications include the capability to save documents in HTML format. A user can, for example, create a Word document or Excel workbook and save it as an HTML file that will display in a browser the same as any page created in Dreamweaver.

■ Office files that are saved in HTML format can be opened in the same way as any Dreamweaver page, using the File>Open command. Office HTML files are opened as complete pages, rather than being inserted on an existing page, as happens with importing or copying.

■ Pages opened this way take their file names (and page titles, for Word files) from the original HTML page, but must still be saved in the site.

■ Word HTML pages may contain coding that is not necessary in Dreamweaver. To strip out unnecessary codes, use the Commands>Clean Up Word HTML menu command.

■ The Clean Up Word HTML dialog box (see the following illustration) shows what steps Dreamweaver takes to streamline the Word code.

Clean Up Word HTML dialog box

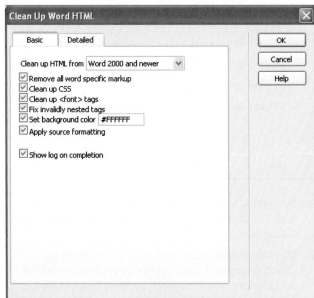

■ After the cleanup has been completed, Dreamweaver displays another dialog box to show you what cleanup operations it has undertaken (see the following illustration).

Results of cleanup operations

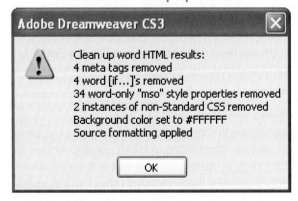

■ When you add a page that has been created in another program, such as a Word HTML page, it is a good idea to convert the code to the version of XHTML in use in the site. This ensures that all the pages in your site meet the current coding standards.

■ To convert a page, use the File>Convert command and select the code option you're using for other pages. In this course, the standard is XHTML 1.0 Transitional.

Modify Font Formats

■ Text entered in a Dreamweaver document is formatted with a default appearance, size, and color (black). Dreamweaver also applies a default style (Paragraph). You can change text appearance, size, style, and color using tools in the Property inspector.

✔ *You can also use commands on the Text menu to apply formats. Using the Property inspector can be quicker—as are available keyboard shortcuts.*

■ By default, Dreamweaver will create new cascading style sheet (CSS) styles when you apply some font formats to text. This default gives you a list of CSS styles that you can then easily apply elsewhere in your site, but it can be confusing for first-time Dreamweaver users. You can tell Dreamweaver to use regular HTML formatting rather than CSS formatting in the Preferences dialog box.

Select New Font Combination

■ A **font** is a design of type. When text is first entered in a Dreamweaver document, it is formatted with the current default font, usually Times New Roman.

✔ *You can change the default font using the Edit>Preferences command.*

■ You can specify a new **font combination** using the Property inspector's font list (see the following illustration). The first font in each combination is your first display choice. If the browser does not support that font, it will use the next font in the combination, and so on.

Apply new font combination

■ To apply a new font combination to existing text, select the text and then click the Font list arrow on the Property inspector to display the available font combinations. Click a combination to apply it to the selected text.

■ You can also apply a font combination before typing text. After the new combination is selected, all text you type will use that combination.

Add Fonts to the Font List

■ By default, the Dreamweaver font list offers only a few popular fonts that display well in most browsers. You can, however, add fonts to the list using the Edit Font List option at the bottom of the Property inspector's font list (or click Text>Font>Edit Font List).

■ When you issue this command, the Edit Font List dialog box opens (see the following illustration), showing the current font list and the fonts available in your system's Font folder.

Edit Font List dialog box

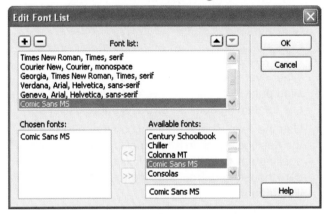

■ Select a font from the Available fonts list and click the [<<] button to add it to the Chosen fonts list. It will then be available in the font list of the Text menu and the Property inspector.

Apply Font Styles

■ **Font styles** are changes to the appearance of a font. Font styles add emphasis to text so it stands out from surrounding text.

■ Font styles used most often are **bold** and *italics*. You can easily apply bold or italic formatting (or both formats) to selected text using the **B** Bold or *I* Italic button on the Property inspector. These styles can also be applied from the Text tab on the Insert bar.

■ These font styles can also be turned on before you type text. Click the appropriate button on the Property inspector and begin typing.

Change Font Size

■ When used in a regular text document (such as a word processing document), font sizes are measured in **points**. (There are 72 points to a vertical inch.)

■ You can apply a different font size by selecting text and clicking the Size list arrow to display the list of available font sizes. Or, change the size first and then start typing.

■ By default, Dreamweaver displays the font size options used in CSS formatting, shown at left in the following illustration. If you have chosen to display HTML tags rather than CSS tags, you will see the font size options shown at the right.

Choose new font size

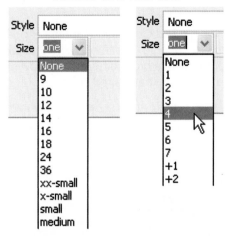

■ CSS font sizes look more like those available in a word processing program, but you can specify units of measurement such as pixels or points. You can also select a relative option such as x-small, medium, or large.

✔ *You will learn more about CSS font options in Lesson 5.*

■ HTML tags use font sizes that run from 1 to 7. The default size is 3, which equates to a regular font size of 12 points. The default font size is shown in the Property inspector as None.

■ The Size list on the Property inspector also includes relative font size measurements you can apply to selected text to increase or decrease the text size.

■ Sizes marked with a + sign (such as +3) increase the font size by increments from the base font size (default is 3), no matter what size the text is currently. Sizes marked with a - sign (such as -2) decrease the font size by increments.

■ If text is size 2, for example, applying the +2 relative font size increases the text size to 5 (not size 4), because the +2 is "added" to the default font size of 3.

■ HTML font sizes can also be selected using the Text>Size command. Select a size from the list to apply it. Relative font sizes can also be applied using the Text>Size Change command.

✔ *Many text formatting commands can also be used by selecting and right-clicking the desired text and clicking a formatting command in the shortcut menu.*

Apply Font Color

- The default text color in Dreamweaver is black. Black text provides the greatest contrast to most backgrounds and thus is easiest for visitors to read.

- To add visual interest to a Web page, you can select a new color for text using the Property inspector.

- Click the ▮▾ Text Color button on the Property inspector to open a palette of colors that will display properly in a browser (see the following illustration). Click on the desired color.

Select new font color in Dreamweaver

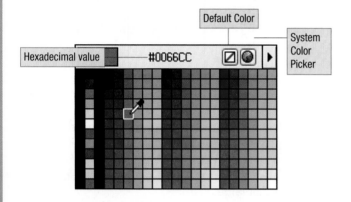

- Click the ▨ Default Color button to restore the page's default text color (usually black). You can change color palettes by clicking the right-pointing arrow in the palette and selecting a palette such as Continuous Tone.

  ✔ *Only the default Color Cubes and Continuous Tone palettes are considered Web-safe; that is, colors selected from these palettes will display correctly in any browser.*

- Each color in the Text Color palette has a hexadecimal—six-digit number—value. If you know the hexadecimal value of a color, you can type it directly in the text box to the right of the Text Color button on the Property inspector.

- To "mix" a custom color, click the ⬤ System Color Picker button to open the Color dialog box. However, it is best to use only Web-safe colors for creating your Web site, even though the latest browsers can support a vast array of color ranges.

Insert Special Characters

- As you create your Web page text, you may need to use special characters such as em dashes (—), copyright symbols (©), currency symbols (£), or foreign language characters (¿).

- Common special characters are listed on the drop-down menu that displays when you click the BR↲ Line Break button in the Text tab of the Insert bar. If you don't see the character you need, click Other Characters at the bottom of this list to display the Insert Other Character dialog box.

  ✔ *The button on the Insert bar will change to show the last character you used, so you may see a button other than the Line Break button in this position on the Insert bar.*

Check Spelling

- Whenever you type more than a few words on a Web page, you should check your spelling. A Web site containing spelling errors is unprofessional.

- Use the Text>Check Spelling command to launch the spelling checker. If the spelling checker finds spelling errors on the page, it lists alternatives you can choose to correct spelling (see the following illustration).

Check document spelling

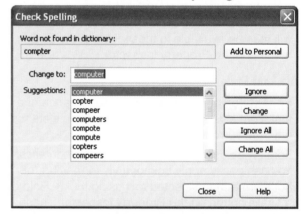

- Use the Add to Personal button to add proper names or other terms from your site to the dictionary so they will not be flagged as errors in the future. Choose Ignore or Ignore All to skip words you know are not misspelled. Use Change or Change All to replace misspelled words with correct words.

E-Commerce Connection

Copyrights and Trademarks

Two special characters you may use on an e-commerce Web site are the copyright symbol and the registered trademark symbol. These symbols can indicate that information is protected from unauthorized use by others.

Obtaining Copyrights and Registering Trademarks

Use the Internet to search for information on how to obtain a copyright or register a trademark. Write a report summarizing the procedures you identify.

Find and Replace Text

■ Dreamweaver offers a Find and Replace feature on the Edit menu that allows you to locate and change text or tags in the current page or throughout a site. When used to find and replace text, this feature works much the same way as in a word processing program.

■ In the Find and Replace dialog box (see the following illustration), choose to search for text, type the text to find, and type the replacement text. Then use Find Next to begin replacing instances of the found text with the replacement text.

Find and replace text

■ You can also choose to find all instances and replace all instances to speed the process. Select options at the bottom of the dialog box to help refine the search to specific cases or whole words.

■ This dialog box also offers an advanced Text setting that allows a user to search for text that is either inside a specified tag or not inside a tag. This gives the user some additional control over which instances of text to locate and replace.

■ Besides finding and replacing text, this feature gives the designer the option of locating and replacing specific tags and their attributes. You will learn more about this option later in the course.

Save Edits

■ As you enter and format text, you should save your work from time to time to guard against computer or power failures that can result in the immediate loss of hours of work. You can use the File>Save command on the menu bar, press the shortcut Ctrl + S, right-click the document tab and click Save, or click the 🖫 Save button on the Standard toolbar. Make a habit of using one of these methods frequently.

> ✔ Display the Standard toolbar by right-clicking the Document toolbar and selecting Standard, or by clicking View>Toolbars>Standard.

■ Use the Save All command—in the File menu, document tab shortcut menu, and Standard toolbar— to save all the pages open in Dreamweaver at once when you have made a series of changes to more than one Web page.

■ Dreamweaver displays an asterisk after a page name in the Dreamweaver (or Document) window title bar if changes have been made since the last save. An asterisk will also be visible in the document tab.

PROCEDURES

Import Office Text

1. Click **File** . . . . Alt+F
2. Click **Import** I
3. Click **Word Document**. . . . W

   OR

   Click **Excel Document** . . . E
4. Navigate in the Open dialog box to the location where the file is stored.
5. Click the file name and click ⬚Open⬚.

Copy Office Text (Ctrl + C, Ctrl + V)

1. Open an Office document, such as a Word document or an Excel worksheet.
2. Select desired information.

3. Click **Edit** . . . . Alt+E
4. Click **Copy** C
5. Switch to Dreamweaver and position the insertion point where the copied information should appear.
6. Click **Edit** . . . . Alt+E
7. Click **Paste**. . . . . P

   OR

   a. Click **Paste Special** . . . S
   b. Choose an option to paste: **Text only**, **Text with structure**, **Text with structure plus basic formatting**, or **Text with structure plus full formatting**.
   c. Select **Retain line breaks** when using the **Text only** option to maintain separate rows of data.

   d. Select **Clean up Word paragraph spacing** to remove extra spaces between Word paragraphs.
   e. Click ⬚ OK ⬚.

Create a Link to an Office Document

1. Display the file to link in a program such as Windows Explorer, and if necessary arrange the screen so that Windows Explorer and Dreamweaver are both in view.
2. Drag the Office file icon from the file list to the Dreamweaver page.
3. In the Insert Document dialog box, choose **Create a link**.

✔ Click **Insert the contents** in this dialog box to copy file contents at the insertion point. You can then select one of the pasting options described for Paste Special in the previous set of instructions.

4. Click ☐ OK ☐.

Open Office HTML Files

1. Click **File** . . . . Alt+F
2. Click **Open** . . . . O
3. Click the **Look in** arrow . . . . Alt+I, ↓
4. Select drive or folder.

   ✔ If necessary, double-click folder name.

5. Click file name to select.
6. Click ☐ Open ☐.

Clean Up Word HTML

1. Click **Commands** . . . . Alt+C
2. Click **Clean Up Word HTML** . . . . U
3. Click ☐ OK ☐ to run the clean-up operation.
4. Click ☐ OK ☐ to close the information dialog box.

Convert HTML to XHTML Code

1. Click **File** . . . . Alt+F
2. Click **Convert** V
3. Click the code option to convert to, such as XHTML 1.0 Transitional.

Display HTML Formatting Tags (Ctrl + U)

1. Click **Edit** . . . . Alt+E
2. Click **Preferences**. . . P, P, ↵Enter
3. In the General settings, deselect **Use CSS instead of HTML tags**.
4. Click ☐ OK ☐.

Select New Font Combination

Select text or position insertion point:

1. Click the **Default Font** list arrow in the Property inspector.
2. Select new font combination.

   OR

1. Click **Text** . . . . Alt+T
2. Click **Font** . . . . N
3. Select new font combination on submenu.

Add Fonts to the Fonts List

1. Click **Text** . . . . Alt+T
2. Click **Font** . . . . N
3. Click **Edit Font List** . . . . . . E

   OR

   Click **Edit Font List** on the Property inspector's font list.
4. Choose font from **Available fonts** list.
5. Click <<.
6. Click ☐ OK ☐.

Apply Font Style

Select text or position insertion point:

- Click **Bold** button **B** on the Property inspector to apply bold formatting.
- Click **Italic** button *I* on the Property inspector to apply italic formatting.

   OR

1. Click **Text** . . . . Alt+T
2. Click **Style** . . . . S

   Click **Bold** . . . . B

   Click **Italic** I

   ✔ Or click another font style on submenu.

   OR

- Press Ctrl+B for **bold**.
- Press Ctrl+I for *italic*.

Change Font Size

Select text or position insertion point:

1. Click the **Size** list arrow in the Property inspector.
2. Select new size.

   OR

1. Click **Text** . . . . Alt+T
2. Click **Size** . . . . Z
3. Select size number on submenu.

   OR

1. Click **Text** . . . . Alt+T
2. Click **Size Change** . . . . H
3. Select size number on submenu.

Apply Font Color

Select text or position insertion point where new font color should take effect:

1. Click **Text Color** button ☐▾ in the Property inspector to display Web-safe color palette.
2. Click desired color in color palette.

   OR

   Type exact hexadecimal value for color in text box to right of Text Color button.

   OR

1. Click **Text** . . . . Alt+T
2. Click **Color** . . . . R
3. Select color or create color in Color dialog box.

Insert Special Characters

1. Position insertion point at location where character should appear.
2. Display Text Insert bar (click list arrow next to current category name in Insert bar and select **Text**).
3. Click list arrow to right of 𝐁𝐑𝐉 (or to right of special character currently displayed at far right of Text tab of the Insert bar).

4. Select desired character on drop-down list.

OR

a. Click **Other Characters** on drop-down list to display Insert Other Character dialog box.

b. Click desired character.

c. Click [OK].

Check Spelling (Shift + F7)

1. Click **Text** . . . . Alt+T

2. Click **Check Spelling** . . . . . K

3. Review each flagged word:

- Click [Ignore] or [Ignore All] to skip words.

- Click [Change] or [Change All] to replace incorrect words with correct ones.

■ Click [Add to Personal] to add terms to your personal dictionary.

4. Click [OK] to end spelling check.

Find and Replace Text (Ctrl + F)

1. Click **Edit** . . . . Alt+E

2. Click **Find and Replace** . . . . F, ↵Enter

3. Select location to search: **Selected Text**, **Current Document**, **Open Documents**, **Folder**, **Selected Files in Site**, **Entire Current Local Site**.

4. Select what to search for: **Source Code, Text, Text (Advanced), Specific Tag.**

5. Type text to search for in **Find** box.

6. Type replacement text in **Replace box**.

7. Click [Find Next] to find first instance.

8. Click [Replace] to replace instance with replacement text.

OR

a. Click [Find All] to display all instances in a panel below the Property inspector.

b. Click [Replace All] to replace all instances at once.

EXERCISE DIRECTIONS

1. Start Dreamweaver and open the Preferences dialog box from the Edit menu. In the General settings, deselect *Use CSS instead of HTML tags.*

2. Open the cincitorial site and then open index.html. You need to add some text to this page:

- Position the insertion point at the beginning of the paragraph that begins *Let us put the pieces together for you.*

- Import the ◉ newtext.doc Word document in the Lesson 2 Data files folder.

- Insert the em dash special character after *1* and *2* in the *Working with CinciTorial is as easy as 123* sentence. (See Illustration A, which shows the top portion of the completed page.)

3. Make the following formatting changes to index.html:

- Change the color of the *We build computer books* heading to the dark maroon with the hexadecimal number #990033.

- Change the font of the *Welcome to CinciTorial* heading to the combination that begins with Georgia. Change its color to the dark blue with the hexadecimal number #000066.

- Change the size of the paragraph *CinciTorial is . . .* to 4.

- Italicize the paragraph that begins *See books we have produced.*

4. Open contactus.html. Change the font combination for the heading to the one that begins with Georgia and change its color to the dark teal with the hexadecimal number #009999.

5. Open ◉ testimonials.html from the data files folder.

✔ *This is an HTML document created in Microsoft Word.*

6. Save the testimonials.html page to your **cincitorial** folder as testimonials.html with the page title **Client Praise**. (Be sure to use Save As to save the page, or you will overwrite the page in the data folder.) If you are prompted to Update Links, click Yes.

✔ *Click the Site Root button in the Save As dialog box to quickly open the cincitorial folder.*

7. Clean up the Word HTML tags (accept default settings).

✔ *After you clean up the page, you will still see a dotted line border around the text that indicates it is enclosed in <div> tags. You will remove the unnecessary tags in a later exercise.*

8. Convert the page to XHTML 1.0 Transitional code. Click OK in the message about not being able to fix the Style tags. You will remove these tags in a later exercise.

9. Format the testimonials.html page as follows:

- Format the *CinciTorial Clients Speak Out* heading the same way as the contactus.html heading.
- Select the three-line group that begins with *Jay Fries*.
- Boldface the three lines.
- Boldface the remaining client names and affiliations.

10. Use Find and Replace to replace all instances of *Cincitorial* on this page with CinciTorial. If the Results panel opens during this operation, close it.

11. Check your spelling on all pages of the site and correct any errors you find.

✔ *You can add CinciTorial to your personal dictionary.*

12. Save and close any open pages and exit Dreamweaver.

Illustration A

We build computer books

Welcome to CinciTorial

CinciTorial is . . .

Application textbooks
Practice manuals
Instructors' notes
CD- and Web-based support materials

Working with CinciTorial is as easy as 1—2—3:

Contact us and set up a consultation.

Establish fee and work schedules

Sit back and relax!

Let us put the pieces together for you. Contact us today to learn how CinciTorial can help you get your compu books to market quickly, efficiently, and affordably.

Contact Us

Client Praise

ON YOUR OWN

1. Start Dreamweaver.

2. Open the gardencenter site and then open the index.html page.

3. Position the insertion point below the heading and import or copy the text from ⊙ indextext.doc from the Lesson 2 Data folder.

4. Format the index.html page as follows:
   - Change the heading color to a dark green and choose a different font combination for the heading, if desired.
   - Change the size of the first sentence of paragraph text to 4.

5. Open contact.html and make the following changes:
   - Change the heading color to one of your choice.
   - Apply italic to the address block. Apply bold-face to the first line of the address.
   - Boldface the phone and fax numbers.

6. Open ⊙ location.html from the Lesson 2 Data folder. Save the file in the gardencenter folder with the same name and the page title Location. Update links when prompted.

7. Clean up the Word HTML in this document. Format the heading the same way as the heading on the contact.html page.

8. Find all instances of *Central Gardens* throughout the site and change them to Civic Gardens. (If the Results panel opens during this process, close it when you have finished.)

9. Check spelling on all pages in the site.

10. Save and close all open pages and exit Dreamweaver.

Skills Covered

- **Adjust Paragraph Alignment**
- **Change Paragraph Indention**
- **Create Lists**
- **Insert a Date**
- **Use the History Panel**

Software Skills Alignment, indention, and lists help to organize areas of a Web page to make text easier to read and understand. Add a date to one or more pages in a site to let visitors know when pages were last updated. The Dreamweaver History panel makes it easy to perform repetitive tasks.

Application Skills In this exercise, you will continue working on the CinciTorial Web site. You will format page text in list format, adjust alignment and indention, and use the History panel to insert dates on site pages.

TERMS

Alignment Horizontal placement relative to the left and right edges of a page.

Bullet An indicator or simple graphic file used to denote individual points or items in an unordered (bulleted) list.

Definition list An HTML list type that includes a term set on one line and its description indented below.

History panel A Dreamweaver feature providing visual maps of past work on Web pages.

Ordered list A list—also called a *numbered list*—whose items must be in a certain order.

Unordered list A list that does not have to be in order. Also called a *bulleted list*.

NOTES

Adjust Paragraph Alignment

- Text in a Dreamweaver document is left aligned by default. This means that the text lines up at the left margin of the page.

- You can change **alignment** to center text or right-align text using the ☰ Align Center or ☰ Align Right button on the Property inspector. Return text to left alignment using the ☰ Align Left button.

- Dreamweaver also supports justified text using the ☰ Justify button, although some browsers may not support justified text.

- Text that has been center aligned is spaced an equal distance from the left and right edges of the page. Right-aligned text lines up evenly at the right margin of the page. Justified text lines up evenly with both margins.

Change Paragraph Indention

- Indent text from the left and right margins (see the following illustration) using the ⬛ Text Indent button on the Property inspector. You can select text to indent or apply the indent and then start typing.

Indent text from both edges of page

CinciTorial Clients Speak Out

CinciTorial has worked with publishers, corporations, and organizations to produce high-quality books, reports, training materials, and other publications. Listen to what our clients say about us:

"I didn't think we had a prayer of meeting our deadline on the training materials we needed for a seminar. CinciTorial took on the job and produced the text and accompanying CDs on schedule."

Jay Fries
Training Coordinator
Training Solutions

Indented text

■ Use the ⬛ Text Outdent button on the Property inspector to return the insertion point or selected text to the left page margin.

Create Lists

■ Web pages often include lists to emphasize text items. You can create two types of lists using buttons on the Property inspector: **unordered lists** and **ordered lists** (see the following illustration).

Unordered and ordered list in Web page

CinciTorial is . . .

- Application textbooks ——— Unordered list
- Practice manuals
- Instructors' notes
- CD- and Web-based support materials

Working with CinciTorial is as easy as 1—2—3:

1. Contact us and set up a consultation.
2. Establish fee and work schedules
3. Sit back and relax! ——— Ordered list

■ Use the ⬛ Unordered List button to create a list whose items do not have to be listed in a specific order. Each item begins with a small character called a **bullet**, so this type of list is often called a *bulleted list*.

■ Use the ⬛ Ordered List button to create a list whose items must be in a specific order. Each item begins with a number, so this list is often called a *numbered list*.

■ To apply either list format, click the appropriate button on the Property inspector. Dreamweaver automatically supplies the bullet or number.

■ The unordered list is formatted using the HTML <ul> (unordered list) tag. The ordered list is formatted using the HTML <ol> (ordered list) tag. Each individual line is formatted using the <li> (list item) tag.

✔ *Remember, you can see—and select—the HTML tags for text you are working on by checking the left side of the Document window's status bar.*

■ You can also apply HTML list tags directly from the Text category of the Insert bar.

■ You can change the properties of ordered lists by clicking on a list item and using the Text>List>Properties command on the menu bar or clicking the ⬚ List Item... button on the expanded Property inspector.

■ Dreamweaver displays the List Properties dialog box (see the following illustration). In this dialog box, you can change the number of the first list item (to start a list with the number 3, for example). You can also change the format of the list from the default numeric order to roman numerals or alphabetic order.

Change properties for ordered (numbered) list

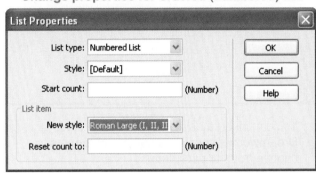

■ Dreamweaver offers a third type of list called a **definition list** that you can create using the Text>List>Definition List command on the menu bar. A definition list consists of a term that is set on one line, and its description that is set on the next line (see the following illustration).

Definition list

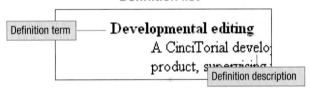

■ When you select the Definition List command, Dreamweaver applies the <dl> and <dt> (definition term) HTML tags.

■ After you have finished typing the term, press the Enter key. Dreamweaver automatically formats the next line with the <dd> (definition description) HTML tag, which indents the description below the term.

■ Definition lists can be used for text other than strict terms and definitions. You can use this type of list to quickly create headings and indented text, a site map or table of contents, and so on.

Insert a Date

■ You can insert the current date on any page in your site using Dreamweaver's Date feature. If you choose, the inserted date updates each time you save the page. This is a good way to keep track of modifications made to a Web site.

■ Use the Insert>Date command or the 🗓 Date button on the Common tab of the Insert bar to open the Insert Date dialog box (see the following illustration).

Insert and format day, date, and/or time

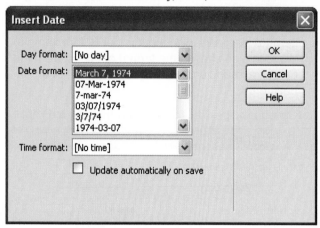

- You can insert a day, a date, and/or a time. Dreamweaver supplies a number of formats to choose from for each item.

- If you want the date/time information to update each time you save the page, select the *Update automatically on save* checkbox. Otherwise, the inserted date will stay the same as when it was inserted.

Use the History Panel

- Dreamweaver's **History panel** is a useful tool for tracking tasks. When displayed, the History panel (see the following illustration) shows a list of tasks that have been performed since the current page was created or opened.

History panel shows recent tasks

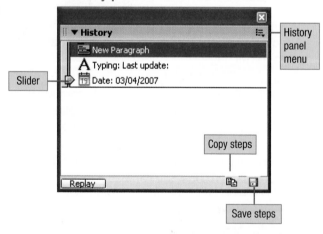

- Not only can you keep track of the tasks you have performed, you can use the History panel to repeat a series of steps or undo a number of recent tasks quickly and easily.

- Display the History panel using the Window>History command.

- As you perform each task, the History panel displays it with an identifying icon. The icon for a text entry, for example, is a capital *A*.

- Select a step by clicking it in the panel. Select more than one step by clicking the first, holding down the Shift or Ctrl key, and clicking additional steps.

- To save time in performing repetitive tasks, you can repeat steps. Select the steps you want to repeat, position the insertion point where you want to begin the steps, and click ⟨ Replay ⟩.

- To reverse a series of steps, drag the slider upward to "gray out" the steps you want to undo. You can redo those steps by dragging the slider back down to activate the steps again.

- The History panel tracks steps on the current page only. If you open another page, the History panel will not show the tasks you performed on the previous page.

- You can, however, copy steps from one page to use on another. Select the series of steps and click the ⌐ Copy selected steps to the clipboard button on the History panel.

- Then activate the page you want to copy the steps to and use the Dreamweaver window's Edit>Paste menu command to paste the steps. The copied steps are replayed as soon as they are pasted.

- You can also, if desired, save a series of steps as a command using the ⌐ Save selected steps as a command button on the History panel.

  ✔ *If you need to later delete the command, use the Commands>Edit Command List menu command, select the desired command, and click Delete.*

- Select the steps, click the button, and supply a name for the command. Your new command displays on the Commands menu so you can issue it at any time on any page.

■ When copying or saving steps, you might want to start with an empty History panel. You can clear the History panel of all entries by clicking the History panel menu and choosing Clear History from the menu.

■ Dreamweaver will warn you that this step cannot be undone. Click Yes in the warning box to clear the History panel.

PROCEDURES

Change Paragraph Alignment

Click in paragraph to align or position insertion point where new alignment should begin:

■ Click **Align Left** button ≣ on the Property inspector to left-align text . . . . . . `Ctrl`+`Alt`+`⬆Shift`+`L`

■ Click **Align Center** button ≣ on the Property inspector to center text . . . . . `Ctrl`+`Alt`+`⬆Shift`+`C`

■ Click **Align Right** button ≣ on the Property inspector to right-align text . . . . . `Ctrl`+`Alt`+`⬆Shift`+`R`

■ Click **Justify** button ≣ on the Property inspector to justify text . . . . . . `Ctrl`+`Alt`+`⬆Shift`+`J`

OR

1. Click **T**ext . . . . `Alt`+`T`
2. Click **A**lign . . . . `A`
   ■ Click **L**eft . . . . `L`
   ■ Click **C**enter . . . . `C`
   ■ Click **R**ight . . . . `R`
   ■ Click **J**ustify . . . . `J`

Indent Paragraphs

Click in paragraph to indent or position insertion point where new indentation should begin:

■ Click **Text Indent** button ⁺≣ on the Property inspector to indent . . . . `Ctrl`+`Alt`+`]`

■ Click **Text Outdent** button ⁺≣ on the Property inspector to remove indent . . . `Ctrl`+`Alt`+`[`

OR

1. Click **T**ext . . . . `Alt`+`T`
2. Click **I**ndent . . . . `I`

OR

Click **O**utdent . . . . `O`

Create Ordered and Unordered Lists

Select text to format or position insertion point where new format should begin:

1. Click **T**ext . . . . `Alt`+`T`
2. Click **L**ist . . . . `I`, `→`
3. Click **O**rdered List . . . . `O`

OR

Click **U**nordered List . . . . `U`

OR

■ Click **Unordered List** button ≣ on the Property inspector.

■ Click **Ordered List** button ≣ on the Property inspector.

   ✔ *To remove unordered list or ordered list formatting, follow the same steps.*

Change List Properties

1. Place the insertion point in the desired list.
   a. Click **T**ext . . . . `Alt`+`T`
   b. Click **L**ist . . . . `I`, `→`
   c. Click **P**roperties . . . . . . `P`

   OR

   Click `List Item...` on the expanded Property inspector.
2. Make the desired changes in the List Properties dialog box.
3. Click `OK`.

Create a Definition List

1. Click **T**ext . . . . `Alt`+`T`
2. Click **L**ist . . . . `I`, `→`
3. Click **D**efinition List . . . . . `D`
4. Type definition term.
5. Press `⏎Enter`.
6. Type definition description.

Insert a Date

1. Click **I**nsert . . . . `Alt`+`I`
2. Click **D**ate. . . . . `D`

   OR

   ■ Click **Date** button 🗓 on Common tab of the Insert bar.
3. Select format for Day, Date, and/or Time.
4. Select **Update automatically on save** checkbox to update date/time information each time page is saved.

Use the History Panel (Shift + F10)

To display the History panel:

1. Click **W**indow . . . . `Alt`+`W`
2. Click **H**istory . . . . `H`

To work with steps in the panel:

■ Click a step to select it.

■ Click step, hold down `Ctrl` or `⬆Shift`, and click additional steps to select more than one step at a time.

■ Select steps and click `Replay` to repeat steps.

■ Drag slider up to undo steps or back down to redo steps.

■ Select steps and click 🖫 to save steps as a command.

To copy steps from one page to another:

1. Select steps to copy and click 📋 on History panel.

2. Open page where steps are to be copied.

3. Click **Edit** . . . . Alt+E

4. Click **Paste**. . . . . P

EXERCISE DIRECTIONS

1. Start Dreamweaver and open the cincitorial site.

2. Open index.html.

3. Create an unordered list as follows:

   ■ Click in the *Application textbooks* line near the top of the page.

   ■ Apply the Unordered List format. Note that only one bullet displays, for the first item, because the items in this list are created using line breaks rather than paragraphs.

   ■ Position the insertion point just to the right of the *s* in the word *textbooks*, press Delete to remove the line break code and any extra space before the next word, and then press Enter to start a new paragraph. Notice that a bullet displays automatically for the new paragraph.

   ■ Repeat the last step to create bulleted items from the last two items in the list.

4. Create an ordered list as follows:

   ■ Click in the *Contact us and set up a consultation* line.

   ■ Apply the Ordered List format. The sentence is now numbered 1.

   ■ Apply the Ordered List format to the next two lines. Your page should look similar to Illustration A.

5. Make the following alignment changes:

   ■ Center the heading *We build computer books*.

   ■ Center the paragraph that begins *See books we have produced* . . .

   ■ Right align the last paragraph on the page. Insert a line break after the second question mark to move the last sentence in the paragraph to a new line.

6. Open the testimonials.html page. Indent the block of three lines that begins with the name *Jay Fries*.

7. Indent the remaining client names, titles, and affiliations.

8. Activate index.html. Display the History panel and clear the contents of the panel.

   ✔ *Dreamweaver may warn you that you will not be able to undo steps if you clear the list. Click* **Yes**.

9. Click to the right of the last sentence on the page. Press Enter and apply left alignment.

10. Type Last update: and press Spacebar.

11. Insert the date and time using formats of your choice. Choose to update the date and time automatically.

12. Deselect the date and time you just entered on the index.html page.

13. Select and replay the last four steps.

14. Use the History panel slider to undo the repeated steps.

15. Copy the last two steps (the last two steps are typing *Last update* and inserting the date) in the History panel.

16. Activate testimonials.html and insert a new blank paragraph below the last line. Paste the copied steps. If the *Last update* text is indented, remove the indent so it is left aligned.

17. Save and close any open pages. Note that the time updates on the pages where you inserted the date and time.

18. Exit Dreamweaver.

Illustration A

We build computer books

Welcome to CinciTorial

CinciTorial is . . .

- Application textbooks
- Practice manuals
- Instructors' notes
- CD- and Web-based support materials

Working with CinciTorial is as easy as 1—2—3:

1. Contact us and set up a consultation.
2. Establish fee and work schedules
3. Sit back and relax!

Let us put the pieces together for you. Contact us today to learn how CinciTorial can help you get your computer books to market quickly, efficiently, and affordably.

Contact Us

Client Praise

History

ON YOUR OWN

1. Start Dreamweaver and open the gardencenter site.
2. Open contact.html. Indent the mailing address on this page.
3. Open location.html. Insert a new paragraph below the existing text paragraph and insert the following text and list. (You can locate the en dash used in the day and time ranges in the last row of the Insert Other Characters dialog box.)

   Garden Center hours are as follows throughout the year:
   - Monday – Friday, 11:00 a.m. – 4:00 p.m.
   - Saturday, 10:00 a.m. – 5:00 p.m.

   From the first weekend in April to the last weekend in October:
   - Monday – Saturday hours as listed above
   - Sunday, 12:00 p.m. – 4:00 p.m.

4. Open index.html. Display the History palette.
5. Insert a new paragraph below the last text paragraph. Change the alignment to center and the text size to 2. Insert the following text. (Insert the copyright symbol from the Text Insert bar, and use your choice of date format.)

   Copyright © Reading Civic Garden Center. Site updated [current date].

6. Copy the steps, or save them as a command, and insert the copyright notice on all other pages in the site. (You may need to turn off the unordered list formatting on the location.html page after you paste the steps and then recenter the copyright notice.)
7. Save and close all pages and exit Dreamweaver.

Exercise | 10

Skills Covered

- **About Dreamweaver's HTML Code Features**
- **Use the Code Inspector**
- **Display Head Content**
- **Use Code Hints and the Tag Chooser**
- **Use the Tag Inspector**
- **Insert Snippets**
- **Use the Reference Panel**
- **Clean Up XHTML Code**
- **Find and Replace Code**

Software Skills   Dreamweaver's Web design tools make it unnecessary for users to work directly with HTML and other Web page programming code. However, you should know how to use Dreamweaver's Code view tools to modify, change, replace, or troubleshoot the tags that make up your site.

Application Skills   In this exercise, you will continue to work with the CinciTorial site. You will use Code view and code editing options to modify code on several pages in the site.

TERMS

Code Inspector Dreamweaver feature that displays HTML code used to create page elements.

Reference panel Dreamweaver panel that supplies reference material about HTML tags, CSS, and JavaScript.

Snippets Predefined HTML forms, tables, menus, and other Web page scripts that can be inserted from the Snippets panel in the Files panel group.

Tag inspector Dreamweaver panel that maps and shows the properties of the tags used in a Web page's code.

NOTES

About Dreamweaver's HTML Code Features

- As you have already learned, you do not need to have a comprehensive grasp of HTML coding to create Web pages. Dreamweaver takes care of the coding "behind the scenes" so that you don't have to.

- Many designers, however, prefer to work directly with HTML code to create page elements. Dreamweaver offers a great deal of support for such designers, making it easy to view code, insert code, and troubleshoot code problems.

- This exercise introduces some of the most common methods of working with HTML code in Dreamweaver. There are additional options for cus- tomizing the code interface that you can explore using Dreamweaver's Help files.

Use the Code Inspector

- If you prefer to work in Design view, you can still keep an eye on a page's HTML code using the **Code Inspector**. The Code Inspector displays the page's code in a floating window, as shown in the following illustration.

Code Inspector

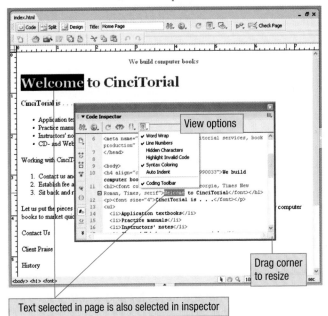

Text selected in page is also selected in inspector

- Use the Window> Code Inspector command to open the Code Inspector, or press F10.

- To work directly in the Code Inspector, click in it.

- You can drag the lower-right corner to increase the Code Inspector's window size. Click the ▦▾ View options button in the Code Inspector to display a menu of options for displaying the code. Selecting the Word Wrap option from this menu causes code to wrap within the window so you do not have to scroll to the right to see line endings.

- By default, the Line Numbers view option is selected to display a number next to each line of code. Line numbers assist in tracking your position in the text. Select the Auto Indent view option to automatically indent lines of code for a neat appearance.

- The Syntax Coloring view option displays HTML tags and attributes in dark blue so you can easily distinguish them from text. This option, too, is selected by default in the other code views.

  ✔ *You can adjust Code Inspector display settings using the Edit>Preferences command to open the Preferences dialog box and then selecting the Code Coloring category.*

- Enter text in the Code Inspector just as you would in the Document window by typing necessary HTML codes and text. You can also edit text or codes in the Inspector by inserting or deleting existing material.

- Changes made to tags in the Code Inspector do not appear in the Document window until you activate the Document window by clicking in it.

- The Highlight Invalid Code view option helps you identify mistakes in your HTML code. If you make a mistake in coding in the Code Inspector, it highlights your error in the code. In the following illustration, for example, Dreamweaver has detected that there is no closing tag for the <font> tag used to apply color to the heading.

Dreamweaver highlights error in code

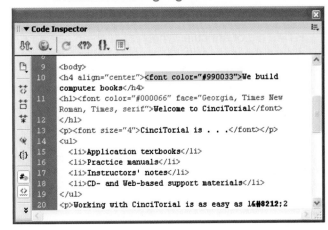

  ✔ *Dreamweaver provides a brief explanation of why the markup code is invalid in the Property inspector.*

- If you want errors in the code highlighted in the Document window when you are in Code view, select the Highlight Invalid Code option in the ▦▾ View options button menu on the Document toolbar. You can then easily find and fix errors in code.

Display Head Content

- Another way to display HTML information for a page without leaving Design view is to display the contents of its Head section in the Document window.

- Use the View>Head Content command to open a pane at the top of the current page with icons representing each HTML tag in the Head section (see the following illustration). Click an icon to see information about that tag in the Property inspector.

Display Head content in page

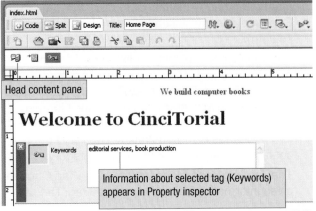

Information about selected tag (Keywords) appears in Property inspector

- You can also display Head content by clicking the 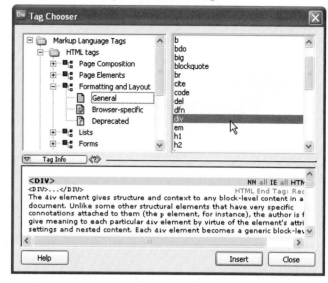 View options button on the Document toolbar and selecting Head Content from the resulting menu.

Use Code Hints and the Tag Chooser

- Dreamweaver offers several features that can make the process of entering code faster and more accurate.

- The code hints feature helps you insert a specific HTML tag or attribute. When you type an opening wicket, the code hints list appears in the code view that you are using (see the following illustration). You can scroll down this list to find the tag you want, highlight it, and press Enter to insert it following the wicket you typed.

Insert a tag using the code hints list

- After you type the closing wicket, you can enter the tag content, such as text or a heading. To insert the proper closing tag, type </. Dreamweaver automatically supplies the tag that needs to be closed and the final wicket.

- Code hints can also help you find an attribute for a tag. If you type a space after entering the h2 tag in the previous illustration, for example, another list displays, containing the attributes that can be used with the tag.

- Another way to find a specific HTML tag and insert it is to right-click at the desired location and select Insert Tag from the shortcut menu (or click the Insert>Tag menu command) to open the Tag Chooser (see the illustration at the top of the next column).

- The Tag Chooser displays a list of tag libraries at the left, including HTML tags, the CFML tags used with ColdFusion files, and ASP and JSP tags used for active server pages and JavaScript. Libraries may have subcategories such as the ones shown for HTML tags in the illustration. The list at right contains the tags available for that category.

- The Tag Info pane at the bottom of the Tag Chooser gives information about the selected tag. The user

Tag Chooser dialog box

can find out what the tag is for and whether it requires an end tag.

- Clicking the Insert button opens the Tag Editor dialog box for that tag (see the following illustration). You can further define the tag in this editor by providing information for the categories listed at the left side of the dialog box. After you have finished with the Tag Editor, the tag is inserted in the page code.

Tag Editor for tag

- You can display a Tag Editor for any code that has already been entered in a page by right-clicking the code and selecting Edit Tag from the shortcut menu.

Use the Tag Inspector

- The **Tag inspector** is in some ways similar to the Property inspector, in that it displays attributes applied to a currently selected tag. Also like the Property inspector, the Tag inspector can be used to select and modify attributes for a tag. Unlike the Property inspector, the Tag inspector can display a list of every attribute available for a tag, allowing a user to fine-tune a tag.

- The following illustration shows a small portion of the attributes list for a table. If you compare this list with the options on the Property inspector, you will see that many—such as bgcolor, border, cell padding—are the same. Scrolling down in the Tag inspector list shows you many more attributes you can change for the current table tag.

Tag inspector for a table tag

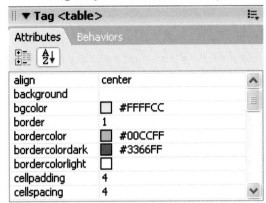

Snippets panel

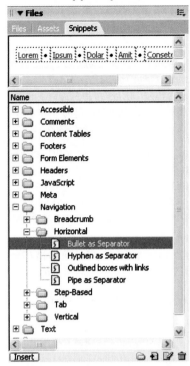

- If an attribute has a value, it displays in the right-hand column of the list. A user can apply values for an attribute by clicking in the right-hand column to see a list of options. As changes are made in the Tag inspector, the HTML code is immediately applied and the appearance of the object changes in Design view.

- The previous illustration shows attributes displayed in an alphabetical list. Display this list by clicking the ⇅ Show list view button in the panel. You can also display attributes organized in categories by clicking the ⊞ Show category view button.

Insert Snippets

- **Snippets** are predefined HTML forms, tables, menus for selecting month and year (handy for credit card order forms), Javascript tools for computing the area of a circle and other shapes, headers, footers, navigation bars, and other complex and/or commonly used code objects that can be selected and inserted using the ⌈Insert⌉ button or dragged directly into your Web page (see the illustration at the top of the next column).

- The Snippets panel is divided into two panes. When you select a snippet in the Snippets panel file tree in the lower pane, the upper pane reveals the snippet's content or code.

- Dreamweaver contains many predefined snippets that you can use as a starting point to customize as you desire.

Use the Reference Panel

- The **Reference panel** (see the second illustration in the next column) is used to find information on HTML tags, CSS (cascading style sheets) tags, and JavaScript objects. The Reference panel is one of the panels in the Results panel group that can be displayed below the Property inspector. The panels in the Results panel group show information

Reference panel

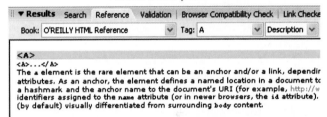

about a number of different site elements. You will use it more extensively in Lesson 7.

- To get help on a specific HTML tag (or other object), select the tag or object and use the Window>Reference command or click the ⟨?⟩ Reference button on the Code Inspector toolbar.

  ✔ *The Reference panel's content is provided by O'Reilly & Associates.*

- Use the two list boxes in the Reference panel to locate the tag or object and its properties and methods for which you want information. The Reference panel provides proper syntax and other important information about the item.

- You can also right-click in any HTML tag in Code view and select Reference on the shortcut menu to see information on that tag.

Clean Up XHTML Code

- One of Dreamweaver's most useful HTML tools is the Clean Up XHTML command, which you can find on the Commands menu. Use this command on your own files, for pages created by other authors that you want to incorporate in your Web site, or for text you have pasted from another source.

> ✔ *If your document is an HTML file created in a previous version of Dreamweaver or in another application, this menu command is Clean Up HTML. You can convert older HTML documents to XHTML using the File>Convert>XHTML 1.0 Transitional menu command if you want all documents in your Web site to meet the latest standards for XHTML.*

- The Clean Up XHTML command removes empty tags, combines nested font tags, and otherwise improves messy HTML coding on a page. This process is similar to cleaning up Word HTML codes, which you learned about in Exercise 8.

> ✔ *The Commands>Clean Up Word HTML command is used when you insert text copied from a Word HTML page or if a Word HTML page has been copied into your Web folder.*

- When you issue the command, you can select specific items to clean up in the Clean Up HTML/XHTML dialog box (see the following illustration). Use the Specific tag(s) box to type specific tag names you want Dreamweaver to clean up.

Specify codes to clean up

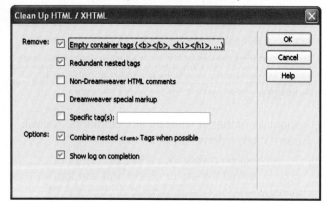

> ✔ *Do not type wickets when entering specific codes. Type only the tag name.*

- You can issue the Clean Up XHTML command at any time while working on page content to make sure your code is always correct and up to date.

Find and Replace Code

- In Exercise 8, you learned how to use the Find and Replace feature to locate and change text on a page or throughout a Web site. You can also use this feature to locate and modify code in a site.

- The illustration below shows how the Find and Replace dialog box looks to replace one code (strong) with another (b).

- To the right of the Search box is a list box you can use to specify the tag you want to find or change. The Action box contains a list of actions that can be performed when the tag is found. You can replace the tag itself, replace the tag and its contents, change the tag, add a tag before or after the start tag, strip (remove) the tag, and so on. Depending on the action you choose, you may need to specify additional information, such as what information to use as a replacement or what attribute to substitute for a specified attribute.

- To refine the search, click the ⊕ button to add another search box containing options such as With Attribute, Containing, or Inside Tag. These options allow you to be very specific about the text or tags you want to find. You can continue to click the button to add search fields, or click the ⊖ button to remove search fields.

- Use the Find Next and Replace buttons just as when finding text to locate instances of code and replace them.

Find and replace codes in Web site

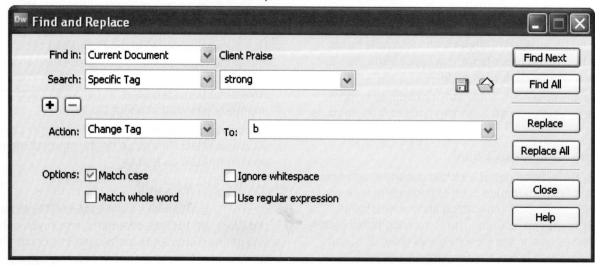

PROCEDURES

Open Code Inspector (F10)

1. Click **Window** . . . . Alt+W
2. Click **Co_d_e Inspector** . . . . . D, D, ↵Enter

Adjust Code Inspector Display

- Resize the Code Inspector window by dragging the lower-right corner.
- Click **View options** button 🗏▾ in the Code Inspector toolbar and select options:
  - Select **Word Wrap** to force code to wrap within the inspector window.
  - Select **Line Numbers** to display numbers to the left of each line of code.
  - Select **Highlight Invalid Code** to highlight coding errors.
  - Select **Syntax Coloring** to display tags and text in different colors.
  - Select **Auto Indent** to enable automatic indenting of code lines.

Enter Text and Codes Using Code Inspector

1. Click in the Code Inspector window to activate window.
2. Position the insertion point as desired and type or edit text or codes.
3. Click in the Document window to record and display changes.

Display Head Content (Ctrl + Shift + H)

1. Click **View** . . . . Alt+V
2. Click **Head Content** . . . . . . H
3. Click icon in the Head content pane to see information in Property inspector.

✔ Follow the same procedure to close the Head content pane.

Enter Tags and Attributes Using Code Hints

In Code view:

1. Position the insertion point where the new tag is to be entered.
2. Type < to begin the tag. The code hints list displays.
3. Scroll down the list to locate the tag to enter.
4. Click the tag to select it and press ↵Enter to insert it.
5. Type > to complete the opening tag.
6. After typing content, type </ to automatically complete the closing tag.

To use code hints to insert an attribute:

1. After entering the tag (step 4 above), press Spacebar. The code hints list of attributes displays.
2. Scroll down the list to locate the desired attribute.
3. Click the attribute to select it and press ↵Enter.

Use the Tag Chooser (Ctrl + E)

In Code view:

1. Position the insertion point where a new tag is to be entered.
2. Click **Insert** . . . . Alt+I
3. Click **Tag** . . . . G
   OR
   a. Right-click at the location to enter a new tag.
   b. Click **Insert Tag** on the shortcut menu.

4. Select the library that contains the desired tag in the Tag Chooser dialog box.
5. Select the desired tag from the list of tags at the right of the Tag Chooser dialog box.
6. Click [Insert].
7. In the Tag Editor, choose additional attributes for the tag if desired.
8. Click [OK] to insert the code.

Use the Snippets Panel (Shift + F9)

1. Click **Window** . . . . Alt+W
2. Click **S_n_ippets** . . . . N
   OR
   Click the **Snippets** panel tab in the Files panel group.
3. Open categories in the Snippets panel to see available snippets.
4. Click a snippet to see its code in the upper pane of the panel.
5. Click [Insert] to insert the snippet at the position of the insertion point.
   OR
   Drag the snippet to the Document window and drop it where it should appear.

Use the Reference Panel (Shift + F1)

1. Select the tag or object to get information on, if desired.
2. Click **Window** . . . . Alt+W
3. Click **Reference** . . . . F
   OR
- Click **Reference** button ‹?› on the Code Inspector toolbar.
   OR
- Click the **Reference** panel tab in the Results panel group.

Use the Tag Inspector Panel (F9)

To display the Tag Inspector panel:

1. Position the insertion point in the tag to inspect.
2. Click **Window** . . . . Alt + W
3. Click **Tag Inspector** . . . . . . T

To work with Tag inspector options:

- Click ⬛ to see a list of attributes for the current tag in an alphabetical list.
- Click ⬛ to see attributes organized in categories.
- Click to right of attribute to see values that can be specified for that attribute.

Clean Up XHTML Code

1. Click **Commands** . . . . Alt + C
2. Click **Clean Up XHTML** . . . L

---

3. Select specific items to clean up.
4. Select **Show log on completion** checkbox to see a report on items fixed.

   ✔ *This command may appear as Clean Up HTML for some pages.*

Find and Replace Code (Ctrl + F)

1. Click **Edit** . . . . Alt + E
2. Click **Find and Replace** . . . F
3. Select location to search: **Selected Text**, **Current Document**, **Open Documents**, **Folder**, **Selected Files in Site**, **Entire Current Local Site**.
4. Select **Specific Tag** in the **Search** box.
5. In list box to right, type the tag to search for, or click the list arrow and select the tag from the drop-down list.

---

6. Click **Action** and select the appropriate action for the identified tag.
7. Supply additional information for the action if necessary, such as the tag that will replace the specified tag.
8. Click Find Next to find first instance.
9. Click Replace to change the tag as indicated by the action.

   OR

   a. Click Find All to display all instances in the Results panel below the Property inspector.
   b. Click Replace All to change all instances at once.

EXERCISE DIRECTIONS

1. Start Dreamweaver and open the cincitorial site.
2. Open index.html.
3. Display the Head content pane and click the Keywords icon to see the keywords in the Property inspector.
4. Click the Meta icon to see the information on this tag in the Property inspector.
5. Look up information in the Reference panel on the <meta> tag.
6. Close the Head content pane and the Results panel group.
7. Open testimonials.html. Edit the page in the Code Inspector as follows:
   - Select and delete all text between the <style> </style> tags and the tags themselves in the Head section of the page.
   - Delete the blank line 6 of the code.
   - Delete any attributes that follow the opening body tag, such as *bgcolor* and its value and any lang=EN-US attributes.

8. Click in the Document window to record your changes.
9. Now use Find and Replace to clean up the code of the page as follows:
   - Change the strong tag to b.
   - Strip the div tag from the page. (This will eliminate the dotted line border around the page content.)
   - Strip the span tag from the page.
10. In the Code Inspector, view line 41 (or the line that contains the text *Lennie Makarios*). If you see a </b> closing tag after the name *Lennie* and a <b> opening tag before the name *Makarios*, remove these two tags, which are unnecessary.
11. Use the Clean Up HTML command to check coding on this page. (Use the default options; the clean-up process may find no mistakes to fix.) Then save and close the page.

12. Open the ⊙ services.html page from the Lesson 2 Data folder and save it in the current site. Update links when prompted.

   ✔ *The definitions at the bottom of this page could be displayed better as a definition list.*

13. Make the following formatting changes in the Code Inspector or any Code view option:

   - Scroll down to locate the *Developmental editing* paragraph. Click to the left of the word *Developmental* and press Backspace three times to remove the <p> tag.
   - Type < to begin the definition list. The code hints list displays. Scroll down to locate the dl tag and enter it. Type >.
   - Press Enter. Type <dt><b> to start and bold the first term, using the code hints list if desired.
   - Move the insertion point to the end of the line, just to the right of *editing*.

   - Delete the </p> tag.
   - Type </ to close the <b> tag, and then type </ to close the <dt> tag.
   - Move to the beginning of the next line and delete the <p> tag. Type <dd>.
   - Delete the </p> tag at the end of the definition and type </ to close the <dd> tag.

14. Format the next term (*Project management*) the same way you formatted *Developmental editing* and provide the proper codes for its definition.

15. Below the last definition, create a new line and type </ to end the list.

16. Click in the Document window or switch to Design view to inspect your changes. Your page should look similar to Illustration A.

17. Use the Clean Up XHTML command to check your coding.

18. Save and close all open pages and exit Dreamweaver.

Illustration A

Our Services

CinciTorial can jump into a project at almost any stage, including before the first word is written. Our services include:

- Topic research
- Writing from notes or outline
- Developmental editing
- Standard copyediting
- Art and permissions management
- Project management
- Proofreading
- Indexing

You might find the following definitions helpful.

Developmental editing
   A CinciTorial developmental editor coordinates with the client and the designated author to produce the desired product, supervising the art program and the schedule and preparing supplementary materials.

Project management
   A CinciTorial project manager oversees all aspects of a project, including client contact, scheduling, production team selection and supervision, quality control, permissions management, and budget management.

ON YOUR OWN

1. Start Dreamweaver and open the gardencenter site.

2. Open location.html. This page was created from a Word HTML page and needs the same kind of code fixes that the testimonials.htm page needed in the Exercise Directions. Use cleanup instructions for that page to make the following changes. You can use the Code Inspector or any Code view.

   ▪ Convert the page to an XHTML 1.0 Transitional page.

   ▪ If you have not already done so, convert the page to XHTML 1.0

   ▪ Delete the unnecessary <style> </style> tags and all information between them.

   ▪ Delete any attributes and values following the opening <body> tag.

   ▪ Remove the <div> tags.

   ▪ Word created SmartTags for the place name and address on this page. The code for these tags begins <st1. Locate all these unnecessary tags and delete them. (You cannot use Find and Replace for this action because <st1> is not in the list of standard HTML tags.)

3. Open index.html and display the Snippets panel in the Files panel group.

4. Position the insertion point to the left of the word *Welcome* in the first text paragraph.

5. In the Snippets panel, open the Navigation folder, open the Horizontal folder, and select the *Outlined boxes with links* snippet.

6. Click ⌈Insert⌋ in the Snippets panel to insert the navigation bar between the main heading and the first text paragraph.

   ✔ *You will edit the links in this navigation bar in the next exercise.*

7. Open contact.html and select the main heading *Contact Us.*

8. Display the Tag inspector and use it to change the color of the heading to #CC3300.

   ✔ *Hint: Click to the right of the color attribute to display the Text Color box. Deselect the text to see the color change.*

9. Activate location.html and change the heading color as you did in step 8.

10. Use the Clean Up XHTML command to check code on all pages.

11. Save and close all open pages and exit Dreamweaver.

DREAMWEAVER IN DEPTH

You can use code snippets to write and read *cookies*, small programs that store information about your system on your computer rather than on a server. You can try the process of inserting cookies to write and read data about your system in the following steps. These steps allow you to select a page color and store your selection as a cookie. When the cookie is read on the next page, the page color changes to the one you selected.

1. Create a folder named Exercise10 on your computer to store the files you will work with in this exercise.

2. Start Dreamweaver and open ◉ DID10_write.html from the data files for this lesson.

3. Save the file with the name cookie.html in the Exercise10 folder. (Click Yes when asked if you want to update links.)

4. Click on the red dashed outline that surrounds the form on the page to select the form. When the form is selected, form properties display in the Property inspector.

5. Click in the Action box and type My_Cookie.html.

6. Display the page in Code or Code and Design view, and click just to the left of the first tag on the page, <!DOCTYPE. You will insert the cookie snippet at this location.

7. Type < and scroll down to locate and insert the **script** tag. Type >.

8. Display the Snippets panel, click the + sign next to JavaScript, click the + sign next to cookies, click the Write Cookie snippet, and click Insert. The JavaScript is inserted on the page.

9. Type </ to close the <script> tag and then save the page.

10. Open ◉ DID10_read.html from the data files for this lesson and save the file with the name My_Cookie.html in the Exercise10 folder. Update links if prompted.

11. Display the page in Code or Code and Design view, and click just to the left of the first tag on the page, <!DOCTYPE.

12. Type < and scroll down to locate and insert the **script** tag. Type >.

13. Click the Read Cookie snippet, and click Insert. The JavaScript is inserted on the page.

14. Type </ to close the <script> tag and then save the page.

15. Activate cookie.html and use the Preview/Debug in browser button on the Document toolbar to preview the page in your default browser. You may need to allow active content if prompted.

16. Choose one of the page background colors in the form list, and then click the Submit button. The My_Cookie.html page should open using the color you chose.

The snippet you inserted uses a function to store a cookie name, value, and duration in hours. If you want to see the actual cookie information, look at line 47 of cookie.html. The onClick action is followed by the writeCookie function, and in parentheses are the cookie's name (pagecolor), value returned by the selection you made in the colormenu form, and its duration. See if you can locate the code in the My_Cookie.html page that sets the background color (bgColor) according to the value returned by readCookie.

17. Close all open Dreamweaver pages, the browser, and Dreamweaver.

Exercise | 11

Skills Covered

- About Links
- Create Text Links
- Link to Named Anchor

- Link to E-Mail Address
- Other Ways to Link

Software Skills   Links provide connections between Web pages that allow visitors to navigate your site. You can set links within a Web page, from page to page in a site, to an e-mail address, and from your site to other Web sites.

Application Skills   In this exercise, you will create links among the pages in the CinciTorial Web site using all the link options discussed in this exercise.

TERMS

Absolute link Link that uses the complete URL. Used for linking to outside Web sites.

Link Connection between locations in the same file or different files.

Named anchor Named location in a Web page used for links on the same page.

Relative link Link set within a specific site that does not include the domain name.

URL (uniform resource locator) Server and path information used to locate documents on the Internet.

NOTES

About Links

- Web sites rely heavily on **links**. Links are the means by which visitors "jump" and "browse" from one location on a page to another, one page to another within a site, or one site to another.

- Links work by directing a browser to open a page at a specific World Wide Web address called a **URL (uniform resource locator)**. The URL www.cincito-rial.com/, for example, would direct a browser to locate the site and open its home page on the cincitorial server on the World Wide Web (www)— or the server that hosts the CinciTorial Web site, since one Web server can host more than one Web site.

- Links are generally formatted in such a way that they stand out from surrounding text so visitors can easily recognize them. They are usually in a different color and underlined.

- You can create several types of links in Dreamweaver:

    - *Text links*—links created using a word or phrase.

    - *Named anchor links*—links from one location on a page to another location on the same page.

    - *E-mail links*—links that open an e-mail program so a visitor can send a message to a Web site's e-mail address.

    - *Graphic links*—links created using an image or icon on a page.

    - ✔ *You will learn about the first three types of links in this exercise. Graphic links are covered in Lesson 3.*

- Links can be either *relative* or *absolute*.
  - A **relative link** is a link to a page within your Web site. As you know, all Web site pages are stored together in a single folder. These pages remain in the same locations relative to each other even after a Web site is published to a Web server.
  - An **absolute link** takes a visitor from a page within your site to a different Web site. Because the browser must open a new Web site, it needs the full URL for the page it is to open.

Create Text Links

- To create a text link, you select the text you want to use as the link and then use the Property inspector's Link text box to set up the link.

- For a relative link to a page in your site, you can type the address of the page you want to link to directly in the Link text box (see the illustration below) or use the 📁 Browse for File button to the right of the Link text box to open the Select File dialog box for a list of your Web site pages from which to select.

- As soon as you complete the page name, Dreamweaver underlines and changes the color of the selected text to indicate it is a link.

- Relative links do not need to include the entire URL in the link address, only the actual page name. Note in the illustration, for example, that the Link text bar shows simply contactus.html.

- Another way to create a relative link to a page in your site is to use the 🔘 Point to File icon on the Property inspector to point directly to a page you want to link to:

- Select the text for the link and then click the 🔘 Point to File icon on the Property inspector.
- Drag the icon to an open page or to the file name in the Files panel (see the illustration at the top of the next page).

- The Link box updates with the name of the page you point to. Release the mouse button to complete the operation.

- Another easy method to create a link is to select the text and right-click it. Then click Make Link from the shortcut menu and select the desired file in the Select File dialog box.

  ✔ *Yet another method is to select the text for the link and then hold down Shift and drag to the file name in the Files panel or to an open page that is not maximized.*

- You must use the Property inspector to create an absolute link. Type the complete URL in the Link text box, including the proper protocol such as http:// or ftp://.

- Remove a link by selecting the text used as the link and clicking the Link list arrow on the Property inspector. On the list of links that displays, click in the blank area at the bottom of the list.

- You can also right-click a link and select Remove Link from the shortcut menu.

Link to Named Anchor

- A **named anchor**—also called a *bookmark*—is a specific location in a Web page (such as the top of the page). After you create a named anchor, you can set a link to it to help visitors navigate on a page.

Select text and type the link in the Link text box

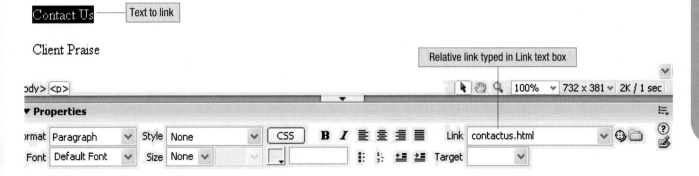

63

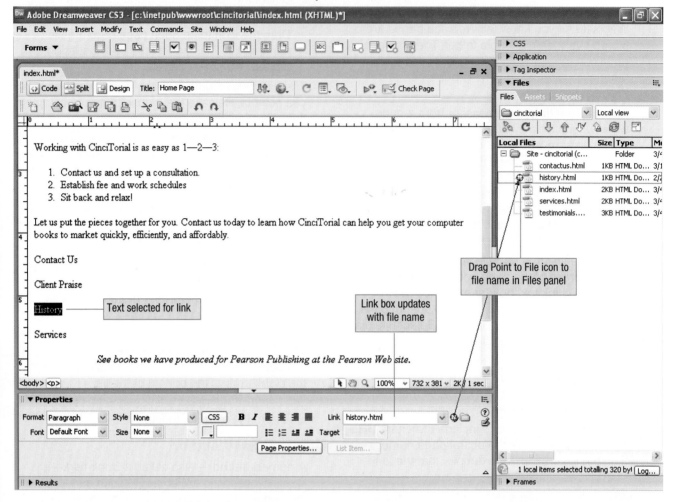

- Create a named anchor by positioning the insertion point at the location for the anchor (or select text to use as the anchor). Then use the Insert>Named Anchor command to open the Insert Named Anchor dialog box.

- You can also insert a named anchor by clicking the Named Anchor button from the Common category of the Insert bar.

- You can enter any name for the anchor (see the following illustration). If you have selected text as the anchor, that text appears in the Anchor name text box. You can change the displayed text if desired, however.

- Dreamweaver inserts an anchor marker at the location where you created the named anchor and the Property inspector changes to show the name of the anchor when it's selected.

- Create the link to the named anchor by selecting the text that will form the link and then typing a pound sign (#) followed by the anchor name in the Property inspector's Link box (see the following illustration).

  ✔ *When you select text for the link, the Property inspector changes back to its default view.*

Insert name for anchor

Named anchor link in Link box

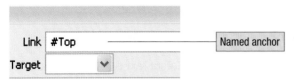

Email Link dialog box

Link to E-Mail Address

- One of the most helpful items to place on your site is a link to an e-mail address where your site visitors can send you questions, feedback, comments—even complaints.

- When creating an e-mail link, you can type the e-mail link directly in the Property inspector. Select the text you want to use as the link and then type mailto: followed by the designated e-mail address in the Property inspector's Link box (see the following illustration).

Link to e-mail address

- You can also insert an e-mail link using the Insert>Email Link command or the ⊞ Email Link button from the Insert bar's Common tab.

- When you use one of these options, Dreamweaver opens the Email Link dialog box (see the following illustration). Here you can type the text for the link and the e-mail address to link to.

- When a visitor clicks an e-mail link in a Web page, the default e-mail program opens with the designated e-mail address already displayed in the To box.

Other Ways to Link

- The links you have learned about in this exercise are not the only ways to link pages in Dreamweaver. In the next lesson, you will learn about the following link options:

  - Graphic links—Use a graphic as the link so that when a site visitor clicks the graphic, a new page opens. The graphic may be a button or any other image, including photos.

  - Image maps—Also called *hotspots*, image maps are portions of an image used as links.

  - Navigation bars—A navigation bar is a collection of links often organized using a table. You can specify images to accompany each link.

E-Commerce Connection

Linking Pages in a Site

One of the most important parts of planning a site is determining how pages will be linked within the site and what links will be created to other Web sites. Search programs such as Google often evaluate links among sites as a way of weighting search results. You can plan a site and its links using a storyboard.

Create a Storyboard

Use the Internet to search for information on what a storyboard is and how a storyboard can be used to plan a site. Then create a storyboard that will show the pages of a site for a club or organization and the links among the pages and to external sites.

PROCEDURES

Create Text Links (Ctrl + L)

To create a relative link:

1. Select text or graphic for link.
2. Type page address in Link text box on Property inspector.

   OR

   a. Click **Browse for File** button 🗀 on Property inspector and navigate to page.
   b. Click page and click
      [OK].

   OR

   a. Click **Point to File** button 🎯 on Property inspector.
   b. Drag Point to File icon to open page or to file name in Files panel.

To create an absolute link:

1. Select text or graphic to act as link.
2. Type complete URL in Link text box on Property inspector.

   ✔ You must include a protocol such as http:// or ftp://.

Create a Named Anchor (Ctrl + Alt + A)

1. Position the insertion point at location for anchor, or select text for anchor.
2. Click **Insert** . . . . [Alt]+[I]
3. Click **Named Anchor** . . . . . [N]

   OR

   Click or drag **Named Anchor** button ⚓ from Common tab of Insert bar.
4. Type name for anchor in Named Anchor dialog box.
5. Click [OK].

Link to Anchor

1. Select text or graphic to act as link.
2. Type # followed by anchor name in Link text box on Property inspector.

Link to E-Mail Address

1. Select text or graphic to act as link.
2. Type **mailto:** followed by e-mail address in Link text box on Property inspector.

   OR

1. Click **Insert** . . . . [Alt]+[I]
2. Click **Email Link** . . . . [L]

   OR

   Click or drag **Email Link** button 📧 from Common tab of Insert bar.
3. Type text to act as link in Text box of Email Link dialog box.
4. Type e-mail address in E-Mail box.
5. Click [OK].

EXERCISE DIRECTIONS

1. Start Dreamweaver and open the cincitorial site.
2. Open testimonials.html.
3. Create an anchor named Top to the left of the main heading on this page.
4. Link the *Back to Top* text at the bottom of this page to the Top named anchor.
5. Save and close the page.
6. Open the index.html page.
7. Create relative links from the *Contact Us* paragraph to contactus.html, from *Client Praise* to testimonials.html, from *History* to history.html, and from *Services* to services.html.

8. Create an absolute link to the Pearson Education Web site (http://www.pearsoned.com/) using the words *Pearson Web site* in the italicized paragraph.
9. Select the words *Contact us* in the last line on the page and use them to create an e-mail link to the e-mail address cincimail@cincitorial.com. The bottom of the page should look similar to Illustration A.
10. Save and close any open pages and exit Dreamweaver.

Illustration A

1. Contact us and set up a consultation.
2. Establish fee and work schedules
3. Sit back and relax!

Let us put the pieces together for you. Contact us today to learn how CinciTorial can help you get your computer books to market quickly, efficiently, and affordably.

Contact Us

Client Praise

History

Services

See books we have produced for Pearson Publishing at the Pearson Web site.

Questions? Comments on this site?
Contact us with your queries and suggestions.

ON YOUR OWN

1. Start Dreamweaver and open the gardencenter site.

2. Open the contact.html page and create an e-mail link to the e-mail address given in the *Leave a message for us* text paragraph.

3. Open ⊙ events.html from the Lesson 2 Data folder and save the page in the current site with the page title Garden Center Events. Update links if prompted.

4. Insert a named anchor to the left of the main heading and to the left of each of the season headings (*Spring, Summer, Autumn, Winter*).

5. Link the references to the four seasons in the last sentence of the first text paragraph to the named anchors.

6. Insert a new paragraph following the last text paragraph (and before the centered copyright notice) and insert the text Top of page. Link this text to the named anchor you inserted in the first text paragraph.

7. Locate the words *contact us* at the end of the first text paragraph and link them to the contact.html page.

8. Open index.html. You inserted a navigation bar on this page in the last On Your Own exercise. Modify the default links in the navigation bar as follows:

   - Select the word *Lorem* in the first table cell and type Home. You will not create a link for this text, because you are already on the home page.

   - Select the word *Ipsum* in the second table cell, and change the text to Contact Us. Link the page to contact.html.

   - Select the word *Dolar* in the third table cell, change the text to Events, and link to events.html.

   - Select the words *Sic Amet* in the fourth table cell, change the text to Location, and link to location.html.

   - Delete the last dummy entry, *Consetetur*.

9. Save and close any open pages and exit Dreamweaver.

Exercise | 12

Skills Covered

- **Preview a Site in a Browser**
- **Preview a Site in Device Central**
- **Work in the Files Panel**

Software Skills   Use the Preview in Browser feature at any time to see how a Web page will look when viewed by a site visitor. Once you have set up links, you can move from page to page in the browser to make sure the links are correct. Adobe Device Central makes it easy to view Web content as it will appear on a mobile device. Use the Files panel—collapsed and expanded—for site maintenance and to display the site map that shows how your pages are linked.

Application Skills   In this exercise, you will preview your CinciTorial site in a browser and on a mobile device to check how the pages look and test the links you created in the last exercise. You will also work with the Files panel to view site information.

TERMS

Broken link A link to a page that is not available in the site because it has been deleted, renamed, or not yet created.

Device Central A feature that allows a designer to preview various types of content on simulated mobile devices.

NOTES

Preview a Site in a Browser

- Links are not active in Dreamweaver's Document window. To test a link, you must preview a Web page in a browser.

- To preview a Web page, use the File>Preview in Browser command. You can select a browser from the pop-out submenu.

- You can also click the 🌐 Preview/Debug in Browser button on the Document toolbar. Click the button to display a short menu of options for previewing or debugging the page in a browser.

  ✔ *You can use the Preferences dialog box to add browsers to the preview list. It is a good idea to test your pages on several popular browsers to avoid display problems. You learn more about checking browser compatibility in Lesson 7.*

- The latest versions of browsers such as Internet Explorer and Mozilla Firefox support tabbed browsing, which allows you to display a whole series of visited pages as tabs at the top of the browser win-

dow, making it easy to move from page to page. Dreamweaver pages will preview correctly in a tabbed environment, so you can easily review all pages in a site by simply opening them as new tabs.

  ✔ *Check your browser's Help files to find out if you have tabbed browsing capability, or try right-clicking a link to see if you have the option of opening the page as a new tab.*

Preview a Site in Device Central

- Increasingly, Web visitors are viewing Web content on mobile devices such as PDAs and cell phones. Web designers need to consider how their Web pages will appear when viewed on a mobile device.

- Adobe **Device Central**, new in Dreamweaver CS3 (and other CS3 suite applications such as Photoshop and Flash), allows a designer to preview content for mobile devices. To open Device Central, click Preview in Device Central on the

Preview/Debug in browser list, or use the File>Preview in Browser>Device Central command.

- The Device Central window, shown in the illustration below, shows how Web content looks on sample mobile devices. Choose a manufacturer to see a list of devices available for testing. Double-click a device and then open the file you want to view to see how content looks in the device's screen.

- The Emulator panel shows the simulated device and allows you to view content and also interact with the device using its buttons and keypad.

- Use the Device Profiles tab to view specifications for the selected device and see the kind of content it supports.

- Device Central adjusts the Content Type list in the right pane according to what you are previewing. When previewing a Web page, for example, the Content Type list contains only the Browser option.

- If your page contains links, you can click them in the device's screen just as you would in a browser to verify that they work correctly.

- An in-depth examination of designing for mobile devices is beyond the scope of this book, but there are some general guidelines that a designer should keep in mind when creating content that might be viewed on a mobile device:

  - Opera Small-Screen Rendering, used to display content in the mobile devices, does not support some standard Web features such as frames and pop-up menus, and some font features such as underlining, strikethrough, and blink effects.

- The simpler the Web page, the better it will look on a mobile device. Fonts and colors should be kept to a minimum.

- Images should be sized to exact dimensions using CSS or HTML tags to ensure they will appear at a size appropriate for the mobile screen. Previewing in Device Central can help you select the best sizes for graphics.

Work in the Files Panel

- The Files panel is an extremely important interface in the creation of a Dreamweaver Web site. The Files panel is one of three panels in the Files panel group that is by default docked on the right side of the Dreamweaver window.

  ✔ You have already been introduced to the Snippets panel, one of the other Files panels. The remaining panel, the Assets panel, may contain image files, URLs, Flash movies, and other "assets" you might use throughout your site. You will use the Assets panel later in this course.

- The Files panel is designed to make it easy to perform maintenance operations such as creating new HTML documents, renaming files, creating folders, and deleting files. You can also view the Web site's navigation layout with a site map in the left pane.

Device Central displays a simulated device in the Emulator pane

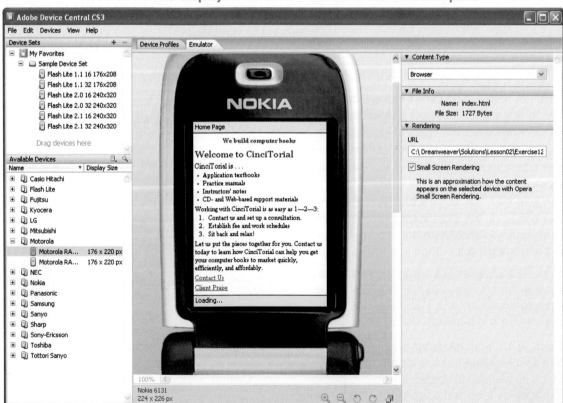

■ The Files panel is also where you set up and control the transfer of files between a local and remote site when publishing your site.

■ If the Files panel does not automatically open with the Web site, you can open it from the Window menu.

Displaying Files in the Files Panel

■ All files for the current Web site display in the Files panel's window, making it easy for you to access pages and other files.

■ You already know that you can switch to a different Dreamweaver site by selecting the site name on the Files panel's Site pop-up menu. This menu also gives you access to the computer's desktop and all drives on your system (see the following illustration).

Use the Site pop-up menu to access files on all drives

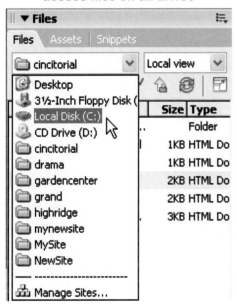

■ Clicking a drive (such as Local Disk (C:) in the preceding illustration) displays all files on that drive in the Files panel window. You can open folders to view their contents just as when working in a program such as Windows Explorer.

■ Using this feature, you can easily locate materials you need for your Web site that are not currently stored in your site.

Basic Files Panel Operations

■ With the files of the current Web site displayed in the Files window, you can perform a number of basic operations.

  ■ Open a page from the list of site files by double-clicking the file name.

  ■ Add a new page to the site by right-clicking on an existing page and selecting New File.

Dreamweaver creates a blank page with a selected placeholder name that you can change by simply typing a new name.

  ✔ *If you are using an application server, the new page will be created with its particular file extension.*

■ Rename a file by clicking on its name twice, slowly, to select the name, or right-click the file, select Edit, and then select Rename on the pop-out menu. Once the file name is selected (see the following illustration), type the new name.

Selected file name

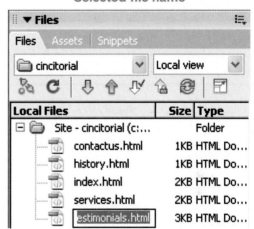

■ Delete a file by clicking its icon to select all information about the file and pressing the Delete key (or right-click and select Edit>Delete).

  ✔ *You cannot undo actions in the Files panel. However, if you delete a file you didn't intend to, you can restore it from the Windows Recycle Bin.*

■ When you rename a file, you can also change the file extension, but use caution when you do so. Specific types of pages such as ASP pages contain code required for that page's function. Simply renaming an .html page as an .asp page will not apply that code.

■ If you rename a file that is linked to other pages in a Web site, Dreamweaver will ask if you want to update links with the new page name (see the following illustration).

Update links when renaming pages

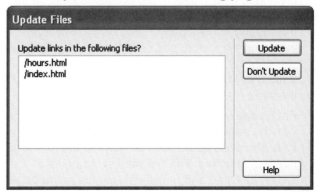

- You will generally want to click the [Update] button and allow Dreamweaver to update the links for you.

- Dreamweaver will also caution you if you delete a page that is linked to other pages in the site (see the illustration below).

Dreamweaver warns about deleting a linked page

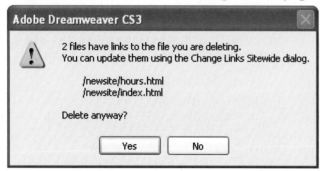

- Deleting a linked page results in a **broken link**; that is, a link that doesn't take you where it is supposed to. You can identify broken links easily in the site map, discussed in the next section.

View the Site Map

- The site map enables you to view your file structure as a graphic representation (see the following illustration).

Site map in the expanded Files panel

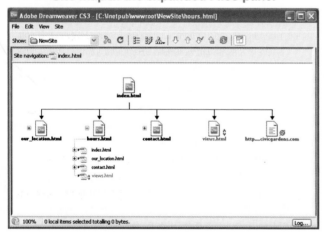

- You can view the site map in either the collapsed or expanded Files panel. In the collapsed Files panel, click Map View on the Site View pop-up menu. In the expanded Files panel, click the ⚒ Site Map button on the toolbar and select either Map Only (to see only the map, as shown in the preceding illustration) or Map and Files (to see both the map and the site's files in side-by-side panes).

- Each page in the site is represented by a page icon with the page's name (or title) shown below the icon. The site's home page displays at the top of the map structure. The site map structure also shows absolute and e-mail links on the home page.

- Organization chart–type lines show the relative links between the home page and its subordinate, or *child*, pages.

- Child pages that contain links display a ⊞ plus sign. Click this symbol to expand the site map and show links from the child page. After you click the plus sign, it becomes a ⊟ minus sign you can click to collapse the portion of the site map under the current page.

- The site map identifies absolute links to pages outside the site to make it easy to keep track of these links. External links are shown in blue, with the ⊘ Web symbol above the link.

- The site map can help you eliminate problems in your Web site such as broken links. The page name or title of a page with a broken link displays in red, with a broken link symbol above the name (see the following illustration).

Page with broken link

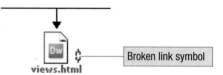

- If you delete a linked page from the Local Files pane of the Files panel, the page remains in the site map, displaying the broken link symbol, until you remove it by selecting it and choosing the Site>Remove Link command on the Files panel menu bar.

- Modify the site map layout using one of the Site Definition wizard's screens on its Advanced tab. Use the Site>Manage Sites command on either the Dreamweaver menu bar or the Files panel menu bar. This opens the Manage Sites dialog box. Select the desired site to edit and click the Edit button.

- Click the Advanced tab and select the Site Map Layout category in the Site Definition dialog box (see the following illustration).

Change site map layout

✔ *You may get an error message if you try to click the Basic tab when you are in the edit site mode.*

- You can make the following adjustments to the layout:
  - Change the number of columns from the default value of 200. Columns equate to the number of pages displayed below the home page.
  - Change the column width from the default value of 125. Column width is the amount of space in pixels taken up by each page displayed in the site map. You must enter a value between 70 and 1000 for this option.

- Change the label for the pages from the default of the file name to the page title. For example, you can change the label of the top-level page from index.html to Home Page.

- Choose to display files that are normally hidden or dependent files such as a page's images.

E-Commerce Connection

Internet Security

From the moment you begin preparing to post Web files online, you need to think about Internet security. An e-commerce site often handles sensitive information that cannot be allowed to fall into the hands of hackers, phishers, or other e-criminals.

Investigate Internet Security

Use the Internet to find information on Internet security issues and legislation designed to keep the Internet safe. Write a report in which you analyze threats to Internet security and how current legislation can be used to prevent or punish criminal activity on the Internet.

PROCEDURES

Preview a Site in a Browser (F12)

1. Click **File** . . . . (Alt)+(F)
2. Point to **Preview in Browser** . . . . . . (P), (P), (↵Enter)
3. Select a browser from the submenu.

   OR

   Click **Preview/Debug in Browser** button on the Document toolbar and select a browser from the menu.

Preview a Site in Device Central (Ctrl + Alt + F12)

1. Click **File** . . . . (Alt)+(F)
2. Point to **Preview in Browser** . . . . (P), (P), (↵Enter)
3. Click **Device Central** . . . . . (D)

OR

Click **Preview/Debug in Browser** button on the Document toolbar and then click **Preview in Device Central**.

4. Click a Manufacturer name in the Available Devices list, then double-click a specific device from that manufacturer.
5. Click **File** . . . . (Alt)+(F)
6. Click **Open** . . . . (O)
7. Navigate to the location of the file you want to display in the selected device.
8. Select the file and click Open .

   ✔ *The page opens in the Emulator tab.*

9. To see the page in a different device, double-click the new device name.

Display Files in the Files Panel

- Click the Site pop-up menu and select a drive or Web site.

Files Panel Operations

To open a page from the current Web site:

- Double-click the file name in the Files panel window to open a page in the Document window.

To add a new page to the site:

1. Right-click on any existing page to display a shortcut menu.
2. Click **New File**.
3. Type a name for the new file.

To rename a page:

1. Click the file name twice, slowly, in the Files panel window to open the file name for editing.

OR

a. Right-click the file name to display a shortcut menu.

b. Point to **Edit**.

c. Click **Rename** from the shortcut menu.

2. Type the new name (and file extension if necessary).

3. Press `↵Enter`.

4. If the renamed page is linked to other pages, click [Update] to update links.

To delete a file:

1. Click the file name once to select and press `Del`.

   OR

   a. Right-click the file name to display a shortcut menu.

   b. Point to **Edit**

   c. Click **Delete**.

2. If the deleted page is linked to other pages, click [Yes] to delete.

3. Click the deleted page icon in expanded site map.

4. Click **Site**.

5. Click **Remove Link**.

Modify Site Map Layout

1. Click **Site** . . . . `Alt`+`S`
2. Click **Manage Sites** . . . . . . `M`
3. Select the site name in Manage Sites dialog box and click [Edit...].
4. Click the **Advanced** tab.
5. Click **Site Map Layout** category.
6. Change **Number of columns** or **Column width** value.
7. Specify **File names** or **Page titles**.
8. Choose to display hidden files and/or dependent files.
9. Click [OK].
10. Click [Done].

EXERCISE DIRECTIONS

1. Start Dreamweaver and open the cincitorial site.

2. Open index.html and display this page in your default browser.

3. Test the links on the Home Page. Use the browser's Back button as necessary to return to the Home Page.

4. Click the e-mail link to see how it opens your e-mail program, but do not send a message.

5. Test the link to the named anchor on the Client Praise page.

6. Close the browser.

7. Preview the home page in Device Central:

   ■ Expand the Nokia list in the Available Devices list.

   ■ Double-click Nokia 6300.

   ■ Use the File menu to open the index.html page from the current site.

   ■ Change the device to another (try your own mobile phone if you have one).

8. Click the *Contact Us* link on the displayed Web page to see how the linked page displays.

9. Close Device Central.

10. Open the Files panel, if necessary.

11. Rename the testimonials.html file to praise.html. Update links when Dreamweaver prompts you to do so.

12. Expand the Files panel and select to display the entire site map.

13. Modify the site map layout to set 15 columns and a column width of 90. Choose to show page titles rather than file names.

14. Show both the site files and site map in the expanded Files panel.

15. You have decided you do not need a history page in the Web site. Delete the history.html page in the Local Files pane and answer Yes when asked if you really want to delete it.

16. Remove the History page link in the site map.

17. Collapse the Files panel.

18. Open the index.html page from the Files panel, if necessary, and remove the History link text from the text on this page. Notice that it is no longer underlined. (Also remove the blank line that remains after you delete the text.)

19. Save and close any open pages and exit Dreamweaver.

ON YOUR OWN

1. Start Dreamweaver and open the gardencenter Web site.

2. Open index.html and change the *Location* link text in the navigation bar to Information.

3. Point to the outside border of the navigation bar table and click to select it. You will know it is properly selected when a heavy black border displays around the outside of the table.

4. Copy the navigation bar table and paste it below the main heading on the contact.html page.

5. On the contact.html page, create a link from the word *Home* in the navigation bar to index.html.

6. Copy this revised navigation bar and paste it below the main heading on the other two pages in the site.

7. In the Files panel, change the name of the location.html file to info.html and update links.

8. On the info.html page, change the first heading from *Location* to Location and Hours, and make the same change to the page title.

9. View the site map in expanded view, and click the plus signs for the pages that have them to see the links on each page.

10. Collapse the site map.

11. Save changes to all pages, and preview index.html in the browser.

12. Test each link on the home page, using the *Home* link on each page to return to the home page. When you reach the events.html page, test all links to named anchors and to the contact.html page.

13. On the contact.html page, test the e-mail link, but do not send a message.

14. Close the browser.

15. Preview the site in Device Central, choosing several of the sample devices to check pages. Try the page links in the Emulator screen.

16. Close Device Central.

17. Close all open pages and exit Dreamweaver.

Exercise | 13

Summary Exercise

Application Skills In this exercise, you will continue to work on the High Ridge Swim & Tennis Club site. You will add a new page, create a link to a Word membership form, and format the pages.

DIRECTIONS

1. Start Dreamweaver and open the highridge site you created in Exercise 4.
2. Open the ⊙ membership.html file from the Lesson 2 Data files. Save it in your highridge site and change the page name to Membership.
3. Clean up the code on this page:
   - Convert the page to an XHTML 1.0 Transitional page.
   - Use the Clean Up Word HTML command to remove unnecessary Word HTML code.
   - Use the Code Inspector to remove unnecessary codes such as the <style> tags and remove unnecessary attributes in the opening body tag.
   - Use Find and Replace to strip any <div> tags.
   - Remove the <st1> tags and attributes for the address information.
   - Clean up XHTML to make sure the page code is up to date.
   - Insert a line break at the end of the first line of the mailing address.
4. In the Files panel, display the drive that contains your data files.
5. Copy the ⊙ memberform.doc file from the Lesson 2 Data files to the highridge site folder.

   ✔ Select the file, right-click and choose Edit, and then choose Copy. Open the highridge site again, right-click in the Files panel, choose Edit, and choose Paste.

6. On the membership.html page, link the text *Membership Form* to the memberform.doc file. (Type the link in the Link text box, rather than using the Point to File feature.)
7. Under the *Fees* heading, create an ordered list from the three fees.
8. In the last two lines on the page, insert an em dash special character between the words *Family* and *Blood*, and between the words *Individual* and *Single*.
9. Select all text on the page and change the font combination to the one beginning with Verdana.
10. Apply text formats on the page as follows:
    - Choose new colors for the main heading and the two subheadings.
    - Boldface and indent the address information. Change the size of this text to 2.
    - Italicize the text *applied toward initiation fee* at the end of the first numbered item under the *Fees* heading. Your page should look similar to Illustration A.
11. Open index.html and change the default font for all text on the page to the font combination that begins with Verdana.
12. Choose a new color for the main head, and make the *Club Features* heading the same color as the first heading on the membership.html page.
13. Make the list of club features into an unordered list. Use any Code view to replace the <br> tags so that each line of the list has a bullet.
14. Create a link from the last two words on the page, *membership page*, to the membership.html file.

15. Save and preview the index.html page in the browser. Test the link to the Membership page.

16. On the Membership page, test the link to the membership form. A File Download box should display asking if you want to open or save the file.

Choose to open it to see the form linked to your site.

17. Close the browser.

18. Close all open pages and exit Dreamweaver.

Illustration A

Membership

High Ridge Swim & Tennis Club is currently accepting applications for new members. If you wish to apply, please fill out the application form below and send to the address listed below along with a $50 application fee.

Applications are reviewed by the board of directors and require two signatures of existing members.

Membership Form

Please mail to:

> **High Ridge Corporation**
> **P.O. Box 3005**
> **High Ridge, OH 45213**

Fees

1. Application Fee: $50 (non-refundable) paid with application (*applied toward initiation fee*)
2. Initiation Fee: $600 (non-refundable)
3. Yearly Dues: $490 (family) and $315 (individual) payable by due date

Types of Membership

Family—Blood relatives living fulltime in member's home

Individual—Single person at least 21 years of age, in a single-person household

Exercise | 14

Application Exercise

Application Skills   In this exercise, you will continue to work on the Web site for the Grand Theatre that you began in Exercise 5. You will add page content, format pages, and create links to start setting up site navigation.

DIRECTIONS

1. Start Dreamweaver and open the grand Web site.
2. Use the Files panel to create a new file and name it show.html. Give it the page title Now Showing.
3. Enter the following text on the show.html page.

   Bargain Tuesdays - All seats, all shows, all day, $5.50
   Matinee any day, $6.00
   Children under 10 (after 6:00 p.m.), $5.50
   Seniors with AARP card (after 6:00 p.m.), $6.00
   General evening admission, $8.00

   Shows and Times Last Updated:

   Screen 1

   Screen 2

   Screen 3

   Screen 4

   For external reviews of shows, click here.

   Back to Top

4. Center and boldface the first five lines on the page. (Use line breaks rather than paragraphs for this list.)
5. Apply a heading tag of your choice to the *Shows and Times Last Updated* heading, and then insert a date after the colon. (You should specify automatic update.)
6. Format the four Screen headings with a heading tag of your choice.
7. Under each Screen heading, insert several film titles and show times for each film. You can use films that are currently playing, create themed showings such as classic science fiction, or simply make up film names.

8. In the second-to-last line on the page, select the words *click here* and create an absolute link to the Internet Movie Database at http://www.imdb.com.
9. Insert a named anchor to the left of the first line on the page, and then link to it using the *Back to Top* text at the bottom of the page.
10. Use Clean Up XHTML to check coding on the page.
11. Open the index.html page. Set up links as follows:
    - Select *show times* in the paragraph below the first heading and link it to the show.html page.
    - Select *Click here* in the second sentence of the paragraph below the second heading and link it to the location.html page.
12. Create an unordered list from the Special Features list.
13. *Dolby* is a registered trademark. Insert the ® special character following the word *Dolby* in the unordered list.
14. Format all three pages of the site:
    - Select a new font combination if desired.
    - Create a color scheme for the headings throughout the site.
    - Adjust font sizes if desired.
15. Display head content on the index.html page and check your keywords for this site.
16. Check spelling on all three pages.
17. Save all pages and then display the home page in the browser and check links in the site.
18. Close all open pages.
19. Exit Dreamweaver.

Exercise | 15

Curriculum Integration

Application Skills   Your American Literature class has decided to create a Web site on which each class member will publish his or her favorite poem from a nineteenth or twentieth century author, along with a brief structural analysis of the poem. Before you begin this project, gather the following information about the poem you have chosen:

- The poem's meter, if it is not free verse
- The poem's rhyme scheme, if there is one
- The poem's structure, if it has a formal structure such as couplets or quatrains

DIRECTIONS

Define a new site with the name poetry. Create a new page for the site and name it mypoem.html. Give it a page title the same as the poem's title.

If you have Microsoft Word available, open it and type your poem in a new Word document. (This gives you the advantage of instant spell checking.) Import the Word document to the mypoem.html page.

Format the poem as desired. For example, boldface the title or italicize the author's name. Make any other adjustments to the layout of the poem necessary to preserve the author's structure.

Create a new Web page and give it a name such as analysis.html. Add an appropriate page title and a heading. On this page, you will provide some metrical information about your poem.

Begin creating a definition list, using the word Meter as the first term. For the definition, explain the meter of your poem. Continue the definition list with the term Rhyme scheme and give the rhyme scheme of your poem. The final term should be Structure, in which you explain how your poem is structured. If your poem does not have a formal meter, rhyme scheme, or structure, indicate this below the appropriate term.

Below the last term, insert text to direct readers back to the poem. Below the poem, insert a link to the analysis page.

Below the link on each page, insert text giving your name, the current date, and the name of the poem. Format this text as desired. Use the History panel to record this information on the first page and then copy it on the second page.

When the pages are published, they should have unique names. Use the Files panel to rename your pages so they reflect the title of the poem you chose. Use one or two words from the poem title in the page names so it is obvious what poem each page represents. Be sure to update links when alerted.

Save pages and then preview the pages in the browser. Make any final changes necessary and save all pages.

Exit Dreamweaver.

Exercise | 16

Critical Thinking

Application Skills   In this exercise, you will continue to work on your personal Web site. You will format existing page content, add new content to the site, use a snippet to create a navigation bar, and insert other links to improve site navigation.

DIRECTIONS

- Review the pages you have already created for your Web site and modify them as desired. For example, create ordered or unordered lists from some of the page text, change text formats (font combination, font size, font style, font color), modify paragraph alignments and indentions to improve the look of the pages, insert special characters if needed, and so on. Illustration A shows a sample home page for a personal Web site.

- Create additional text for the site in Microsoft Word. You may save the new material in default Word format and then import it, or save it as a Word Web page and open it directly in the site. (Don't forget to save the page in the site if you use the second option.)

- Clean up XHTML coding as needed for the new material you added.

- Insert a navigation bar snippet on the home page and modify it to link to the pages currently in your site. Copy the navigation bar to other pages in the site and make sure all links are correct.

- Create other links from page to page in the site as desired. You may want to add links to named anchors or links from text to other pages. You may also want to insert links to pages outside the site.

- Add an e-mail link somewhere in the site using your school or personal e-mail address so that site visitors can contact you with questions or comments.

- Check spelling on all pages.

- Save all pages and preview the site in the browser.

- Preview the site in Device Central using several devices of your choice.

- Save all open documents and close them.

- Exit Dreamweaver.

Clifton Drama Club

Home   <u>Outings</u>

Welcome to the Drama Club!

The Clifton Drama Club is a group of people who love everything about the theater, including:

- Acting in dramas
- Writing drama
- Production design
- Costume design
- Makeup design
- Stage management
- Lighting and other technical support

If you're interested in any of these areas, the Drama Club is for you.

What We Do

The Clifton Drama Club sponsors four plays a year and contributes expertise and support for the school's musical production. When we're not working on school dramatics, we schedule visits to <u>local and regional theater productions</u> to see how the pros do it. The Drama Club also arranges for seminars and workshops with local theater groups to learn the nuts and bolts of production design, costumes and makeup, and the behind-the-scenes technical skills without which the show would never be able to go on.

For more information on the Drama Club, contact <u>studentname@website.net</u>.

Lesson | 3
Work with Graphic Elements and Templates

Exercise | 17

Skills Covered

■ **Change Page Background Color**

■ **Insert Horizontal Rules**

■ **Use Web-Safe and Custom Colors**

Software Skills   Use a solid color background to liven up a Web page or emphasize it among other pages in a site. Horizontal rules divide pages to emphasize parts of the page content. When selecting colors for a Web site, you can use Dreamweaver's palette of Web-safe colors or create your own colors.

Application Skills   In this exercise, you will add some graphic interest to the CinciTorial Web site by applying a background color to a page and inserting horizontal rules.

TERMS

Web-safe colors   A palette of 216 colors that will display the same in any browser, regardless of the operating system.

NOTES

Change Page Background Color

■ A simple way to add graphic interest to a Web page is to change its background color. By default, Web pages have a white background. You can use any of the colors in the Dreamweaver color palette as a page background color—but Web-safe colors are recommended.

■ To change page background color, use the Modify>Page Properties command to open the Page Properties dialog box (see the following illustration). If you have the Property inspector expanded, you can also click [Page Properties...] to open the Page Properties dialog box.

Page Properties dialog box

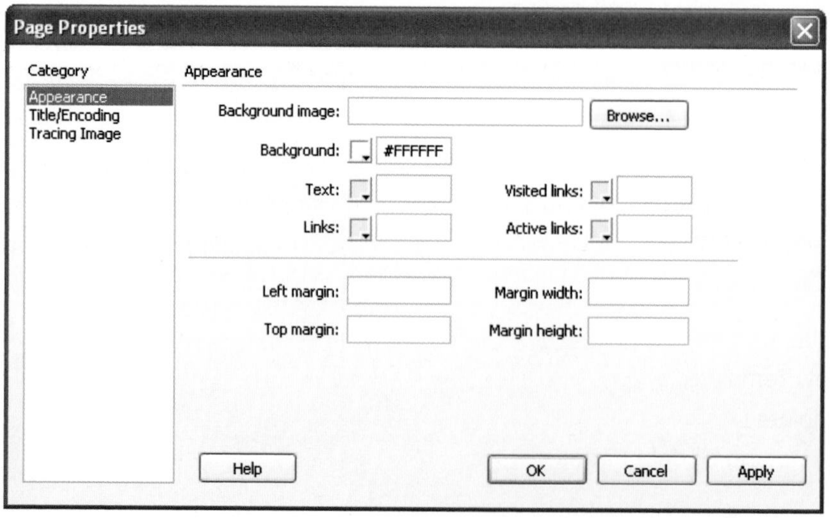

- Click the ▢ Background color button to display the color palette and use the eyedropper to select a color.

- You can use the Apply button to apply your color choice without closing the Page Properties dialog box. If you do not like the applied color, you can open the color palette and choose a different color.

- Notice the other color buttons in this dialog box. You can use them to change the color of all links on the page, as well as change colors of visited links and links in the process of being clicked (active links).

- You can also apply margin settings from this dialog box. You will learn why you might want to set page margins in a later exercise.

Insert Horizontal Rules

- You can insert horizontal rules on your Web pages to separate sections of text. Position the insertion point at the beginning or end of a paragraph and use the Insert>HTML>Horizontal Rule command.

  ✔ *If you position the insertion point at the end of a paragraph, the horizontal rule is inserted below the paragraph. If you position the insertion point at the beginning of a paragraph, the horizontal rule is inserted above the paragraph.*

- You can change horizontal rule formats by selecting the horizontal rule and changing settings in the Property inspector (see the illustration below).

- By default, the rule runs the full width of the Web page. You can specify a width in the W text box using either a pixel measurement or a percentage of the page width. If you specify a width less than the full page, you can choose an alignment option of left, center, or right.

- Use the H box to specify a height for the rule in pixels. Selecting the Shading checkbox adds shading to the rule that makes it look three-dimensional. Deselect this checkbox to make the rule a solid color.

- The Properties panel does not have a feature to change the horizontal rule's color. However, you can change the color of the horizontal rule by editing the HTML <hr> tag in the Tag inspector's property sheet or in Code view, as follows:

  ```
  <hr color="009999">
  ```

- The rule color does not display in Design view. You must preview the page in the browser to see the color.

  ✔ *If you specify a color for the rule, you cannot also display shading. Regardless of whether Shading is selected, the rule will display as a solid color.*

- The color attribute for horizontal rules may not display correctly in all browsers. To make sure the rule displays as you want it to, you can modify the HTML tag using a CSS style, as you will learn in Exercise 39.

- Although horizontal rules are easy to insert, you may want to consider using CSS styles to apply rules because you have many more options about where to position rules and how to format them.

Use Web-Safe and Custom Colors

- As has been discussed in an earlier exercise, the color palette shown when a user clicks a color box in a panel or dialog box displays **Web-safe colors**. The 216 color blocks in this palette display the same regardless of browser or operating system, which means that a designer who chooses color #990000 for a heading can be confident that the color will appear as the same dark red in Internet Explorer, Netscape, Firefox, or Opera running on a Windows, Macintosh, or Linux operating system.

- When this palette of colors was developed, most computers could display a maximum of 256 colors. Now that many systems are capable of 16-bit and 32-bit display, allowing them to display thousands of colors, it is not as important to stick to the Web-safe color palette as it once was.

- An exception to this freedom of color expression is if a user is designing for Web devices such as cell phones or PDAs. Adobe's Device Central makes it easy for you to check how colors will display on your chosen mobile device.

- To choose a color outside the Web-safe spectrum click the ⬤ System Color Picker icon at the upper-right side of the color palette to open the Color dialog box (see the illustration on the next page).

- Select one of the basic color blocks or create a custom color as follows:

  - Enter values for Hue, Saturation, and Luminescence or for Red, Green, and Blue.

  - Drag the pointer in the continuous color palette and then adjust intensity in the vertical slider.

- The custom color can be added to the Custom colors palette to be available for future use.

Change horizontal rule formats

Color dialog box

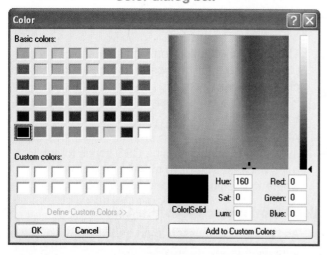

- The Web-safe color palette that displays when a user clicks a color box offers an options arrow at the upper-right edge of the palette. Click this arrow to display additional options. A user can display the Continuous Tone palette, or palettes especially for Windows or Macintosh systems. A grayscale palette is also available on this menu.

E-Commerce Connection

The Internet and Businesses

The development of the Internet has had an enormous impact on business. Communications, marketing, and sales have undergone striking changes since the advent of fast Internet connections.

Investigate Effects of the Internet on Businesses

Use the Internet to search for information on how businesses use the Internet. Write a report that explains the ways that the Internet has affected businesses around the world.

PROCEDURES

Change Background Color (Ctrl + J)

1. Click **Modify** . . . . (Alt)+(M)
2. Click **Page Properties** . . . . (P)

   OR

- Click [Page Properties...] on the expanded Property inspector.

In the Page Properties dialog box:

1. Click **Background** color box ☐ to display color palette.
2. Use the eyedropper to pick a color.
3. Click [Apply] to apply color without closing the dialog box.
4. Click [OK] when finished in the dialog box.

Insert a Horizontal Rule

Position insertion point at beginning or end of paragraph:

1. Click **Insert** . . . . (Alt)+(I)

2. Point to **HTML** . . . . (H)
3. Click **Horizontal Rule** . . . . (Z)

To modify rule properties:

In Property inspector or Tag inspector:

- Specify width in pixels or percent measurement.
- Specify height in pixels.
- Select alignment if rule is less than 100% of page width.
- Turn shading on or off.
- Specify color in one of the code views or in the Tag inspector using the color attribute and a hexadecimal value.

   ✔ *The Tag inspector uses a color palette if you prefer that method of picking a color.*

To copy rule to new location:

1. Right-click rule and select **Copy**.

2. Right-click at location to place copy and select **Paste**.

Create a Custom Color

1. Click any color box ☐ in any panel to display the Web-safe color palette.
2. Click **System Color Picker** ◉ to display the Color dialog box.
3. Specify values for **Hue**, **Sat**, and **Lum** or **Red**, **Green**, and **Blue**.

   OR

   Drag the pointers in the continuous tone palette and vertical intensity slider.

4. Choose to add the color to the Custom colors palette, if desired.
5. Click [OK].

EXERCISE DIRECTIONS

1. Start Dreamweaver and open the **cincitorial** site.

2. Emphasize the **praise.html** page by applying the lightest yellow background color to the page (#FFFFCC).

3. Open the ⦿ **people.html** page from the Data folder and save it in the current Web site. Update links if prompted. *Lesson 3*

4. Insert a horizontal rule above the heading *Caitlin Preston*.

5. Remove the rule's shading and change its height to **3**.

6. Use the Tag inspector to modify the horizontal rule's color to #990033. *~ Read page 85*

7. Save the page and preview it in the browser to see the color applied to the rule. Close the browser.

8. You would like the rule color to be a little darker. Create a custom color:
   - Click the color box for the rule in the Tag inspector, and then click the System Color Picker icon to open the Color dialog box.
   - Change the Lum setting to **60**.
   - Add the color as a custom color.

9. Copy the rule and paste it above the *Tyler Meadows* heading.

10. Save the page and view it in the browser again. The top of your CinciTorial People page should look similar to Illustration A.

11. Save and close any open pages and the browser, and exit Dreamweaver.

Illustration A

CinciTorial People

Any company is only as good as its people, and we have some of the best. To contact any staff member directly, use the supplied e-mail address or call (513) 555-9909.

Jim Horner

Jim Horner has had a long and varied editorial career. With degrees in English and German literature and publications in German as well as English, he has fine-tuned manuscripts of all kinds, from plays to poetry to legal tomes. The dawn of the computer age encouraged Jim to master many software applications, starting with primitive DOS applications and moving ever onward through version after version of Microsoft Windows and Office. He refined his editorial skills on computer books at a number of publishing and full-service editorial companies before co-founding CinciTorial. Jim has considerable experience with Web publishing programs such as FrontPage and Dreamweaver.
jhorner@cincitorial.com

Caitlin Preston

Caitlin Preston began her publishing career by editing children's magazines, a far cry from the modern and contemporary English literature of her Master's degree. (She was glad to have the money, after seven years of university life.) Caitlin soon moved on to Northeast Publishing, a well-respected and venerable educational publisher specializing in business and economics textbooks, where she learned the nuts and bolts of publishing as it was practiced in the era of computerized typesetting. The advent of personal computers changed her editorial life as it changed so many other aspects of publishing. Caitlin enthusiastically mastered word processing, spreadsheet, database, and page layout programs. She co-founded CinciTorial with Jim Horner to build better computer books. Caitlin's areas of expertise are word processing and database programs.
cpreston@cincitorial.com

Tyler Meadows

ON YOUR OWN

1. Start Dreamweaver and open the gardencenter Web site.

2. Open index.html.

3. Choose a new background color for this page. Choose a color that contrasts well with the main heading color.

   ✔ You can either choose a Web-safe color or mix your own custom color.

   ✔ Notice that the table cells that create the navigation bar do not fill with color. You will learn how to change table background color in a later exercise.

4. Open events.html.

5. Insert horizontal rules above the Spring and Summer headings. Format the rules as follows:

   ▪ Specify that the rules are 75% of the page width.

   ▪ Center the rules.

   ▪ Use your judgment about the height, shading, and color of the rules.

6. Save and close all open pages and exit Dreamweaver.

Skills Covered

- About Adobe Bridge
- Insert an Image on a Page
- Modify Image Properties
- Position an Image on a Page

- Edit Graphics within Dreamweaver
- Insert and Edit a Photoshop Image
- Manage Graphic Files

Software Skills   Use Adobe Bridge to view and organize images on your computer. Place images on a page to illustrate or emphasize text. Images can be positioned so that text wraps to the left or right. Use Fireworks tools to edit graphics without leaving Dreamweaver. Insert Photoshop images and optimize them for use in a Web site. Use folders in a Web site to manage graphic files.

Application Skills   In this exercise, you will add images to the CinciTorial Web site, modify their properties and position, and edit a graphic in Dreamweaver. You will also create a folder in the site to hold all graphic files.

TERMS

Adobe Bridge A file management application included with the Adobe Creative Suite that allows a user to view and manage image files.

GIF (Graphics Interchange Format) A bitmapped image format designed for onscreen viewing of images.

JPEG (Joint Photographic Experts Group) A file format particularly suited for Web graphics, such as photos.

NOTES

About Adobe Bridge

- As part of the Adobe Creative Suite 3, Dreamweaver CS3 can access **Adobe Bridge**, a file management program that makes it easy to work with image files.

- To open Adobe Bridge, use the File>Browse in Bridge command or click the 🖼 Browse in Bridge button on the Standard toolbar. Adobe Bridge opens and displays the contents of the current folder, as shown in the illustration at the top of the next page.

- The Bridge window is divided into three panes. The left and right panes contain several panels that allow you to navigate to a specific folder, display files according to various criteria (such as all GIF images or files created on a specific date), see a preview of the currently selected file, and view metadata about the file.

- Bridge displays images as thumbnails and other files as icons in the center Content pane. Click an image in the Content pane to select it.

- You can easily insert an image from Bridge to a Dreamweaver Web site. Use the File>Copy to command and then select the current Web site's root folder, or click Choose Folder and navigate to the folder into which you want to copy the image.

- For more information on how you can use Adobe Bridge to manage your files, consult the Adobe Bridge Help files.

Insert an Image on a Page

- Images can be used in a Web site to illustrate its text, to provide additional information, or simply to add decorative elements for visual interest.

- To display properly in a browser, images should be saved in a standard format such as **JPEG** or **GIF**

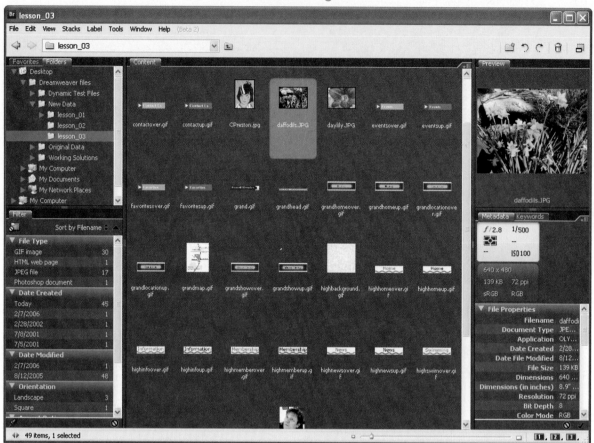

format. Dreamweaver will not automatically convert image files in other formats such as BMP or TIFF to JPEG or GIF.

- You can use the Insert>Image command to open the Select Image Source dialog box, or you can click the 🖃 ▾ Images button from the Common tab of the Insert bar and then select Image from the drop-down list to open this dialog box.

  ✔ *You can also simply drag the Image button to the desired location on the page to open the Select Image Source dialog box.*

- In the Select Image Source dialog box, select the image you want to insert and then save the image file in your Web site.

  ✔ *The Manage Graphic Files section in this exercise gives you more information about organizing graphic files in your Web site.*

- After you tell Dreamweaver where to store the image, the Image Tag Accessibility Attributes dialog box opens to allow you to specify alternate text or a long description for the image (see the following illustration). This dialog box encourages a designer to include accessibility information when an image is first inserted, rather than wait and supply this information later when fine-tuning the site using accessibility reports.

Image Tag Accessibility Attributes dialog box

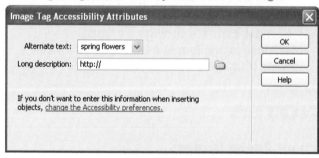

✔ *You will work with accessibility reports in Lesson 7.*

- Alternate text displays in place of the image in text-only browsers. If a site visitor is using a screen reader, the alternate text is read aloud so the visitor knows the content of the image.

- Some browsers display alternate text as a ScreenTip when you rest the mouse pointer over the image, while other browsers, such as Firefox and Mozilla, do not. Best practice suggests that alternate text should be used only as an alternative to the image, not as a method of labeling an image or other object.

  ✔ *To create text that will display as a ScreenTip in all browsers, use the title attribute. You can find information about using this attribute by searching for it online.*

- Alternate text should be kept fairly short; Dreamweaver suggests no more than 50 characters. If an image is especially complex or meaningful to the site and needs more description, the designer can create a document to describe the image and store the document in the Web site. Use the Long description box to type the path to the explanatory document, or use the 🗁 Browse icon to navigate to the location of the document.

- Some images that you insert, such as those used to create a navigation bar, may not require alternate text. However, you may still need to specify a value for the Alt attribute to satisfy accessibility standards. You can do so by clicking the Alternate text list arrow and selecting <empty>.

- After the picture has been inserted, you can modify its appearance and position it on the page using the Property inspector.

- As you add images to a page, keep an eye on the page size/download time measurements `143K / 21 sec` shown in the right side of the status bar at the bottom of the Document window.

- Images can significantly increase the size of a page and, even if a visitor is using a broadband connection, increase its download time. (This is especially true with digital photographs, which have also increased in size as quality digital cameras become more affordable.) A page that loads too slowly is an inconvenience to the visitors to your site, so you should try to keep download times low by eliminating large image files.

- The download time is based by default on a connection speed of 56.0kbps. You can set a different connection speed for this measurement in the Preferences dialog box in the Status Bar category.

  ✔ *See Appendix A for more information about the Status Bar category in Preferences.*

Modify Image Properties

- An image must be selected to display its properties. Click once on the image to select it. The selected image displays a black border with square black sizing handles at the bottom, right, and lower-right corner of the image.

- The Property inspector displays a number of properties for an image (see the following illustration). To see all properties, use the Expander arrow in the Property inspector.

- Notice that a thumbnail-size version of the image appears at the left side of the Property inspector. On pages that have more than one image or where images may be layered, this thumbnail helps you to be sure you are editing properties for the correct image.

- Next to the thumbnail is the Name text box, which by default is empty. You can supply a name for the image if you need to refer to the image in a script.

- You can use an image to link to other pages or sites in the same way you use text. Select the image and then type the link address in the Link text box, or use the ⊕ Point to File icon or 🗁 Browse for File button to specify the link target.

Image properties in Property inspector

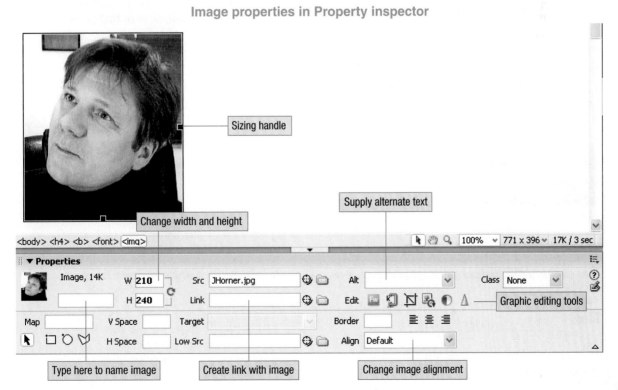

- If you chose not to supply alternate text when inserting an image, you can use the Alt box on the Property inspector to supply the text or the <empty> value.

Resize Image

- You can use the sizing handles on the picture to adjust its size. Click on a handle and drag out or down to enlarge, or in or up to reduce size. Dragging a corner handle adjusts both width and height at the same time.

  ✔ *If you need to resize proportionately, hold down the Shift key as you drag the corner handle.*

- To resize an image to exact measurements, use the W and H text boxes on the Property inspector. You must supply both a width and a height— Dreamweaver does not automatically resize proportionally if you supply only one dimension.

- If you need to go back to the original proportions, click the ↺ Reset Size symbol to the right of the W and H text boxes.

- Sizing measurements are supplied in pixels. Pixel measurements allow you to size exactly. This measurement is also a Web design standard.

About Image Borders

- By default, an image does not display a border. You can if desired use the Border text box on the expanded area of the Property inspector to specify a border width such as 1 or 2. Border measurements are in pixels.

- An image border is always black, unless the image is being used as a link. When used as a link, the image's border becomes the default link color.

- If you are really interested in applying a border to an image, you are advised to do so using the CSS Border property, which allows you to specify width as well as color for each side of an image.

Position an Image on a Page

- You have several options for positioning an image on a page. You can use alignment buttons or settings in the Align list.

Position Standalone Image

- If the image appears on a line by itself (not on the same line with text), you can use the Align Left, Align Center, or Align Right text alignment options to position it just as if it were a text paragraph.

- Select the image and use the alignment buttons that appear in the expanded area of the Property inspector to left align, center, or right align the image.

  ✔ *You can also use keyboard shortcuts such as Ctrl + Alt + Shift + C or Ctrl + Alt + Shift + R to center or right align an image.*

Wrap Text Around Image

- When an image is inserted in the same line as text, you use the options on the Align list on the Property inspector to position the image. Options on this list allow you to wrap text around the image or position it precisely relative to the text on the same line.

- Dreamweaver selects the Default position for a new image. This setting positions the image at the left edge of the page with the bottom of the picture aligned with the baseline of text (see the following illustration).

Default alignment

Jim Horner

Jim Horner has had a long and varied editorial career. With degrees in English and German literature and publications in German as well as English, he has fine-tuned manuscripts of all kinds, from plays to poetry to legal tomes. The dawn of the

`<body> <h4> <b> <font> <img>`   100%   771 x 396   17K / 3 sec

▼ Properties

Image, 14K   W 150   Src JHorner.jpg   Alt   Class None

H 173   Link   Edit

Map   V Space   Target   Border

H Space   Low Src   Align Default

- The Align list offers nine other alignment options, but you need to take care when selecting from among these options. Some of the alignment options Dreamweaver offers are supported by only a few browsers, and others do not meet some XHTML standards.

- Valid XHTML alignments include Top, Bottom, Middle, Left, and Right.

  - Top alignment aligns the top of the image with the top of the text's tall letters. If the text is a paragraph of several lines, only the first line aligns at the top; the remaining lines of the paragraph display below the image.

  - The Bottom alignment aligns the image and text the same way as Default.

  - The Middle alignment aligns the middle of the image with the text baseline. Only the first line of text is aligned at the middle; remaining lines display below the image.

  - The Left alignment positions the image at the left margin and wraps text around it on the right side.

  - The Right alignment positions the image at the right margin and wraps text around it on the left side.

- The Align list also offers Text Top, Baseline, Absolute Middle, and Absolute Bottom, but you will probably find that you can achieve the desired alignment effect using one of the options above, with the added security of knowing these alignments will display correctly in all browsers.

- When you apply the Left or Right alignment option, Dreamweaver places an anchor ⬧ at the location where the image was inserted. Selecting this anchor is the same as selecting the image itself.

  ✔ *You may need to select Anchor points for aligned elements in the Invisible Elements settings of the Preferences dialog box to display the anchor.*

- You can drag and drop the anchor to pinpoint the graphic file's position in the text and change the way text wraps around the image (see the illustration below).

About Spacing Around Images

- When you wrap text around an image, Dreamweaver doesn't apply any standoff spacing between the image and the text, so text may run right to the edge of an image, especially if Left alignment has been applied.

- The V Space and H Space text boxes on the Property inspector allow you to add space around an image, but the options in the Property inspector do not provide very flexible control of the space.

- For example, the H Space box adds space to both the left and right sides of an image, when you may want to add space on only one side, to provide a buffer between text and an image. Likewise, the V Space option adds space both above and below an image even if you only want space below the image.

- For best appearance, you are advised to use CSS properties to adjust spacing around an image. The CSS padding property, for example, allows you to specify space as desired on each side of an image.

Use Rulers and Guides to Help Position Graphics

- As you arrange objects on a page, you may want to display rulers and guides to help you position the page content.

- If the rulers are not already displaying, you can show them using the View>Rulers menu command. Rulers display at the top and left sides of the Document window. You have the option of setting the unit of measurement for the rulers.

Text wraps around image

Drag anchor to adjust right alignment

Jim Horner

Jim Horner has had a long and varied editorial career. With degrees in English and ⬧German literature and publications in German as well as English, he has fine-tuned manuscripts of all kinds, from plays to poetry to legal tomes. The dawn of the computer age encouraged Jim to master many software applications, starting with primitive DOS applications and moving ever onward through version after version of Microsoft Windows and Office. He refined his editorial skills on computer books at a number of publishing and full-service editorial companies before co-founding CinciTorial. Jim has considerable experience with Web publishing programs such as FrontPage and Dreamweaver.

jhorner@cincitorial.com

Drag anchor to change wrap

Right alignment applied to image

- You can add guides to the display by dragging down from the horizontal ruler or to the right from the vertical ruler. As you drag, a ToolTip displays the current vertical or horizontal position in pixels, as shown in the first illustration below.

- You can also set guidelines to indicate the *fold* area of a Web page—the area that displays in the browser at a specific screen resolution. The second illustration below shows guides set to show the screen area at a resolution of 640 by 480 pixels.

- Using guides can help a designer plan a page so that important content displays when the page opens, rather than being positioned so that a visitor has to scroll to reach it.

- Use the View>Guides pop-out menu commands to control guides on the page. This pop-out menu allows you to hide, lock, edit, and clear guides, as well as adjust snapping options for the guides. You can also select the browser window size if displaying fold guides like those shown in the following illustration.

Edit Graphics within Dreamweaver

- As part of Adobe's suite of Web design applications, Dreamweaver has built-in graphics-editing

capabilities that rely on other Adobe programs such as Photoshop and Fireworks. You can use these editing tools to modify graphics right in Dreamweaver, which can save a great deal of formatting time in a complex Web site.

- The graphic editing tools are located on the Property inspector, as shown in the following illustration.

Graphic editing tools on the Property inspector

- Use the tools as follows to edit a selected image.
  - Use the Edit button (Fw or Ps) to open the image in Fireworks or Photoshop, where you can use tools in that application to edit the image. The appearance of the Edit button depends on the file type of the image you want to edit. By default, the Fireworks Edit button displays if you select a GIF image, and the Photoshop Edit button displays if you select a JPEG image.

Display a guide to help position page content

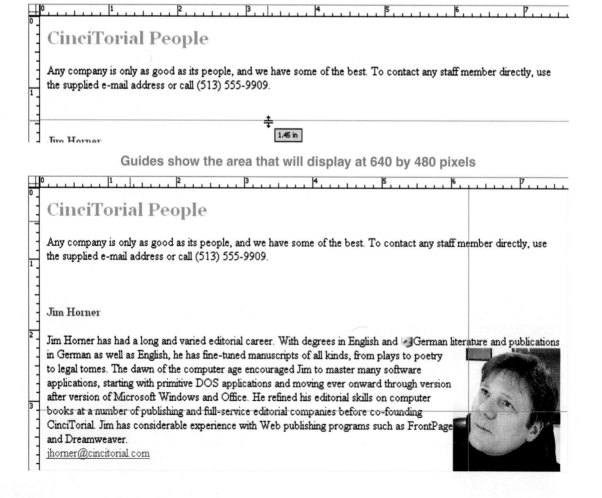

Guides show the area that will display at 640 by 480 pixels

✔ *You can adjust settings to specify which application opens which type of graphics.*

▪ Use 🔲 Optimize to open an Image Preview dialog box such as the one shown in the next illustration, where you can modify settings for the best appearance on the Web page. The settings available in the Image Preview dialog box differ depending on the file type of the selected image.

▪ Use 🔲 Crop to remove portions of the image you don't need. This action cannot be reversed except by using the Edit>Undo menu command.

▪ Use 🔲 Resample after resizing an image to make sure the pixel size matches the display size. Resampling keeps the image looking sharp and can reduce image file size.

▪ Use ◑ Brightness and Contrast to adjust these attributes for the selected image. This action cannot be reversed except by using the Edit>Undo menu command.

▪ Use △ Sharpen to adjust the contrast of pixels at the edges of image areas to give a clearer, more precise image.

Insert and Edit a Photoshop Image

▪ Adobe has built another attractive graphic-handling feature into Dreamweaver CS3: A designer can

now insert an image in Photoshop's PSD format directly onto a Dreamweaver page and then use Photoshop to edit that image.

▪ Use the Insert>Image or Images button on the Common tab of the Insert bar to insert the Photoshop file. Dreamweaver then displays the Image Preview dialog box shown in the illustration below. In this dialog box, you can specify the file format and settings to optimize the image for Web use.

▪ Select a format from the Format list, such as JPEG, GIF, or PNG. The dialog box options change to allow you to adjust settings specific to the chosen format type. The Saved settings list offers some common settings predefined for you so that you merely have to click one of the list options to optimize the image.

▪ Tools below the preview let you crop or magnify the image. You can also display several versions of the image and change optimization settings for each view to compare how the images look with different settings applied.

▪ The File tab allows you to specify exact dimensions for the image or scale it to a percentage of its original size.

Image Preview dialog box

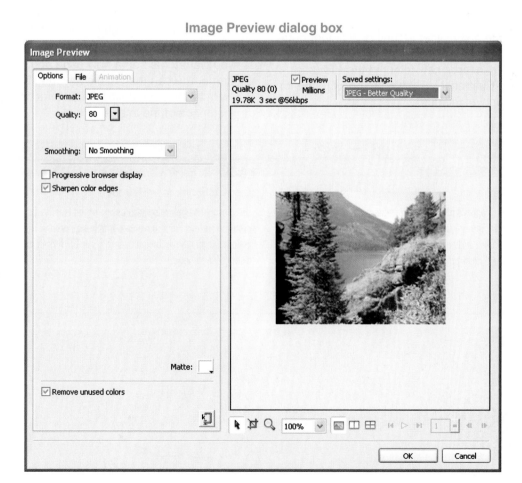

- If you have Photoshop CS3 available, you can edit the image in Photoshop using the Modify>Image>Photoshop command, or by clicking the **Ps** Edit button in the Property inspector. The image opens in Photoshop, where it can be modified using any of Photoshop's tools.

- The edited image can then be pasted back into Dreamweaver to update the image on the Web page.

- Photoshop images can also be inserted using a copy and paste process. All or part of an image can be copied in Photoshop and then that copy can be pasted directly on a Dreamweaver page. This process opens the Image Preview dialog box for optimization.

  ✔ *Using the Copy Merged command in Photoshop allows you to merge all layers of the Photoshop image for easy transport to Dreamweaver.*

Manage Graphic Files

- As you add graphic files such as pictures to your Web site, Dreamweaver will prompt you to save the graphics to your Web site's root folder so they will be available to display in the browser.

- You can store the files loose in the Web folder. However, for larger sites that may include many files, it is better site management to create a subfolder for graphic files.

- You can create a subfolder in the Local Folder pane of the Files panel. Right-click any file and select New Folder to insert a new folder in the site (see the following illustration). Then type a new name for the folder, such as images.

Create a subfolder in the Files panel

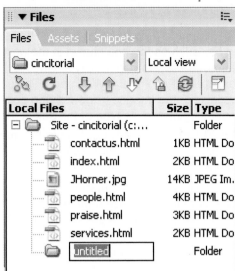

- When you are prompted to save graphic files, save them in your images folder. Be sure to include this folder when copying files for publication so the browser will be able to locate them.

- If you intend to use an image on more than one page in a site, you should be aware that modifying an image on one page may change it on other pages as well. If, for example, you insert a full-size image on one page, then insert it again on another and resize it to thumbnail size, you may find that all instances of the image are now thumbnails.

- To avoid this kind of problem, copy the image file you want to use on a new page and give it a unique name. You can then make any modification you want to the copied file without affecting other instances of the image.

PROCEDURES

Use Adobe Bridge (Ctrl + Alt + O)

To open Adobe Bridge:
1. Click **File** . . . . Alt+F
2. Click **Browse in Bridge**. . . B

OR

■ Click the **Browse in Bridge** button 📷 on the Standard toolbar.

To display images in a folder:
1. Click the **Folders** tab in the upper-left corner of the left pane.
2. Navigate to the desired folder and click it to display its images in the Content pane.
3. Click an image in the Content pane to preview it in the Preview panel.

To insert an image into Dreamweaver:
1. Click the image to select it.
2. Click **File** . . . . Alt+F
3. Click **Copy to** . . C, C, ↵Enter
4. Select the current root folder on the pop-out list.

OR

a. Click **Choose Folder** . . C
b. Browse to the desired folder to select it.
c. Click OK .

Insert an Image on a Page (Ctrl + Alt + I)

1. Click **Insert**. . . . . Alt+I
2. Click **Image** I

OR

a. Click the drop-down arrow on **Image** button 📷 ▾ from the Common tab of the Insert bar.
b. Select **Image**.

OR

Drag the **Image** button 📷 ▾ to the page to open the Select Image Source dialog box.
3. Locate and select image file.
4. Click OK .
5. Click Yes to copy file to root folder.
6. Open folder in which images will be stored and rename file if necessary.
7. Click Save .
8. Type a short description of the image in the **Alternate text** box.

OR

Type a path to a document that contains a more lengthy description of the image in the **Long description** box, or click 📁 and navigate to location of document.
9. Click OK .

Modify Image Properties

To name an image:
1. Click image to select it.
2. Click in the **Name** box and type name for image.

To use an image as a link:
1. Click image to select it.
2. Type page or site address in the **Link** text box on the Property inspector.

OR

Use **Point to File** icon ⊕ or **Browse for Folder** 📁 to locate link page.

To add alternate text for image:
1. Click image to select it.
2. Click in the **Alt** text box and type alternate text.

OR

Click the **Alt** box list arrow and select **<empty>**.

To resize an image:
1. Click image to select it.
2. Click sizing handle and drag to expand or reduce size.

OR

a. Click in the **W** text box on the Property inspector and type pixel size for width.
b. Click in the **H** text box on the Property inspector and type pixel size for height.

To reset image size:
■ Click **Reset Size** button ⟲.

Align a Standalone Image

Click image to select it and expand Property inspector.

■ Click **Align Left** button ☰ on the Property inspector to left align.
■ Click **Align Center** button ☰ on the Property inspector to center.
■ Click **Align Right** button ☰ on the Property inspector to right align.

Wrap Text Around an Image

Click image to select it.

1. Click the **Align** list arrow on Property inspector.
2. Select alignment option:
   ■ Default
   ■ Top
   ■ Middle
   ■ Bottom
   ■ Left
   ■ Right

   ✔ *The above options will display correctly in any browser. You can also choose other options that may not be supported by all browsers or XHTML standards.*

To adjust wrap alignment:

- Click the anchor ⬧ and drag to new location in text.

Display "Visible Area" Guides

1. Click **View**. . . . . ⌐Alt⌐+⌐V⌐
2. Click **Guides** . . . . ⌐U⌐
3. Select the browser size from the pop-out list.

Clear Guides

1. Click **View**. . . . . ⌐Alt⌐+⌐V⌐
2. Point to **Guides** . . . . ⌐U⌐
3. Click **Clear Guides** . . . . . . ⌐C⌐

Edit Graphics within Dreamweaver

With the image selected:

- Click **Edit** button (⌐Fw⌐ or ⌐Ps⌐) to open the image in Fireworks or Photoshop for modification.

  ✔ *Fireworks and/or Photoshop must be installed to use this command.*

- Click **Optimize** button ⌐ to open the Image Preview dialog box and change settings.

- Click **Crop** button ⌐ and then drag the crop outline to select the portion of the image to keep; click outside the image, or press ⌐Enter⌐, to complete the crop.

- Click **Resample** button ⌐ after resizing an image to adjust pixel size to match new image size.

- Click **Brightness and Contrast** button ⌐ and drag sliders to adjust brightness and/or contrast of image.

- Click **Sharpen** button ⌐ and drag slider to adjust contrast of edge pixels in image objects.

Insert and Edit a Photoshop Image

To insert a Photoshop image:

1. Click **Insert**. . . . . ⌐Alt⌐+⌐I⌐
2. Click **Image** . . . . ⌐I⌐

   OR

   a. Click the drop-down arrow on **Image** button ⌐ from the Common tab of the Insert bar.

   b. Select **Image**.

   OR

   Drag **Image** button ⌐ to page to open the Select Image Source dialog box.

3. Locate and select image file.
4. Click ⌐ OK ⌐.

In Image Preview dialog box:

5. Click **Format** list arrow and select a format type.
6. Change settings for image:

   - For JPEG image, click Quality slider arrow and drag to set quality of imported image, or click **Saved settings** list arrow and select a quality option.

   - For GIF image, select desired palette and desired number of colors.

7. Make other desired adjustments to image:

   - Click **Crop** button and drag crop borders to set the import image area.

   - Click the **File** tab in the dialog box and specify a **Scale** percentage or exact measurements for the imported image.

8. Click ⌐ OK ⌐.
9. Type a new name for the imported image, and then click ⌐ Save ⌐.

10. Type a short description of the image in the **Alternate text** box.

    OR

    Type a path to a document that contains a more lengthy description of the image in the **Long description** box, or click ⌐ and navigate to location of document.

11. Click ⌐ OK ⌐.

To edit a Photoshop image in Photoshop:

1. Click the image to select it.
2. Click the **Edit** button ⌐Ps⌐ on the Property inspector to open Photoshop.
3. Modify the image as desired using Photoshop tools.

To reinsert an edited Photoshop image:

1. In Photoshop, use a selection tool to select the area you want to reinsert.
2. Click **Edit** . . . . ⌐Alt⌐+⌐E⌐
3. Click **Copy** . . . . ⌐C⌐
4. In Dreamweaver, click **Edit**. . . . . ⌐Alt⌐+⌐E⌐
5. Click **Paste**. . . . . ⌐P⌐

   ✔ *The pasted image replaces the original image in the Files panel.*

Create a Folder in Site Window

In Local Files pane of Files panel:

1. Right-click any file name.
2. Click **New Folder**.
3. Type name for new folder.

EXERCISE DIRECTIONS

1. Start Dreamweaver and open the **cincitorial** site.
2. Display the Files panel, if necessary.
3. Create a new subfolder in the **cincitorial** folder named **images**.
4. Open Adobe Bridge and navigate to the folder that contains the Lesson 3 data files.
5. Locate the 🔘 **CinciTorial_logo.gif** image in the folder and then copy it to the **cincitorial** site.
6. Switch to Dreamweaver. You should see the image you just copied in the site files. (If you don't see the logo, click ⟳ on the Files panel toolbar.) Drag the **CinciTorial_logo.gif** file into the **images** folder.
7. Open **index.html**.
8. Position the insertion point to the left of the first heading on the page (*We build computer books*) and press Enter to create a new line.
9. Move the insertion point up into the new line.
10. Drag the **CinciTorial_logo.gif** image from the Files panel to the location of the insertion point. When prompted, supply the alternate text **CinciTorial logo**.
11. Apply the Default alignment to the image. (Remove center alignment if necessary to move the image to the left margin.)
12. Create a copy of the logo image to use on other pages in the site as follows:
    - Open the images folder if necessary, right-click the **CinciTorial_logo.gif** file, select Edit, and then select Copy to create a copy of the image file.
    - Right-click on the images folder, select Edit, and select Paste.
    - Rename the copied image **small_logo.gif**.
13. Open **services.html** and insert the **small_logo.gif** file from the images folder to the left of the first heading. Supply the alternate text **link logo**.
    - Reduce its size to 257 pixels wide by 44 pixels high.
    - Resample the logo image.
    - Link the image to **index.html**. (If a blue border surrounds the image, click in the Border box on the expanded Property inspector and type **0** to eliminate the border.)
    - Click to the right of the picture and press Enter to move the heading to a new line.
14. Select and copy the image, then save and close the page.
15. Open **praise.html** and paste the copied image between the named anchor and the first heading.

Move the heading to the next line. Save and close the page.

16. Open **people.html** and paste the copied image to the left of the first heading. Move the heading to the next line.
17. Position the insertion point to the left of the paragraph under the *Jim Horner* heading. Use the Image button on the Insert bar to insert the 🔘 **JHorner.jpg** image from the Data folder. Save the image in your images folder. Supply the alternate text **Photo of Jim Horner**.
18. Insert the 🔘 **CPreston.psd** image to the left of the Caitlin Preston paragraph. Accept the default JPEG settings and save the image in the images folder. Supply the alternate text **Photo of Caitlin Preston**.
19. Insert the 🔘 **TMeadows.jpg** image to the left of the Tyler Meadows paragraph. Save the image in the images folder and supply the alternate text **Photo of Tyler Meadows**.

    ✔ *In both cases, "paragraph" means the body copy under the name headings.*

20. Format the pictures as follows:
    - Change the size of Jim's picture to 150 by 170 pixels. Change the size of Caitlin's illustration to 150 by 170 pixels.
    - Resample both images after resizing.
    - Crop Tyler's picture to remove unnecessary background above her hair and on the left side of the picture. It should show only her head and shoulders.
    - Change the size of Tyler's picture to 150 by 170 pixels and then resample.
    - Adjust the contrast of Tyler's picture to 20.
    - Apply Right alignment to Jim and Tyler's pictures and Left alignment to Caitlin's.
    - If necessary, drag the anchor for each picture up and to the left of the person's heading, so the anchor is just to the left of the heading.

    ✔ *If you don't see anchors, use Edit>Preferences and select Invisible Elements from the list at left. Select Anchor points for aligned elements. You can adjust Caitlin's picture by simply dragging the image to the left of the heading.*

    ✔ *The text may run very close to the pictures. If you know CSS coding, you may want to create CSS rules to add padding to the left or right side of each picture. You can see how the CSS padding improves the look of the page in Illustration A.*

21. Save and close the page.

22. On the **index.html** page, insert a blank paragraph above the *Services* link and type **Our People** in the blank paragraph. Link this text to the **people.html** page.

23. Display guides to show how the page will break using a browser size of 800 by 600.

24. Clear the guides.

25. Preview the **index.html** page in the browser and test the link to the **people.html** page. The top of your CinciTorial People page should look similar to Illustration A.

26. Close the browser.

27. Save and close any open pages and exit Dreamweaver and Adobe Bridge.

Illustration A

CinciTorial People

Any company is only as good as its people, and we have some of the best. To contact any staff member directly, use the supplied e-mail address or call (513) 555-9909.

Jim Horner

Jim Horner has had a long and varied editorial career. With degrees in English and German literature and publications in German as well as English, he has fine-tuned manuscripts of all kinds, from plays to poetry to legal tomes. The dawn of the computer age encouraged Jim to master many software applications, starting with primitive DOS applications and moving ever onward through version after version of Microsoft Windows and Office. He refined his editorial skills on computer books at a number of publishing and full-service editorial companies before co-founding CinciTorial. Jim has considerable experience with Web publishing programs such as FrontPage and Dreamweaver.
jhorner@cincitorial.com

Caitlin Preston

Caitlin Preston began her publishing career by editing children's magazines, a far cry from the modern and contemporary English literature of her Master's degree. (She was glad to have the money, after seven years of university life.) Caitlin soon moved on to Northeast Publishing, a well-respected and venerable educational publisher specializing in business and economics textbooks, where she learned the nuts and bolts of publishing as it was practiced in the era of computerized typesetting. The advent of personal computers changed her editorial life as it changed so many other aspects of publishing. Caitlin enthusiastically mastered word processing, spreadsheet, database, and page layout programs. She co-founded CinciTorial with Jim

ON YOUR OWN

1. Start Dreamweaver and open the gardencenter Web site.

2. Create a new subfolder in the site named images to hold all image files.

3. Open index.html.

4. Use Adobe Bridge to insert the ⊙ daylily.jpg image from the Lesson 3 Data files to the left of the main heading. Save the image in your images folder and supply appropriate alternate text. Resize the image to a size you think appropriate. Be sure to resample after resizing.

5. Wrap text around the image.

6. Modify the image as you think necessary. You may want to crop it or adjust its brightness and contrast.

7. Open info.html.

8. Insert the ⊙ daffodils.jpg image from the Lesson 3 Data files and save it in your images folder. Supply appropriate alternate text. Resize the image to 280 W and 210 H and then resample it. Position it to the right of the first text paragraph and wrap text around it.

9. Create a copy of the daylily.jpg image in the images folder and rename the copy link_lily.jpg.

10. Drag the link_lily.jpg image from the images folder and position it above the first heading on the info.html page. Provide appropriate alternate text. Resize to a small size, such as about 63 pixels wide by 49 pixels high. Create a link from this image to the index.html page. Copy the link image.

11. Open events.html and paste the link image above the first heading.

12. Paste the image above the first heading on the contact.html page.

13. Save all open pages and preview the Web site in the browser. Don't worry if your navigation bar runs off the right side of the home page. You will fix it in a later exercise.

14. Close the browser and all open pages and exit Dreamweaver.

DREAMWEAVER IN DEPTH

If you are working with the Adobe Creative Suite 3 Premium or have Photoshop CS3 installed, you can get a better idea of how Photoshop and Dreamweaver are designed to work together in the following exercise.

1. Create a folder named Exercise18 on your computer to store the files you will work with in this exercise.

2. Start Photoshop and open ⊙ DID_mountain.psd. Save the image in the Exercise18 folder as mountain.psd. Close the image file, but leave Photoshop open.

3. Start Dreamweaver and create a new HTML page. Save it in the Exercise18 folder as glacier_views.html.

4. Insert the mountain.psd image on the Web page. Accept default JPEG settings, and choose to save the image in the Exercise18 folder as a JPEG file. Give the image alternate text if desired.

5. Select the image on the page and click the Edit button on the Property inspector to open it for editing in Photoshop.

6. In Photoshop, click the Filter menu, click Filter Gallery, and then select a filter to apply to the picture to give it a different look, such as one of the Artistic filter effects. (Click the triangle to the left of Artistic in the center panel to display the various effects; click an effect to see how it looks on the picture.)

7. Click OK when you have found a look you like to close the gallery and apply the filter.

8. Click the Rectangular Marquee selection tool in the upper-left corner of the Photoshop tool box and drag the selection marquee to enclose the entire picture.

9. Click Edit>Copy to copy the modified picture.

10. Switch back to Dreamweaver and click Edit>Paste. The revised version of the picture should replace the original photo.

11. Switch to Photoshop and save and close the picture.

You can also insert a Photoshop image using Copy and Paste from Photoshop to Dreamweaver, as in the following steps.

1. Open ⊙ DID_lake.psd in Photoshop. Save the image in the Exercise18 folder as lake.psd. Click OK if you are asked to maximize compatibility.

2. Click the Rectangular or Oval Marquee tool in the Photoshop toolbox and drag a selection of the picture to copy.

3. Click Edit>Copy.

4. Switch to Dreamweaver and click Edit>Paste. The Image Preview dialog box opens and shows only a white preview. What happened?

5. Click the Cancel button and then switch back to Photoshop. Look at the Layers panel in the lower-right corner of the Photoshop window. It shows that an adjustment layer has been added on top of the background. When you copied the picture, you copied only the adjustment layer.

6. Click Edit>Copy Merged. This command merges all layers in the area inside the selection marquee and copies them.

7. Switch back to Dreamweaver and click Edit>Paste. This time the Image Preview dialog box should show the complete image. Accept default settings by clicking OK.

8. Save the picture in the Exercise18 folder as a JPEG with the name lake.jpg, and supply alternate text if desired.

9. Save the Dreamweaver page and close it. Close the image in Photoshop. Exit both programs.

Skills Covered

- **Insert Background Picture**
- **Create Image Maps**
- **About Rollover Images**
- **Use the Assets Panel**

Software Skills   Another way to add graphic impact to a Web page is to use a background picture behind the text. Use images to create image maps and navigation bars that improve navigation in a Web site. Rollover images add a dynamic touch to a Web page. The Assets panel makes it easy to view and access objects in a Web site.

Application Skills   In this exercise, you will continue to work with graphic images in the CinciTorial Web site. You will add a page background, create image maps and navigation bars, and view the site's assets in the Assets panel.

TERMS

Assets panel In Dreamweaver, a panel in the Files panel group that displays the "assets" of the site: images, colors, URLs, library items, templates, and other objects used in a Web site.

Element Entry in a Dreamweaver navigation bar.

Hotspot Region on an image map that provides a link to another Web page.

Image map GIF or JPEG images with a corresponding set of coordinates designed to select specified areas and set hyperlinks to other documents or areas of the Web site.

Navigation bar A set of links to pages in a Web site.

Rollover image An interactive effect created by specifying two images, one of which loads with the page and the other that displays when the mouse rolls over the image.

NOTES

Insert Background Picture

- You can use an image, or picture, as a background. Background images can create an attractive and unobtrusive appearance that gives a Web site identity while keeping the Web file size small and download times minimal.

- Insert the background image from the Page Properties dialog box. You can use the Browse... button to the right of the Background image text box to open the Select Image Source dialog box and locate the file you want to use for the background image (see the following illustration).

- If the Preview images checkbox is selected in the Select Image Source dialog box, you can see a

Locate graphic image file

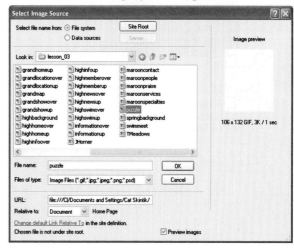

preview of the image at the right side of the dialog box when you click the image's file name.

- After you choose the file, Dreamweaver prompts you to save the image in your root folder. When you click Yes, Dreamweaver displays the Copy File As dialog box, where you can rename the file and specify a folder to store the image if desired.

- You can then apply the background image from the Page Properties dialog box to see the effect without having to close the dialog box, or you can close the dialog box to see the background image in place on the page.

- If the image is not large enough to cover the entire page area, Dreamweaver *tiles* the image—repeats it across and down the page to fill the entire page area.

- The background image information appears as an attribute of the <body> opening tag in the HTML code.

Create Image Maps

- As you know from the last exercise, you can use an entire image to create a link. You can also use an image to create an **image map,** which contains a **hotspot** that links the current page to another location. Image maps are creative ways to add both visual interest and navigability to your Web site.

- To create image maps, you use the hotspot tools (see the following illustration) on the expanded portion of the Property inspector to draw an area on the image.

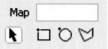

- Use the ▭ Rectangular Hotspot tool to create a square or rectangular area on the image.
- Use the ⬯ Oval Hotspot tool to create a circular area.
- Use the ⬠ Polygon Hotspot tool to create an irregular-shaped area.

✔ *The Polygon Hotspot tool will not work on an image that has been absolutely positioned either at the left or right with text wrapped around it.*

- After you click the appropriate tool, Dreamweaver reminds you to supply alternate text for the image map. The insertion point changes to a crosshair you use to draw the area on the image. Drawing a hotspot is the same as drawing an object in a program such as Paint or Word.

- The area you draw fills with a blue shading to indicate the hotspot and the Property inspector changes to display settings for the hotspot (see the following illustration below).

Oval hotspot

Hotspot

Jim Horner

Alt text box

Jim Horner has had a long and varied editorial career. With degrees in English and German liter

`<body> <h4> <b> <font> <map#Map> <area>`

▼ Properties

Hotspot	Link	services.html
	Target	
		Alt	How can Jim help y

Map Map

✔ *The blue shading will not appear when the image map is viewed in the browser.*

■ Type the link address in the Link box, or use the ⊕ Point to File icon or 📁 Browse for File button to select the page or site to which you want to link.

■ Dreamweaver automatically inserts a pound sign (#) in the Link box. Delete the # sign in the Link box before typing a file name to create a link to another page or another Web site, or use the 📁 Browse for File button to locate the page.

✔ *An interesting use for an image map is to reduce an image to thumbnail size and link it to a larger version of the image.*

■ You can type a name in the text box next to Map on the Property inspector to name each image map on a page. This is helpful if you create more than one hotspot on an image.

■ As for any image, you can use the Alt box to supply text for text-only browsers to inform a site visitor of the link. Some browsers, such as Internet Explorer, will display this text as a ScreenTip when a visitor rests the mouse on the hotspot.

■ Adjust a hotspot's size by selecting it with the ▶ Pointer Hotspot tool. Drag any sizing handle on the hotspot to change its size.

✔ *You cannot adjust the size of a hotspot on an image that has been positioned absolutely with text wrapped around it.*

■ Click on a hotspot and hold down the mouse button while dragging the shape to move it to another position.

■ To delete a hotspot, select it and press the Delete key.

■ If you do not like the look of the blue-shaded hotspot on your image, you can hide the hotspot. Use the View>Visual Aids>Image Maps command or click the 👁 Visual Aids button on the Document toolbar and deselect Image Maps.

About Rollover Images

■ The Images list on the Insert bar offers two options that can add interactivity to a Web page: Rollover Image and Navigation Bar.

■ Both of these options are designed to replace one image with another when a mouse pointer rolls over the original image in a browser or clicks on an image.

■ The process of inserting rollover images and navigation bars is quite similar, as you will discover in the following sections.

Insert a Rollover Image

■ A **rollover image** is composed of two images that are controlled by JavaScript. The original image loads with the page. When a site visitor hovers the mouse over the image, the original image is replaced by another.

■ The illustration below shows how one image replaces another in the browser. The original image, at left, is an overexposed version of a photo to give a dreamy effect. When the mouse pointer rolls over the image, it changes to a brightly colored version of the photo.

A rollover image in a browser

■ Rollover images can be used in a number of ways on a Web site. Use them to show two different versions of an image, as shown above, or to display related images. Rollover images can also be used to create navigation buttons.

■ To create a new rollover image, click the 🖾 ▾ Images list arrow from the Common category of the Insert bar and select 🖾 ▾ Rollover Image from the list of image options. Or use the Insert>Image Objects>Rollover Image command.

■ The Insert Rollover Image dialog box displays, as shown in the illustration at the top of the next page.

■ Supply a name for the rollover image and then specify the original image and the rollover image. Use the Browse... buttons to locate the images, and then save the images with the other images in your site.

■ Note that you can also create a link from the rollover image so that when you click the image in the browser, a new page displays.

■ When creating images to use for rollovers, it is customary to make the original and rollover images the same size so that one will replace the other precisely.

Insert a Navigation Bar

■ A **navigation bar** is a set of links to pages in a Web site. Navigation bars arrange text or image links horizontally or vertically in a group to make it easy for a visitor to jump to other pages in the site. The links in a navigation bar are often included in a table structure to make it easy to position the links.

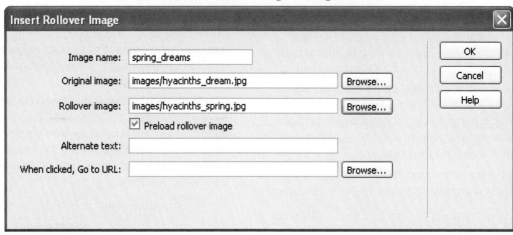

✔ *You have already worked with text navigation bars available as snippets in previous exercises.*

■ The Navigation Bar option on the Images list allows you to create a graphic, interactive navigation bar that, as for rollover images, uses JavaScript to replace original navigation images with other images depending on the action of the mouse pointer in the browser.

■ You can provide up to four images for each element in a navigation bar:

  ■ *Up*—This image is the one that displays when a page opens.

  ■ *Over*—This image displays when the mouse pointer moves over the element.

  ■ *Down*—This image displays when the navigation bar element is clicked.

  ■ *Over While Down*—This image displays if the pointer is moved over the element after it has been clicked.

■ To create a new navigation bar, click the 🖳 ▾ Images list arrow from the Common category of the Insert bar and select 🗒 ▾ Navigation Bar from the list of image options. Or use the Insert>Image Objects>Navigation Bar command.

■ The Insert Navigation Bar dialog box opens (see the following illustration) with a default unnamed element displayed in the *Nav bar elements* list.

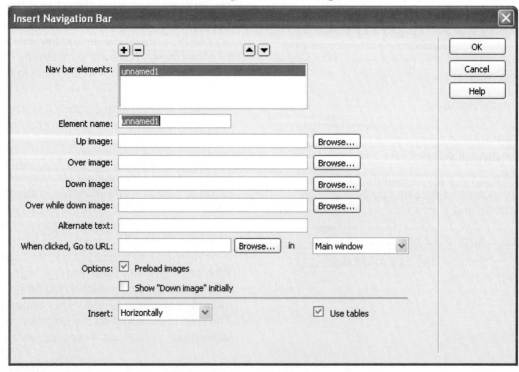

- A navigation bar **element** is the image that will appear in the navigation bar. Each element must have a unique name.

- To add the first navigation bar element, replace the *unnamed1* default element with your first navigation bar element. When creating a navigation bar to link pages in a Web site, the elements should reflect the names of the site's pages.

- Add other elements by clicking the ⊞ button and typing new element names. Remove an element from the Nav bar elements list by selecting it and clicking the ⊟ button. Move an element in the list by selecting it and clicking either ▲ or ▼.

- As you add each element, you specify images for the various appearances of the element. Use the ⌈Browse...⌋ buttons for each image to locate the image, and then save the images with the other images in your site.

  ✔ *A navigation bar image can be a GIF or JPEG file of a button or bullet—although virtually any kind of Web-compatible image file can be used.*

- You can choose a graphic for each selection—Up, Over, Down, and Over While Down. A common option is to use the same image in a different color for each state.

- For each element, type a relative or absolute address in the *When clicked, Go to URL* text box, or use the ⌈Browse...⌋ button to locate the page or site that should open when the element is clicked.

- By default, Dreamweaver will preload the images with the page so they are available immediately. You can also choose to have the "down" image displayed initially rather than the "up" image.

- You can choose to insert the navigation bar horizontally (the default) or vertically on the page, and in a table or freestanding.

- After you click OK to finish the navigation bar, the images you selected display on the page, as shown in the following illustration.

Completed navigation bar

Contact CinciTorial

| Contact | People | Praise | Services |

- If you have created the navigation bar in a table, you can make some adjustments to the table, such as changing column widths, but you cannot format the table in the same ways you format other tables. You cannot, for example, add cell borders, although you can change the background color of cells or the entire table.

- Images used to create navigation bars generally include labels, as shown in the previous illustration, to let visitors know what page will open when the navigation button is clicked. If the image used for the navigation element is merely decorative, such as a button or arrow, you will have to supply a text label beside the image to identify the link. To create a label with the same link properties as the image, select the image, press the right arrow key, and begin typing. The label is automatically formatted as a link to the same page the image is linked to.

- To modify a navigation bar after creating it, click anywhere in the navigation bar and use the Modify>Navigation Bar menu command.

- Creating a navigation bar in a Web site with a number of pages can take time. Fortunately, after you create the navigation bar you can select it, copy it, and paste it on other pages in the site. You can also make it part of a template so that it appears whenever a document is created with the template.

  ✔ *You will learn about creating templates in the next exercise.*

- You can also copy the navigation bar and then create a new library item. The copied navigation bar is automatically "pasted" in the Library when you name the new library item.

  ✔ *You will learn about the Library in Exercise 21.*

- There are several advantages to making a navigation bar a library item. Not only is it easy to insert on other pages, it cannot be changed accidentally on a page.

- Most important, when new pages are added or old pages deleted, the navigation bar can be modified in the Library and then updated easily on all pages.

Use the Assets Panel

- The **Assets panel** is a tab in the Files panel group that also includes the Files panel. It is divided into two panes. The lower pane is a list of asset files available for your site. The upper pane is a viewing window in which to inspect a selected asset (see the illustration at the top of the next page).

- To display the Assets panel, use the Window>Assets command, or click the Assets tab of the Files panel group.

- As you work with a Web site, the Assets panel collects information that makes it easy for you to keep track of objects and other elements. For example, all graphic files you add to a site display in the Images category of the Assets panel. Each color you apply in the Web site displays in the Colors category of the Assets panel.

Assets panel

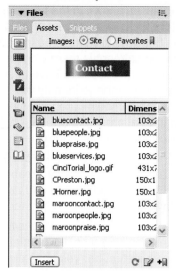

- The Assets panel's vertical toolbar lets you choose the different categories of objects and style elements available to your Web site.
- Click a category button to see assets of that type listed in the bottom pane of the panel. Further information about or a representation of the asset may be displayed in the top pane when you click an asset listed in the bottom pane.
- The Assets panel collects and displays the following items:
  - Images (🖼) stored in the site.
  - Colors (🎨) used in the site.
  - External URLs (🔗) that pages in the site link to.
  - Flash (🗹) and Shockwave (🎞) movie files present in the site.
  - Other movie files (🎦), such as QuickTime or MPEG movies, used in the site.
  - Scripts (📜) used in the site.
  - Templates (📄) present in the site.
  - Library items (📖) stored in the site.
- The Assets panel makes it easy to insert objects and format pages throughout a site. For example, to insert an image that you have already saved in the site, simply position the insertion point, click the image file in the Assets panel, and click the [Insert] button on the Assets panel. To format text in a color you have already used in the site, select the text, select the color in the Assets panel, and click the [Apply] button.
- By default, the Assets panel displays objects for the current site (the Site option is selected just below the Assets tab at the top of the panel). However, you also can add assets to a Favorites list to make it easy to locate specific assets.

  ✔ *The Site and Favorites options are not available in the Templates and Library categories.*

- Click the asset you want to make a favorite and then click the ➕ Add to Favorites button on the Assets panel. To view your favorites, select the Favorites option at the top of the Assets panel. You can right-click any item in the Assets panel to access a shortcut menu with commands that allow you to add the item to the Favorites panel, edit the item, or insert it in a document.
- If desired you can create folders within the Favorites list to store items that you want to group. With Favorites displayed, click the 📁 New Favorites Folder button and name the new folder. You can then drag assets into the folder to store them.

PROCEDURES

Insert a Background Picture (Ctrl + J)

1. Click **Modify** . . . . (Alt)+(M)
2. Click **Page Properties** . . . . (P)

   OR

   Click [Page Properties...] in the expanded Property inspector.

In the Page Properties dialog box:

1. Click [Browse...] to open the Select Image Source dialog box.

2. Locate image file to use for background.
3. Click [OK].
4. Click [Yes] to copy file to root folder.
5. Open folder in which images will be stored and rename file if necessary.
6. Click [Save].
7. Click [OK].

Create an Image Map

Click image to select it and expand Property inspector.

1. Click desired hotspot tool on the Property inspector:
   - **Rectangular Hotspot** tool 🔲
   - **Oval Hotspot** tool ⭕
   - **Polygon Hotspot** tool 🔷

2. Click [OK] when prompted to add alternate text.

3. Draw hotspot:

- For rectangle or circle, position pointer above and to the left or right of area to map. Hold down the mouse button and drag to create hotspot.

- For polygon, click to start and click to change direction.

  ✔ *Drag a blue handle to adjust the polygon's shape.*

4. Type page or site address in the **Link** box on the Property inspector.

  ✔ *Remember to delete the pound sign (#) that Dreamweaver automatically puts in the Link box if you are typing the page or site address.*

  OR

- Use **Point to File** icon ⊕ or **Browse for Folder** 📁 to locate link page.

To modify hotspot:

- Modify size or location of hotspot by clicking outside the picture and then using the **Select Hotspot** pointer ▶ to drag the hotspot or one of its handles.

To hide hotspot:

1. Click **V**iew . . . . Alt + V

2. Point to **V**isual Aids V

3. Click **I**mage Maps I

  OR

1. Click 👁 on the Document toolbar.

2. Click **Image Maps**.

Insert a Rollover Image

1. Position insertion point at the location to insert the rollover image.

2. Click **I**nsert . . . . Alt + I

3. Point to
Image Objects . . . G, ↵Enter

4. Click **Rollover Image**. . . . . R

  OR

- Click **Rollover Image** tool 🖼 ▾ from the Common category of the Insert bar 🖼 ▾ Images button list.

In the Insert Rollover Image dialog box:

1. Type name for rollover image.

2. Type path to image for Original image, or click [Browse...] and navigate to image.

3. If necessary, save image in current site.

4. Type path or browse to image for Rollover image, and save image in current site.

5. Type path for page to link to in **When clicked, Go to URL** box, or click [Browse...] and navigate to page.

6. Click [OK].

Insert a Navigation Bar

1. Position insertion point at the location to insert the navigation bar.

2. Click **I**nsert . . . . Alt + I

3. Point to
Image Objects . . . G, ↵Enter

4. Click **Navigation Bar** . . . . . G

  OR

- Click **Navigation Bar** tool 🖼 ▾ from the Common category of the Insert bar 🖼 ▾ Images button list.

In the Insert Navigation Bar dialog box:

1. Type name of first element for navigation bar.

2. Type path to image for Up image, or click [Browse...] and navigate to image.

3. If necessary, save image in current site.

4. Select other or same image for Over, Down, and/or Over While Down images.

5. Type path for page to link to in **When clicked, Go to URL** box, or click [Browse...] and navigate to page.

6. Click ⊞ to add elements or ⊟ to remove elements.

7. Use ▲ or ▼ to move elements in list.

8. Click [OK].

Modify a Navigation Bar

1. Click **M**odify . . . . Alt + M

2. Click **Navigation Bar** . . . . . B

Display the Assets Panel (F11)

1. Click **W**indow . . . . Alt + W

2. Click **A**ssets . . . . A

  OR

- Click the Assets tab on the Files panel group.

Manage Assets

- Click the category button in the Assets panel to see assets for that category.

- Apply or insert an asset on any page by selecting the asset and clicking [Insert] or [Apply].

Work with Favorites

- Display Favorites by clicking the **Favorites** option in the Assets panel.

To add an asset to Favorites:

1. Click asset to select it.

2. Click +📗 in the Assets panel.

  OR

  Right-click an asset's name and then choose **Add to Favorites** from the shortcut menu.

To create folder in Favorites:

1. Display Favorites in the Assets panel.

2. Click 📁 in the Assets panel.

3. Type name for new folder.

4. Drag favorite assets into folder to organize.

Complete Steps 1-11 only!

EXERCISE DIRECTIONS

1. Start Dreamweaver and open the cincitorial site.
2. Open index.html.
3. Apply the ⊙puzzle.gif image from the Lesson 3 Data folder as a background picture on this page. Save the image in the images folder.
4. Open people.html. Select Jim's picture on this page and use the Oval Hotspot tool to create a hotspot area about the size of Jim's head. Cancel the dialog box that asks you to enter alternate text (you will enter it in the next step).
5. Link the hotspot to services.html and type the following text in the Alt box: Click here to see how Jim can help you.
6. Create similar hotspots on Caitlin's illustration and Tyler's picture.
7. If desired, hide the hotspots on the image maps.
8. Click to the left of the first text paragraph on this page and create a navigation bar as follows:
    - For the first element, type the name contact.
    - For the Up Image, browse to the Lesson 3 Data folder and select ⊙bluecontact.jpg. For the Over image, select ⊙marooncontact.jpg. When prompted to copy each image to the root folder, click Yes and navigate to the images folder, then save the image there.
    - Link the element to contactus.html. (Use the When clicked, Go to URL box to set up the link.)
    - Add additional elements named people, services, and praise. Use the appropriate images for each element. For example, use bluepeople.jpg and maroonpeople.jpg for the people element and blueservices.jpg and maroonservices.jpg for the services element.
    - Link the elements to people.html, services.html, and praise.html, respectively.
    - Move the praise element up in the list until it is below the people element.
    - Choose to create a horizontal navigation bar, and deselect the Use tables checkbox.
    - Click OK to create the navigation bar.
9. Click to the right of the navigation bar on the page and press Enter to move the paragraph to a new line.
10. Save the page and open it in the browser. Check the links in the navigation bar and the image map links on this page. The top of your page should look like Illustration A.

    ✔ If Internet Explorer displays the Information bar to tell you it has blocked some content on the page, click the bar and select Allow Blocked Content. If you are using a browser other than Internet Explorer, you may not see the ScreenTip when you rest your pointer on a picture.

11. Close the browser.
12. Open the Assets panel. View the images that have been added to the site. Then view the site's colors.

    ✔ Click the Refresh button in the Assets panel toolbar if necessary to see the images that you have added to the site in the Assets list.

13. Add the small_logo.gif file to your Favorites.
14. Save and close any open pages and exit Dreamweaver.

only chg is end at 11.

Illustration A

CinciTorial People

| Contact | People | Praise | Services |

Any company is only as good as its people, and we have some of the best. To contact any staff member directly, use the supplied e-mail address or call (513) 555-9909.

Jim Horner

Jim Horner has had a long and varied editorial career. With degrees in English and German literature and publications in German as well as English, he has fine-tuned manuscripts of all kinds, from plays to poetry to legal tomes. The dawn of the computer age encouraged Jim to master many software applications, starting with primitive DOS applications and moving ever onward through version after version of Microsoft Windows and Office. He refined his editorial skills on computer books at a number of publishing and full-service editorial companies before co-founding CinciTorial. Jim has considerable experience with Web publishing programs such as FrontPage and Dreamweaver.
jhorner@cincitorial.com

Caitlin Preston

Caitlin Preston began her publishing career by editing children's magazines, a far cry from the modern and contemporary English literature of her Master's degree. (She was glad to have the money, after seven years of university life.) Caitlin soon moved on to Northeast Publishing, a well-respected and venerable educational publisher specializing in business and economics textbooks, where she learned the nuts and bolts of publishing as it was practiced in the era of computerized typesetting. The advent of personal computers changed her editorial life as it changed so many other aspects of publishing. Caitlin enthusiastically mastered word

Click here to see how Caitlin can help you

ON YOUR OWN

1. Start Dreamweaver and open the gardencenter site.

2. Open index.html. Replace the existing navigation bar with a new one:

- Click in the first cell of the navigation bar table (the Home cell).

- In the status bar at the bottom of the Document window, click the first <table> tag to select the entire table. Press Delete to remove the navigation bar.

- Create a new navigation bar at the same location with the following elements: contact, events, and information.

- Use the following images in the Lesson 3 Data folder to associate with the elements listed above: contactup.gif, contactover.gif, eventsup.gif, eventsover.gif, informationup.gif, and informationover.gif. Save all images in your images folder.

- Associate each element with the correct page in the site.

3. Create a hotspot on the daylily picture on this page that links to the events.html page. Add the alternative text: Click here to see upcoming events.

4. Open events.html. To set this page apart, apply the springbackground.jpg file from the Lesson 3 Data folder as a page background. Save the image file in your images folder.

5. Open info.html. Replace the current daffodils picture with a rollover image as follows:

- Delete the daffodils picture from the page. (It should remain in the images folder.)

- Position the insertion point to the left of the first text paragraph on the page and insert a rollover image with the name spring_flowers. Use daffodils.jpg as the original image, and use hyacinths.jpg as the rollover image. Save hyacinths.jpg in the images folder.

- Add the alternate text Spring events are coming up! Link the rollover image to events.html.

- Apply Right alignment to the image.

6. Save all open pages. Preview index.html in the browser and test links in the new navigation bar. Test the image map on the Civic Garden Center Home page.

7. Go to the Information page, test the rollover image, and click it to open the Events page.

8. Close the browser and all open pages and exit Dreamweaver.

Skills Covered

- **About Templates**
- **Create a New Template**
- **Apply a Template**
- **Edit a Template and Update Pages**

Software Skills   Templates maintain a uniform look and feel across the entire Web site. Dreamweaver provides flexible template design features. You can control individual sections of your page without affecting the basic design.

Application Skills   In this exercise, you will create a template for the CinciTorial site, apply the template to several pages, and then modify and update the template.

TERMS

Editable region In a template, an area that an author can change in a page to which the template is applied.

Noneditable region In a template, an area that is locked so that the author cannot change its content.

Template A collection of formats and page elements that can be used to give pages in a Web site a consistent look.

NOTES

About Templates

- A **template** is a collection of formats and page elements that can be used to give pages in a Web site a consistent look.

- For example, a template could include a background image or color, images, headings, and text styles and formats. Using a template can save you considerable development time.

- When you create a template, you can specify **noneditable** and **editable regions**:

  - Noneditable regions contain items that should remain the same on each page, such as a copyright notice or a logo.

  - Editable regions contain items such as text or headings that can change on a page.

- The value of creating and using templates is that you can easily adjust formats over an entire Web site. When you modify a template, you can update all pages that use that template at the same time to show the modifications.

Create a New Template

- You can create a template from a new, blank page or an existing page that contains text and other page elements. If your pages contain complex layouts, it makes sense to use a page you have already formatted as the basis for the template.

- You have several options for creating a new template:

  - In an open document, use the File>Save As Template command. Dreamweaver opens the Save As Template dialog box (see the following illustration) where you can name the template. This option creates a template of the same page type as the page you are saving. If you are saving an ASP page, for example, your template will also be an ASP page.

Save As Template dialog box

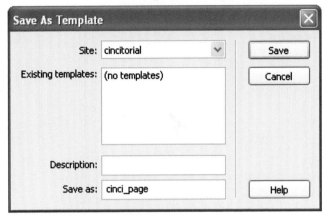

- Click the 📄 ▾ Templates button from the Common tab of the Insert bar and then click Make Template on the drop-down list. This option will create a template of the same page type as the currently active page.

- In the Assets panel, click the 📄 Templates button. Then click the 🔂 New Template button at the bottom of the panel and provide a name for the template.

- Dreamweaver stores templates automatically in the Templates folder in the current site. If no templates have been created, Dreamweaver will create the Templates folder as well.

- If you used the File>Save as Template method, the new template opens automatically after you save the template. If you have created the template in the Assets panel, you must click the 📝 Edit Template button to open the template.

- A Dreamweaver template looks like any other Web page. The title bar, however, shows the page title <<Template>> so you know you are working in a template page.

- If you are creating the template from scratch, add and modify page elements as you would on any Web page.

- You can use the objects and style elements in your Assets panel or insert or format new ones.

- You can specify a background color or picture, format levels of headings, format paragraph text, add a logo, and so on.

  ✔ *You can also create a layout with frames or absolutely positioned elements or attach cascading style sheets (CSS). You will learn about these features in Lesson 5.*

- As you create the template, you must give some thought to editable and noneditable regions. Noneditable regions are locked on any page created using the template. That is, an author will not be able to change anything in a noneditable region. This helps to protect items such as logos, official

photographs, and the like from being changed without authorization.

- All items on a template are noneditable unless you specify that they be editable. To create an editable region, select the item such as a heading or text paragraph. For best results, select while in Code and Design view so that you select the tags around the text as well. Not doing so may result in error messages requesting that you edit your code.

- Click the Templates button list arrow on the Common tab of the Insert bar. Then click the 📝 Editable Region button on the drop-down list. Dreamweaver opens the New Editable Region dialog box (see the following illustration), where you can supply a name in place of the default name for the editable item.

Name an editable item

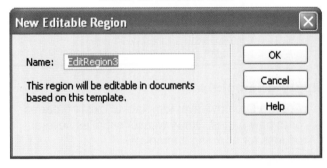

- You can also create an editable region using the Insert>Template Objects>Editable Region command.

- The editable region name displays on the template page surrounded by a light blue box that has a tab containing the editable item name.

- In pages based on templates, the entire page is bordered in yellow with the template name in the upper-right corner (see the following illustration).

Editable items in a template document

Logo   Template:cinci_page
Logo
Heading 2
Contact CinciTorial
Navigation
Navigation

- An author can click on an editable region placeholder in a page based on the template to add new content to the page. If you move the mouse over any other region, the mouse pointer turns to a 🚫 "not permitted" symbol to inform you that the region cannot be edited.

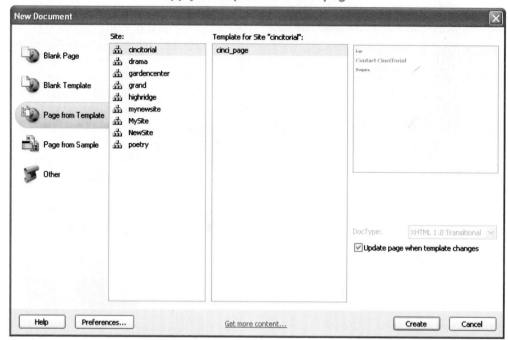

Apply a Template

- Apply a Dreamweaver template to existing pages or to new pages. Dreamweaver supplies several options for applying a template.

- To apply a template at the time you create a new page, use the File>New command, and click Page from Template in the New Document dialog box.

- Dreamweaver displays templates available for sites on your server so you can select the template to use on the new page from a list of templates available for your site (see the illustration above).

  ✔ *The New Document dialog box offers the* Update page when template changes *checkbox. This checkbox is selected by default and allows you to automatically update the page if changes are made to the template.*

- After you select the desired template, click the Create button to open the new page in the Document window.

- You have two options for applying a template to an existing page:

  - Use the Modify>Templates>Apply Template to Page command and then select the template in the Select Template dialog box (see the following illustration).

  - If the Assets panel is open, click the 🖹 Templates button if necessary, select the desired template, and drag it onto the page.

Select Template dialog box

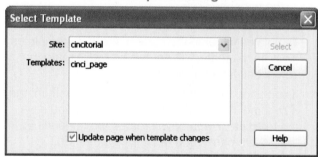

- Applying a template to a page that already has text may require that you "resolve" what to do with that text. Dreamweaver analyzes the page and then displays the Inconsistent Region Names dialog box similar to the one shown in the illustration at the top of the next page to alert you to the fact that it does not know what editable region to use for the preexisting text.

- Choose one of the editable regions in the *Move content to new region* list, shown in the following illustration, to relocate existing text.

- Choosing the Nowhere option in the *Move content to new region* list throws away all content on the page and inserts the template's content. If you have only a few lines of text on the page and its format matches an editable region in the dialog box, choose that editable region.

- You can detach a page from a template using the Modify>Templates>Detach from Template command. All template formatting remains, but the page will not update if changes are made to the template.

Applying editable regions to existing text

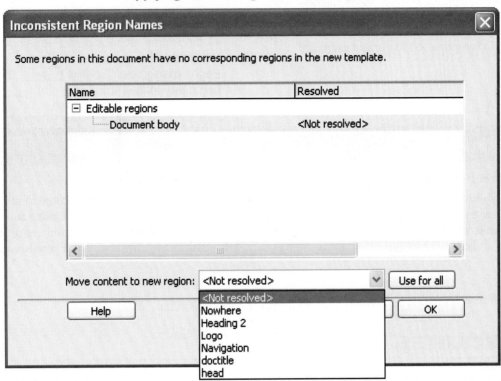

Edit a Template and Update Pages

■ After you have created a template, you can edit it at any point by opening it from the Assets panel. You can make changes to both editable and noneditable regions—and remove them, too.

✓ *To open a template to edit it, double-click on the template file name in the Assets panel. Make sure the page title <<Template>> appears in the title bar.*

■ When you save revisions to a template that has been applied to pages in a Web site, Dreamweaver asks if you want to update the pages that use the template (see the following illustration).

Dreamweaver prompts you to update pages

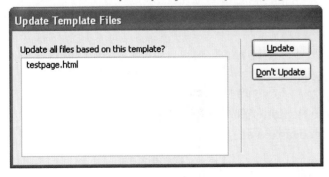

■ If you click [Update], Dreamweaver performs the updates for you and displays a report to tell you what pages have been updated (see the following illustration).

Update Pages report

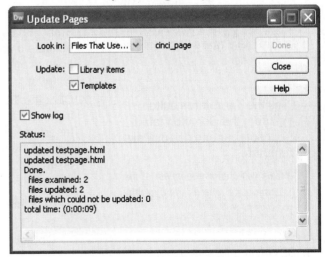

■ If you deselected the *Update page when template changes* option in the New Document or Select Template dialog box, pages attached to a template will not be changed automatically when changes to the template are saved and you will not see either dialog box prompting you to update.

- If you choose [Don't Update], you can update pages individually using the Modify>Templates>Update Current Page command. This command essentially reapplies the template to the current page only.

- If you have chosen not to update pages immediately after saving changes to the template, you can at a later time update all pages using the Modify>Templates>Update Pages command. When you do so, Dreamweaver displays an empty Update Pages dialog box. Click the [Start] button to begin the update process.

PROCEDURES

Create a New Template

Using existing page:

1. With the page active you want to base the template on, click **File** . . . . Alt+F
2. Click **Save as Template**. . . M

   ✔ *This will create a template of the same page type as the page you are saving.*

   OR

- Click the **Templates** button 📄 ▾ from the Common tab of the Insert bar and select **Make Template**.

   ✔ *This will create a template of the same page type as the currently active page.*

   OR

1. Display the Assets panel.
2. Click **Templates** button 📄.
3. Click **New Template** button 🔁.

For templates created with any of the above options:

1. Type name for template.
2. Click 🗑 if necessary.

3. Edit and modify formats as desired.
4. Save the template after editing.

Create an Editable Region (Ctrl + Alt + V)

1. Select text or graphic to make editable or position insertion point in area of page to make editable.
2. Click the **Templates** list arrow from the Common tab of the Insert bar and select **Editable Region** button 📝 on the drop-down list.

   OR

   a. Click **Insert** . . . . . . Alt+I
   b. Point to **Template Objects**. . . . . O
   c. Click **Editable Region** . E
3. Supply name for editable area.
4. Click [OK].

   ✔ *To remove an editable region, select the region by right-clicking its tab and then clicking Remove Tag.*

   ✔ *Make an editable area noneditable by selecting it and clicking Modify>Templates> Remove Template Markup.*

Apply a Template

To apply when creating page:

1. Click **File** . . . . Alt+F
2. Click **New** . . . . N
3. Click **Page from Template**.
4. Select the site, if necessary.
5. Select the desired template.
6. Click [Create].

   ✔ *Update page when template changes is selected by default. If you want to control when to update pages, deselect this check box.*

To apply to existing page:

1. Click **Modify** . . . . Alt+M
2. Point to **Templates** . . . . E, E, ↵Enter
3. Click **Apply Template to Page** . . . . A
4. Select the desired template.
5. Click [Select].

   OR

- Drag the template name from the Assets panel to the page.

Detach a Page from a Template

1. Click **Modify** . . . . Alt + M
2. Point to **Templates** . . . . E, E, ↵Enter
3. Click **Detach from Template** . . . . D

Edit a Template

From Files panel:

1. Open the **Templates** folder.
2. Double-click the template file.
3. Make changes to editable and noneditable regions as desired.
4. Save the template file and update attached files, if desired.

From Assets panel:

1. Click **Templates** button in the toolbar.

2. Double-click the template file.
   OR
   a. Select the template.
   b. Click **Edit** button.
3. Make changes to editable and noneditable regions as desired.
4. Save the template file and update attached files, if desired.

Delete a Template

From Files panel:

1. Open the **Templates** folder.
2. Right-click the template file.
3. Press **Delete**.

From Assets panel:

1. Click **Templates** button in the toolbar.
2. Right-click the template file.
3. Click **Delete**.
   OR

1. Select template.
2. Click **Delete** button.

Update Template Pages

After making changes to template:

- Click Update in the Update Template Files dialog box to update all files that use the template.
   OR

If files have not been updated after changes:

1. Click **Modify** . . . . Alt + M
2. Point to **Templates** . . . . E, E, ↵Enter
3. Click **Update Current Page** C
   OR
   Click **Update Pages** . . . . . U
4. Click Start.

EXERCISE DIRECTIONS

1. Start Dreamweaver and open the **cincitorial** site.
2. To save time, you want to create a template that contains a space for the logo link to the home page, a formatted Heading 2, and a placeholder for a navigation bar. Create the template as follows:

   - Use the Assets panel to make a new template named **cinci_page.dwt**. Open the template page for editing. (You may need to open one of the site pages before the Assets panel's tools become available to create the new template.)
   - Open **contactus.html**. Click in the heading, then select the <h2> tag in the status bar to select the heading and its tags. Copy the heading.
   - Paste the heading in the template page.
   - Apply the **puzzle.gif** image as a page background.
   - Position the insertion point to the left of the heading and press Enter to create a new line.

   - Move up into the new line and type **Logo**.
   - Position the insertion point at the end of the *Contact CinciTorial* heading, press Enter, and type **Navigation**.

   ✔ *Don't worry about the formats of the paragraphs you have just typed. You will change these formats later.*

   - Create editable regions from each of the three lines in the template, using the names **Logo**, **Heading 2**, and **Navigation**.

   ✔ *To avoid error messages, work in Code and Design view (Split view) so that you can select the <p> and <h2> tags as well as the text between them when you create the editable regions.*

3. Format the editable regions as follows.

   ✔ *Try this shortcut. Right-click anywhere in the text and click Paragraph Format from the shortcut menu and select the desired format.*

   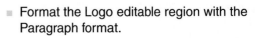

   - Format the Logo editable region with the Paragraph format.

- Format the Heading 2 editable region with the formats you used for Heading 2 on other pages, if necessary.
- Format the Navigation region with Paragraph formatting. If necessary, change the font to Default Font and the font color to black.

4. Save and close the <<Template>> page. If you are asked to update, do so. (No pages will be changed.)

5. Apply the cinci_page template to the contactus.html page.

6. The Inconsistent Region Names dialog box opens because the page already has content. Click Document body, and then choose Heading 2 to receive the existing content on the page.

7. Enter the page title Contact Us for this page.

   ✔ *The previous page title disappeared when you applied the template, because the template does not have a page title.*

8. Create a new page that uses the cinci_page template. Name the page specialties.html and give it the page title Our Specialties.

9. Replace the Heading 2 placeholder with Our Specialties.

10. You have decided not to use the page background image for the template. Open the cinci_page template and remove the puzzle.gif background from the <<Template>> document. (Clear the Background image path in the Page Properties dialog box.)

11. Save and close the template. Update the pages with the revised template.

12. Now that you have basic formatting in place for contactus.html and specialties.html, detach these pages from the template.

13. Save and close any open pages and exit Dreamweaver.

ON YOUR OWN

1. Start Dreamweaver and open the gardencenter site.

2. Create a new template for the site using the events.html page. Name the template appropriately. Your template should include:
   - The main page heading and the daylily image link back to the home page.
   - The navigation bar.
   - The text paragraph below the navigation bar.
   - A second-level heading.
   - The copyright information at the bottom of the page.
   - The current page background.

3. Make the main heading, the text paragraph, and the second-level heading editable areas. (You may want to combine the text paragraph and the second-level heading into one editable area to make it easy to insert new content.) Save and close the template.

4. Create a new page using the template and save it as favorites.html with the page title Regional Plant Favorites.

5. Change the main heading to Regional Plant Favorites.

6. Insert the following text paragraph:

The following table lists flowers, shrubs, and trees that do especially well in our region. These plants not only withstand our hot, dry summers and cold winters but actually thrive in these conditions.

7. Save and close the new page.

8. Open index.html. Add a new button named favorites to the navigation bar that uses the ☼ favoritesup.gif and ☼ favoritesover.gif image files from the Lesson 3 Data folder. Link the navigation images to the new favorites.html page.

9. Preview index.html in the browser and test the link to the new page.

10. Save and close all open pages and exit Dreamweaver.

Exercise | 21

Skills Covered

- ■ **Use the Library**
- ■ **Use Design Notes**

Software Skills The Assets panel's Library feature helps automate the insertion and changing of elements on multiple pages in your site. You can use the Design Notes feature to track your project.

Application Skills In this exercise, you will work with library items and add design notes to the CinciTorial Web site.

TERMS

Key In the Design Notes feature, an identifier for a set of information, such as *status*.

Library Dreamweaver feature that stores text, images, or other objects for easy insertion on any page in the Web site.

Library items Items stored in the Library.

NOTES

Use the Library

- ■ The **Library** feature in the Assets panel is a wonderful tool for saving time and using the same elements repeatedly—but with the ability to update and change them in every Web page that uses the element in a Web site. This tremendously reduces ramp-up time when working with a team possessing different kinds of skills.

- ■ When you place a library item on a page, Dreamweaver inserts a copy of the HTML source code for that item into the document and adds an HTML comment containing a reference to the original, external item—a link from the page item to the library item.

- ■ You can modify that library item wherever it appears in the Web site by modifying the item in the Library. In this way, a library item differs from an item inserted from the other Assets panels.

- ■ A proficient designer can create a logo and save it to the Library, for example, allowing a less experienced team member to go to the Library and use the element. This assures consistency and eliminates the need for redevelopment.

- ■ You can store images, text, or other elements in the Library and then use these **library items** on any page in a Web site.

Add Items to the Library

- ■ To view the Library, click the 📖 Library button in the Assets panel toolbar.

- ■ Library items display in the upper pane of the palette. Click the library item's name in the lower pane to display it in the upper pane, as shown in the following illustration. You can use the scroll bars if necessary to display the entire item.

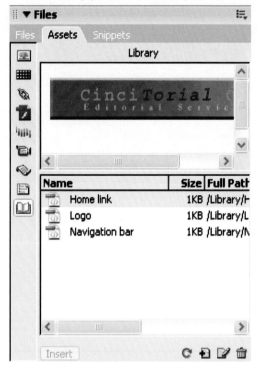

Dreamweaver automatically creates a Library sub-folder in the site's root folder to contain the library items.

You can create library items from existing text or images by selecting the object in the document and clicking Modify>Library>Add Object to Library.

When selecting items, it can be helpful to view the status bar in the Document window to make sure you are selecting a complete item, such as the complete paragraph or table in which a navigation bar is contained.

You can also create new library items. Click the New Library Item button and then the Edit button on the Library pane of the Assets panel to open a new <<Library Item>> in the Document window.

Use this Document window to type text or insert images or other elements to create the library item. When you are finished, click on File>Save As to save the library item, and then close the <<Library Item>> window.

You can remove an item from the library at any time by right-clicking its name in the Library pane and then clicking Delete—or selecting it and clicking the Delete button on the Library pane.

Insert Library Item on Page

Inserting library items on a page is even easier than adding them to the Library. Position the insertion point where you want the library item to appear in the Document window, select its name in the Library pane of the Assets panel, and click the Insert button.

You can also simply drag a library item or its name from the Library pane of the Assets panel to the desired position on the Web page.

Inserted images are initially shaded but will look normal as soon as you click in the Document window. Inserted text retains a yellow shading to remind you it is a library item.

You cannot edit a library item once it has been inserted on a page unless you break the link between the item on the page and the Library. You can detach an item from the Library by clicking it on the page and then clicking the Detach from Original button in the Property inspector.

Modify Library Item and Update Pages

As for templates, the value of using library items is that all library items inserted throughout a Web site can be modified at once by modifying the item stored in the Library.

Edit a library item by double-clicking either the item itself or its name in the Library pane of the Assets panel. Or, select the item name and click the Edit button.

The library item opens in a <<Library Item>> window. You can then edit or modify it using Dreamweaver's editing tools.

After you save the modified item, Dreamweaver will ask if you want to update all pages on which that library item appears (see the following illustration). You can choose to update all pages or not update.

Choose to update library items

Update Library Items

Update library items in these files?

contactus.asp
people.html
services.html
specialties.html
index.html
praise.html

Update
Don't Update

- If you choose not to update, you can use the Modify>Library>Update Current Page or Update Pages commands to update a single page or all pages with Library changes.

- Dreamweaver displays an Update Pages dialog box similar to that displayed when a template is updated to show you which pages have had a library item updated.

Use Design Notes

- Design notes work much like comments in Word, but you have much more control over who sees your notes.

- This is especially helpful when designing your site with sensitive data that must be shared only with your team members. Design notes are never displayed in a browser but travel with your files.

- Add design notes to a page using the File>Design Notes command. Or click the ⬍⬆ File management button on the Document toolbar and select Design Notes from the menu.

- On the Design Notes dialog box's Basic info tab, you can specify the page's status, insert the current date, and add comments (see illustration below).
    - Click the Status list arrow to display a list of status options, including draft, revision1, and final.
    - Click the 🗓 date icon to insert the current date in the Notes box.
    - Type comments or insert other necessary information in the Notes text box.

- If you want the design notes to appear each time the page opens, select the *Show when file is opened* checkbox.

- To see more design note information, click the All info tab. This tab shows information as sets of **keys** (identifiers) and values. In the illustration at the top of the next page, status, notes, and author are keys. The = sign separates a key from its value.

Add basic design notes information

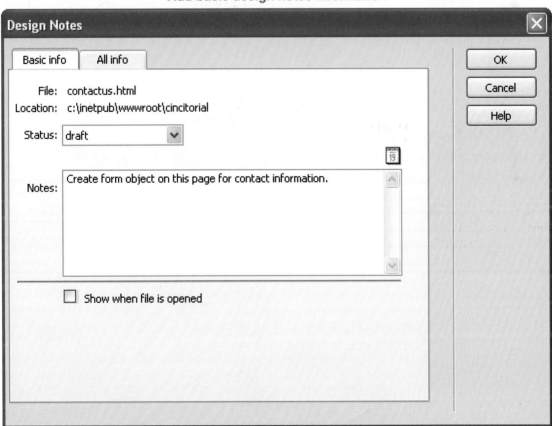

- Add new keys (such as *author* in the illustration below) by clicking the ⊞ button. The Name and Value boxes at the bottom of the tab empty so you can type the name of the new key and its value.

- Select a key/value combination in the Info list and click ⊟ to remove the key/value.

- In addition to Web pages, design notes can also be added to objects such as image files.

Viewing Design Notes

- The same steps used to create a design note can be used to view a design note. However, to easily see that a page has a design note attached to it, expand the Files panel.

- Design notes that are attached to a Web page or object are shown with a 💬 note icon in the Notes column in the Local Files pane of the expanded Files panel window. The Notes column is hidden by default. To display it, click the View>File View Columns command in the expanded Files panel, choose the Notes column, and select the Show checkbox.

- To open the note, double-click the 💬 icon.

Add new keys on All info tab

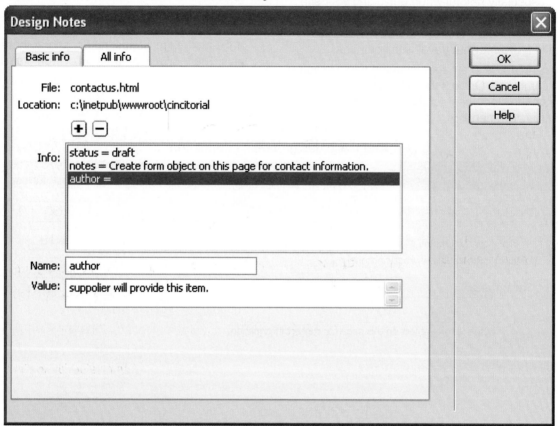

PROCEDURES

Add Items to the Library

1. Select object.
2. Click **Modify** . . . . `Alt`+`M`
3. Point
   to **Library** . . . . . `↓`, `↓`, `↵Enter`
4. Click **Add Object
   to Library** . . . . `O`
5. Type a name for the new item.

   OR

1. Select object
2. Click **Window** . . . . `Alt`+`W`
3. Click **Assets**. . . . . `A`
4. Click **Library** button 📖 on the Assets toolbar.
5. Select and drag item from the Document window to the lower pane in the Library.
6. Type a name for the new item.

Insert Library Item on Page

1. Position insertion point where library item should appear.
2. Select library item in the Library pane.
3. Click `Insert`.

   OR

   ▪ Drag library item from Library pane to the desired location on the page.

Modify Library Item

From the Assets panel:

1. Click **Library** button 📖 on the Assets toolbar.
2. Double-click the library item.

   OR

   a. Select the library item.
   b. Click **Edit** button 📝.
3. Make changes to the library item as desired.

Delete Library Item

From Assets panel:

1. Click **Library** button 📖.
2. Right-click the library item.
3. Click **Delete**.

   OR

1. Select the library item.
2. Click **Delete** button 🗑.

Update Library Items on Pages

After making changes to the library item:

   ▪ Click `Update` in the Update Library Items dialog box to update all files that use the library item.

   OR

If items have not been updated after changes:

1. Click **Modify** . . . . `Alt`+`M`
2. Point to
   Library . . . . `↓`, `↓`, `↵Enter`
3. Click **Update
   Current Page**. . . . . `C`

   OR

   Click **Update Pages** . . . . . `P`

Enable Design Notes

If the Design Notes command does not appear on the File menu:

1. Click **Site** . . . . `Alt`+`S`
2. Click **Manage Sites** . . . . . . `M`
3. Click name of the site to edit.
4. Click `Edit...`.
5. Click the **Advanced** tab and then click **Design Notes** in the Category list.
6. Select the **Maintain Design Notes** checkbox if necessary.

7. Select **Upload Design Notes for sharing**, if desired.
8. Click `OK`.
9. Click `Done` to close the Manage Sites dialog box.

Add Design Notes to Page

1. Select the desired Web page or object.
2. Click **File** . . . . `Alt`+`F`
3. Click **Design Notes** . . . . . . `G`
4. Click the **Status** list arrow and choose status for page.
5. Click 📅 to add current date to the Notes box.
6. Type comments in the **Notes** box.
7. Select the **Show when file is opened** checkbox to see design notes each time the file opens.
8. Click `OK`.

To add a new key:

In the Design Notes dialog box:

1. Click the **All info** tab.
2. Click ➕.
3. Type name for key in the **Name** box.
4. Type value for key in the **Value** box.
5. Click `OK`.

To remove a key:

In the Design Notes dialog box:

   ▪ Select a key and click ➖ to delete it, if desired.

View Design Notes

To display the Notes field:
1. Expand the Files panel.
2. Click **View** . . . . Alt+V
3. Click **File View Columns** . . F

4. Click **Notes** in the File View Columns list.
5. Click the **Show** option to select it . . . . Alt+S
6. Click ⌐ OK ⌐.

To view a design note:
- Double-click the Note icon 💬 in the Notes column of the Local Files pane in the expanded Files panel.

EXERCISE DIRECTIONS

1. Start Dreamweaver and open the **cincitorial** site.
2. Display the Library pane in the Assets panel and add—and update—items to the Library as follows:
   - Open **index.html** and drag the logo image to the Library. Name it **Logo**.
   - Open **people.html** and drag the small logo that links to the home page to the Library. Name it **Home link**.
   - Still on **people.html**, select the navigation bar by clicking on the first button and then selecting the <p> tag in the tag selector to make sure you have selected the entire paragraph. Add the navigation bar to the Library. Name the item **Navigation bar**.

   ✔ *If your navigation bar is created within an <h2> tag, you may want to replace that tag and any attributes and values with the <p> tag to eliminate unnecessary code around the navigation bar.*

   ✔ *If you are asked to update library items, do so.*

3. Create a new library item named **Copyright** that contains the text **Copyright © CinciTorial Co. All rights reserved**.
4. Insert library items as follows:
   - Insert the Home link library item in place of the Logo placeholder on **contactus.html** and **specialties.html**.
   - Insert the Copyright library item below the last paragraph of type on all pages in the site.

   ✔ *Make sure the Copyright library item is left aligned on all pages. You may need to adjust HTML code in the Code view or Code inspector.*

   ✔ *In the contactus.html and specialties.html documents, the Copyright library item should go under the Navigation bar placeholder.*

   - Insert the Navigation bar library item below the first heading on **contactus.html** (remove the Navigation placeholder), **praise.html**, **services.html**, and **specialties.html** (remove the Navigation placeholder).
   - The white background of the navigation bar does not look good on the **praise.html** page with its light yellow page background. Remove the light yellow background on this page.

5. Cut the *Last update* paragraph on **index.html** and delete it on **praise.html**. You will add this information to the Copyright library item. Remove the blank paragraph that remains after you delete the *Last update* text.
6. Modify the Copyright library item by pasting the cut *Last update* information following the *All rights reserved* sentence. Change the font color of the text to #990033.
7. Don't update pages automatically. Instead, view each page in the site and update it to see the change to the library item.
8. Save and close each page after you update it.
9. Open **contactus.html** and create the following design notes:
   - Set the status as draft.
   - Insert the following comment: **Create form on this page**.
   - Add a new key named **author** and assign the value **Ellen**.
10. Open **specialties.html** and create the following design notes:
    - Set the status as draft.
    - Insert the following comment: **Create table on this page**.

11. Expand the Files panel and view the design notes. (Display the Notes field if necessary to see the design note icons.) Collapse the view to the File panel.

12. Open index.html and add the words Our Specialties below *Services* in the list of links. Use these words to create a link to specialties.html.

> ✔ *You realize you do not have a link in the navigation bar to the specialities.html page.*

13. Open the Navigation bar library item. Choose to modify the navigation bar and add the specialties

element using the  bluespecialties.jpg and maroonspecialties.jpg images in the Lesson 3 Data folder. Save the new images in your site's images folder. Link to the specialties.html page.

14. Update all pages with the new navigation bar.

15. Preview index.html in the browser. Check navigation to and from all pages in the site. Your Contact Us page should look like Illustration A. (The date on your page will be different.)

16. Close the browser.

17. Close any open pages and exit Dreamweaver.

Illustration A

Contact CinciTorial

| Contact | People | Praise | Services | Specialties |

Copyright © CinciTorial Co. All rights reserved. Last update: 03/10/2007 3:44 PM

ON YOUR OWN

1. Start Dreamweaver and open the gardencenter site.

2. Open contact.html. Select the small flower above the main heading and add it to the Library with an appropriate name.

3. Move the pointer near the border of the navigation bar until you see the ScreenTip *Press control key to see table structure*, and then click to select the entire table that holds the navigation bar links.

4. On the Property inspector, locate the W box and type **75** to reduce the navigation bar to 75% of the page width.

5. Boldface the links so they stand out in the table.

6. Add the navigation table to the Library with an appropriate name. (Hint: When selecting the table, click the <table> tag in the status bar to make sure you have selected the entire table.)

7. Remove the existing navigation bars on events.html and info.html, and then insert the Library navigation bar.

8. Remove the existing navigation bar on the template page, insert the Library navigation bar, and update the template. (You may need to create a space between the editable regions in a code view: Insert code such as <p>space</p>, refresh the Design view, and then insert the navigation bar in place of the *space* text.)

9. You notice a couple of problems with the Library navigation bar. It doesn't have a link for the regional favorites page, and it has a white background that looks odd on the pages that have a background image. Modify the navigation bar library item as follows:

   ▪ Open the navigation bar library item and add a link in the last table cell that reads Favorites. Make sure the new text has the same format as the other links in the navigation bar, and link the text to the favorites.html page.

   ▪ Display the Code Inspector for the library item page. Locate the <table> tag and remove the bgcolor attribute and its value (remove bgColor="FFFFFF").

   ▪ Update all files that use the navigation bar, and update the page based on the template.

   ✔ *After you update the pages, you will notice that the Library navigation bars are filled with yellow. This color simply indicates the library item; the yellow background will not show in the browser.*

10. Open favorites.html and add a design note with the status needs attention. Insert the following note:

    Add a table to this page that lists flowers, shrubs, and trees that grow well in our region.

11. Save all open pages. Test the site in the browser, clicking each link to make sure the navigation bars work and look correct on each page.

12. Close the browser and exit Dreamweaver.

Exercise | 22

Summary Exercise

Application Skills In this exercise, you will continue to work on the High Ridge Swim & Tennis Club site. You will add and modify images, create a template and a navigation bar, and add items to the Library.

DIRECTIONS

1. Start Dreamweaver and open the highridge site.

2. Create a new folder in the site named graphics to store the graphic images you will add to the site.

3. Open index.html. Position the insertion point to the left of the paragraph below the bulleted list and insert ⊙ swimmeet.psd from the Lesson 3 Data files. Optimize the image as a JPEG using default settings. Save the file in the graphics folder and add the alternate text High Ridge swimmers at a recent meet.

4. Modify the image as follows:

   ▪ Resize the image to **320** by **240** and resample the image after resizing.

   ▪ Change the contrast to **20**.

   ▪ Apply right alignment to the picture.

5. Open membership.html. Apply the ⊙ highbackground.gif image as a background picture on this page. Save the page.

   ✔ *You are ready to add more pages to the site. Create a template to make this process easier.*

6. Create a new template based on the membership.html page and save it as high_page. Update links if prompted. Format the template as follows:

   ▪ Create an editable region for the main head with an appropriate name.

   ▪ Create another editable region that includes paragraph text and the second-level heading.

   ▪ Below the last editable region, insert a horizontal rule and then the following text:
   Copyright © High Ridge Swim & Tennis Club. For more information, contact manager@highridgeswim.net.

   ▪ Format the text as desired and create an e-mail link from the e-mail address. Save the page.

7. Save the horizontal rule and copyright information as a library item with an appropriate name, and then insert it on the index.html and membership.html pages.

8. Create three new pages based on the template:

   ▪ Save the first page as info.html with the page title Club Information. Change the main heading to Club Information and the page text to Text in progress.

   ▪ Save the second page as news.html with the page title Club News. Change the main heading to News and Updates and the page text to Text in progress.

   ▪ Save the third page as swimdive.html with the page title Swimming and Diving. Change the main heading to Swimming and Diving and the page text to Text in progress.

9. Activate index.html and create a navigation bar as follows:

   ▪ Insert a blank line below the main heading for the navigation bar.

   ▪ Create the following navigation bar elements: home, info, news, members, swimming.

   ▪ For each element, find and insert the corresponding GIF file in the Lesson 3 Data folder, such as ⊙ highhomeup.gif and ⊙ highhomeover.gif. Save all images in your graphics folder.

- Link each element to the appropriate page in the site.
- Make sure to create a horizontal navigation bar that does not use a table.

10. Save the navigation bar as a library item and then insert it on membership.html and on the page template. (You may want to use a code view to make sure the navigation bar is inserted between the two editable areas.) Update all template files.

11. Activate index.html and create an image map on the photo that links to the swimdive.html page. The alternative text for the image map should read Join the High Ridge Swimming and Diving Team!

12. Save all pages, then preview the index.html page in the browser. Test all links in the navigation bar and image map. The Club Information page should look similar to Illustration A.

13. Open the Copyright library item and modify the text color as desired and then save the item and update all files.

14. Close all open pages and exit Dreamweaver.

Illustration A

Club Information

Home   Information   News   Membership Swimming

Text in progress.

Copyright © High Ridge Swim & Tennis Club. For more information, contact manager@highridgeswim.net.

Application Exercise

Application Skills In this exercise, you will continue to work on the Web site for the Grand Theatre. You will add graphic images to the site and create a navigation bar that you can insert on all pages.

DIRECTIONS

1. Start Dreamweaver and open the grand Web site.
2. Create a folder in the site to hold your site graphics.
3. Open index.html. Insert at the top of the page the 💿 grand.gif image from the Lesson 3 Data folder and save the image in your site. Add appropriate alternate text.

    ✔ *The colors used in this graphic are adapted from the Grand's historic marquee. You may want to modify colors in the Web site to match the Web-safe colors used in this graphic and the other graphics you will add to the site.*

4. Open location.html. Insert at the top of the page the 💿 grandhead.gif image from the Lesson 3 Data folder. Add appropriate alternate text. Create a link from this graphic to the home page. (Set the border to 0 if necessary to remove the link outline.) Add this image to your Assets panel favorites.
5. Insert the image from the Favorites list at the top of show.html and create a link to the home page.

    ✔ *One of the maps for the site is now available.*

6. Insert and format the map page as follows:
    - Create a new blank HTML page in the Web site and save it as jeffersonmap.html with the page title Jefferson Map.
    - Insert the grandhead.gif image from your Favorites and link it to the home page.
    - Insert a heading on the page that reads Finding Madison Village. Use the Assets panel's Colors panel to select and apply one of the colors you have already used in the site.
    - Below the heading, insert text that reads Back to Location. Link this text to the location.html page.
    - Below the link, insert the 💿 grandmap.gif image from the Lesson 3 Data folder, adding appropriate alternate text and saving the image in your site.
7. Activate location.html. In the fourth sentence in the first text paragraph, locate the words *Click here* and use them to create a link to jeffersonmap.html.
8. Add a design note to this page that reminds you to check the status of the Madison Village map.
9. Create a navigation bar for the site as follows:
    - Activate index.html and insert a blank line above the first heading (*Now Showing . . .*) to contain the navigation bar.
    - Create a horizontal navigation bar that includes home, location, and show elements. For each element, find and insert the correct navigation bar images in the Lesson 3 Data folder.
10. Save the navigation bar as a library item and insert it on the location.html and show.html pages below the *Grand* heading.

    ✔ *If you receive an error message when trying to insert the library item on the show.html page, try deleting the automatically updating date and then restore it after inserting the library item.*

11. Activate the index.html page. Display the page in the browser and check links in the site.
12. Close all open pages and exit Dreamweaver.

Exercise | 24

Curriculum Integration

Application Skills   Your biology class is about to begin a unit on endangered species, and your instructor has asked the class to create a Web site containing information on endangered species in your state. To make sure the contributions are uniform, the class will use several of Dreamweaver's Starter pages. Before you begin this project, gather the following information:

- Locate a list of species identified as endangered in your state (or a neighboring state if you can't find information for your state).

- Choose one of the species from the site to be the focus of your contribution to the Web site.

- Find pictures of several of the species on the list, including the one you are focusing on, and save them to your computer.

- Review how to open one of Dreamweaver's Starter pages; these pages can be accessed from the Welcome Screen.

DIRECTIONS

Define a new site with the name endangered. Create your first page for the site using the Starter Page (Theme) page identified as Lodging – Home Page. This page will be your general introduction to the topic of endangered species in your state. Save the page as introxx.html, replacing *xx* with your initials. As you save the page, create a new folder to contain the images and other files associated with the page. Change the page title to a more appropriate title.

Replace the main heading on the page with a title such as OHIO ENDANGERED SPECIES. Select the image at the left side of the page and delete it.

Insert one of the images you saved in place of the picture you just deleted. Resize the picture to fit in the space used by the default picture (your picture should be about 230 pixels wide and a corresponding height). Resample the image after resizing, and adjust brightness and contrast as necessary. Be sure to supply alternative text for this and any other images you add to the site.

Replace the placeholder text below the image with a brief description of the new image and a link to the page where you found the picture as a credit line.

Replace the heading to the right of the image with new text, and then replace the placeholder text below the heading with some general remarks about why you think species have become endangered in your state.

Create a second page using the Starter Page (Theme) page identified as Lodging – Product Page. Save the page using the name of your chosen species, and save any associated files in the images folder. Give the page an appropriate page title.

If you have located several pictures of your species that are roughly the same size and orientation, create a rollover image: Insert the pictures on the page to adjust size, contrast, brightness, or sharpness and resample as necessary. Then create the rollover image in the placeholder supplied for an image.

Replace the main heading on the page with the same main heading you used on the previous page. Change the subheading to the name of your species, and use the third-level heading for the species' Latin or scientific name if available.

Replace placeholder text with some facts about your species and why it is endangered.

Create a link from the *Home* text below the main heading that returns a site visitor to your intro page. On the intro page, delete all placeholder link text except the first (*OUR ROOMS*) and change the text to the name of your species. Create a link to the species page.

Save all pages and view them in the browser. Test links.

Close all open pages and exit Dreamweaver.

www.state.nj.us/dep/fgw/tandespp.htm
lists –

Then find another site : not wik....
ex www.allaboutbirds.org

use ext. of org/edu...
remember credibility!

www.projectseven.com

on left >
horizontal
glider magic.
↳>

★Review pg 105
"Rollover Image"
first...

Exercise | 25

Critical Thinking

Application Skills   In this exercise, you will continue to work on your personal Web site. You will create a template and a new page based on the template, add images to the site and format them, and work with the site's navigation bars.

DIRECTIONS

- Create a template for your Web site to make it easy to add new pages to the site. Create at least one new page using the template and insert content on the page.

- Add a graphic background to at least one page, using either an image or a background color.

- Add an image to at least one page, using clip art or a photo you located on the Web. Resize the image(s) as necessary and position them as desired on the page(s). Be sure to save the images in a folder in your site and add alternative text.

- Update one of the navigation bars with links to any pages you added, and then save the navigation bar as a library item. Insert the new library item on all pages.

- You may wish to detach the navigation bar library item from the page that has a background color so you can adjust or remove the fill color of the table to match the page background. (Use the Tag inspector to do so.)

- Create any additional links necessary to and from your new pages(s).

- Preview the site in the browser.

- Save all open documents and close them.

- Exit Dreamweaver.

Lesson | 4

Work with Tables and Forms

Skills Covered

- **About Tables**
- **Create a Table**
- **Insert Text and Images in Table Cells**
- **Adjust Table Structure**

Software Skills   A table in a Web document is the best and most structured way to organize graphics, text, and other objects such as forms in your Web pages. A table can be designed to be an obvious part of the page—as an object itself— or invisible so that it simply supports nested elements such as graphics.

Application Skills   In this exercise, you will add a table to the CinciTorial site to organize information. You will change the table structure and insert text and graphics in the table cells.

TERMS

Cell The intersecting point of a row and column.

Cell padding Space between cell content and the cell border.

Cell spacing Space between cells.

Columns Divisions that run across the table's width.

Merge cells Combining several cells to create one larger cell.

Rows Divisions that run down the table's length.

Split cell Dividing a single cell into multiple rows or columns.

NOTES

About Tables

- Tables are used on Web pages to organize related data in a grid made up of **rows** and **columns**. A table may consist of only a few rows and columns, or it may be used to organize an entire Web page.

- Though there are other, more elaborate ways of organizing Web page data, such as the AP elements and frames you will learn about in later exercises, tables provide the most dependable framework for Web page layout. All browsers can display the HTML codes used to create tables, so if you want to make sure your page layout will work for all visitors, structure it using a table.

  ✔ You will use a table to create a page layout in Exercise 28.

- Once a table has been inserted on a Web page, it can be restructured very easily. Change the look of a table by adjusting row height or column width, adding or deleting rows or columns, or merging or splitting **cells** (a cell is the intersecting point of a row and a column).

Create a Table

- Create a table on a Web page using Insert bar options or a menu command. Position your insertion point where the table should appear and then use one of these methods:

  - Click the ▦ Table button from the Common or Layout tab of the Insert bar.

  - Use the Insert>Table command.

  ✔ You can also draw a table in Layout view. You will work with Layout view and table drawing tools in Exercise 28.

- The Table dialog box opens after you perform either of these actions (see the following illustration). In this dialog box, you can specify several kinds of information for the new table.

Table dialog box

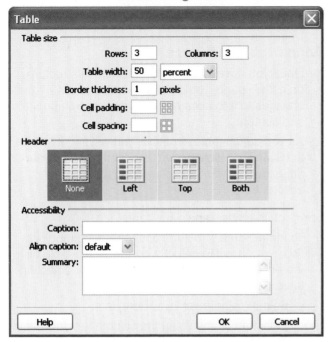

✔ *The Table dialog box shows the settings chosen for the last table. Make sure you check all settings in the Table dialog box before clicking OK.*

- Your first task in this dialog box is to specify the numbers of rows and columns for the table.

- You can also specify a width for the table as it is being created. Type a width in the Table width box and choose to measure that width either as a percentage of the page width or in pixels.

- Using the percentage value in the Table width text box allows you to maintain the ratio of table-to-page text when the page is viewed in different types of browsers. Using pixel values ensures that the table will be exactly the same physical size in any browser or screen resolution.

  ✔ *Current Web standards prefer percentage widths over exact table sizes, so that a table's content can "flow" according to the size of the browser window.*

- Either measurement option is appropriate for tables used to format the entire Web page. A pixel value, however, is the best choice for tables that you don't want to be resized in the browser.

- You can select border thickness in the Table dialog box. Border thickness is measured in pixels.

  ✔ *Leaving the Border thickness box empty results in a border-less—or invisible—table that can be used to format an entire Web page or other data.*

- If desired, you can insert values for **cell padding** and **cell spacing** when creating the table. Cell padding is the distance between cell text and a cell border. Cell spacing is the amount of space between cells.

  ✔ *You can change these values at any time after creating a table using the Property inspector.*

- Use the Header options in the Table dialog box to apply basic formatting to some areas of the table. The Left header option applies bold, centered formatting to the first column of the table, as indicated in the thumbnail in the dialog box. The Top header option applies this formatting to the first row of the table. The Both header option applies formatting to the left column and top row.

- The Accessibility options in the Table dialog box allow the user to insert a caption for the table that displays outside the table grid at the top, bottom, left, or right of the table. Use the Summary text box to describe the table for visitors who use a screen reader.

  ✔ *Text you insert in the Summary box does not display in the browser.*

- A new table displays on the Web page with default border options (see the following illustration) if you have specified a border thickness. The table is selected when inserted.

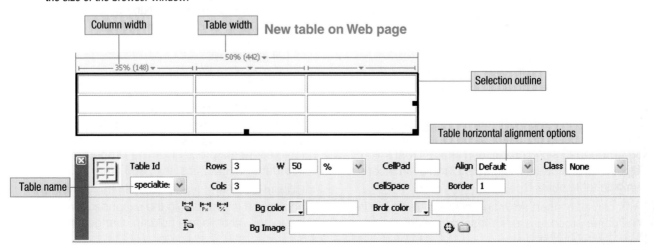

New table on Web page

- Note the green lines and text above the selected table and table columns. The top line tells you the table width as a percentage or pixel value (depending how you specified table width when creating it). If you set specific column widths, the lines above each column give you that information.

- This table width information can be toggled on and off using the 🔍 Visual Aids list on the Document toolbar.

- The table and column width lines also display small green downward-pointing arrows that, when clicked, display either the table header menu or the column header menu. These menus give you quick access to commands that allow you to select the table or restructure the table by adjusting column widths and spacing, inserting new columns at the left or right, and so on.

- While the table is selected, you can also use the Property inspector to make a number of changes to the table:

  - Identify (name) the table if desired.

  - Change the number of rows and columns in the table.

  - Change the width and/or height of the table in percentage of page width or pixel measurements.

  - Specify cell padding and cell spacing.

  - Specify a border width (or delete the border measurement to remove borders altogether).

  - If the table is less than the full page width, you can use the Align list to center, left align, or right align the table in the page.

- In the expanded portion of the Property inspector, you will find properties relating to the table's appearance. You can change column widths and row heights, and add border and background colors—or a picture to be used as a table background. (Individual cells can have backgrounds, too, allowing for creative effects.)

  ✔ *You will learn about borders and backgrounds in the next exercise.*

Insert Text and Images in Table Cells

- To enter text in a table, click in a table cell and begin typing. Use the Tab key or an arrow key to move from cell to cell in the table.

- Format text in a table cell just as you would on a Web page using the buttons and other options on the Property inspector. You can change font style, size, and color; adjust alignment; and even insert links in table cells.

- You can also insert an image in any table cell using the same procedure as for inserting an image on a

Web page. If the image is larger than the table cell, the cell automatically expands to accommodate the image.

Adjust Table Structure

- Once you have inserted the basic table structure on a Web page, you can make a number of changes to it to accommodate data as you begin to add content.

- As you adjust table structure, you will find it helpful to display the History panel so you can view your adjustments. You can easily undo a series of actions from this panel.

Select Table Elements

- To make some structural and formatting modifications, you need to select a portion of the table or the entire table. Use these guidelines for selecting table elements:

  - Select a single cell by clicking in it.

  - Select a column using the column header menu (see the following illustration). Or, place the mouse pointer so it touches the top edge of the column. When the pointer becomes a solid black arrow, click the mouse button to select the column. You can also select a row this way—position the pointer so it touches the left edge of the row and click.

Use the column header menu to select a column

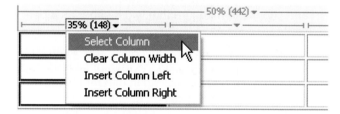

  - To select noncontiguous elements, such as cells, rows, and columns in a table, hold the Ctrl key and make the desired selections.

  - To select the entire table, use the table header menu or click on any outside border with the sizing pointer. Or click inside the table and then click the <table> tag in the tag selector on the left side of the status bar.

Change Cell Width and Height

- You can easily resize column widths or row heights by clicking on a column or row border and then dragging to the desired size. You can also resize table elements precisely in the Property inspector in order to fit graphics, text, and other objects.

- Click in a cell and type a value in the W (Width) and/or H (Height) box in the expanded Property inspector. All cells in a column change when a new width is entered, and all cells in a row change when a new height is entered.

✔ *If you want the cell value in percentages rather than in the default pixels, immediately follow the value with a percentage sign (%). You can also use the pixel-to-percentage conversion buttons in the expanded Property inspector.*

▪ If your width and height changes do not look the way you want, you can select the table and use the 🖫 Clear Column Widths or ▣ Clear Row Heights buttons on the expanded Property inspector. Clear Row Heights returns any rows to their default height. Clear Column Widths reduces column width to exactly fit the widest entry in the column.

✔ *You can also find these commands on the table header menu or use Modify>Table>Clear Cell Heights or Clear Cell Widths to adjust row height and column width in a selected table.*

Insert and Delete Rows and Columns

▪ You may need to add or delete rows and columns after you have created a table. You can insert a new row as you are adding content to a table by simply pressing the Tab key when you are in the last cell of the table.

▪ To add a new row elsewhere in the table or a new column, use the commands on the Modify>Table submenu:

  ▪ Click Modify>Table>Insert Row to insert a new row above the currently selected cell.

  ▪ Click Modify>Table>Insert Column to insert a new column to the left of the currently selected cell. You can also use the column header menu to insert a new column to the right or left of the currently selected cell.

  ▪ Click Modify>Table>Insert Rows or Columns to open the Insert Rows or Columns dialog box (see the following illustration) where you can specify a number of rows or columns and their position.

Select number of rows or columns to insert

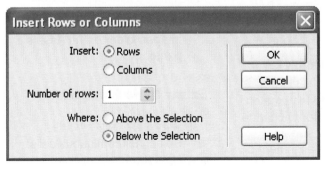

✔ *You can also access these commands by right-clicking in a cell and then pointing to Table on the shortcut menu.*

▪ If you prefer to use toolbar buttons to insert rows and columns, you can find them on the Layout tab of the Insert bar.

▪ To delete a row or column, select it and then press Delete.

Split and Merge Cells

▪ Tables are generally considered symmetrical elements, with rows stacked on rows, cells stacked on cells. Although this is beneficial for tabular or mathematical data, you may need to split and merge the cells to emphasize headers, labels, and other design elements.

▪ When you **split cells**, you break one cell into more than one column or row. When you **merge cells**, you combine more than one cell to create a single, larger cell.

▪ To split a cell, select the cell and then click the 🞨 Splits cell into rows or columns button on the Property inspector (or use the Modify>Table>Split Cell command). The Split Cell dialog box opens to allow you to split the cell into the desired number of rows or columns (see the following illustration).

Split cell into rows or columns

▪ To merge cells, select the cells and click the ▣ Merges selected cells using spans button on the Property inspector (or use the Modify>Table>Merge Cells command).

Span Rows and Columns

▪ The Modify>Table submenu also features commands for merging columns or rows so that they span across one or more columns or down one or more rows. In the following illustration, for example, the text has been set to span down one row.

Text spans down one row

Editor Specialties	

- Use Modify>Table>Increase Row Span or Increase Column Span to span rows or columns.

- Choosing a span command causes the current cell to merge with the one to its right (if you span columns) or below it (if you span rows). Increase the span by issuing the command more than one time.

- Use the Decrease Row Span or Decrease Column Span command to decrease the number of rows or columns spanned.

- Spanning is much the same as merging, but it is easier to do "on the fly" than merging. If you decide you want text to span three columns rather than two, for example, just increase the span. Decreasing the span is likewise easier than splitting a cell you have already merged.

  ✔ *You can achieve interesting effects with tables if you do some experimenting. For example, you can nest a table within a table cell to provide more layout options.*

E-Commerce Connection

Business and E-Business

E-commerce businesses perform many of the same functions as brick-and-mortar businesses. Both types of businesses, for example, must deal with issues of securing a location to do business, hiring staff, payroll and banking, marketing the business, and so on.

Explore E-Commerce Functions

Use the Internet to locate information on basic business functions and common e-business activities. Write a report that compares basic functions of both brick-and-mortar businesses and e-businesses.

PROCEDURES

Create a Table (Ctrl + Alt + T)

1. Position insertion point at location for new table.
2. Click **Insert** . . . . (Alt)+(I)
3. Click **Table** . . . . (T)

   OR

- Click **Table** button from the Common (or Layout) tab of the Insert bar.

In the Table dialog box:

1. Specify number of rows and columns.
2. Specify width as percentage of page width or in pixels.
3. Specify border thickness and cell padding and spacing.
4. Specify header option.
5. Specify caption, if desired, and position of caption.

6. Add Summary text for accessibility.
7. Click [OK].

Align Table

1. Select entire table (see *Select Table Elements* below).
2. Click the **Align** list arrow in the Property inspector.
3. Select desired alignment.

Insert Text and Images in a Table

- Click in cell and begin typing.
- Use (Tab↹) or an arrow key to move from cell to cell.
- Use buttons and features on Property inspector to change the format, font, size, font style, color, and alignment of text.

To insert images in table cells:

1. Click **Insert** . . . . (Alt)+(I)
2. Click **Image** . . . . (I)

   OR

- Click **Image** button from the Common tab of the Insert bar.

In the Select Image Source dialog box:

1. Navigate to the location of the image and select the image.
2. Click [OK].

   OR

- Drag the image from the site's images folder or the Assets panel.

Select Table Elements

- Select cell: Click in cell.
- Select noncontiguous cells: Hold down (Ctrl), click in first cell, and then click other cells.

- Select column or row: Position mouse pointer just above column or just to left of row (pointer becomes a solid black arrow) and click, or click column header menu and click **Select Column**.
- Select table: Click on table border or click in the table and then click the <table> tag in the tag selector on the status bar, or click table header menu and click **Select Table**.

Change Cell Width and Height

- Drag a column or row border in the direction to resize.

  OR

1. Click in cell to resize.
2. Expand Property inspector, if necessary.
3. Type desired width in **W** text box on Property inspector.
4. Type desired height in **H** text box on Property inspector.

Return to Default Row Height

- Select table and click **Clear Row Heights** button ⓘⓒ on Property inspector to restore default row height, or click table header menu and select **Clear Row Heights**.

Return to Default Column Width

- Select table and click **Clear Column Widths** button ⓘⓔ on Property inspector to set column width to accommodate widest entry in column, or click table header menu and select **Clear Column Widths**.

Delete Rows and Columns (Ctrl + Shift + M, Ctrl + Shift + -)

1. Select row or column to delete.
2. Press Ⓓⓔⓛ.

Insert Rows and Columns (Ctrl + M, Ctrl + Shift + A)

1. Position insertion point in cell below where new row should appear or to right of where new column should appear.
2. Click **Modify** . . . . Alt+M
3. Point to **Table** . . . . Ⓣ
4. Click **Insert Row** . . . . Ⓝ

   OR

   Click **Insert Column** . . . . . Ⓒ

   OR

   a. Click **Insert Rows or Columns** . . . . Ⓘ
   b. Select **Rows** . . . . . Alt+R
      or **Columns** . . . . . . Alt+C
   c. Type or choose number of items.
   d. Click **Above the selection** . . . . Alt+A
      or **Below the selection** . . . . Alt+B
   e. Click Ⓞⓚ.

   OR

1. Position insertion point in cell.
2. Click column header menu and select **Insert Column Left** or **Insert Column Right**.

   OR

- Use buttons from the Layout tab of the Insert bar to insert a column to left or right or insert a row above or below.

Split Cells (Ctrl + Alt + S)

1. Click in cell to split.
2. Click **Modify** . . . . Alt+M
3. Point to **Table** . . . . Ⓣ
4. Click **Split Cell** . . . . Ⓟ

   OR

- Click **Splits cell into rows or columns** button 🔧 on Property inspector.

In Split Cell dialog box:

1. Select **Rows** . . . . Alt+R
   or **Columns** . . . . Alt+C
2. Type or choose number of rows or columns to create.
3. Click Ⓞⓚ.

Merge Cells (Ctrl + Alt + M)

1. Select cells to merge.
2. Click **Modify** . . . . Alt+M
3. Point to **Table** . . . . Ⓣ
4. Click **Merge Cells** . . . . Ⓜ

   OR

- Click **Merges selected cells using spans** button ⬜ on Property inspector.

Span Text in Rows and Columns

1. Click in cell to span.
2. Click **Modify** . . . . Alt+M
3. Point to **Table** . . . . Ⓣ
4. Click **Increase Row Span** . Ⓡ
   to span down one row.

   OR

   Click **Increase Column Span** . . . . Ⓐ
   to span to right across one column.

5. Repeat to span additional rows or columns.

To remove span:

1. Click in cell to remove span.
2. Click **Modify** . . . . Alt+M
3. Point to **Table** . . . . Ⓣ
4. Click **Decrease Row Span** . . . . Ⓦ

   OR

   Decrease Column Span . . . . Ⓤ
   to remove span.

EXERCISE DIRECTIONS

1. Start Dreamweaver and open the cincitorial site.

2. Open specialties.html.

3. Create a blank paragraph below the navigation bar and above the library item if necessary. (You may need to create the blank paragraph in a code view.)

4. Type the following paragraph:

   CinciTorial editors have worked with most widely used software applications. Each editor has areas of specialization, as shown in the table below. All three editors are certified in one or more applications.

5. Press Enter to create a new paragraph.

6. Create a new table at the insertion point consisting of 5 rows and 2 columns. Set the table width at 75 percent of the page width. Set the border thickness at 1 if necessary. Insert the following summary text:

   The table displays word processing, spreadsheet, database, and programming applications and lists CinciTorial editors proficient with each application.

7. In the selected table on the page, drag the border between the two columns to the left until the left column header reads about 35%. Center the table.

8. Format the table heading area:
   - Click in the first cell and type Editor Specialties.
   - Click to the left of the text. Insert the ⊙book.gif image from the Lesson 4 Data folder and save it in your images folder. Add the alternate text Book clip art.
   - Resize the image so it is 88 pixels wide and 40 pixels high. Resample the image. Use Bottom alignment.
   - Use the column span command to make the heading span both columns.
   - Format the text as Heading 4 and change its color to #990033. Insert a space between the image and the heading.

9. Using Illustration A as a guide, insert text in the next four rows of the table as follows:
   - Use the split cell feature to split the three cells below the *Word Processing* cell into three columns.
   - Adjust column width as necessary to display the names on one line.
   - Insert the bullet characters using the Other Characters command on the Characters list from the Text tab of the Insert bar. Change the character size to **4** and its color to #990033. Copy the bullet character and use Paste to insert it elsewhere in the table.

10. After entering the bullets for Caitlin, press Tab repeatedly to create 13 more new rows. Merge the three smaller cells in the appropriate rows to create one wider cell for the *Spreadsheets*, *Databases*, and *Programming* headings. Enter the remaining text and characters.

11. Merge the empty cells above the names in the first column.

12. Format the table as follows:
    - Use Illustration A as a guide for boldfacing and centering table text.
    - Adjust column widths for the split columns as necessary to look attractive.
    - Enter a nonbreaking space (use the Insert Non-breaking Space button on the Characters list from the Text tab of the Insert bar or press Ctrl + Shift + Spacebar) in any empty cells.

    ✔ If you do not enter a nonbreaking space, the borders may not display correctly for the cells that do not have entries.

13. Save the page and then preview it in the browser. The table should look similar to Illustration A.

14. Close any open pages and exit Dreamweaver.

Illustration A

 Editor Specialties

	Word Processing		
	Word	**WordPerfect**	**StarOffice Writer**
Jim Horner	•	•	•
Caitlin Preston	•	•	•
	Spreadsheets		
	Excel	**Quattro Pro**	**Lotus 1-2-3**
Jim Horner	•	•	•
Caitlin Preston	•		
	Databases		
	Access	**SQL**	**Oracle**
Jim Horner	•	•	•
Caitlin Preston	•		•
Tyler Meadows	•		•
	Programming		
	ColdFusion	**Java**	**PowerBuilder**
Caitlin Preston	•	•	
Tyler Meadows	•	•	•

ON YOUR OWN

1. Start Dreamweaver and open the gardencenter site.

2. Open contact.html.

3. Insert a new paragraph below the last paragraph on the page (and above the copyright paragraph) and type the following text:

   To ask a specific question about horticulture, use the following contact information:

4. Create a table to contain the following information. Use your own judgment about how to set up the data and format the table information. You may format the e-mail addresses as e-mail links if desired.

   Questions about Annuals and Perennials

   Mary Matthews Ext. 135 mmatthews@readinggarden.net

   Tom Gilb   Ext. 142 tgilb@readinggarden.net

   Questions about Groundcovers

   Mary Matthews Ext. 135 mmatthews@readinggarden.net

   Questions about Shrubs

   Jin Tsang   Ext. 140 jtsang@readinggarden.net

   Pat Harte   555-3389

   pat_harte@hartedesign.net

   Questions about Trees

   Lynne Fairchild   Ext. 138 lfairchild@readinggarden.net

   Olivia Bauer   555-7800

   obauer@stateextension.oh.gov

5. If you have access to clip art files, locate a picture of a flower, shrub, or tree and add it to a cell in the table. Adjust size as necessary (don't forget to resample and save the image in your site).

6. Save changes and preview the page in the browser.

7. Make any necessary revisions to the table, then close all open pages and exit Dreamweaver.

Exercise | 27

Skills Covered

- Modify Table Borders and Backgrounds
- Import Table Data

- Sort Table Data
- Insert Table-Related Tags

Software Skills   Use table borders and backgrounds to emphasize portions of a table. If you have tabular data stored in another application, you can import it to create a table in Dreamweaver. After importing the data, you can sort it.

Application Skills   In this exercise, you will enhance the table you created in the last exercise, import tabular data to create a new table, and sort the table.

TERMS

Delimited format Format for saving application data that separates columns of data with characters such as commas, tabs, or colons.

NOTES

Modify Table Borders and Backgrounds

- New tables usually display default gray borders and no background (the page background displays in the table cells). To improve the look of a table, you can modify the weight and color of the table borders and add a color or background image to the table or cells.

Set Border Colors

- Note that a Dreamweaver table displays a border around each cell as well as a border around the table to give a three-dimensional look. You have two options for applying color to these borders:
  - You can use a single color for all borders in the table.
  - You can set one color for the outside table border and another color for individual cells in the table. (Or give each cell its own border color, if desired.)

  ✔ *Cell border colors may not appear the same way in all browsers. See the information on targeting browsers in Lesson 7.*

- To set table border colors, first select the entire table and then click ⬚ Brdr color to open the color palette and pick the color.

  ✔ *You can also type the hexadecimal value for any color in the provided text box or select a color already used in the site from the Colors category in the Assets panel by first clicking on the Brdr color box and then clicking on the desired color in the Assets panel with the eyedropper tool.*

- To set cell border colors, click in the cell to which you want to apply the color. Click ⬚ Brdr to display the color palette.

- You may need to experiment with border colors to find a combination that provides visual appeal without overwhelming the table text.

  ✔ *Empty cells may not display all border lines when viewed in a browser. To prevent this, insert an invisible object such as a nonbreaking space from the Characters list or by pressing Ctrl + Shift + Spacebar.*

Add Background Color to Cells

- Color cell backgrounds in a Web page can draw the eye to information you want emphasized. You can add a color background to one cell, a row, a column—or even the entire table.

■ Select the table element you want to add color to and then click ▭◞ Bg color (the Bg color option is available when the entire table is selected) or ▭◞ Bg (the Bg option is available when a cell, column, or row is selected) on the Property inspector. Then choose a color from the color palette using the eyedropper. If you select the color from the Assets panel, the Colors category must already be selected.

■ Applying a background color to an entire table will fill not only the cells but the small spaces between inner and outer borders. You can override the table background color by applying color to individual cells, but the table background color will still show in the border spaces.

■ Take care when choosing background colors for table cells. A dark color may make text difficult to read. If you want to use a dark cell background, change text color to white, light gray, or light yellow to contrast with the background.

Insert Background Image in Cell

■ You can select background images for your table or individual cells to add visual interest in much the same way that you add background images that tile for entire Web pages.

■ Select the table elements you want to format with the background image. In the Bg box on the Property inspector, type the path to the image, or use the ◉ Point to File icon or 🗀 Browse for File button (or Background URL of cell button) to locate the image.

■ You can insert any Web graphic into a table cell or cells, from texture GIFs to JPEG photographs, which, if smaller than the cell, tile inside the table cells just as page backgrounds do. Make sure, however, that the image you choose does not overwhelm any text in the table.

Import Table Data

■ You may think that most tables are created from scratch on a Web page. However, with collaborative projects, you can also use existing data from a word processing program or spreadsheet to create a table. Importing can eliminate data entry errors or the tedium of reentering long columns of numbers.

■ Data to import must be saved in a **delimited format**. That is, columns must be separated by delimiters such as commas, tabs, semicolons, or colons.

✔ *Dreamweaver can use spaces as delimiters, but you may need to do a lot of cleanup on the table if you are importing text with spaces between words.*

■ Most spreadsheet and word processing applications allow you to save a file in a delimited form. Save a word processing document using the TXT format or a spreadsheet using the CSV format.

■ These formats save only the data, so formatting such as fonts and font styles will not be imported. This formatting can be applied easily in Dreamweaver.

■ Use the File>Import>Tabular Data command or the Insert>Table Objects>Import Tabular Data command to import the data into a new table. Either option displays the Import Tabular Data dialog box (see the following illustration).

Import Tabular Data dialog box

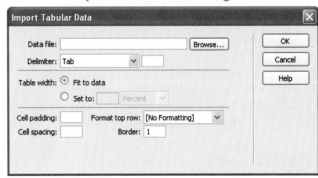

■ Use the [Browse...] button to locate the file to import. If necessary, choose from the Delimiter list the delimiter format used in the file you want to import.

✔ *Dreamweaver will recognize some common file types such as CSV and set the delimiter automatically.*

■ As when creating a table from scratch, you can choose formats such as size, cell padding, cell spacing, and border width.

■ Note in the illustration of the Import Tabular Data dialog box that Dreamweaver will also fit the table cells to the imported data and allow you to choose a font style for the top row.

Sort Table Data

■ You can sort table data by row or column to further organize your data. Data presented in alphabetical or numerical order can be easier for site visitors to read and understand.

■ To sort data in a table, click in the table and use the Commands>Sort Table command to open the Sort Table dialog box (see the following illustration).

Sort Table dialog box

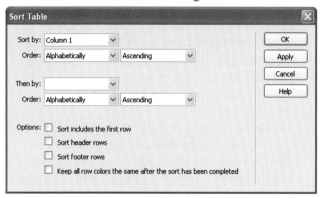

- The *Sort header rows* and *Sort footer rows* options apply to special tags that contain one or more rows used to repeat the headers or footers of tables that will print on more than one page. They are not covered in this book, but typically you would not want to sort them.

- Select *Keep all row colors the same after the sort has been completed* if you want to keep row attributes intact after a sort.

- You cannot sort data in a table that has spanned columns or rows. If you know you want to sort data and also want to create spanned columns or rows, sort the data first.

- Select a column to sort by (or select more than one column) and choose to sort Alphabetically or Numerically. You also can set the direction of the sort as Ascending (A to Z, 1 to 10) or Descending (Z to A, 10 to 1).

- If you do not want to sort the first row of the table along with the remaining rows, make sure the *Sort includes the first row* checkbox is *not* selected.

Insert Table-Related Tags

- Dreamweaver provides tools for editing—and even creating—tables in Code and Code and Design views. The Insert>Table Objects command displays a submenu of tags for creating rows (<tr>), headings (<th>), data (<td>), and captions (<caption>).

- To use these commands, you must switch to a code view.

PROCEDURES

Set Border Colors

To set border colors for entire table:
1. Select entire table.
2. Set same-color borders in the Property inspector:
   a. Click **Brdr color** .
   b. Select color with eyedropper.

To set border color for cell(s):
1. Click in cell.
2. Click **Brdr** .
3. Select color from palette with eyedropper.

   ✔ *When selecting a color from the Assets panel, the Color category pane must be in view.*

Add Background Color to Cells

1. Click in cell to add background color to, or select table or group of cells.

2. Click **Bg color** or **Bg** and select color for background.

   OR

- Type hexadecimal value for color in box to right of color box.

Insert Background Image in Cell

1. Click in cell to add background image to, or select table or group of cells.

2. Type relative or absolute address for background image in **Bg** or **Bg Image** box.

   OR

   a. Click **Background URL of cell** button on Property inspector and navigate to image.
   b. Click image and click OK .

Import Table Data

1. Position insertion point at location for imported table.
2. Click **File** . . . . Alt+F
3. Point to **Import** I
4. Click **Tabular Data** . . . . . . T

   OR

1. Click **Insert** . . . . Alt+I
2. Point to **Table Objects** . . . A
3. Click **Import Tabular Data** T

In the Import Tabular Data dialog box:

1. Type path to data file or click Browse... and navigate to data file.
2. Specify delimiter, if necessary.
3. Set table width, cell padding, cell spacing, border width, and format for top row, if desired.
4. Click OK .

   ✔ *Data file must be saved as delimited text, with columns separated by a delimiter such as commas, tabs, semicolons, or colons.*

Sort Table Data

1. Click in table to sort.
2. Click **C**ommands . . . . Alt+C
3. Click **S**ort Table . . . . S
4. Choose column(s) to sort by.
5. Specify alphabetical or numerical sort.
6. Choose Ascending or Descending sort.
7. Select options to include first row in sort and keep attributes after sort.
8. Click [OK].

Insert Table-Related Tags

1. Switch to Code or Code and Design view.
2. Click **I**nsert . . . . Alt+I
3. Point to **T**able Objects . . . A
4. Click the desired tag to insert it in the code view pane.

EXERCISE DIRECTIONS

1. Start Dreamweaver and open the cincitorial site.
2. Open specialties.html.
3. Complete the table formatting as follows:
   - Change the table border width to **2**. Set a border color of #003399.
   - Fill the subject heading cells (such as *Word Processing, Spreadsheets*, etc.) with background color #CCFFFF and change the font color to #990033.
   - Fill the application heading cells (such as *Word, Quattro Pro,* and *ColdFusion*) with background color #0066CC and change font color to white (#FFFFFF) in these cells.
   - Select all cells in the first column, excluding the first row, and apply the background image ⊙ blueshade.jpg from the Lesson 4 Data folder. (Save the file in the images folder.)
4. Open praise.html. Scroll to the bottom of the page and click to place the insertion point to the left of the *Back to Top* link.
5. Import the tabular data in ⊙ contacts.txt from the Lesson 4 Data folder. Choose to fit the table to the data and make sure Tab appears as the delimiter.
6. Sort the table data in ascending order according to the first column. Do not include the first row in the sort.
7. Apply border and cell formatting as desired to make the table stand out on the page. You may also want to adjust text formatting and alignment.
8. Insert a new column to the left of the current first column. Type the following text in the first cell of the new column:
   Contact our best clients for more info on our services.
9. Span this text down all rows in the column and boldface the text.
10. Adjust the first column width to 85 pixels, and adjust other column widths to best fit their data, if necessary.
11. Adjust the font color, if necessary.
12. Switch to Code and Design view. Locate the first table tag, <table border="*x*">. (Your border value may vary, depending on the table format you chose.)
13. In the code pane, click to the right of the <table border="*x*"> tag and use the Insert>Table Objects menu to insert a caption tag. Insert the caption **Our Clients** between the opening and closing caption tags.

    ✔ *If you have trouble inserting the caption because of a message about locked code or a template, detach the copyright notice from the library and try again.*

14. Format the caption in bold. Your table should look similar to Illustration A.
15. Save and close any open pages and exit Dreamweaver.

Lennie Makarios
Project Coordinator
Peters Press

Our Clients

Contact our best clients for more info on our services.	Client	Contact	E-mail
	Lion Press	Maggie Jenkins	Maggie_Jenkins@lionpress.com
	Peters Press	Lennie Makarios	lmakarios@peterspress.com
	Quentin-Stevens	Tyler Stanislowski	tylerstan@qspub.com
	Training Solutions	Jay Fries	jfries@trainingsolutions.com

Back to Top

Copyright © CinciTorial Co. All rights reserved. Last updated: 03/17/2007

ON YOUR OWN

1. Start Dreamweaver and open the **gardencenter** site.
2. Open **favorites.html** and detach this page from the template.
3. Import the tabular data in ⊙ **favorites.txt** from the Lesson 4 Data folder to create a table below the paragraph text.
4. Sort the data by plant type and then by common name (specify both sort criteria at the same time in the Sort Table dialog box).
5. Modify and format the table as desired. For example, you may want to:
   - Apply a background color to the entire table and/or column heading cells.
   - Apply a specific cell color to all cells for a particular plant type.
   - Insert blank rows to separate parts of the table by plant type.
   - Adjust cell padding and cell spacing.
   - Eliminate or modify the table borders.

6. Botanical names are usually set in italics. Apply italics to all botanical names in the second column except the name surrounded by single quotes ('Hicksii').
7. Preview your finished table in the browser, and then make any adjustments you think necessary.
8. If desired, apply similar formats to the table on **contact.html**.
9. Close the page and exit Dreamweaver.

Skills Covered

- **Use a Table for Page Layout**
- **Work in Layout Mode**
- **Format Layout Cells**

Software Skills   Using a table for page layout allows you to create a sophisticated design that will display in all browsers. Use Dreamweaver's layout tools to draw the table and its cells. Working in Layout view makes it easier to add content to a layout table.

Application Skills   In this exercise, you will create a new page for the CinciTorial Web site and organize the page content using a layout table.

TERMS

Autostretch Dreamweaver feature that allows you to specify that a table column will adjust automatically to full browser window width.

Expanded Tables mode Dreamweaver view that gives you an enlarged view of table contents.

Layout mode Dreamweaver view that allows you to build layout tables.

NOTES

Use a Table for Page Layout

- Tables are useful not only for organizing data on a Web page but also for laying out a page's content. An advantage to using a table for page layout is that all browsers can display tables. Laying out a page with a table allows you to create a complex page design without the use of sophisticated layout features such as frames or AP (absolutely positioned) elements.

  ✔ *You will learn how to create frame pages and AP elements in the next lesson.*

- Creating a table for page layout is the same process as creating a table to organize data, except that you work on a larger scale to fill the page. For best results, maximize the Document window and collapse unnecessary panels before you begin creating the page layout.

- A layout table frequently fills the entire width of the page. You can then insert rows or columns and merge as necessary to create areas to insert text and images.

- You can apply color and design to the page creatively by adding a background color or image to specific table cells. When laying out an entire page, you will probably not want to use table borders, but applying a cell border to an individual cell can draw attention to its content.

Work in Layout Mode

- To create a layout table, you need access to Dreamweaver's layout tools, which display on the Layout tab of the Insert bar.

- The Layout tab offers two buttons that allow you to choose a layout mode.

  - Standard mode gives you access to tools for creating and restructuring a standard table, inserting <div> tags, drawing an AP div, inserting Spry objects, or inserting a frame.

  ✔ *You will work with Spry interactive elements in Lesson 6.*

- **Expanded Tables mode** enlarges a table structure so that you can more easily work with the contents of the table cells. This mode does not represent the way a browser will display the table, so be sure to return to Standard mode before completing your work on a table to make sure all content displays as you want it to.

- To create a layout table, you must be in Layout mode. Use the View>Table Mode>Layout Mode command to change to Layout mode. In this mode, you have access to the ▦ Draw Layout Table and ▦ Draw Layout Cell tools that you can use to draw the layout table structure.

- The first time you switch to Layout mode, Dreamweaver displays the dialog box shown in the following illustration to give you further information about Layout mode.

Dreamweaver supplies information about Layout mode

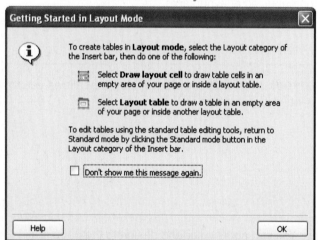

- ✔ If you don't want to see this message each time you switch to Layout mode after you start Dreamweaver, select the Don't show me this message again *checkbox.*

- Creating a layout on a page using a layout table and layout cells (see illustration below) gives you a great deal of flexibility in inserting and positioning cells precisely where you need them within the table.

- After you create a layout table and layout cells, you can move or resize cells by dragging. You can specify exact dimensions for cells or let them "stretch" to conform to the browser window's size.

Draw a Layout Table

- Begin a new page layout by drawing a layout table. You can create a table the full size of your page, or you can create several different layout tables on a page. You can also create one layout table within another.

  - ✔ You can draw a layout cell without first drawing a layout table; Dreamweaver will automatically create the layout table to surround the layout cell.

- Draw a layout table by clicking the ▦ Draw Layout Table button from the Layout tab of the Insert bar and then use the crosshair pointer to drag the outline of the table on the page. This procedure is the same as drawing an object in a program such as Illustrator. The area in which you want to draw the layout table must be empty.

Layout mode showing layout table and a layout cells

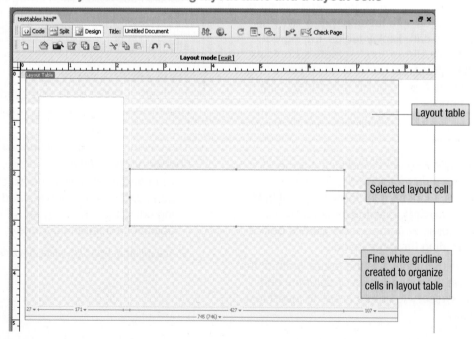

- To help you size layout objects, Dreamweaver displays dimensions near the right side of the status bar as you draw.

- The new layout table displays a green border with sizing handles and a green tab containing the label *Layout Table*. The table's width in pixels is shown in the table header area at the top or bottom of the table. The table area itself is light gray.

- You can modify the table width by dragging a sizing handle or you can use the Width and Height boxes in the Property inspector to set exact measurements. You can also adjust cell spacing and cell padding values just as you do in a standard table.

- If a layout table appears on a page by itself, you do not have to take any special step to select it. Because the table is the only object on the page, it is selected by default.

- Once you insert cells in the table, the table itself is deselected. If you have inserted the table on a page with other content (or within another layout table), you can deselect the table by clicking on other page content.

- To select the table again, click on its green outline or its green tab.

Draw Layout Cells

- Use the same general method to draw layout cells. Click the ▥ Draw Layout Cell button from the Layout tab of the Insert bar and use the crosshair pointer to draw the cell anywhere on the page or within the layout table.

- Dreamweaver automatically creates a grid of rows and columns in the remaining portion of the layout table relative to the inserted cell (see the previous illustration). You can use this grid to guide you in inserting other cells.

- The changes you can make to a layout cell depend on whether the cell is *active* or *selected*.

- To make a cell *active*, click in it. An active cell displays a light blue border and a white background. When a cell is active, you can add content to it by typing text at the insertion point or by pasting text. Insert graphics in the cell just as you would in a standard table.

- To *select* a layout cell, move the pointer on the border (the border turns red when the pointer is on it) and then click the border. When selected, the cell border displays sizing handles on the light blue border.

- When a cell is selected, you can change its background color and the horizontal and vertical alignment of its content.

- Modify a selected cell's width by dragging its border or by using the Property inspector's Width and Height boxes. You can also specify the autostretch option for a selected cell, as discussed next.

Use Autostretch

- Tables and columns within tables can be sized to fixed widths or you can use the **autostretch** feature. Autostretch allows a table column (or the entire table) to resize automatically to fill the browser window.

- Typically, you will use both fixed-width columns and an autostretch column in a table. Use fixed widths for columns that contain cells you want to remain the same size, such as those containing images, a menu, or links. Use the autostretch column for text that can wrap flexibly.

  ✔ *Only one column in a table can be set to autostretch.*

- Fixed-width columns display the width in pixels in the cell's column header in the table border. Autostretch columns display a -⌄⌄⌄- zigzag line in the column header to indicate that the size can change.

- To make a column autostretch, select a cell in the column and select the Autostretch option in the Property inspector. Or, choose Make Column Autostretch from the column header menu.

- If you have not used the autostretch feature previously in the current site, Dreamweaver asks if you want to create a spacer GIF file to insert in the fixed-width columns (see the following illustration). The spacer image prevents fixed-width columns from resizing, allowing the autostretch column to adjust freely in the browser window.

Dreamweaver suggests a spacer file

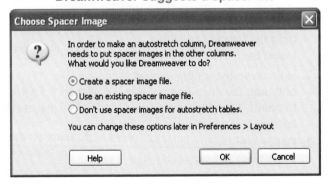

- The default option is to create the spacer image file. If you select this option, Dreamweaver will create the file for you and allow you to save it in your Web site. You can save the spacer image with your other images.

- You need to create a spacer file only once in a Web site. After you have created the file, Dreamweaver will not prompt you to create one in any other layout table in the site.

Format Layout Cells

- You can apply some formats to layout cells in Layout view using the Property inspector. You can, for example, adjust cell width and height, apply a background color, and set both horizontal and vertical alignment. You can also, if desired, prevent text from wrapping in the cell, a good choice if you have a list of links in a cell that you want to display on one line.

- You can apply standard table formats to layout cells by clicking the Standard button from the Layout tab of the Insert bar to display the layout table as a standard Dreamweaver table.

- You then have access to the same formatting options as for a standard table, such as cell borders and backgrounds, fonts and styles, and so on.

E-Commerce Connection

Marketing and the Internet

Target marketing is the process of choosing customers to serve. The Internet can make it easy for an e-business to define customer groups and position products or services for target markets.

Explore Target Marketing

Use the Internet to locate information on important aspects of target marketing. Write a report in which you analyze how an e-business could use the Internet to define target markets for its goods.

PROCEDURES

Switch to Layout Mode (Alt + F6)

1. Click **View** . . . . (Alt)+(V)
2. Point to **Table Mode** . . . . . (T)
3. Click **Layout Mode** . . . . . . (L)

   ✔ *When finished working in Layout mode, click the **Standard** button.*

Draw Layout Table

1. Click **Layout Table** button ▣ from the Layout tab of the Insert bar.
2. Hold down the mouse button and drag the crosshair pointer to create the table's outside border.
3. Release the mouse button when table is the desired size.

Draw Layout Cell

1. Click **Draw Layout Cell** button ▤ from the Layout category of the Insert bar.
2. Hold down the mouse button and drag the crosshair pointer to create a cell of the desired size.
3. Release the mouse button.

   ✔ *If you have not already created a layout table when you draw a layout cell, Dreamweaver will automatically create the table for you.*

Modify Layout Table or Cell Dimensions

1. Click on the outside border of the table or cell to select it.
2. Drag a border to resize.

   OR

   Use the Width and Height boxes in the Property inspector to set exact dimensions.

Use Autostretch

1. Select the cell to autostretch.
2. Click the **Autostretch** option on Property inspector.

   OR

   Click the down arrow in column header in table border for column to autostretch and select **Make Column Autostretch**.
3. Choose **Create a spacer image file** in the Choose Spacer Image dialog box.
4. Click [OK].
5. Save spacer image in site's images folder.

EXERCISE DIRECTIONS

1. Start Dreamweaver and open the cincitorial site.

2. Open a new, blank HTML page. Save the page as mission.html with the page title Our Mission.

3. Create the page layout table shown in Illustration A as follows:

   ▪ Switch to Layout mode. Draw a layout table about 750 pixels wide and 500 pixels high.

   ▪ Draw a layout cell in the upper-left corner of the layout table that is 200 pixels wide and 300 pixels high. (You can see the measurement as you draw at the right side of the status bar.)

   ▪ Draw the remaining cells as shown in Illustration A. The first cell in the second column should be about 75 pixels high, Cell 4 should be about 85 pixels high, and Cell 5 should be about 100 pixels high.

   ▪ Make the right column an autostretch column.

   ▪ Select the table and set cell spacing at 7.

4. Add content to the layout table as follows:

   ▪ In Cell 1 (see Illustration A), insert the ◉ Laura_Brater-Reidel.jpg image from the Lesson 4 Data folder. Save the image in your images folder and add the alternate text Photo of Laura Brater-Reidel.

   ✔ *Click in another cell to readjust the cell size around the photo if necessary.*

   ▪ In Cell 2, insert the **Home link** library item and center it horizontally in the table cell.

   ▪ In Cell 3, insert the text shown in Illustration B. Use the Heading 2 format for the centered heading.

   ▪ In Cell 4, insert the following text and center it:
   We dedicate this site to Laura Brater-Reidel, the smartest one in the family, and to Bertha Richards, who taught her family never to settle for second best.

   ▪ In Cell 5, type the text Quality products on time at a fair price. Center the text horizontally and apply the Middle vertical alignment and the Heading 4 style. (Select the cell to see the vertical alignment option.)

   ▪ Fill Cell 5 with the background color #336699 and change the text color to white.

5. Drag Cell 5 upward about a half an inch. If two new cells appear below the cell you moved, remove them in Standard view.

6. Open index.html and position the insertion point after the *We build computer books* heading at the top of the page. Press Enter and type Read Our Mission Statement. Link this text to mission.html.

7. Save changes. Preview the page in the browser and check the link to the Our Mission page.

8. Close the browser.

9. Close any open pages and exit Dreamweaver.

Layout Table

Cell 1

Cell 2

Cell 3

Cell 4

Cell 5

200 ▾   550 ▾

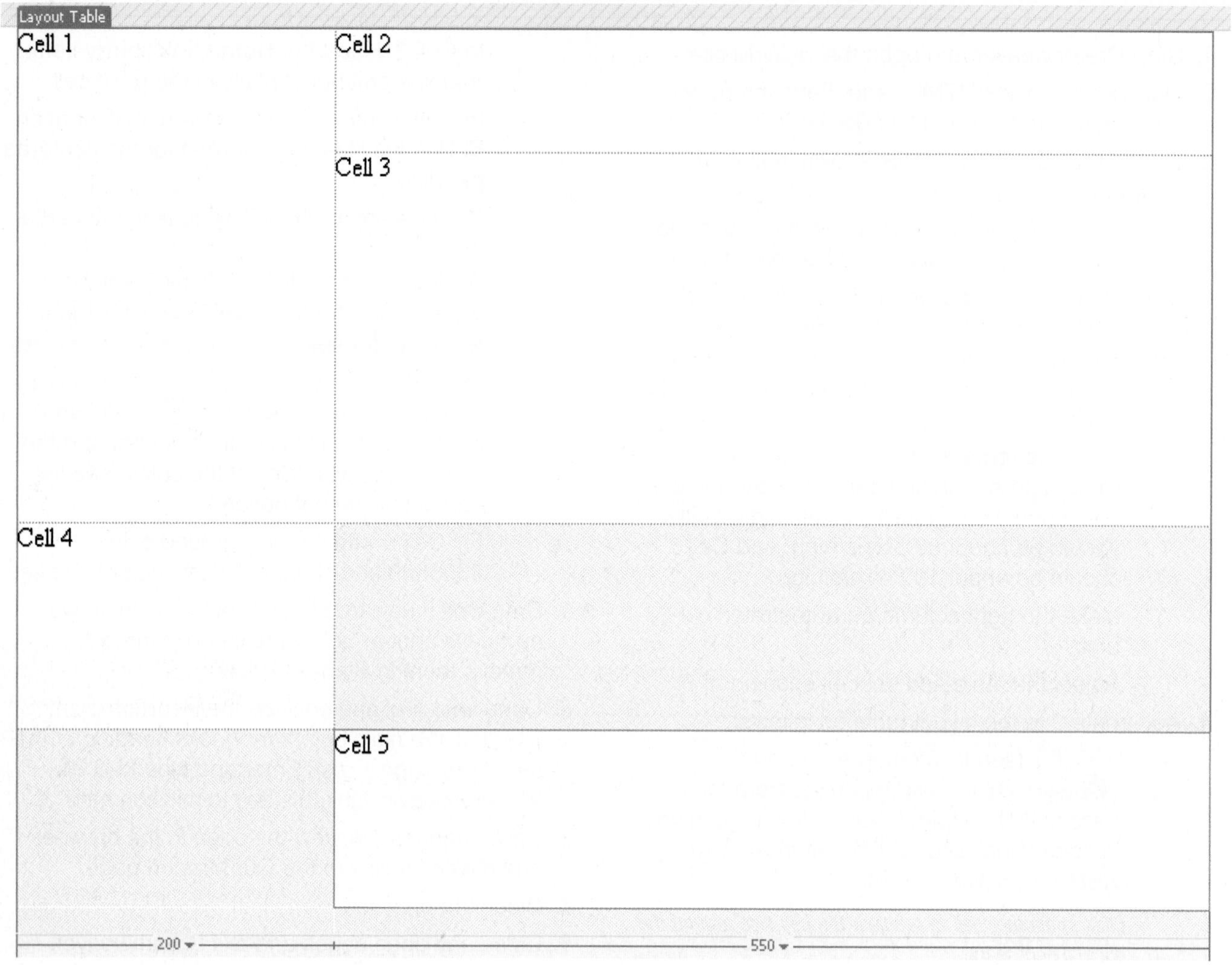

Illustration B

Our Mission Statement

Every job is an important job.

At CinciTorial, we believe every job is an important job. No matter how big. No matter how urgent.
When you work with CinciTorial staff, you can rest assured we'll do our best for you. We learn from
every job and every client, and you benefit from that learning process.

ON YOUR OWN

✔ *If you completed Curriculum Integration Exercise 24, you worked with pages organized using layout tables. In this exercise, try your hand at copying the layout from another Starter page in this group.*

1. Start Dreamweaver and create a folder to hold the files you work with in this exercise.

2. In the Start window, display the Starter Page (Theme) files and select the one named Lodging – Text Page. Save the file in your solutions folder and copy all required files to that location.

3. Switch to Layout mode and view the various layout tables and cells that were used to create this text page.

4. Open a new, blank HTML page and save it in your solutions folder as mytext.html. Using information about the Starter page's layout tables and cells you gather from the Property inspector, recreate the page:

   ▪ Select layout tables and cells to determine their size and then duplicate those sizes and approximate positions in your page.

   ▪ You can attempt to duplicate colors, or use your own. Note that some elements in the Starter page are formatted using CSS codes, but you can determine attributes by viewing the HTML code for Starter page elements.

   ▪ If you do not know how to insert some elements, such as the fine white horizontal lines between layout cells at the top of the page, you can copy the code from the Starter page and insert it in the code of your page.

5. You may find it helpful to create elements in this order:

   ▪ First apply a page background color for the color that surrounds the main layout table and forms the background of the Web site name layout cell.

   ▪ Create the main layout table that organizes the entire page. It is about 550 pixels high and is an autostretch column.

   ▪ Then create the layout cell that holds the Web site name and the layout cell that contains the *HOME* link.

   ▪ Create a layout table in the center of the page that is 440 by 450. Then insert the layout cell that contains the page name and the layout cell that contains the page text.

6. You can insert background colors for the layout cells in layout mode, but you should switch to Standard mode to apply colors to the spacer cells around the layout cells.

7. Insert text placeholders to indicate what kind of content goes in each layout cell, such as the Web site name, the Home link, the page title, and the page text.

8. Save your page and view it in the browser. Make any changes necessary, and then save and close the page.

9. Use the Files panel to access your solution files and delete the Starter page you used as a guide.

10. Exit Dreamweaver.

   ✔ *You probably learned while doing this exercise that even a relatively simple layout design can take quite a bit of tweaking to get right!*

Exercise | 29

Skills Covered

Software Skills   Creating a form in Dreamweaver is a simple process that uses many of the skills you already have, such as inserting and formatting text. Dreamweaver offers many types of form fields for collecting various kinds of information. To best serve all visitors to your site, you can create an accessible form that meets current XHTML coding standards.

Application Skills   In this exercise, you will add an accessible form to the CinciTorial site that includes a number of common form field types.

TERMS

Form Interactive area on a Web page that allows a visitor to supply information or answer questions.

Form field Object inserted in a form that gathers a specific type of data, such as a text field or checkbox.

Initial value In a form field, the text or value that will appear in the form field by default when the form page is opened in a browser.

Jump menu A menu that supplies a list of values which, when clicked in the browser, takes a visitor to a specific Web page.

Label In a form, text that identifies the function of a form field.

Value In a form field, the actual result that will be returned to a server after a visitor types text or makes a choice.

NOTES

About Forms

■ You can use a **form** to collect information from visitors to your Web site. You can create forms for surveys, contact information, feedback, searching, ordering products, or even an online job application.

■ Forms can vary greatly in complexity, but all forms consist of a form area in which you insert form fields such as text boxes, radio buttons, and submit buttons. The skills you learn in this exercise will enable you to create both simple and complex forms in Dreamweaver.

■ You can build a form on an HTML page or on a specific server-type page such as ASP or PHP. The type of page you use for a form depends on the server technology you will use to process the form.

■ In many cases, you will not have a choice in what technology to use—it will be determined by the server on which you intend to put your site files. Before you build a form for a real-world site, make sure you know how the form data will be processed by your server.

■ *Form data* is the information gathered from a form that a visitor fills out on a Web page. You have a number of options for viewing and storing form data. You can specify that it be sent to you via e-mail, or you can send the data to a database for future manipulation. You can also set up a page in your site to display form data in HTML format.

✔ *You will learn more about form handling and databases in the next exercise.*

Create a Form

- Create a form using commands on the Insert menu or using buttons from the Forms tab of the Insert bar.

- It is a good idea to insert a descriptive paragraph or caption above the form to make the purpose of the form clear. You can also use this paragraph to give specific directions for filling out the form if necessary, such as which entries are required.

- With the insertion point where you want the form to begin, use the Insert>Form>Form command, or click the ☐ Form button from the Forms tab of the Insert bar.

- A red dashed outline appears on all sides of the insertion point and as wide as the page. This outline marks the borders of the form. The Property inspector allows you to specify information about the form (see the illustration below).

- You should name the form using the Form name text box. If you know the path to the script or application file that will be used to process the form data, enter it in the Action box.

- The Method list choices are used to define the way the form data will be handled. If you are not sure what method will be used by your server, leave the setting as POST (the default setting for a new form).

- For certain kinds of forms, such as the kind that send personal data and credit card information, there are also advanced properties to select. The Enctype drop-down list lets you specify the type of data encoding that is submitted to the server for processing. The Target drop-down list allows you to choose a window in which to display data returned by a form handler application.

- To create a tidy-looking form, you can insert a table directly in the form area. Using a table allows you to align labels and form fields and maintain that alignment on any browser.

- Once your form area is set up, you are ready to enter form objects: **labels** and **form fields**. Labels are text words or phrases that tell a visitor what kind of information to enter. Form fields are the boxes and buttons visitors type in or click to supply information.

- Dreamweaver supplies a number of different form fields you can add to a form, but you will use the following five field types most often:

  - *Text fields* allow the visitor to type text in a box. A text field can consist of a single line or multiple lines.

  - *Radio buttons* allow the visitor to choose only one option from a group of options.

  - *Checkboxes* enable a visitor to select an option or select more than one option from a group of options.

  - *List/menu fields* give visitors a list or menu of options to choose among.

  - *Buttons* and *button groups* perform a specific action when a visitor clicks them.

Handle Accessibility Issues

- By default, Dreamweaver prompts you to make your forms accessible to those using screen readers, just as you were prompted to supply alternate text when inserting images so they could be described by a screen reader.

  ✓ *Dreamweaver is set to prompt for accessibility information for forms, frames, images, and media objects. You can deselect any of these options in the Preferences dialog box if you prefer not to supply accessibility information for them. See Appendix A for more information on setting preferences.*

- To make a form accessible, Dreamweaver uses the <label> tag to supply information about each form field that can then be read in a text-only browser or by a screen reader. The <label> tag allows you to associate the form's label with its other coding (such as name and value) so that a visitor using a screen reader can easily determine how a form is structured.

- To create an accessible form, first make sure that Form objects is selected in the Accessibility category of the Preferences dialog box. Then insert a form field in a form, as described in the following sections for each type of field. Dreamweaver displays the Input Tag Accessibility Attributes dialog box, shown in the following illustration.

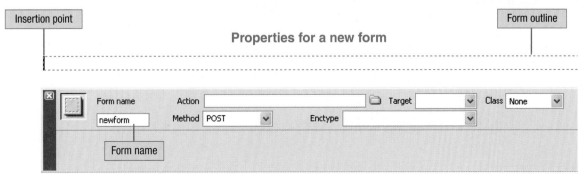

Insertion point

Form outline

Properties for a new form

Form name

Input Tag Accessibility Attributes dialog box

Type the label to be associated with the form field in the Label box. You can use the Position options to set the label before the form field (that is, to the left of the field) or after the field (to the right of the field).

Choose a style for how the <label> tag is associated with form elements.

- The *Wrap with label tag* option encloses the form field name within the <label> tags, as shown in the first illustration at the bottom of the page. Note how the label (*First Name*) and the field name ("first_name") display between the <label> and </label> tags.

- The *Attach label tag using 'for' attribute* option attaches the label tag to the form field using the 'for' attribute, as shown in the second illustration at the bottom of the page. Note that the <label> tag uses the 'for' attribute to identify the specific tag ("payment") and encloses the label text (*Credit Card*). When this accessibility option is used, a visitor can click either the radio button or

its label to select the form element. For example, in the form shown in the code at the bottom of the page, a visitor could click either the Credit Card button or the Credit Card label to choose the payment option.

✔ *The Attach label tag using 'for' attribute is the preferred accessibility option, because it makes it easier for visitors to select an option. However, browsers vary in their support for this functionality, so be sure to test in your target browsers before using this option.*

- You can also choose the *No label tag* option if you don't want to use the <label> tag for a particular field or in a particular form.

After you complete the Insert Tag Accessibility Attributes dialog box, the new form field appears in the form. You must still supply specific information for the field, such as its name, size, and value. The following sections detail the information you must supply for the most common form field types.

Insert Single-Line Text Fields

Single-line text fields are used to hold a modest amount of text data that can appear on one line, such as names, e-mail addresses, and street addresses.

Insert a single-line text field using the Insert>Form>Text Field command. Or, click or drag the ⬚ Text Field button from the Forms tab of the Insert bar. Supply accessibility information if you are creating an accessible form.

Dreamweaver inserts the default text field. Click on the field to select it so you can modify its properties. Use the Property inspector to display and modify properties for the field, as shown in the illustration at the top of the next page.

You should supply a name for every field in a form. The script or application used to handle the form data uses these field names—as well as the name you give to your form—to store data correctly. The field name should be only one or two words. If you

Code showing the Wrap with label tag style

```
<form id="newform" name="newform" method="post" action="">
  <label>First Name
  <input type="text" name="first_name" id="first_name" />
  </label>
</form>
```

Code showing the Attach label tag using 'for' attribute style

```
<form id="form1" name="form1" method="post" action="">
  <input type="radio" name="radio" id="payment" value="payment" />
  <label for="payment">Credit Card</label>
</form>
```

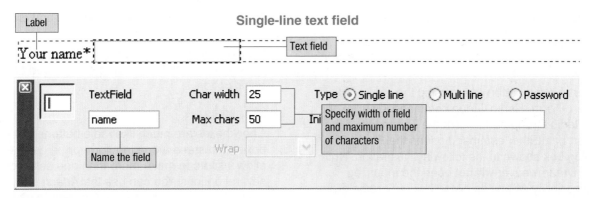

Single-line text field

Label | Text field

Your name*

TextField | name | Char width 25 | Max chars 50 | Type ● Single line ○ Multi line ○ Password | Ini... Specify width of field and maximum number of characters | Wrap

Name the field

use two words, join them with an underscore, such as street_address.

- You can specify how many characters wide the field should be, as well as how many characters it can hold.

- If your data is being stored in a database, you will need to make sure that your fields are not incompatible with the size and type of data used by the database.

- If you want the field to show an **initial value** (text that displays each time the form is opened, such as *Type full name here*), insert this text in the Init val box in the Property inspector.

- The Password option is selected for text boxes in which passwords are typed so that onlookers cannot see the form user's password, which appears as a series of black dots.

Insert Radio Buttons

- Radio buttons are small circles that visitors click to select a single option from a group of options. Radio buttons allow simple selections to supply data. If you have ever participated in an online poll, you have used this kind of form object.

- Insert a radio button using the Insert>Form>Radio Button command. Or use the ⦿ Radio Button button from the Forms tab of the Insert bar. If you are creating an accessible form, you will probably want to use the *Attach label tag using 'for' attribute* style option, so that visitors can select the option using the radio button or its label.

- Dreamweaver inserts the radio button and the Property inspector shows properties for the radio button field (see the illustration below).

- Radio buttons are generally inserted in groups. (Creating grouped buttons is discussed in the next topic.)

- If you insert more than one radio button to gather responses to a particular area of a form, all radio buttons in the group must have the same name. Only the **value** changes for each button. The value entered in the Checked value box is the data that will actually be shown in the form results.

- For example, if you create a group of three radio buttons for a credit card field, each button will be named card_type, but one button will have the value *MasterCard*, another will have the value *Visa*, and the third may have a value such as *Discover*.

- If a visitor selects the *Visa* radio button, the form results will show an entry of *Visa* for the card_type field.

  ✔ *Some servers will not correctly process data in which more than one field element has the same name, as described above for radio buttons. In this case, you may need to redesign a form so that all fields have a unique name.*

- If you want one of the radio buttons to be selected each time the form opens, select the Checked option for Initial state. Visitors will still be able to change their selection even if one radio button is selected by default.

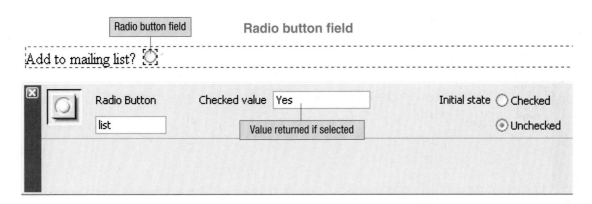

Radio button field

Radio button field

Add to mailing list?

Radio Button | list | Checked value Yes | Value returned if selected | Initial state ○ Checked ● Unchecked

Insert Radio Groups

- A radio group allows you to create two or more radio buttons quickly either on separate lines or in a table.

- Insert a radio button group using the Insert>Form>Radio Group command. Or, click the ▤ Radio Group button from the Forms tab of the Insert bar. Either command opens the Radio Group dialog box shown in the following illustration. Note that Dreamweaver will not open the Input Tag Accessibility Attributes dialog box for a radio group; the *Wrap with label tag* option is used automatically for this type of form field.

Radio Group dialog box

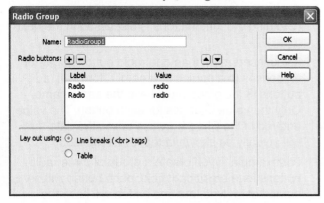

- In the Radio Group dialog box, you can enter a name for the radio group. In the Radio buttons list, two buttons are created by default, with default labels and values. Labels display to the right of each button in the form. The value is the data that will be sent to the server when the form data is recorded.

- To customize the button labels and values, simply click on the label name or value and enter your own information. Values should be similar to item labels, with no spaces or capital letters.

- Use the ➕ button to enter additional labels and values (or simply press Tab to create a new label). Click the ▲ and ▼ buttons to change the radio group order.

- To remove a list item, select the item and click the ➖ button.

- You can lay out a radio group either in separate lines or in a table by selecting the desired *Lay out using* option.

Insert Checkboxes

- Checkboxes are much like radio buttons, but checkboxes can stand alone in a form or be grouped to allow visitors to make more than one selection from several options. You can use the *Attach label tag using 'for' attribute* accessibility option to make it possible for a visitor to click either the checkbox or its label to select the field.

- Insert a checkbox using the Insert>Form>Checkbox command. Or, use the ☐ Checkbox button from the Forms tab of the Insert bar.

- Dreamweaver inserts the checkbox and the Property inspector displays properties for the field (see the illustration below).

- Name the checkbox as you would for any other form field if it is standing alone in the form. If you are offering visitors a number of selections for the same form item, give each checkbox the same name, as when creating radio buttons, to create a group of checkboxes.

- For grouped checkboxes, make sure each checkbox has a unique value. This value is usually similar to the label used for the checkbox. Because a visitor can select more than one checkbox, the form results can show multiple values for the checkbox field name.

- As for radio buttons, you specify whether checkboxes are checked by default when the form opens.

  ✔ *Checkboxes are usually not checked by default, to save visitors from unintentionally choosing an option.*

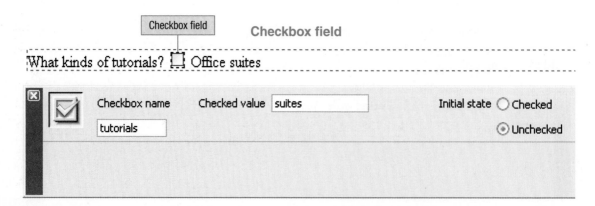

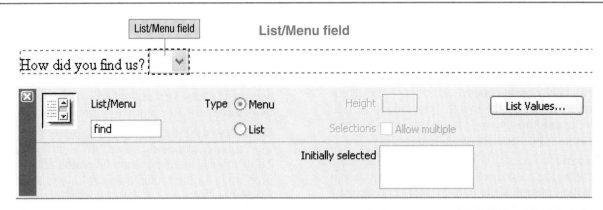

List/Menu field

Insert Lists and Menus

- Dreamweaver's List/Menu field allows you to place several options on a scrollable list or drop-down menu. Visitors click the list or menu to display choices and then select one (or more, if you allow multiple selections).

- Lists and menus are generally used for three or more options. For fewer options, radio buttons or checkboxes are preferred.

- Using a list or menu can save room in a form because the options are stored in one field rather than in multiple radio buttons or checkboxes.

- Insert a list or menu using the Insert>Form>List/Menu command. Or, use the List/Menu button from the Forms tab of the Insert bar.

- Dreamweaver inserts the List/Menu field and the Property inspector displays properties for the field (see the illustration above).

- The List/Menu field is only a few characters wide when first inserted. Its final size is determined by the choices you add to the list or menu.

- Name the field as you would for other form fields. Then you must choose whether to create a menu or a list:

  - A menu displays a single choice by default and drops down when clicked to display a menu of choices. Visitors can select only one choice.

  - A list can display more than one choice by default, and visitors can scroll the list to see additional choices. Visitors may be allowed to select more than one choice.

- If you choose to create a list, you can specify the height of the list (that is, how many items will display by default) and select the Allow multiple checkbox to let visitors choose more than one option from the list.

- For both menus and lists, you must create the choices visitors will see on the menu or list. Click the List Values... button to open the List Values dialog box (see the following illustration).

Add choices in the List Values dialog box

- Type the item labels (the actual list items visitors will see in the form) and a value for each label. As in other form objects, the value is the data that will be sent to the server when the form data is recorded.

- Use the + button to enter additional labels and values (or simply press Tab to create a new label) and the ▲ and ▼ buttons to change the list order.

- To remove a list item, select the item and click the − button.

- If desired, you can select one of the choices to appear in the list or menu box (if Height is set to 1). Expand the Property inspector, if necessary, and click the desired label in the Initially selected box (see the following illustration) in the expanded Property inspector.

Select an item for default display

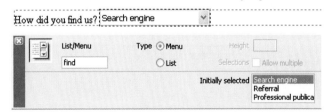

- If you do not select one of the choices to appear initially, Dreamweaver displays the first choice in the list when the form is opened in the browser.

- You can insert another type of list/menu field in a form called a **jump menu**. A jump menu supplies a list of values that, when clicked in the browser, takes a visitor to a specific Web page.

- Insert a jump menu using the Insert>Form>Jump Menu command or use the ⬈ Jump Menu button from the Forms tab of the Insert bar.

- In the Insert Jump Menu dialog box (see the illustration below), you specify text for each URL you want to include on the menu. Then type the URL itself, or use the [Browse...] button to browse to the location of the page you want to open.

- You can also specify where to open the page and a name for the menu, and you can choose to add a go button after the menu that visitors can use to make the jump. If you have included a general instruction such as *Choose an item below* as the first option on the menu, you can select the *Select first item after URL change* to display this informational item again after a visitor has selected one of the other URLs on the list.

Insert Multiple-Line Text Fields

- As you have already learned, text fields are used for single-line entries. Text fields can also be set to allow for multiple-line entries. A multiple-line text field can be used to request more information from site visitors or allow them to answer questions.

- Use a Text field to create a multiple-line text field. In the Property inspector, select the Multi line option. The Property inspector then activates additional properties for the multiple-line field (see the second illustration below).

- You can also shortcut this process somewhat by using the Insert>Form>Textarea command, or by using the ▦ Textarea button from the Forms tab of the Insert bar. These commands insert a multiline text area in the form so that you don't have to select the Multi line option in the Property inspector.

Specify properties for a jump menu field

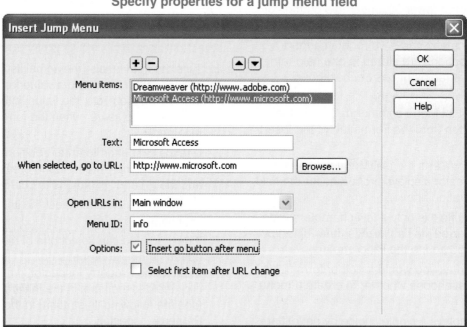

Specify properties for multiple-line text field

■ As for other Text fields, you must specify a name. You can also specify a width in characters and the number of lines visitors can use for their comments.

✔ *Defining the character width and number of lines allows you to limit user responses to a reasonable length.*

■ You can change the way text wraps in the multiple-line text field, but the Default option is suitable for most form uses.

■ The Init val text box allows you to enter initial value text to ask a question or make a request.

Insert Buttons

■ You must give your site visitors a way to send the information they have provided in the form. Use Dreamweaver's Button fields to create Submit and Reset buttons.

■ Insert a button using the Insert>Form> Button command. Or, use the ▭ Button button from the Forms tab of the Insert bar.

■ Dreamweaver inserts a Submit button by default (see the following illustration). You will generally accept the default properties for this button.

■ To insert another button to be used for resetting or clearing the form, use the same procedure. You will then need to change the button's name to reflect its purpose, change its label, and choose the appropriate action (Reset form for a Reset button).

✔ *The text you type in the Label box is the label that will appear on the button in the form.*

■ It is not strictly necessary to include a Reset button in a form. Rather than start completely over, most form users can simply modify the fields they want to correct. It is also possible for a user to accidentally click the Reset button rather than the Submit button, requiring the user to start all over. Use your own judgment as to whether you want to use a Reset button.

About Spry Form Fields

■ The Form tab on the Insert bar shows several additional tools you can use to insert form fields with names such as Spry Validation Text Field and Spry Validation Checkbox.

■ The Spry framework is new in Dreamweaver CS3. Dreamweaver offers a number of Spry *widgets* that provide interesting dynamic effects for Web pages, including form tools.

■ The Spry form tools allow you to insert interactive form elements that change color as a visitor enters the correct type of data.

■ You will work with Spry widgets in Lesson 6.

About Validating a Form

■ Part of the process of creating any form is supplying validation criteria for the form's fields. Validation ensures that a visitor enters data in required fields and inserts the correct type of data in fields where format makes a difference.

■ In Dreamweaver, you can use behaviors to validate fields, or you can insert Spry form fields that have validation built in.

■ You will work with validation options in Lesson 6.

Test a Form

■ After creating a form, you should test it to make sure your values are set up correctly. If your form is linked to a script or application, you can display the form in the browser and fill in the form fields. Your form results will show you if you need to modify your fields or values.

■ Even if you don't have a script or form handler for your form, you should preview it in the browser to check its appearance. By entering sample data in the form, you can determine if your text fields are wide enough or positioned logically in the form.

About Dynamic Data

■ *Dynamic data* is data that is not fixed but changes according to circumstance such as what selections a user makes in a form.

Dreamweaver inserts Submit button

Click here to submit the form Submit

| Button name | Value | Submit | Action ⦿ Submit form ◯ None |
| submit | | | ◯ Reset form |

- Form fields can be linked to database recordsets to display dynamic data in a form field that can help a visitor choose options in the form. For example, a list field can pull data on a list of items from a database, so the designer does not have to enter into the List Values dialog box a long series of entries. When a product line changes, the database can be modified, while the form can remain the same.

- To create dynamic data and recordsets, you must establish a link to a database. You will learn more about how to do this in the next exercise.

PROCEDURES

Create a Form Area

1. Position insertion point where form will begin.
2. Click **Insert**. . . . . ⟨Alt⟩+⟨I⟩
3. Point to **Form** . . . . ⟨F⟩
4. Click **Form** . . . . ⟨↵Enter⟩
   OR
   - Click or drag **Form** button ⌷ from the Forms tab of the Insert bar.

To set properties for form:
   - Type form name in Property inspector
   - Type script or application file name in **Action** box, or click 🗁 and navigate to location of script.
   - Specify method, if necessary.

Create an Accessible Form

1. Click **Edit** . . . . ⟨Alt⟩+⟨E⟩
2. Click **Preferences**. . . ⟨P⟩, ⟨P⟩, ⟨↵Enter⟩
3. Click the **Accessibility** category.
4. Make sure **Form objects** is selected.
5. Click ⟨ OK ⟩.

After selecting a form element to insert:

1. Type a label for the form field.

2. Select a style for the <label> tag:
   - Use Wrap with label tag to enclose all information about the field, including the label, inside the <label> </label> tags.
   - Use Attach label tag using 'for' attribute to make it possible to click either the label or a button or checkbox to select the field.
   - Use No label tag if you do not want a label attached to a field.
3. Select a position for the label **Before form item** or **After form item**.
4. If desired, provide a key combination in the Access box that can be used to access the element.
5. If desired, specify a number in the Tab Index box the order in which the field will become active when the Tab key is pressed to move through the form.
6. Click ⟨ OK ⟩.

Insert a Single-Line Text Field

1. Click **Insert**. . . . . ⟨Alt⟩+⟨I⟩
2. Point to **Form** . . . . ⟨F⟩
3. Click **Text Field** . . . . ⟨T⟩
   OR
   - Click or drag Text Field button ⌶ from the Forms tab of the Insert bar.

To set properties for the text field:
1. Click the Text field to select it.
2. Type name in TextField box if you have not already supplied one.
3. Type value in Char width field for width of field if desired.
4. Type value in Max chars for maximum number of characters allowed if desired.
5. Type value in Init val that will display as the initial value if desired.

Insert Radio Buttons

1. Click **Insert**. . . . . ⟨Alt⟩+⟨I⟩
2. Point to **Form** . . . . ⟨F⟩
3. Click **Radio Button** . . . . . . ⟨R⟩
   OR
   - Click or drag **Radio Button** button ◉ from the Forms tab of the Insert bar.

To set properties for the radio button:
1. Click the radio button to select it.
2. Type name in Radio Button box if you have not already supplied one.

   ✔ *In a group of radio buttons, all buttons should have the same name.*

3. Type value to send when radio button is selected.
4. Select **Checked** initial state to show radio button selected by default if desired.

Insert a Radio Group

1. Click <u>I</u>nsert . . . . Alt+I
2. Point to <u>F</u>orm . . . . F
3. Click <u>R</u>adio Group . . . . . . G
   OR
   - Click or drag **Radio Group** button ⊞ from the Forms tab of the Insert bar.

To set properties for the radio group:

1. Specify items for radio group in Radio Group dialog box:
   a. Type group name in the Name box.
   b. Click **Radio** in label column and replace this text with desired label.
   c. Press Tab⇄ and type a value.
   d. Click ⊕ to add items to list or ⊖ to remove items.
   e. Click ▲ or ▼ to reorder list.
   f. Select the desired **Lay out using** option:
      - Click Line breaks to place the radio buttons on lines with <br> tags.
      - Click Table to place radio buttons in table.
2. Click [OK].

Insert Checkboxes

1. Click <u>I</u>nsert . . . . Alt+I
2. Point to <u>F</u>orm . . . . F
3. Click <u>C</u>heckbox . . . C, ↵Enter
   OR
   - Click or drag Checkbox button ☑ from the Forms tab of the Insert bar.

To set properties for the checkbox:

1. Click the checkbox to select it.
2. Type name in Checkbox box if you have not already supplied one.

   ✔ *In a group of checkboxes, all boxes should have the same name.*

3. Type value in Checked value to send when checkbox is selected.
4. Select **Checked** initial state to show checkbox selected by default if desired.

Insert a List or Menu

1. Click <u>I</u>nsert . . . . Alt+I
2. Point to <u>F</u>orm . . . . F
3. Click <u>L</u>ist/Menu L
   OR
   - Click or drag **List/Menu** button ▤ from the Forms tab of the Insert bar.

To set properties for the list or menu:

1. Click list/menu field to select it.
2. Type name in List/Menu box if you have not already supplied one.
3. Select **Menu** or **List**.
   - For List, specify number for **Height** and, if desired, select **Allow multiple** checkbox.
4. Specify items for list:
   a. Click [List Values...].
   b. Type label for first item.
   c. Press Tab⇄ and type a value.
   d. Click ⊕ to add items to list or ⊖ to remove items.
   e. Click ▲ or ▼ to reorder list.
   f. Click [OK].
5. Set initial selection by expanding Property inspector, if necessary, and choosing item from Initially selected list.

Insert a Multiple-Line Text Field

1. Click <u>I</u>nsert . . . . Alt+I
2. Point to <u>F</u>orm . . . . F
3. Click Text<u>a</u>rea . . . . A
   OR
   - Click or drag **Textarea** button ▭ from the Forms tab of the Insert bar.

To set properties for the text area:

1. Click the multiple-line text field.
2. Type name in TextField box if you have not already supplied one.
3. Type value for field width if desired.
4. Type value for number of lines in text box if desired.
5. Type initial value if desired.
6. Change wrap option if desired.

Insert Buttons

1. Click <u>I</u>nsert . . . . Alt+I
2. Point to <u>F</u>orm . . . . F
3. Click <u>B</u>utton . . . . B
   OR
   - Click or drag **Insert Button** button ▭ from the Forms tab of the Insert bar.

To set properties for the button:

1. Click button to select it.
2. For Submit button leave all default properties as is.
3. For Reset or other button:
   a. Type button name.
   b. Type label to appear on button.
   c. Select **Reset form** action for Reset button.

EXERCISE DIRECTIONS

1. Start Dreamweaver and open the cincitorial site.

2. Open contactus.html. On a new paragraph below the navigation bar, type the following text:
   To learn more about CinciTorial, fill out the form below and click Submit. We'll respond to your submission within 24 hours. Fields marked with * are required!

3. Boldface the last sentence in the paragraph and change its color to #990033.

4. Insert a form below the paragraph you just typed.

5. Name the form ctform. Set the Method setting to POST if necessary.

   ✔ You do not need to enter anything in the Action text box. When you create a link to a database in the next exercise, Dreamweaver will automatically add the correct action in this box.

   ✔ Refer to Illustration A as you create the accessible form in the following steps.

6. Insert single-line form fields as follows:
   - Insert a text field with the ID **name** and the label Your name*. Use the *Wrap with label tag* accessibility option. Specify a width of 35 characters and a maximum of 50 characters.
   - Click to the right of the first form field and press Enter. Insert a text field with the ID country and the label Country*. Use the *Wrap with label tag* accessibility option. Specify the same properties as the *name* field.
   - In the next paragraph, insert a text field with the ID **email** and the label E-mail address*. Specify the same properties as the *name* field.

7. Insert a checkbox:
   - In a new paragraph, type Would you like to be added to our mailing list? Insert a line break to move to a new line.
   - Insert a checkbox with the ID **list** and the label Yes. Select the checkbox in the form and in the property inspector, type Yes in the Checked value box.

8. Insert a list:
   - In a new paragraph, insert a list/menu field with the ID **tutorials** and the label What kinds of tutorials do you need.
   - Select the list/menu field and choose the **List** option in the Property inspector. Change the height value to **3**.

   - Click the List Values button and enter the following labels and values:

Office suites	suites
Internet and Web publishing	web
Programming	programming

   - After inserting these values, click to the left of the list box and insert a line break to move the list below the label.

9. Insert a menu:
   - In a new paragraph, insert a List/Menu field with the ID find and the label How did you find us? Use the current accessibility options.
   - Select the list/menu field and choose the Menu option..
   - Click the List Values button and enter the following labels and values:

Search engine	search_engine
Professional publication	publication
ExpoPub	expopub
Referral	referral

   - Select *Search engine* as the initially selected item.

10. Insert the multiline text box:
    - Click to the right of the menu field and press Enter to move to a new paragraph.
    - Insert a Textarea field with the ID **comments** and the label What additional services should we offer. Use the *Wrap with label tag* option.
    - Specify a width of 50 characters and 5 lines.
    - Insert a line break after the label to move the field to a new line below the label.

11. Insert a Submit button:
    - Move to a new paragraph and insert a Button field.
    - Specify *No label tag* and make no changes to the button's properties.

12. Save your changes to this page and preview it in a browser. Your form should look similar to Illustration A.

13. Enter sample data in the form to make sure the fields are large enough for a typical entry. You do not have to click the Submit button when testing.

14. Close the browser and all open pages and exit Dreamweaver.

Illustration A

To learn more about CinciTorial, fill out the form below and click Submit. We'll respond to your submission within 24 hours. Fields marked with * are required!

Your name* [   ]

Country* [   ]

E-mail address* [   ]

Would you like to be added to our mailing list?
☐ Yes

What kinds of tutorials do you need?
| Office suites |
| Internet and Web publishing |
| Programming |

How did you find us? [Search engine   ▼]

What additional services should we offier?
[   ]

[Submit]

ON YOUR OWN

1. Start Dreamweaver and open the **gardencenter** site.
2. Create a new page name **mailing.html** and insert an appropriate heading. Above the heading, insert from the library the small daylily picture used as a link to the home page. Below the heading, insert text that you can use as a link to the **contact.html** page.
3. Insert an accessible form on the **mailing.html** page. Use your judgment about what information to gather with this form, but you should use as many of the form field types that you learned about in this exercise as you can.
   - Be sure to name each field and supply labels and values as needed.
   - Add a Submit and a Reset button to the form.

4. On **contact.html**, create a link from the text *mailing list* in the fifth text paragraph to the **mailing.html** page.
5. Close all open pages and exit Dreamweaver.

Exercise | 30

Skills Covered

- **About Form Handling**
- **Create a Database Connection**
- **Insert Records in a Database**
- **Create a Recordset for a Results Page**

Software Skills Dreamweaver's Application panel group includes several panels that allow you to connect to a database, send form data to the database, and display form results on another page.

Application Skills In this exercise, you will learn how to create a connection to an Access database, insert data from your CinciTorial form into a database, and create a recordset that allows you to see stored form data.

TERMS

Application Program that performs a task for the user; spreadsheet, word processing, database, and presentation programs are common examples of applications.

Application server A computer that runs applications or delivers applications to client computers.

Form handler A script or application that controls how form data is processed.

Recordset A collection of data from a database.

Script A series of instructions to perform specific steps.

NOTES

About Form Handling

- What happens to the information a visitor supplies in a form after he or she clicks the Submit button? The information is sent to the Web site server, where it is processed by a **script** or **application** on the server.

- The server may then send information back to the client (the Web server) or perform some other action that the form requests, such as interacting with a database server to store or retrieve information.

- The following illustration shows this process in a simplified form. Keep in mind that not all form data proceeds to a database. Some designers set up forms to return results by e-mail, and some forms are set up to request input from a database.

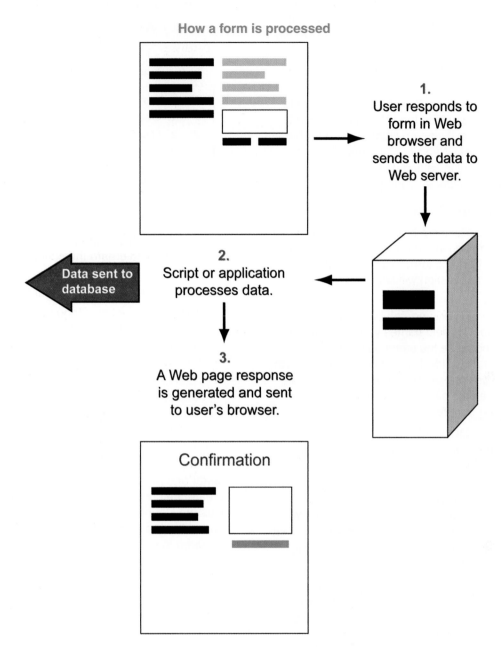

How a form is processed

1.
User responds to form in Web browser and sends the data to Web server.

Data sent to database

2.
Script or application processes data.

3.
A Web page response is generated and sent to user's browser.

Confirmation

- A program that controls the process of dealing with form data is called a **form handler.**
- Dreamweaver does not include a default form handler that you can use to process or store information from your forms, but the program includes powerful tools to help you create the connections you need in order to handle your form data.
- Some Web hosts offer generic scripts a designer can customize for his or her form. If a generic script is not available, a designer may need to write a script from scratch or download one of the thousands of scripts available on the Internet.

- Scripting languages include Perl, VBScript, JavaScipt, ColdFusion Markup Language, and PHP.
- A form may also require that the Web server communicate with an **application server** if an application is necessary to process the form data. When you build a form on an ASP page, for example, you need a server that uses ASP technology to handle the form.

- The IIS built into recent Windows versions is not only a Web server but an application server that can handle both VBScript and JavaScript. You can use the IIS not only to test a form but to set up a connection to a database that allows you to send data to and retrieve data from the database.

- In the following sections, you learn how to create such a connection using the IIS and a Microsoft Access database. If you are using a server other than the IIS to test Web sites, you may find the information useful in setting up form handling procedures that will work for your server.

Create a Database Connection

- After you have created a form that you want to use to store information in a database, you must create a connection from the form to the database, so your script or application will know where to send the data.

- You must have an existing database file in which to store the data. The field names you use in the database table should be the same as the names you used for the form fields. If you have created a form field named *list* for example, your database table should have a field named *list* that will store the data from that form field.

- You create a database connection using the Databases panel in the Application panel group, shown in the illustration at the top of the next column.

- This panel offers a checklist of tasks you must complete before you can make a connection: You have to create a site, choose a document type that supports your current task, and set up a testing server that will be able to process the data.

  ✔ If you want to process a form using ColdFusion, you do not have to specify a document type or testing server until this point. You can click the links in the tab to specify the page type or set up the server.

Databases panel in Application panel group

- When the first three items are properly checked, you are ready to create the connection.

- You have two connection options: Custom Connection String and Data Source Name (DSN).

  - Custom Connection String allows you to type a string of code that tells the server how to connect to a database and where the database is stored.

  - A DSN connection relies on drivers that are pre-installed in most Windows computers. To use this type of connection, you must create a new data source and supply a name that you can then refer to when making the connection.

- Connection strings are generally considered to be faster and more reliable than DSN connections. To create the connection, you type the string in the Custom Connection String dialog box. The illustration at the top of the next page shows the string required to connect to an Access database.

E-Commerce Connection

CGI and Perl
CGI (Common Gateway Interface) is a standard protocol used to communicate between an application and a Web server. The programming language Perl is commonly used to write CGI scripts.

Explore CGI and Perl
Use the Internet to locate information on CGI and Perl. Write a report that summarizes the history and common uses of the CGI protocol and the Perl language.

Creating a custom connection string

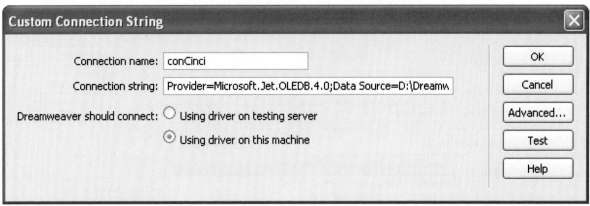

- You can click the Test button in the dialog box to check that you have entered the string correctly.

- When the connection is made, it displays in the Databases panel as shown in the following illustration. You can see the database itself, its tables and other objects, and the fields in each table, by expanding view levels in the tab.

A database connection
displays in the Databases panel

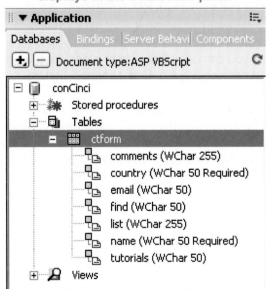

- Once you have established a connection, you are ready to tell Dreamweaver how to insert form data into the database. For this task, you use the Insert Record behavior.

  ✔ *You will learn more about behaviors in Lesson 6.*

- If you are using the IIS testing server, you need to make sure the IIS can access the folder in which you have stored the database, or you will not be able to submit form results properly. You can find instructions for adjusting sharing and permissions for Windows 2000, XP, and Vista in the Procedures section.

Insert Records in a Database

- You have two options for inserting records in a database for which you have already established a connection. You can use the Record Insertion Form Wizard or you can use the Insert Record behavior.

- The Record Insertion Form Wizard is a quick way to set up both a form and the scripting required to store data from that form. The Wizard creates a simple-looking form in a table that you cannot customize, so if you have already built a form, this is not your best option.

- The Insert Record behavior allows you to specify the database connection, what table should receive the data, how fields in the form and the database match up, and other options. You make these sections in the Insert Record dialog box, shown in the illustration at the top of the next page.

- Note that the Form elements list shows how the form fields insert data into the database fields. You have the option of changing how data is submitted.

- For a form field that contains a checkbox, for example, such as the list field in the illustration, you can specify that the data be submitted as checkbox data or text data. You can also specify numeric or date formats for form fields that contain numbers.

Insert Record dialog box

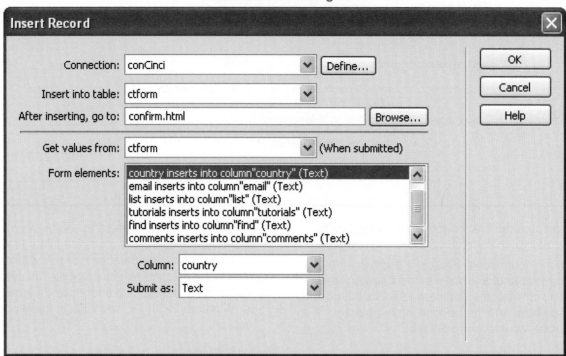

- This dialog box also allows you to tell the server what page to display after inserting the form data. Generally, you will want to create a confirmation page that will display to tell the visitor the form data was submitted correctly.

- Once you have completed the Insert Record setup, the form fields display a blue shading and the Action box in the Property inspector for the form shows an action such as <%=MM_editAction%>.

- You have now specified the database connection and told Dreamweaver to insert form data into that database as records. Once visitors begin submitting data with your form, you can open your database at any time and see the records that have been stored there.

- Dreamweaver gives you another way to view stored data without having to leave Dreamweaver. You can create a recordset on a site page to display data from the database, as you learn in the next section.

Create a Recordset for a Results Page

- A **recordset** is a collection of data—literally a set of records—from a database. When creating a recordset, you can use all data from a database table, or you can use a query to specify only certain records.

- Customizing recordsets to return exactly the right data can be an absorbing but complex subject. One simple application of the process is to use a recordset to display on a form results page the data captured when visitors fill out an online form.

- You use the Bindings panel in the Application panel group to insert a new recordset.

- Use the Recordset dialog box (see the illustration at the top of the next page) to specify a name for the recordset, the connection name, and the table that contains the data you want to display in the recordset.

Recordset dialog box

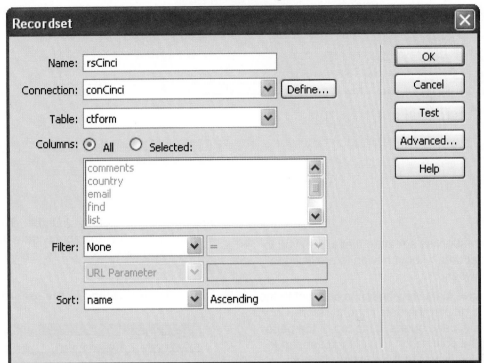

- You can use an existing database connection, or you can use the [Define...] button to create a new connection from this dialog box.

- You can choose to display all the columns from the database in the recordset or only selected columns, and you have the option of filtering the data to match specific parameters as well as sort the data in the recordset.

Insert Recordset Data Fields

- After you create the recordset, it displays in the Bindings panel as shown in the illustration at right. The data fields in the recordset are displayed in a tree structure below the recordset name. The lightning bolt icon for each data field indicates that this is dynamic data.

- To insert a recordset data field, drag it to the page, or use the Insert button to insert a selected data field.

- When creating a results page, you can set up a table that displays meaningful column headers and then insert the recordset data fields in the second row of the table, as shown in the following illustration.

New recordset in the Bindings panel

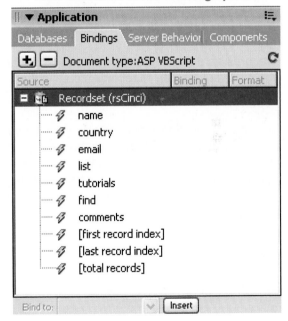

Recordset data fields inserted into a table

CinciTorial Form Results

Name	Country	E-mail	List	Tutorials	Find us	Comments
{rsCinci.name}	{rsCinci.country}	{rsCinci.email}	{rsCinci.list}	{rsCinci.tutorials}	{rsCinci.find}	{rsCinci.comments}

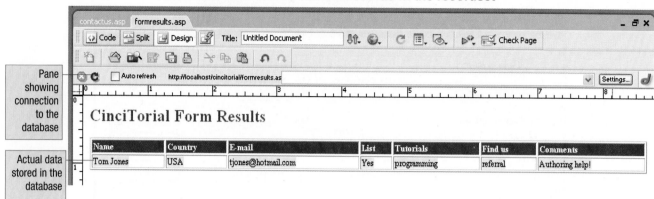

Pane showing connection to the database

Actual data stored in the database

CinciTorial Form Results

Name	Country	E-mail	List	Tutorials	Find us	Comments
Tom Jones	USA	tjones@hotmail.com	Yes	programming	referral	Authoring help!

Display Live Data

- Dreamweaver supplies a feature that allows you to view recordset data without having to preview the page in a browser.

- Click the 📝 Live Data view button to connect to the database and display the data currently stored in the database. A pane opens at the top of the page to show you the connection to the database, and the form results display at the location of each recordset data field, as shown in the illustration at the top of this page.

Create a Repeat Region and Add Recordset Navigation Links

- A recordset's data fields show only one record at a time by default. To see all records stored in the database, you must create a repeating region in the recordset.

- To create a repeating region, select the recordset fields you want to repeat and click the 🔲 Repeat Region button on the Data tab of the Insert bar.

- Dreamweaver displays the Repeat Region dialog box shown in the following illustration to allow you to specify how many records to show at a time.

- The repeat region is indicated by a tab as shown in the following illustration.

Repeat region dialog box

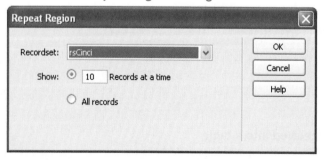

- If you anticipate storing a number of records that you will want to be able to navigate through easily, you can add navigation controls below the record-set.

Repeat region in the recordset

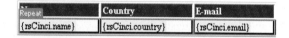

Repeat	Country	E-mail
{rsCinci.name}	{rsCinci.country}	{rsCinci.email}

- Click the ⚌ Recordset Paging button on the Data tab of the Insert bar and select a single navigation control or the navigation bar from the list. Dreamweaver displays a dialog box to ask if you want to use text or images, and then inserts the navigation controls, as shown in the following illustration.

  ✔ The navigation bar will not display until you have more than the number of records you specified in the Repeat Region dialog box.

Navigation bar for a recordset

PROCEDURES

Connect to a Database

✔ *Database file must already be created and stored in a folder that allows file sharing; see Allow the IIS to Access the Database Folder, at the end of the Procedures section.*

1. Click **Databases** panel in Application panel group.

2. If steps 1–3 are checked, click ➕ button, then click **Custom Connection String**.

3. Click in the Connection name box and type a name for the connection.

4. Click in the Connection string box and type the string used to connect to your database. For a Microsoft Access database, the string should be: Provider=Microsoft.Jet. OLEDB.4.0;Data Source=[path to database].

5. Click **Using driver on this machine** if necessary.

6. Click the ⬚Test⬚ button to test the connection.

7. Click ⬚ OK ⬚ if the connection is successful.

✔ *If the connection is not successful, check your typing to make sure you have the string properly inserted.*

Use Insert Record Behavior

1. Select the form to which you wish to attach the behavior.

2. Click **Server Behaviors** panel in Application panel group.

3. Click ➕ button, then click **Insert Record**.

OR

1. Click **I**nsert . . . . (Alt)+(I)

2. Point to **Data Objects** . . . . (J)

3. Point to **I**nsert Record . . . . (I)

4. Click **I**nsert Record . . . . . . (I)

In the Insert Record dialog box:

1. Click the **Connection** list arrow and select an existing database connection.

OR

a. Click ⬚Define...⬚.

b. Click ⬚ New ⬚.

c. Click **Custom Connection String**.

d. Follow steps 3–7 in *Connect to a Database*, at left.

2. Click the **Insert into table** list arrow and select the table to receive the data.

3. Type the path of the page to display after the form is submitted in the **After inserting, go to** box, or use the ⬚Browse...⬚ button to navigate to the page.

4. Check to make sure the form fields are set to submit into the correct database fields. If fields do not match exactly:

a. Select the form element in the Form elements list that does not match.

b. Click the **Column** list arrow and select a database column to receive the data.

5. Check to make sure the data will be submitted in the correct way. If you need to change the way data will be submitted:

a. Select the form element in the Form elements list that does not match.

b. Click the **Submit as** list arrow and select a new format for the data.

Create a Recordset

1. Click **Bindings** panel in Application panel group.

2. Click ➕ button, then click **Recordset (Query)**.

3. Click in the **Name** box and type a name for the recordset.

4. Click the **Connection** list arrow and select an existing database connection.

OR

a. Click ⬚Define...⬚.

b. Click ⬚ New ⬚.

c. Click **Custom Connection String**.

d. Follow steps 3–7 in *Connect to a Database*, at left.

5. Click the **Table** list arrow and select the table from which the recordset data will be retrieved.

6. To choose only selected columns from the database table, click the **Selected** option, click the first column to include, then hold down ⬚⬆Shift⬚ or ⬚Ctrl⬚ and select additional columns.

7. To filter data from the database:

a. Click **Filter** list arrow and select the column to filter.

b. Click the comparison operator box's list arrow and choose an operator for the filter.

c. Choose the source of the comparison value in the list box below the Filter list box.

d. If necessary, enter the comparison string in the fourth Filter box.

✔ *For example, to display only records in which the country is USA, choose to filter by country, select the = comparison operator, choose the Entered Value source, and type USA in the box.*

8. To sort data in the recordset, click the **Sort** list arrow and select the column to sort by.

9. Click ⬚ OK ⬚.

Insert Recordset Data Fields

1. Display the **Bindings** panel if necessary.
2. Click the ⊞ button to expand the recordset.
3. Click on a data field and drag it to the desired location on the current page.

   OR

   a. Position the insertion point where the data field should appear.

   b. Click the data field you want to insert to select it.

   c. Click ⌜Insert⌟.

Display Live Data

- On a page that contains a recordset, click the **Live Data view** button ✒️.

  ✔ It may take a while to create the connection and display the data.

  ✔ To turn off Live Data view, click the button again.

Add a Repeat Region

1. Select the recordset data fields you want to repeat.

   ✔ If the data fields are stored in a table row, for example, select the entire table row.

2. Click the **Repeat Region** button 🔁 on the Data tab of the Insert bar.
3. Specify the number of records to show at a time.
4. Click ⌜ OK ⌟.

Add Recordset Navigation Controls

1. Position the insertion point on the page where you want the navigation controls to display.
2. Click the **Recordset Paging** button ⟨⟩ list arrow on the Data tab of the Insert bar.
3. Click a navigation option:

Recordset Navigation Bar

Move To First Record

Move To Previous Record

Move To Next Record

Move To Last Record

Move To Specific Record

4. Select **Text** or **Images**.
5. Click ⌜ OK ⌟.

Allow the IIS to Access the Database Folder

✔ If you receive an error when you attempt to insert records in a database connection, follow these steps to adjust permissions for the folder in which the database is stored.

In Windows 2000:

1. Right-click on the folder that contains the database (right-click the actual folder icon, not the folder name) and click **Properties**.
2. Click the **Security** tab.
3. Deselect the **Allow inheritable permissions from parent to propagate to this object** at the bottom of the dialog box.
4. Click the ⌜ Add... ⌟ button in the upper-right corner of the dialog box to open the Select Users or Groups dialog box.
5. Locate the entry that begins with IUSR, such as IUSR_[computer name].
6. Click the entry and then click ⌜ Add... ⌟ in the middle of the dialog box. The [computer name]\IUSR_[computer name] displays in the box in the bottom half of the dialog box.
7. Click ⌜ OK ⌟ to return to the Properties dialog box for the database folder.

   ✔ The top box list should contain a highlighted name such as Internet Guest Account ([computer name]).

8. Click the Internet Guest Account entry and then click the **Read** and **Write** check

boxes in the Allow column in the Permissions section of the dialog box.

✔ You may also select Full Control if you are certain your system is safe from intruders.

9. Click ⌜ OK ⌟ and then restart the computer.

In Windows XP Professional:

1. Right-click the 🏁 start button and click **Explore** to open Windows Explorer.
2. Click **Tools** . . . . ⌜Alt⌟+⌜T⌟
3. Click **Folder Options** . . . . . ⌜O⌟
4. Click the **View** tab.
5. Scroll down in the Advanced settings list to locate the Use simple file sharing (Recommended) checkbox and deselect it.
6. Click ⌜ OK ⌟.
7. Right-click on the folder that contains the database (right-click the actual folder icon, not the folder name) and click **Properties**.
8. Click the **Security** tab.
9. Click the ⌜ Add... ⌟ button.
10. Click the ⌜ Advanced... ⌟ button in the Select Users or Groups dialog box.
11. Click the ⌜ Find Now ⌟ button in the Select Users or Groups dialog box.
12. Scroll down to find the entry that begins with IUSR, such as IUSR_[computer name].
13. Click the entry and then click ⌜ OK ⌟ twice to return to the Properties dialog box for the database folder.

    ✔ The Group or user names list should contain a highlighted name such as Internet Guest Account ([computer name]).

14. Click the Internet Guest Account entry and then click the **Full Control** check box in the Allow column in the Permissions section of the dialog box.

15. Click [OK] and then restart the computer.

In Windows Vista:

1. Right-click the Start button and click **Explore** to open Windows Explorer.

2. Right-click on the folder that contains the database (right-click the actual folder icon, not the folder name) and click **Properties**.

3. Click the **Sharing** tab and then click the **Share** button.

4. Click the list arrow and then select the entry that begins with IUSR, such as IUSR_[computer name].

5. Click [Add...], click **Share**, and then click **Done**.

6. Click the **Security** tab.

7. Click the **Edit** button.

8. Scroll the Group or user names list and select the entry that begins with IUSR.

9. In the Permissions section of the dialog box, click the **Full Control** check box in the Allow column.

10. Click [OK] to return to the Properties dialog box for the database folder.

    ✔ *The Group or user names list should contain a highlighted name such as IUSR_[computer name].*

11. Click [OK] and then restart the computer.

EXERCISE DIRECTIONS

✔ *In this exercise, you will create a site to test the CinciTorial form and view form results. You will use new pages and pages based on those you have been working with to speed the testing process. This exercise requires you to use the IIS Web server.*

Prepare the Site

1. Create a new site named cinci_form with the following site definition:
   - Choose to use the ASP VBScript server technology.
   - Choose to edit and test locally, and store files in C:\Inetpub\wwwroot\cinci_form\.
   - Set the URL to http://localhost/cinci_form/.
   - Do not use a remote server, and do not enable check in/check out.

2. Open the following files from the Lesson 4 Data files folder and save them in the cinci_form site: form_confirm.html, form_contactus.asp, form_index.html, and form_results.asp.

3. Set up links on these pages as follows:
   - On the form_confirm.html page, link the text *CinciTorial Home* to form_index.html.
   - On the form_contactus.asp and form_results.asp pages, use the entries in the navigation tables at the top of each page to link to form_index.html, form_contactus.asp, and form_results.asp.
   - On the form_index.html page, change the *Contact Us* link to point to form_contactus.asp.

4. Save all pages.

Store the Database

1. Create a folder on your hard drive with a name such as Dreamweaver_Databases.

2. Copy ⊙ cincitorial.mdb from the Lesson 4 Data files to this folder.

3. If directed by your instructor, adjust file sharing and permissions to allow the IIS to access this folder.

   ✔ *See the Procedures section for information on how to adjust permissions.*

Create the Database Connection

1. In the cinci_form site, open the form_contactus.asp page.

2. Create the database connection as follows:
   - Open the Application panel group and click the Databases panel. Steps 1–3 should be checked.
   - Click the [+] button in the Databases panel and then click Custom Connection String.
   - Type the name conCinci for the new connection.
   - Type the following connection string: Provider=Microsoft.Jet.OLEDB.4.0;Data Source=C:\Dreamweaver_Databases\cincitorial.mdb

   ✔ *If your Dreamweaver_Databases folder is on another drive, or inside another folder, adjust the path accordingly.*

   - Make sure **Using driver on this machine** is selected.
   - Click the Test button to make sure you have a valid connection, then click OK.

   ✔ *You should see the new connection in the Databases panel.*

Attach the Insert Record Behavior

1. Attach the Insert Record behavior to the form as follows:
    - Click the form border to select the entire form.
    - In the Application panel group, click the Server Behaviors tab.
    - Click the ⊞ button in the panel and then click Insert Record.
    - In the Insert Record dialog box, click the Connection list arrow and select **conCinci**. The ctform table should display in the Insert into table box.
    - Click the Browse button and select **form_confirm.html** for the page that will display after the form is submitted.
    - Click OK to close the dialog box.

    ✔ *Notice that the Action box now contains a script.*

2. Save changes to the **form_contactus.asp** page.

Insert and Modify a Recordset

1. Insert a recordset as follows:
    - Open the **form_results.asp** page.
    - In the Application panel group, click the Bindings panel.
    - Click the ⊞ button in the panel and then click Recordset (Query).
    - Type the name **rsCinci** for the recordset.
    - Click the Connection list arrow and select **conCinci**.
    - Click OK to accept all remaining defaults and close the dialog box.

2. Add recordset data fields as follows:
    - Expand the recordset in the Bindings panel.
    - Drag each data field to the proper column in the table.

3. Create a repeating region as follows:
    - Select the entire second row of the table, using the <tr> tag if necessary.
    - Click the Data tab on the Insert bar.
    - Click the 🖺 Repeat Region button.
    - Change the number of records to display to **5**.

4. Add navigation controls as follows:
    - Click below the table to position the insertion point.
    - On the Data tab of the Insert bar, click the ⟨⟩«» Recordset Paging button's list arrow, and then select Recordset Navigation Bar.
    - Choose to display text.

5. Save the **form_results.asp** page.

Create and View Data Records

1. Activate the **form_contactus.asp** page and preview it in the browser. (You may find the browser takes a long time to display the pages in this site because of the server technology being used.) Test the form by entering the following responses in the appropriate form fields.

Your name*	Todd Tedesco
Country*	Canada
Email address*	ttedesco@maplexpo.org
Add your name to our mailing list?	Yes
What kinds of tutorials do you need?	Office suites
How did you find us?	ExpoPub
Additional services	Please consider branching out into graphics!

2. Click Submit. After a pause, you should see the Confirmation page that lets you know the form data submitted correctly.

    ✔ *If you receive an error page, see your instructor for troubleshooting options.*

3. Click the link from the Confirmation page to the CinciTorial home page, and navigate to the Contact Us page.

4. Fill out the form again, entering your name and varying your responses. Repeat this process until you have entered data at least six times.

5. In Dreamweaver, activate the **form_results.asp** page and click the Live Data view button to view the data you have entered.

6. Preview the page in the browser and test the navigation buttons below the results table. Your first form results page should look similar to Illustration A.

7. Close the browser, close all open documents, and then exit Dreamweaver.

Illustration A

Home   Contact Us   Form Results

CinciTorial Form Results

Name	Country	E-mail	List	Tutorials	Find us	Comments
Tom Jones	USA	tjones@hotmail.com	Yes	programming	referral	Authoring help!
Todd Tedesco	Canada	ttedesco@maplexpo.org	Yes	suites	expopub	Please consider branching out into graphics!
Mark Jones	USA	mark_jones@hotmail.com	Yes	web	publication	Flash tutorials would be nice.
Jessica Hogarth	England	jesshogarth@howarthpress.com	N	suites	search_engine	Okay so far . . .
Kelly Unvers	USA	k_unvers@juno.net	N	web	referral	Please consider conducting seminars.

Next Last

ON YOUR OWN

1. Start Dreamweaver and open the gardencenter site.
2. Create a confirmation page that will display after visitors submit the form data from the mailing.html page. Give the page an appropriate name and add a link that will take visitors back to the site.
3. Open the mailing.html page you created in the last exercise. To test how the confirmation page will work:
   - Select the form.
   - Type the confirmation page's name in the Action box. This will open the confirmation page as soon as the form is submitted.
   - Click the Target list arrow and select _blank to open the confirmation page in a new browser window.
4. Preview the form in your browser and insert at least one record. Click the Submit button to open the confirmation page in a new window.
5. Close the browser, close any open documents, and exit Dreamweaver.

Summary Exercise

Application Skills In this exercise, you will import tabular data to create a calendar in the High Ridge Swim Club site.

DIRECTIONS

1. Start Dreamweaver and open the **highridge** site.

2. Open **swimdive.html**. Delete the *Text in progress* placeholder and import the Word text in the **swimpage.doc** file from the Lesson 4 Data folder. Modify the page as necessary after importing by adjusting paragraph tags and applying a new font if necessary.

3. On a blank line below the new information, import the tabular data in **calendar.txt** from the Lesson 4 Data folder. Set the table width to 700 pixels.

4. Modify the table as follows:
   - Change the font of the table data if necessary to match the font on the page.
   - Change the size of all events, such as Home Meet, to 2. Center all events.
   - Merge all cells in the first row and apply an appropriate format to the June text.
   - Boldface and center the day headings.
   - Boldface and right align the day numbers.
   - Merge cells vertically to create the calendar blocks, so that there are no borders between the dates and the cell or cells below. You can use Illustration A as a guide to how to merge cells in the table. (Check this illustration carefully; for the first week of June you merge two rows, and for the remaining weeks you merge three rows.)
   - Use Top vertical alignment for all cells that have dates.

5. Adjust column widths so they are more equally sized. You may break lines in the events to reduce the size of some columns.

6. Format the text of the events as desired.

7. Format the table cells and borders as desired.

8. Preview the table in the browser. Make any necessary changes to the table layout.

9. Close all open pages and exit Dreamweaver.

Illustration A

June

Sun	Mon	Tue	Wed	Thu	Fri	Sat
				1 Team Suit-Up 6-8 pm	2	3
4	5 Morning practices begin	6	7	8 Home MeetHR hosts Valley View	9	10
11	12	13 Tie Dye Day!	14	15 Away MeetHR @ Mt. Adams	16	17
18	19	20 Pancake Breakfastafter every practice	21	22 Home MeetHR hosts Shady Grove	23	24
25	26	27	28	29 Away MeetHR @ Fairmont	30 Overnight730 pm – 800 am	

Exercise | 32

Application Exercise

Application Skills   In this exercise, you will add an accessible mailing list form to the Grand Theatre site.

DIRECTIONS

1. Start Dreamweaver and open the grand Web site.
2. Open index.html. Below the unordered list on this page insert a new heading that matches the other headings on the page. Type the heading text **Mailing List**.
3. Below the heading, type the following text:

   Join our weekly movie e-mail list for updated schedules, summaries of new movies, and news on upcoming events. The Grand Theatre Movie List will be sent to you every week. Sign up here!

4. Create a new page named movielist.html and insert an appropriate heading for the page, along with the grandhead.gif image from your Assets favorites list. Link the graphic to the home page, and supply alternate text if prompted.
5. Below the heading, insert the following text:

   Please fill out and submit the following form to sign up.

6. Insert a form and add the following fields. Create an accessible form that uses <label> tags. Be sure to name each field appropriately.

E-mail	Insert a text field
What types of movies do you prefer?	Create a list or menu with the options Foreign Films, Classic Films, New Releases, Family Films, Art Films
How often do you go to the movies?	Create a list or menu with the options Once a week, Once a month or more, Once every two months, About four times a year
What do you like best about the Grand? (choose all that apply)	Create checkboxes for Ambience, Film choices, and Location
First name	Insert a text field
Last name	Insert a text field
Zip/postal code	Insert a text field
Gender	Create a radio button group that gives options for Male and Female
Age	Create a list or menu with the options Under 18, 18 - 25, 26 - 29, 30 - 39, 40 - 49, 50 - 59, 60 or over
Submit	Create a Submit button

   ✔ When creating the lists/menus, you may want to add a choice at the top of the list such as Please Select One to let visitors know they must choose from a menu.

7. Preview the form in the browser to make sure all fields work correctly.
8. On the home page, create a link from the text *Sign up here!* to the form page.
9. Create a confirmation page that will open when the form is submitted, and set the Action on the form page to display the confirmation page (type the name of the confirmation page in the form's Action box).
10. Preview the home page, test the link to the form page, and submit a form to test the confirmation page.
11. Save and close all open pages.
12. Exit Dreamweaver.

Exercise | 33

Curriculum Integration

Application Skills   For your American History class, you have been assigned the task of creating a Web page that shows how many Americans have died in various wars throughout American history. To present your research, you will create a Web page, format it using a layout table, and insert your findings in tabular form within one of the layout cells. Before you begin this project, locate:

■ A Web site that gives information on deaths in all the wars in which Americans participated

■ A historic war picture you can use to illustrate the site

DIRECTIONS

Create a new site with an appropriate name. Create a new HTML page and save it in the site with the name warcasualties.html.

Create a layout table to organize the page layout. You may want to review some of the Starter pages for ideas on how to lay out the page and use color blocks for effect.

Insert an appropriate page heading in a layout cell. Create a cell to hold the data on war deaths. Within this cell, create a table to organize the data you found. Use your judgment on what data to present. You may want to include the number of service personnel who participated in the war and the number of nonfatal casualties as well as deaths. It might be interesting to determine what percentage of the total number of service members were killed in battle in each war. You may also wish to sort the table to show which wars were the costliest in terms of American lives lost.

Format the table as desired to make the data attractive and easy to understand.

Draw a layout cell above or below the table to explain the data in the table.

Draw a layout cell somewhere in the layout table to hold the war image you located. Below the image, draw another layout cell to hold a caption for the picture.

Save the page and view it in the browser.

Close the page and exit Dreamweaver.

Exercise | 34

Critical Thinking

Application Skills   In this exercise, you will continue to work on your personal Web site. Add a form to the Web site to gather information from visitors.

DIRECTIONS

- Open your personal Web site and display the home page.

- Add text somewhere on the page to give visitors the chance to complete a survey form related to the site's subject. For example, you may survey club members on activities they would like to engage in or create a mailing list form for new members.

- Create a new page, if desired, to contain the form. (Modify navigation bar or links as necessary to accommodate the new page.) Use a layout table if desired to organize the page content. Insert an appropriate heading and text indicating any special instructions needed to fill out the form.

- Add a form to the page. You can choose to create an accessible form if desired. Use as many different types of form fields as you can. Name each field appropriately and supply the necessary labels and values.

- Test the form in the browser to make sure all fields are working correctly.

- Close all open pages and exit Dreamweaver.

4th bullet!

2 text fields
ex: name
area (state?)

2 List: choices (at least 3)

1: radio button

email - contact

submit

Lesson | 5

Work with AP Elements, Frames, and Styles

Skills Covered

- **About AP Elements**
- **Create AP Elements**
- **Size and Position AP Elements**
- **Use the AP Elements Panel**
- **Name AP Elements**
- **Add Content to AP Divs**

Software Skills AP elements make it possible for Web designers to create overlapping or perfectly aligned images, text boxes, and other objects. Newer browsers support AP elements, giving designers an alternative to using tables to lay out a Web page. AP elements not only enhance the appearance of a Web site, they also enhance its functionality, directing the visitor's eye to important content, links, images, and so on.

Application Skills In this exercise, you will reconfigure one of the CinciTorial site's Web pages to use AP divs to give it more visual interest.

TERMS

Anchor point Invisible object that marks the location where an element has been inserted.

AP div An absolutely positioned <div> tag that controls a block of content on a page.

AP element An AP (absolutely positioned) element is a page element that has been assigned an absolute or fixed position on a page.

NOTES

About AP Elements

- An **AP element** is any HTML element on a Web page that has been positioned absolutely; that is, it has been assigned specific coordinates on the page at which it will appear in any browser.

- The most commonly used AP element is the **AP div**, an HTML element that controls a block of Web page content, but any HTML element can be an AP element. An absolutely positioned image, for example, is an AP element.

  ✔ AP divs are called layers in previous versions of Dreamweaver.

- AP divs can contain text, graphics, multimedia objects such as sounds, and even other AP divs. You can overlap them for creative layouts (see the illustration at the top of the next page) or convert them to a table.

- An advantage of using AP elements is that, because they can be positioned precisely on a Web

page, your creative design will look the same on any browser that supports AP elements.

  ✔ AP elements are robust Web design elements that require Netscape 4.0 or Internet Explorer 4.0 and higher.

- A disadvantage of using AP elements is that different browsers may interpret the coding required to position and format an element differently. If you plan to use AP elements extensively in a Web site, you are strongly advised to test them rigorously in your target browsers to make sure that the AP elements and their contents display as you want them to.

  ✔ The CSS coding used to fine-tune AP elements so they display correctly in all browsers can be complex. You will learn more about CSS coding in this lesson; you can also find information about working with AP elements by searching online.

Portion of Web page containing AP elements

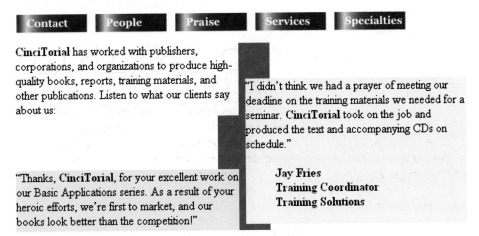

CinciTorial Clients Speak Out

Contact People Praise Services Specialties

CinciTorial has worked with publishers, corporations, and organizations to produce high-quality books, reports, training materials, and other publications. Listen to what our clients say about us:

"I didn't think we had a prayer of meeting our deadline on the training materials we needed for a seminar. CinciTorial took on the job and produced the text and accompanying CDs on schedule."

Jay Fries
Training Coordinator
Training Solutions

"Thanks, CinciTorial, for your excellent work on our Basic Applications series. As a result of your heroic efforts, we're first to market, and our books look better than the competition!"

Create AP Elements

▪ AP elements fall into two general categories: HTML objects such as graphics or tables that you want to position absolutely, and AP divs.

▪ Different methods are used for creating these two types of AP elements.

Position Any Object Absolutely

▪ To position any object absolutely, you must create a CSS (cascading style sheet) rule that specifies the type of positioning and coordinates for the object.

▪ Create the rule in the CSS Rule dialog box, as shown in the following illustration. The Positioning

category in this dialog box allows you to specify absolute positioning and indicate where the object will be positioned on the page.

▪ You will learn how to create new CSS rules in Exercise 39.

Insert AP Divs

▪ You can insert an AP div on a Web page using any of three methods:

  ▪ Insert an AP div using a menu command.

  ▪ Drag an AP div from the Layout tab of the Insert bar.

CSS Rule dialog box

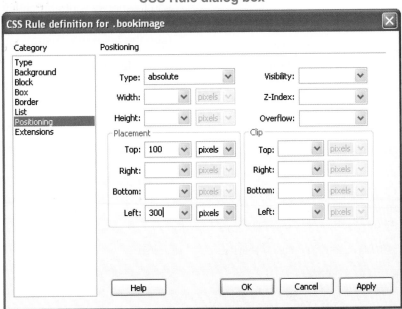

- Draw an AP div using the Draw AP Div button from the Layout tab of the Insert bar.
- To use a menu command to insert an AP div, place the insertion point where you want the element and use the Insert>Layout Objects>AP Div command.

  ✔ *The placement can be an approximation, because the AP div can be dragged to any position on the page.*

- Dreamweaver inserts a default-sized AP div at the position of the insertion point, as well as an AP element ⬛ **anchor point** to indicate the point where the element was inserted (see the following illustration).

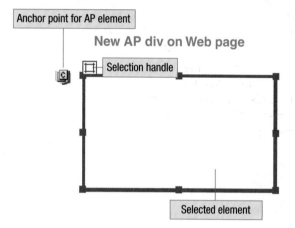

Anchor point for AP element

New AP div on Web page

Selection handle

Selected element

- The remaining two methods of inserting an AP div use the ⬛ Draw AP Div button from the Layout tab of the Insert bar. You can drag the button to the page and release it where you want the element to insert a default-sized AP div element. Or, you can click the button and then use the pointer to draw the element the desired size.

  ✔ *As when drawing a layout cell, you can see the measurements as you draw an AP div by looking near the right side of the status bar.*

Size and Position AP Elements

- You can easily adjust the size and location of an element by dragging. Or, you can use the Property inspector to size and position an element precisely using pixel measurements and coordinates.
- Before you can change the size or location of an element, you must select it. Select an AP element by:
  - Clicking its anchor point.
  - Clicking its selection handle.
  - Clicking its outside border.

Drag to Resize or Relocate

- The easiest way to resize an AP element is to click one of the handles on its selected border and drag in the direction you want to resize. This method may not be suitable, however, for AP elements that are absolutely positioned graphics, because it resizes the graphic as well.
- You can also use dragging to move AP elements to new positions after they have been inserted. Drag the selection handle or click on the outside border of the element and drag with the four-headed arrow pointer.
- Dreamweaver places a <div> tag at the location where you insert an AP element. This tag will remain in its original position in the HTML code no matter where you move the element.
- If you are not happy with your changes to an element, you can easily delete it. Just select the element and press Delete.

Size and Position AP Elements Precisely

- To size or position an element precisely, use the Property inspector. The Property inspector allows you to specify width and height measurements and coordinates for the top-left corner of the element (see the following illustration).

Use Property inspector to size or position precisely

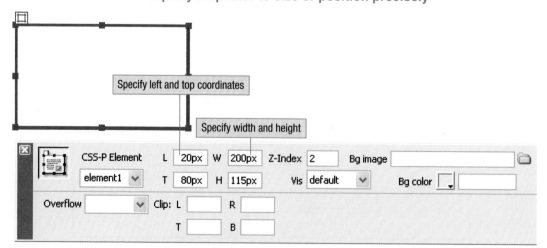

Specify left and top coordinates

Specify width and height

CSS-P Element	L	20px	W	200px	Z-Index	2	Bg image	
element1 ▾	T	80px	H	115px	Vis	default ▾	Bg color
Overflow ▾	Clip: L		R	
	T		B	

■ The L (Left) coordinate measures the distance from the left edge of the page. The T (Top) coordinate measures the distance from the top of the page. Using these positioning coordinates ensures that an element will appear at the same location in any browser.

■ Measurements are in pixels (px) by default. You can also use percentages for size measurements or picas (pc), points (pt), inches (in), millimeters (mm), centimeters (cm), or percentages (%) for the positioning coordinates by using the common symbol or abbreviation for each measurement.

■ Your ability to reposition AP elements freely will depend on whether you have enabled overlap. You can control overlap in the AP Elements panel.

✔ *You will learn more about overlap in the next exercise.*

Use the AP Elements Panel

■ After you have inserted multiple AP elements on a page, you can use the AP Elements panel—a panel in the CSS panel group—to work with the AP elements on your workspace. Launch this panel using the Window> AP Elements menu command.

■ The AP Elements panel (see the illustration below) shows the names of all AP elements on the page and the order in which they are stacked (the Z column). Note from the illustration that this panel shows not only AP divs but other objects that you have positioned absolutely.

✔ *When you create your first few AP elements, their Z numbers reflect the order in which the AP elements were created. As you change the stacking order, the Z number reflects an element's position in the stack.*

■ The AP Elements panel changes as you work with AP elements. When you *activate* an element by clicking anywhere inside it, the element's name is boldfaced in the AP Elements panel. An active AP div is ready for you to enter text or an image and has an insertion point at the left side.

■ When you *select* an element, the element name is highlighted with a color band in the AP Elements panel. You can select an element by clicking its name in the AP Elements panel. This feature is helpful when your page contains many overlapping AP elements.

■ Selected elements display a heavy border with sizing handles. The border color adjusts according to any background color you have added to the element to create a contrast.

■ As you learned earlier, CSS rules are required to position objects absolutely. For this reason, AP elements display not only in the AP Elements panel but also in the CSS Styles panel, as shown in the following illustration.

AP elements display in the CSS Styles panel

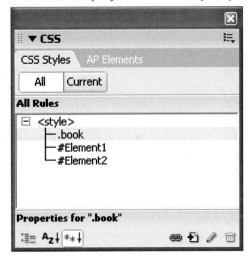

AP Elements panel and AP elements

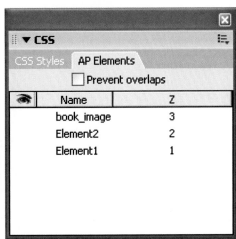

- If you need to modify settings for an AP element, you can do so in this panel in the same way you modify CSS rules.

Name AP Elements

- When you have a number of AP elements on a page, you can help yourself remember what each one contains by naming the elements.

- Name an element by typing a name in the CSS-P Element text box on the Property inspector. As you create names, they appear in the AP Elements panel (see the illustration below).

  ✔ *You can also double-click on the name of the element in the AP Elements panel and change the name there, or right-click the selection handle or anchor point of a selected element, choose ID . . ., and then type the element name in the Change Attribute dialog box.*

Add Content to AP Divs

- AP divs can contain any type of HTML content that you can insert on a Web page. Besides adding text or images, you can format an AP div with a background color or image.

Insert Text

- To insert text in an AP div, click inside the AP div to activate it and begin typing at the insertion point. The AP div behaves very much like a text box in a word processing application. For example, as you resize the AP div, the text wraps to conform to the new shape.

- When you first click in a new AP div to add text or other content, the insertion point will be the same size as the AP div's height and the current format will be listed as None. You can simply begin typing to enter unformatted text, or change the format in the Property inspector to Paragraph or a heading format.

- You can also insert text in an AP div by cutting or copying it from another location and then pasting it in the AP div. After inserting and formatting the text, you can resize the AP div to fit neatly around the text (see the following illustration).

Enter text in an AP div by typing

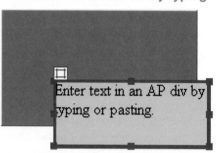

- Notice in the previous illustration that text begins in the upper-left corner of the AP div, with no padding between the edges of the AP div and the text. This can make text in an AP div look somewhat crowded if the AP div has a background color.

- You can improve the look of text in an element by adding padding, just as you do in a table. To add padding to the top, left, right, or bottom of an element, you must use CSS rules. You will learn how to add padding to AP elements in a later exercise.

Name each element

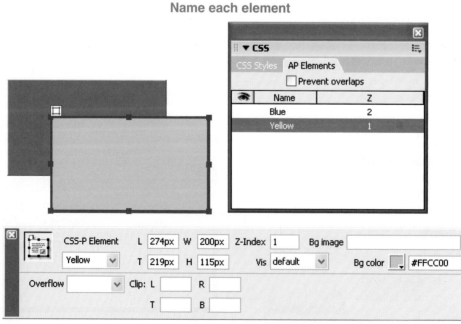

Insert Images

- Inserting an image in an AP div is no different from inserting it on any Web page. Activate the AP div by clicking in it and then use the Insert>Image command or the 🖳 ⋅ Image button from the Common tab of the Insert bar to insert the image.

- An image in an element may be formatted just like any image on a Web page (see the following illustration). You can resize the image, change its alignment, add a border to it, and so on.

Insert image in AP div

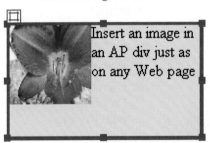

Add Background Color or Image

- Using the Property inspector, you can add color and background images to an AP div to provide contrast with the background of the Web document.

- You must select an AP div to display properties for background color or image in the Property inspector.

- Use the Bg color button to display the familiar palette of background colors. Use the Bg image box to type the name of the image to use, or click the Browse for File button to navigate to the background image file.

E-Commerce Connection

E-Business Marketing
Successful marketing requires attention to four P's: product, place, price, and promotion. Considering that many households now have one or more computers connected to the Internet, e-businesses have unique opportunities to market their services via Web sites.

Analyze E-Business Marketing
Use the Internet to search for information about marketing as it relates to e-commerce. Write a report in which you analyze the marketing functions of an e-business.

PROCEDURES

Insert AP Divs

1. Position insertion point where AP div should appear.
2. Click **Insert** . . . . Alt+I
3. Point to **Layout Objects** . . Y
4. Click **AP Div** . . . . . . A, ↵Enter

   OR

- Drag **Draw AP Div** button 📄 from the Layout tab of the Insert bar to the Document window and release the mouse button.

   OR

1. Click **Draw AP Div** button 📄 on the Layout tab of the Insert bar.

2. Draw AP div of desired size at desired location.

   ✔ *Check the size as you draw near the right side of the status bar.*

Select an AP Element

- Click AP element anchor point 🖸.
- Click element selection handle.
- Click outside border of element.

Drag to Resize or Relocate

To resize an element:

1. Select element.
2. Click on a square handle on any side of the selected element and drag in direction to resize.

To move an element:

1. Select element.
2. Click on a selection handle or outside border.
3. Drag element to new location.

Size and Position AP Elements Precisely

To resize precisely:

1. Select element.
2. Type exact width in the **W** text box on Property inspector.
3. Type exact height in the **H** text box on Property inspector.

To position precisely:

1. Select element.
2. Type measurement from left edge of page in the **L** text box on Property inspector.
3. Type measurement from top of page in the **T** text box on Property inspector.

Display AP Elements Panel (F2)

1. Click **Window** . . . . [Alt]+[W]
2. Click **AP Elements** . . . . . . [L]

Name AP Elements

In the AP Elements panel:

1. Double-click element name.
2. Type new name.

In Property inspector:

1. Select default name in the **CSS-P Element** box.
2. Type new name.

In Document window:

1. Right-click on the element's selection handle or element marker.
2. Click **ID** in the shortcut menu to open the Change Attribute dialog box.
3. Type new name in the **Id** text box.

Insert Text in AP Div

1. Activate AP div by clicking inside AP div.
2. Begin typing at insertion point.
   OR
   ■ Paste cut or copied text at insertion point.

Insert Images (Ctrl + Alt + I)

1. Activate AP div by clicking inside AP div.
2. Click **Insert** . . . . [Alt]+[I]
3. Click **Image** . . . . [I]
   OR
   ■ Click **Image** button ■ ▾ from the Common tab of the Insert bar.

In Select Image Source dialog box:

1. Navigate to the location of the image, select it, and save it in the current Web site.
2. Create alternate text if desired.

In Dreamweaver:

■ Format image as on any Web page.

Add Background Color or Image

To insert background image:

1. Select AP div.
2. Click in the **Bg image** box on Property inspector and type path to image.
   OR
   ■ Click **Browse for File** button 📁 on Property inspector and navigate to image.

To insert background color:

1. Select AP div.
2. Click **Bg color** button and select color from palette.
   OR
   ■ Type hexadecimal value for color in the **Bg color** text box.

EXERCISE DIRECTIONS

1. Start Dreamweaver and open the cincitorial site.
2. Open praise.html. In this exercise, you will create and format AP divs to hold the page's text paragraphs. You will complete the layout in the next exercise.
3. Click to the left of the first text paragraph on the page.
4. Use the Insert menu to insert a new AP div. Name this AP div intro.
5. Select the first paragraph on the page and cut it by right-clicking and selecting the Cut command from the shortcut menu.
6. Activate the intro AP div and paste the cut text into the AP div. Set the format to None if necessary to remove the automatic space above the paragraph.
7. Resize the element to be about 4" wide and 1" high. Insert the puzzle.gif image from your images folder as a background image.

   ✔ *You do not have to be exact about the size and width. You will set the sizes precisely later in the exercise.*

8. Draw a second AP div to the right of the intro AP div, making it about 300 pixels wide and 100 pixels high. Name this AP div training.
9. Move the AP div so the top of the training AP div lines up with the middle of the intro AP div.
10. Add a background color to this AP div using #CCFFFF.
11. Draw a third AP div about 300 pixels wide below the intro AP div and aligned about halfway down the training AP div. Name this AP div lion.

12. Apply a background color of #99FFFF to the AP div.

13. Draw a fourth AP div below the training AP div and name it quentin.

14. Apply a background color of #66FFFF to the AP div.

15. Draw a fifth AP div below the lion AP div and name it peters.

16. Apply a background color of #00CCCC to the AP div.

17. Draw a final AP div to the right of the peters AP div and name it link. Apply the background color #FFCC33.

18. Make the following adjustments to size and position in pixels:

   ■ For the intro AP div, set Left to 9 and Top to 170. Set Width to 300 and Height to 91.

   ✔ *Don't worry if the text obscures the navigation bar. It will look correct in the browser.*

   ■ For the training AP div, set Left to 318 and Top to 217. Set Width to 300 and Height to 115.

   ■ For the lion AP div, set Left to 9 and Top to 335. Set Width to 300 and Height to 115.

   ■ For the quentin AP div, set Left to 318 and Top to 449. Set Width to 300 and Height to 115.

   ■ For the peters AP div, set Left to 9 and Top to 567. Set Width to 300 and Height to 115.

   ■ For the link AP div, set Left to 318 and Top to 661. Set Width to 280 and Height to 90.

19. Save the page and preview it in the browser. The top of the page should look similar to Illustration A. This page still needs work to move the existing text into the AP divs and finalize the layout. You will complete this page in Exercise 36.

20. Close the browser and any open pages.

21. Exit Dreamweaver.

Illustration A

CinciTorial
Editorial Services

CinciTorial Clients Speak Out

| Contact | People | Praise | Services | Specialties |

CinciTorial has worked with publishers, corporations, and organizations to produce high-quality books, reports, training materials, and other publications. Listen to what our clients say about us:

ıdline on the training materials we needed for a seminar. CinciTorial took on CDs on schedule."

Training Coordinator
Training Solutions

"Thanks, CinciTorial, for your excellent work on c   eroic efforts, we're first
                         npetition!"

"We've worked with CinciTorial since the beginni   fessional as well as downright fun. We plan to continue to use their dev   ıtury."

Tyler Stanislowski
Production Manager
Quentin-Stevens Inc.

Torial that it will come back to us on time and ready for the printer. We feel

reters rress

ON YOUR OWN

1. Start Dreamweaver and create a new Web page for a subject of your choice.
2. Practice creating AP divs on the page, using the three methods of inserting AP divs.
3. Position the AP divs by dragging to create a pleasing layout.
4. Add content to the AP divs. Try typing text, pasting text, and inserting both background and other images.
5. Modify some AP divs with background colors.
6. Save the Web page in your solutions folder with a name such as elementpractice.html.
7. Close all open pages and exit Dreamweaver.

Skills Covered

- Manipulate AP Divs
- Control AP Element Visibility
- Advanced AP Element Properties
- Convert AP Divs to Tables

Software Skills   Manipulate AP divs to adjust or modify a page layout. You can change stacking order and nest AP divs within AP divs to organize content. You can also control visibility of AP elements using the AP Elements panel.

Application Skills   In this exercise, you will complete the AP divs page by adding content to the AP divs you created in the previous exercise. You will paste text from the page into AP divs, type new content, and insert an image into a nested AP div. You will adjust visibility to make it easier to add content and change stacking order to finalize the layout.

TERMS

Stacking order Order in which AP elements are added to a page. The lowest number is at the bottom of the stack.

Z-index Stacking order of AP elements on a page.

NOTES

Manipulate AP Divs

- You can manipulate multiple AP divs on a page to create special effects. For example, you can insert AP divs within AP divs to hold related content or images. Before you begin manipulating AP divs, you need to decide whether your AP elements can overlap on the page.

Set Overlap Options

- By default, Dreamweaver allows you to overlap AP divs. This means that you can drag one AP element on top of another or partially obscure one AP element with another.

- For some layouts, you will want to prevent AP elements from overlapping, as, for example, when text in one AP div describes images in an AP element next to it.

- Control AP element overlap in the AP Elements panel. If you click the Prevent Overlaps checkbox, you will not be allowed to overlap one AP element on another.

Change Stacking Order

- When you overlap AP elements, you may need to adjust the **stacking order**. AP elements are stacked on a page in the order they are created, from the first AP div (designated by default as apDiv1) on the bottom to subsequent AP divs on top (see the following illustration).

Stacked AP divs on a page

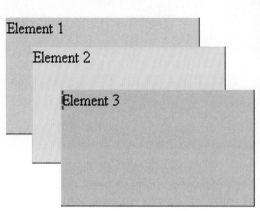

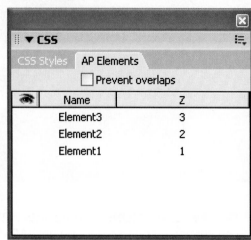

- The stacking order is also called the **Z-index**. The bottommost AP element is given a Z-index number of 1, and subsequent AP elements receive incrementally higher numbers. To change the stacking order of an AP element, you change its Z-index number.

  ✔ *It is possible to assign the same Z-index number to more than one AP element.*

- You can change an AP element's Z-index number by clicking it in the Z column of the AP Elements panel and typing a new number. Or, type a new stacking order number in the Z-Index box on the Property inspector.

- You can also change stacking order by selecting an AP element name in the AP Elements panel and dragging it to the desired level in the AP Elements panel's stack.

Nest AP Divs

- Just as it sounds, a *nested* AP div is an AP div inserted inside an existing AP div. The same meth-

ods you use to insert an AP div on a Web page can be used to insert an AP div in another AP div.

  ✔ *If you draw the AP div with the Draw AP Div button crosshair, you must press Alt to nest the new AP div if nesting is turned off in AP Elements preferences in the Preferences dialog box.*

- The AP div in which you insert a nested AP div is called the *parent AP div*. The nested AP div is called the *child AP div*. The child AP div's anchor point appears within the parent AP div, and the child AP div is listed underneath the parent AP div in the AP Elements panel (see the following illustration).

- Though created within a parent AP div, the child AP div does not have to remain within the parent AP div. It can be moved outside of the nested AP div without its ceasing to be a nested AP div.

- Click the minus sign next to a parent AP div in the AP Elements panel to hide child AP divs. Click a plus sign to display child AP divs.

Nested AP div created in Element3

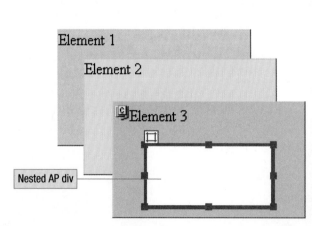

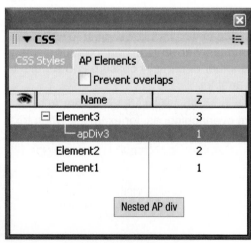

Element3 is hidden

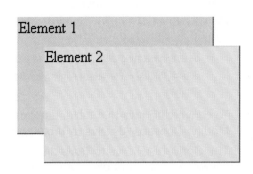

- You can click on the nested AP div's name in the AP Elements panel and drag it out of the parent AP div to break the nested relationship.

- To create or restore nesting in the AP Elements panel, press Ctrl and then drag the AP div's name over the name of the desired parent AP div. When the parent AP div is outlined—selected—release the mouse button to create the nesting relationship.

- Nested AP divs can be stacked in the AP Elements panel just like other AP divs. A nested AP div can even be nested within another nested AP div.

- You can also nest or restore nesting in the Document window by clicking the AP div's anchor point and then dragging it inside the target parent AP div, releasing the mouse button when the anchor is in the desired position. The nested AP div—or its anchor—can be dragged into its final position as desired.

- A child AP div inherits certain properties of the parent AP div, such as the visibility setting (see the next section for more information on visibility).

Control AP Element Visibility

- Making an AP element or elements invisible can be helpful to "quiet" the onscreen complexity of a Web page so that you can work on one AP element at a time.

- Controlling visibility also allows you to set up sophisticated interactive effects in which elements switch or display and disappear as a result of a visitor's actions.

  ✔ *You use behaviors to create effects like these. You learn about behaviors in Lesson 6.*

- You can control AP element visibility from the AP Elements panel or the Property inspector.

- To hide an AP element in the AP Elements panel, click to the left of the AP element's name to display the closed eye icon ☁. When the eye is closed, the AP element is hidden (see the illustration above).

- Note in the previous illustration that the child AP div inserted within Element3 is also hidden. The child AP div inherits the visibility setting of its parent AP div.

- Click the closed eye icon ☁ next to the AP element to show a hidden AP element. The closed eye icon changes to an open eye icon ☁.

  ✔ *To hide or show all AP elements at the same time, click the eye column heading until the desired view is achieved. To reset to the blank default mode, click on the individual eye icon until it is removed.*

- Using the Property inspector gives you greater control over visibility settings for nested AP divs. Select an AP div and click the Vis list arrow on the Property inspector to see a list of visibility attributes.

  - Select *hidden* to make the AP div and its contents invisible.

  - Select *visible* to make the AP div and its contents visible.

  - Select *inherit* to determine the AP div's visibility based on the parent AP div's visibility setting.

  - The *default* setting typically provides the same attributes as the *inherit* setting.

- Using the Vis list, you can set a child AP div's visibility to differ from that of its parent. For example, you can make the child AP div visible while the parent AP div is hidden.

Advanced AP Element Properties

- With an AP element selected, click on the expander arrow of the Property inspector to see advanced settings that control the appearance and functionality of AP divs in different browsers (see the following illustration).

Advanced AP element properties

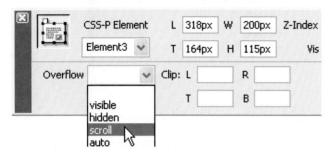

- The Overflow property controls an AP div's behavior when the AP div's content is larger than its size. Choose from the following options:
  - Select *visible* to increase the AP div's size so that all content is visible. The AP div expands down to contain all text or images.
  - Select *hidden* to maintain the AP div's size and crop any content that does not fit. No scroll bars are provided.
  - Select *scroll* to add scroll bars to the AP div regardless of whether the contents exceed the AP div's size.
  - Select *auto* to make scroll bars appear only when the AP div's content exceeds its boundaries.

    ✔ *Scroll and auto settings do not display in the Document window. You must preview the AP div in a browser to see the scroll bars.*

- Use the Clip settings to control the size of AP element content by specifying in pixels (or another measurement system) how much content to remove from each side of the AP div. This is useful when an image is too large for an AP div. You can crop parts of an image that do not contribute to your page.

Convert AP Divs to Tables

- Pre-version 4 browsers do not support AP elements. However, Dreamweaver offers an option to convert an AP div layout to a table so that the page can be viewed by any browser version.

    ✔ *Before converting an AP div layout to a table, you must unnest nested AP divs and make sure AP divs do not overlap.*

- To convert AP divs to a table, use the Modify>Convert>AP Divs to Table command.

- The Convert AP Divs to Table dialog box (see the following illustration) gives you a number of options for the conversion.

Convert AP Divs to Table dialog box

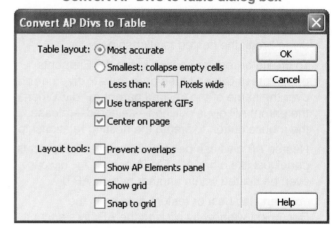

- *Most accurate* creates a table cell for every AP div. Additional table cells are created to replace the original spacing between AP divs.

- *Smallest: collapse empty cells* specifies that the AP divs' edges should be aligned if they are positioned within the number of pixels entered in Pixels wide box. This option results in a table with fewer empty rows and columns.

- *Use transparent GIFs* fills the table's last row with transparent GIFs. This allows for tables that are consistent in appearance from browser to browser.

    ✔ *Transparent GIFs are invisible GIF images used to adjust layout.*

- *Center on page* automatically centers the new table in the page.

- The resulting table layout may still need some work to merge cells and reposition content (see the following illustration), but this option is faster than recreating a layout.
- It is also possible to convert a table to AP divs. In this process, each cell becomes an AP div.

AP divs converted to a table

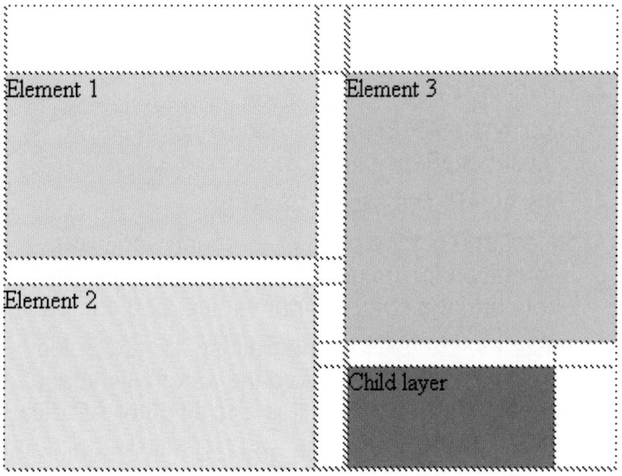

Element 1

Element 3

Element 2

Child layer

PROCEDURES

Set Overlap Options

1. Display the AP Elements panel.
2. Select the **Prevent overlaps** checkbox to prevent overlap.
3. Clear the **Prevent overlaps** checkbox to allow overlap.

Change Stacking Order

In the AP Elements panel:

- Click **Z-index** number and type new number.
- Select AP element name and drag to new position in name list.

In Property inspector:

- Select **Z-Index** number, type new number, and press ↵Enter or click in the Document window.

Nest AP Divs

1. Activate AP div that will become parent element.
2. Insert child AP div using one of AP Elements preferences in the Preferences dialog box.
3. Format nested AP div as any other element.

Change Visibility

To hide AP element:

1. Select AP div to hide.
2. Click to left of AP div name in the AP Elements panel to display 🐛 icon.

   OR
- Click **Vis** list arrow on Property inspector and select **hidden**.

To show hidden AP element:

- Click 👁 icon in AP Elements panel.

   OR
- Click **Vis** list arrow on Property inspector and select **visible**.

To give child AP div a parent AP div's visibility setting:

- Click **Vis** list arrow on Property inspector and select **inherit**.

Convert AP Divs to Table

1. Reorganize any nested AP divs and adjust AP divs to prevent overlap.
2. Click **Modify** . . . . Alt+M
3. Point to **Convert** C
4. Click **AP Divs to Table** . . . . A
5. Select options for table display.
6. Click ☐ OK ☐ .

EXERCISE DIRECTIONS

1. Start Dreamweaver and open the **cincitorial** site.

2. Open **praise.html**.

3. Display the AP Elements panel and clear the Prevent overlaps checkbox if necessary.

4. Hide all AP divs except training.

5. Select and cut the praise paragraph and client information for Training Solutions (this includes the quote and the contact's name, title, and company).

6. Paste the cut text into the training AP div. Select the None format to remove the automatic space above the paragraph in this and all other AP divs.

7. Cut the praise paragraph and client information for Lion Press. Make the lion AP div visible and paste the text into this AP div.

8. Hide the lion AP div and make the quentin AP div visible.

9. Cut the testimonial and client information for Quentin-Stevens and paste this text into the quentin AP div.

10. Cut the last praise paragraph and client information. Make the peters AP div visible and paste the cut text into the AP div.

11. Click below the intro AP div anchor (just below the navigation bar) and insert blank paragraphs at the left edge of the page as necessary to move the link and the table down past the last AP div.

12. Make all AP divs visible.

13. Add the "stripe" AP div down the center of the page as follows:

    ■ Beginning about ½" from the right edge of the intro AP div, draw a new AP div from the top of this AP div to just below the peters AP div. The AP div should overlap the left edge of the training AP div about ½". (See Illustration A.)

    ■ Name the AP div **stripe** and add background color of #CC3333.

    ■ Fine-tune the size and position: Set a Left measurement of 281 and a Top of 170. Set a Width of 70 and a Height of 625.

14. Change the stacking order so the stripe AP div has a Z-index number of 1.

15. Create a nested AP div within the link AP div and name the child AP div **picture**.

16. Create a copy of the JHorner.jpg image and insert the copy in the picture AP div, adding the alternate text **People link**. Resize the picture to 60 by 66 pixels, and then resize the picture AP div to fit closely around the image.

17. Create another nested AP div within the link AP div to the right of the picture. Name the AP div **linktext**.

18. Type the following text in the linktext AP div:

    For more information on our staff, click the picture.

19. Create a link from the image in the picture AP div to **people.html**.

20. Save your changes and preview the page in the browser. Your page should look similar to Illustration A. If the AP divs do not automatically expand in the browser to fit the text, you can delete the Height measurement for each AP div in the Property inspector to allow the AP div to expand in your browser.

    ✔ Note that the text is too close to the edges of the AP divs. You will find out how to fine-tune text position in an AP div when you learn about style sheets in Exercises 39 and 40.

21. If necessary, return to Dreamweaver and add space under the AP divs to move the table and the *Back to Top* link down so they do not obscure the AP divs.

22. Close any open pages and the browser and exit Dreamweaver.

Illustration A

CinciTorial Co.
Editorial Services

CinciTorial Clients Speak Out

| Contact | People | Praise | Services | Specialties |

CinciTorial has worked with publishers, corporations, and organizations to produce high-quality books, reports, training materials, and other publications. Listen to what our clients say about us:

"I didn't think we had a prayer of meeting our deadline on the training materials we needed for a seminar. CinciTorial took on the job and produced the text and accompanying CDs on schedule."

> **Jay Fries**
> **Training Coordinator**
> **Training Solutions**

"Thanks, CinciTorial, for your excellent work on our Basic Applications series. As a result of your heroic efforts, we're first to market, and our books look better than the competition!"

> **Maggie Jenkins**
> **Senior Editor**
> **Lion Press**

"We've worked with CinciTorial since the beginning, and we've always found them to be highly professional as well as downright fun. We plan to continue to use their development and production services into the next century."

> **Tyler Stanislowski**
> **Production Manager**
> **Quentin-Stevens Inc.**

"We know when we hand a project over to CinciTorial that it will come back to us on time and ready for the printer. We feel very fortunate to work with their great people."

> **Lennie Makarios**
> **Project Coordinator**
> **Peters Press**

 For more information on our staff, click the picture.

ON YOUR OWN

1. Start Dreamweaver and open the practice page you created in the last On Your Own exercise.

2. Reposition AP divs as desired to overlap, or add an AP div such as the unifying stripe in the previous Exercise Directions.

3. Change stacking order to display all AP divs attractively.

4. Create at least one nested AP div.

5. Practice with the visibility and overflow settings. (Remember, you can view scroll settings only in the browser.)

6. Save your page and preview your page in the browser, and then make any final adjustments to the layout in Dreamweaver. Use the Property inspector to size and position AP divs absolutely.

7. If desired, convert your layout to a table. (You must make sure no AP divs overlap to use this feature.)

8. Save your page and close it.

9. Exit Dreamweaver.

Exercise | 37

Skills Covered

- **About Frame Pages**
- **Create a Frameset**
- **Work with Frames**
- **Add Content to Frames**

Software Skills   A frame page allows you to display several Web pages at the same time in specified areas on the page. You can set up links in a page in one frame to open pages in another frame or create many other kinds of layouts and uses for frames. Dreamweaver's tools make frame page building easy. You only need to plan the layout and choose the content.

Application Skills   In this exercise, you will create a frameset in place of the CinciTorial home page. As you insert a new frame for the home page, you will name each frame in the frameset to comply with accessibility standards.

TERMS

Frame A container for Web page text displayed within a *frameset*.

Frameset A container for HTML frames.

NOTES

About Frame Pages

- The term *frame page* is used to describe a page that contains several **frames**. Frames are regions on an HTML page that contain a specific HTML page.

- In Dreamweaver, a frame page is known more properly as a **frameset**. The frameset has a name and a page title, but its only content is the frame definitions.

- Each frame in a frameset contains a page that has its own name and page title. Pages displayed in frames consist of text, images, and links just like any other Web page and can be formatted with backgrounds, styles, and other effects.

Create a Frameset

- You have several options for creating a new frameset:
  - Insert frames manually in a new or existing document to create a new frameset.

- Use a page design from the Framesets category on the Dreamweaver Welcome Screen window to create a new frameset with frames in place.

Insert Frames Manually

- You have two options for inserting frames into a new or existing document:
  - Use the Insert>HTML>Frames command and select the frame(s) to insert from the submenu.
  - Click the ▢ ▾ Frames button from the Layout tab of the Insert bar to display the same list of frame options and select one to insert.

- Both options allow you to insert a single frame, such as a left or top frame, or several frames at once, such as the Left and Nested Top Frames option, which inserts both a left and top frame designed to fit neatly together.

- The Frames list on the Insert bar can be more helpful if your page already has some content. Existing content is represented by the blue area of the thumbnail, with new frames shown as white areas (see the following illustration).

**Frames list offers basic
and complex frame layouts**

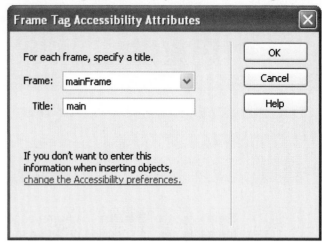

	Left Frame
	Right Frame
	Top Frame
	Bottom Frame
	Bottom and Nested Left Frame
	Bottom and Nested Right Frame
	Left and Nested Bottom Frame
	Right and Nested Bottom Frame
	Top and Bottom Frames
	Left and Nested Top Frames
	Right and Nested Top Frame
	Top and Nested Left Frames
	Top and Nested Right Frame

Frame Tag Accessibility Attributes dialog box

- If you have specified in the Preferences dialog box that you want to be prompted to enter accessibility information for frames, the Frame Tag Accessibility Attributes dialog box displays immediately after you select a new frame option for a page. Use this dialog box to set a title for each frame in the frameset (see the illustration at the top of the next column).

- Click the Frame list arrow to display each default frame name (such as mainFrame) and then type a meaningful title for the frame in the Title text box. The title attribute is used by a screen reader to identify each frame.

- When you insert a new frame in any page, Dreamweaver shows the new frames and any

existing content in a new frameset, with the borders between frames clearly visible on the screen (see the illustration at the bottom of the page). You can drag a frame's border to adjust the size of the frame.

- You can further divide a frame into additional frames using the Modify>Frameset command to display a submenu of split options.

    - Split Frame Left and Split Frame Right insert a border that divides the current frame in half vertically.

    - Split Frame Up and Split Frame Down insert a border that divides the current frame in half horizontally.

    ✔ *Create only two or three frames in a frameset. More than three frames can make the page look confusing.*

- The distinctions between these split directions are more relevant if a frame already contains content.

New page divided into two frames

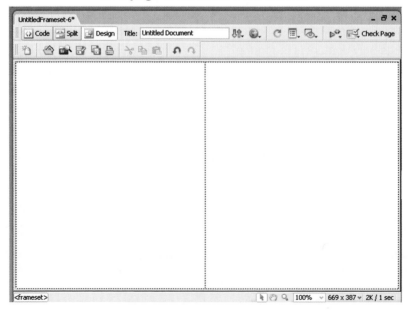

The existing content always moves into the new frame, so choose the split type that will keep your content where you want it.

✔ *If you inadvertently choose the wrong split type, simply use the Edit>Undo command to reverse the split.*

Use a Frameset Page Design

- Another way to create a frameset is to use one of the page designs from the New Document or Welcome Screen's Frameset category. The New Document dialog box offers fifteen frameset choices similar to those listed on the Frames button's drop-down list.

- Selecting one of these page designs opens a new page with the specified frame borders in place.

Work with Frames

- To work with frames, you need to know how to activate and select frames, name frames, and save frames and framesets.

Activate or Select a Frame

- Some operations, such as adding content, require the frame to be active. Other operations, such as changing frame properties, require the frame to be selected.

- To *activate* a frame, simply click in it to position the insertion point. When a frame is active, you can add and format content, save the frame's page, and apply page properties such as background color and a page title.

- To *select* a frame, hold down the Alt key and click in the frame. The frame's borders show a dotted outline to let you know the frame is selected (see the following illustration).

- A selected frame also displays frame information in the Property inspector, such as the frame's name, source, and border options.

- The distinction between activating and selecting is extremely important when working with frames. If you find you cannot perform a specific operation, check the Procedures section at the end of this exercise to determine whether you should activate or select a frame.

Name a Frame

- You will find it helpful to name the frames you create (or change the default names Dreamweaver supplies). Note that even if you have already supplied a title, you still need to provide a name for each frame. Name and title attributes serve different functions in the code.

LeftFrame is selected

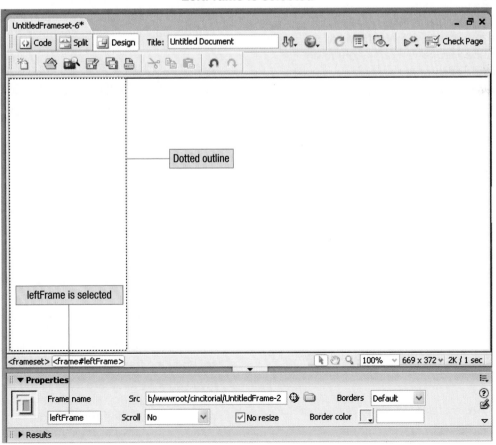

- It is especially important to name frames if you want to link from one frame to another because you must specify the name of the frame in which the linked page will open.

- Name a frame using the Property inspector. *Select* the frame, click in the Frame name text box, and type the desired name. Frame names should reflect the content or function of a frame. A frame that holds a logo at the top of a page, for example, might be named *logo*.

Save Framesets and Frames

- Saving a frameset and its frames pages can be confusing for first-time Dreamweaver users, because the frameset page itself and each frame's page must be named and titled.

- The easiest way to save the frameset is to use the File>Save Frameset command. This command saves only the frameset, not the frame pages within the frameset.

- After saving the frameset, be sure to give the frameset page a title in the Page Properties dialog box. If you issue the Modify>Page Properties command directly after saving the frameset, you can be certain the page title applies to the frameset, not one of its frames.

  ✔ *You can also type a new page title in the Document toolbar's Title box.*

- If you intend to create new content in a frame, you must also name and title the page in that frame. You can do so by clicking in the frame to *activate* it and issuing the File>Save Frame command.

- As you work with the frameset, use the File>Save Frameset command often to save changes to the frameset and its frames. You can also save changes to a specific frame by clicking in it to activate it and then clicking Ctrl + S.

  ✔ *Save changes to all frames at once using the File>Save All command.*

  ✔ *Remember, if the page name within parentheses in the title bar shows an asterisk, changes have been made since the last save. This is your signal to save again.*

Add Content to Frames

- You have two choices for adding content to a frame in a frameset:

  - You can simply begin typing in the frame to insert content in the frame, or you can paste text that has been copied or cut from another location.

    ✔ *Remember, you must activate a frame before you can add content to it.*

- You can link the frame to an existing Web page. When the frameset is opened, that Web page appears in the frame.

- If you intend to link a frame to a Web page, you can save time by creating that Web page before creating the frameset.

- As you begin to add content to frames, you will find the Frames panel extremely useful to manipulate the frames. The Frames panel (see the following illustration) shows the frame layout of the frameset and the names you have assigned each frame.

Frames panel

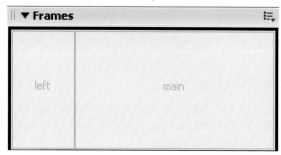

- You can quickly select any frame in the frameset by clicking the corresponding frame in the Frames panel. This operation can be faster than the Alt + click method of selecting a frame.

Set Frame Source

- If you want an existing Web page to open in a frame, you must specify that page as the frame's *source*. Specify a frame source in the Property inspector.

- *Select* the frame to link to a source and type the address of the source page in the Src text box on the Property inspector. You can also click the 📁 Browse for File button and navigate to the source page.

  ✔ *Or, click the ⊕ Point to File icon and drag it to the desired source page in the Files panel.*

- Dreamweaver assumes that you will choose a Web page from the current site folder, but you can select a page at any Internet address.

- The Src text box displays the name of the source page and the page immediately opens in the selected frame (see the illustration at the top of the next page).

- The Src text box will not be empty when you begin this operation. It will contain a placeholder name (such as UntitledFrame-2) for the HTML document set up in the frame when the frame was created.

- If you choose to create a new Web page in the frame, you rename this default placeholder name when you save the frame's page.

Link frame to source page

E-Commerce Connection

E-Commerce Legislation
The increasing importance of e-commerce in world markets has led to a corresponding increase in legislation to deal with issues critical to e-commerce, such as electronic signatures, electronic fund transfers, software piracy, and online privacy.

Investigate E-Commerce Laws
Use the Internet to search for information about e-commerce legislation in this country and around the world. Write a report in which you identify several key pieces of legislation that relate to e-commerce and analyze how that legislation affects e-commerce.

PROCEDURES

Create a Frameset

In a new, blank page or existing document:

1. Click **Insert** . . . . Alt+I
2. Point to **HTML** . . . . H
3. Point to **Frames** . . . . S
4. Click the desired frame option, such as **Left**, **Right**, **Top**, **Bottom**, **Bottom Nested Left**, etc.

   OR

1. Display the Layout tab in the Insert bar, if necessary.
2. Click ▢ ▾ to display list of frame options.
3. Click a predefined frame layout from the drop-down list.

OR

1. In the Welcome Screen window, click **Framesets**.
2. Select the desired option from the Framesets list.
3. Click [Create].

   OR

1. Click **File** . . . . Alt+F
2. Click **New** . . . . N
3. Click **Page from Sample**.
4. Click **Frameset** in Sample Folder list.
5. Select the desired option from the Sample Page list.
6. Click [Create].

Specify Accessibility Tags for Frames

In the Frame Tag Accessibility Attributes dialog box:

1. Click the **Frame** list arrow to display a frame in the current frameset.
2. Type new title for the frame in the **Title** text box.
3. Repeat steps 1 and 2 until all frames have new titles.
4. Click [OK].

Modify a Frame by Splitting into Additional Frames

1. Click **Modify** . . . . Alt+M
2. Point to **Frameset** . . . . . . F
3. Click desired type of split:
   - **Split Frame Left** L
   - **Split Frame Right** . . . . . R
   - **Split Frame Up** . . . . . . U
   - **Split Frame Down** . . . . . D

Activate or Select a Frame

To activate a frame:

- Click anywhere in frame to position insertion point.

To select a frame:

- Hold down Alt and click in frame.

  OR
- Click frame name in Frames panel.

  OR
- Click Frameset Property inspector's RowCol Selection window.

To select a frameset:

- Click any frame border in the frameset, if borders are displayed.

  OR
- Click border that surrounds frames in Frames panel.

Name a Frame

1. Select frame to name.
2. Click in the **Frame name** text box and type a one-word name.
3. Press ↵Enter or Tab⇥ to complete the naming action.

Save and Title a Frameset (Ctrl + S)

Immediately after creating frameset:

1. Click **File** . . . . Alt+F
2. Click **Save Frameset** . . . . . S
3. Type name for frameset as for any other Web page.
4. Click Save.
5. Click **Modify** . . . . Alt+M
6. Click **Page Properties** . . . . P
7. Type page title as for any other Web page.
8. Click OK.

Save a Frame (Ctrl + S)

1. Activate frame to save.
2. Click **File** . . . . Alt+F
3. Click **Save Frame** . . . . . . S
4. Type desired page name.
5. Click Save.

Save Changes to Frames

1. Click **File** . . . . Alt+F
2. Click **Save All** L

Display Frames Panel (Shift + F2)

1. Click **Window** . . . . Alt+W
2. Click **Frames** . . . . M

Add Content to a Frame

- Activate frame and type text or paste text that has been cut or copied from other location.
- Modify frame's page properties as for any other Web page.

Set Frame Source

1. Select frame to link to source.
2. Click in **Src** box on Property inspector and type address of source page.

   OR

   Click **Browse for File** button 📁 on Property inspector and navigate to address of source page.

   OR

   Click **Point to File** button ⊕ on Property inspector and drag it to the desired source page.

EXERCISE DIRECTIONS

1. Start Dreamweaver and open the cincitorial site. You will create a new frameset page with a contents frame at the left to hold links that will open the Web site's pages in a main frame. You will name the frameset index.html so it will operate correctly as the site's home page.

2. Make the following preparations:
   - Open index.html and cut from the page the series of links beginning with *Contact Us*.
   - Create a new blank HTML page and paste the cut links on the page. Save the page as contents.html with the page title **Contents**.
   - Change the page title for the index.html page to Welcome to CinciTorial.
   - Save and close contents.html and index.html.
   - In the Files panel, rename index.html as home.html. Do *not* update links because you will create a new index.html page.

3. Open home.html. If necessary, display the Layout tab of the Insert bar.

4. Display the Frames list and click the ☐ Left Frame button to create a new frame to the left of the current page content. Change the title of *mainFrame* to main and the title of *leftFrame* to contents.

5. Save the new frameset as index.html and supply the page title Welcome to CinciTorial.

6. Name the new frame contents and the frame that holds existing text main.

   ✔ *Remember, specifying a title is not the same as specifying a name. Use the Property inspector to supply a name for each frame.*

7. Select the contents frame and set its source as contents.html. The links you cut from the previous index.html page open in the frame. Adjust the frame width if necessary to display all links on one line. Your page should look similar to Illustration A.

8. Close any open pages and exit Dreamweaver.

Illustration A

Contact Us

Client Praise

Our People

Services

Our Specialties

We build computer books

Read our Mission Statement

Welcome to CinciTorial

CinciTorial is . . .

- Application textbooks
- Practice manuals
- Instructors' notes
- CD- and Web-based support materials

Working with CinciTorial is as easy as 1—2—3:

1. Contact us and set up a consultation.
2. Establish fee and work schedules
3. Sit back and relax!

ON YOUR OWN

1. Start Dreamweaver and open the gardencenter site.
2. Reconfigure the events.html page as a frames page by following these steps:
   - Delete the horizontal rules on this page.
   - Cut the Spring information and paste it in a new document titled springevents.html with the page title Spring Events.
   - Cut the Summer, Autumn, and Winter information and paste it in new documents (a new document for each season) with appropriate names and page titles.
   - Cut the copyright information to remove it from the page.
   - Remove the remaining named anchors and the link to the top of the page and any blank paragraphs below the introductory text.
   - Save changes to events.html and close the page.

3. Rename events.html as intro.html and don't update links.
4. Create a new page and apply the Top Frame option on the Insert bar. Change frame titles to intro for the top frame and main for the main frame.
5. Save the frameset as events.html with the title Garden Center Events.
6. Name the top frame intro and the main frame main.
7. Set the sources for each frame as follows:
   - Link the **intro** frame to intro.html.
   - Link the **main** frame to springevents.html.

   ✔ Don't worry if the frames do not fit the source material very well. You will adjust the frames in the next exercise.

8. Save all open pages and exit Dreamweaver.

Skills Covered

- **Change Frame and Frameset Properties**
- **Set Frame Target for Links**
- **Preview a Frameset**
- **Modify Page Properties**

Software Skills   Change frameset and frame properties to adjust the display of frame content. When setting up links to display pages in a frameset, you must specify the correct frame target. Previewing a frameset can help you avoid errors in linking.

Application Skills   In this exercise, you will continue working on the new CinciTorial home page. You will adjust frame page properties and modify links to open in the proper frames.

TERMS

No new terms in this exercise.

NOTES

Change Frame and Frameset Properties

- By selecting frames and the frameset, you display the Frame Property inspector and the Frameset Property inspector. These panels allow you to change a number of properties, including border properties, frame resize and scroll options, and frame width.

Modify Frame Properties

- In addition to setting a name for a frame and specifying its source, you can change scroll settings, resize options, border properties, and frame margins.
- The frame's Scroll setting controls the display of scroll bars in the frame.
  - Select *No* if you want to prevent scroll bars from displaying. This setting is suitable for frames that have little content.
  - Select *Yes* or *Auto* to display scroll bars if the frame's page is longer than the frame's height. Auto will cause scroll bars to appear automatically if the browser window is resized.
  - The *Default* setting uses whatever the browser's setting is, which is typically Auto.

- Selecting the No resize checkbox prevents users from dragging the frame's borders in the Web browser to resize the frame.
- You can set border options for each frame in a frameset as well as the frameset itself. Frame border properties override frameset border properties, however.
  - Select *Yes* from the Borders drop-down list to display borders for the active frame.
  - Select *No* to remove borders. To remove all borders in a frameset page, you must select the No option for each frame.
  - Selecting *Default* will display or suppress borders depending on the browser's default setting, which is usually Yes.
  - Use the Border Color palette to choose a border color.
- Setting border options for frames can require patience. If you apply one color border in one frame and another in an adjoining frame, for example, only one of the border colors will display. You may need to experiment with frameset and frame border options to achieve a desired effect.
- If you expand the Frame Property inspector, you can set margins—space between the borders and

the frame's content—in pixels for frame width and height.

- If you create a frameset using a predefined frameset, the Scroll setting is No and No resize is selected by default for the new, empty frame or frames. The main frame, which contains existing text, has no scroll or resize limitations. You can modify these settings, however, as discussed previously.

Modify Frameset Properties

- To change frameset properties, you must select the entire frameset rather than one of its frames. Select the frameset using one of the following options:

  If borders are displayed in the frameset, click any border.

  - In the Frames panel, click the heavy border that surrounds all frames.

- The Frameset Property inspector (shown in its expanded form in the first illustration below) allows you to specify border options for the entire frameset and set a width for each frame.

- Choose which frame you want to work on in the RowCol Selection window. The selected frame is shaded.

- You can specify whether the frameset will display borders, the border color, and the border width.

  ✔ If you create a frameset using a predefined frameset, the frameset is set to the No Borders option. You must delete the 0 from the Border width box to display the borders for the frames.

- In the expanded area of the Frameset Property inspector, specify the width of a frame in pixels or

percent. You can also set a relative size for a frame that will change depending on the size of the browser window.

Set Frame Target for Links

- A common use for frames in a frameset is to insert links in one frame that open pages in other frames. For example, you may insert a list of links such as a table of contents in a frame at the left side of a page. Clicking a link in the left frame opens a page in the main frame of the frameset.

- When you create a link from text or an image in one frame that will open a page in another frame, you must tell Dreamweaver which frame to open the page in.

- As you have set up links throughout this course, you have probably been aware of the Target box associated with the Link box in various dialog boxes and panels.

- You use the Target list options (see the second illustration below) in the Property inspector to tell Dreamweaver which frame to open a linked page in.

- To set up a link from one frame to another, follow this procedure:

  - Select the text or image that will be used for the link.

  - In the Link text box in the Property inspector, specify the page that will open when the link is clicked.

  - Click the Target list arrow to display a list of the frames in the current frameset (see the second illustration below).

Frameset Property inspector

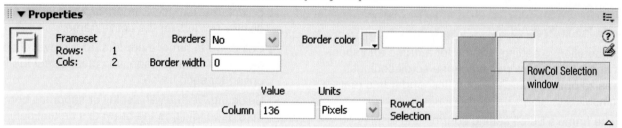

Select a target for link

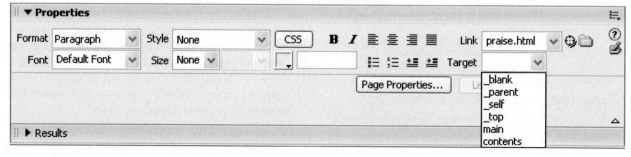

- Select the frame in which you want the page to open.
- In addition to the frames in the current frameset (such as main, contents), the Target list includes four other default targets: _blank, _parent, _self, and _top. Use these targets as follows:
  - Choose the _blank target to open the linked page in a new browser window while also keeping the current browser window open.
    - ✔ *This is a good choice if you are linking to a page outside your Web site.*
  - Choose _parent to open the linked page in the current frameset, replacing all frames.
  - Choose _self to open the linked page in the frame that also contains the link, replacing all content in this frame.
  - Choose _top to open the linked page in the outermost frameset, replacing all frames.
- If you have only one frameset on a page, _parent and _top function in the same way. If you have more than one frameset in a page, _parent replaces the frameset of the current frame and _top replaces all framesets on the page with the linked page.
- Consider the use of each frame on your page as you set up links. If you have a frame that functions as a contents area, it should never display other content. The main frame on the page should be used to display the main content of the site.
  - ✔ *Target settings are most important when working with frames. You can, however, use the _blank Target setting with any link on any kind of Web page to open the linked page in a new browser window.*

Preview a Frameset

- Before you can preview a frameset, you must save all frames and the frameset itself.
- You can click in each frame you have modified and use the Ctrl + S shortcut to save changes, and use the File>Save Frameset. Or simply use the File>Save All command to save everything at once.
- If you have not saved all elements of the frameset before issuing the Preview in Browser command (or pressing F12), Dreamweaver displays the dialog box shown in the following illustration.

Prompt to save changes

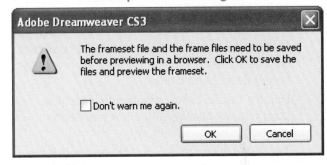

- Clicking [OK] saves all frameset elements so you can preview your frameset page.

Modify Page Properties

- So far, you have used the Page Properties dialog box to create page titles, apply background images, and choose page background colors.
- You can use the options in the Page Properties dialog box (see the following illustration) to make other changes to a page's properties that can improve or control the page's appearance.

Modify page properties in the Page Properties dialog box

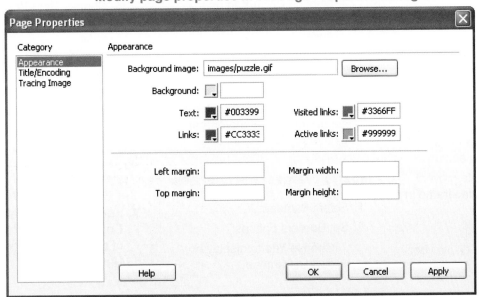

✔ Note that the Page Properties dialog box shown in the previous illustration is the one that displays when Dreamweaver is using HTML tags rather than CSS tags. The dialog box has more categories and somewhat different options when CSS tags are the default.

■ The default text color is black, because black supplies the best contrast to most background colors. You can, however, choose any color for text using the Text color box. Try a dark blue color, for example, for a colorful contrast to a white background.

■ An easy way to customize a page's appearance is to change the color used for links. The default link color is a bright blue.

■ The Page Properties dialog box lets you choose three different colors for a link.

   ■ Use the Links color box to choose the color that will display when you first insert a link on a page, before it has been used.

   ■ Use the Visited Links color box to select the color that will display after a link has been clicked.

   ■ The Active Links color box lets you choose the color that will display when a visitor actually clicks on a link.

■ Choosing different colors for these three states does more than provide additional color and interest on a page. If you choose different colors for Links and Visited Links, visitors to your site can also track which links they have already visited on a page.

■ You can add margins to pages using the four margin setting boxes. If you need to add margins to a page, Internet Explorer requires you to specify Left margin and Top margin settings; Netscape requires you to specify Margin width and Margin height settings.

   ✔ To make sure margins appear as you want them in all browsers, provide settings for all four margin boxes.

■ To change document encoding, click the Title/Encoding option in the Category list. You will most likely accept the default encoding choice of Western (Latin1). This is the encoding used for characters on the page. You can choose from many other encoding options, however, such as Japanese, Chinese, and Cyrillic.

■ If you would like to use a design created in a graphics program as a basis for page layout, you can "trace" the design using the Tracing Image option in the Page Properties dialog box.

■ Specify the file name of the image you want to trace and then use the Image Transparency slider to determine how transparent you want the image to appear.

■ With the image displayed on the page, you can create a table, AP divs, or frames on top of the image to recreate the design. The image being used will not display in the browser.

PROCEDURES

Modify Frame in Property Inspector

1. Select frame to modify.
2. Set Scroll property:
   ■ Choose **No** to prevent scroll bars from displaying.
   ■ Choose **Yes** or **Auto** to display scroll bars when necessary.
   ■ Choose **Default** to use browser's scroll default.
3. Select **No resize** to prevent visitors from resizing frame in browser.
4. Set Border options:
   ■ Choose **Yes** to display border.

   ■ Choose **No** to suppress border.
   ■ Choose **Default** to use browser's border preference.
   ■ Click the **Border color** box 🔲 to display palette and choose border color.
5. Expand Property inspector to set margin width and/or margin height.

Modify Frameset Properties

1. Select frameset.
2. Set Borders options:
   ■ Choose **Yes** to display borders in frameset.

   ■ Choose **No** to suppress borders.
   ■ Choose **Default** to use browser's border preference.
   ■ Specify border width in pixels or type 0 to remove all borders.
   ■ Click **Border color** button 🔲 to display palette and choose border color.
3. Expand Property inspector to click frame to modify in the RowCol Selection window.
4. Specify width for frame in the **Column** box and choose units of measurement from the **Units** list.

Set Frame Target for Links

1. Click in link to select it.
2. Specify page to link to.
3. Click the **Target** list arrow and select a frame name from the current frameset or a default target such as _blank, _parent, _self, or _top.

Preview a Frameset (F12)

1. Click **File** . . . . Alt+F
2. Click **Save All** L
3. Click **File** . . . . Alt+F

4. Click **Preview in Browser** . . . . P, P, ↵Enter

   OR

   Click **preview/Debug in browser** button 🌐.
5. Select browser.

Modify Page Properties (Ctrl + J)

1. Click **Modify** . . . . Alt+M
2. Click **Page Properties** . . . . P
   - Click the **Text** color box and choose a new color for all text on the page or in a frame.

- Click the **Links** color box and choose a color that will display when a link is first inserted.
- Click the **Active links** color box and choose a color that will display when a link is clicked.
- Click the **Visited links** color box and choose a color that will display after a link has been clicked.
3. Click ‾OK‾.

EXERCISE DIRECTIONS

1. Start Dreamweaver and open the cincitorial site.
2. Open the index.html frameset. Use the Page Properties dialog box to make the following property changes to the contents.html page in the contents frame:

   ✔ *To make these changes, activate the frame by clicking in it.*

   - Apply the lightest yellow background color (#FFFFCC).
   - Change the color for active links to #990033 and the color for visited links to #009999.

   ✔ *Because you did not change the Links color, you will not see changes to link colors until you use the links in the browser.*

3. Select the frameset and specify a width for the contents frame of 18 percent. (Use the RowCol Selection window in the Frameset Property inspector to select the proper frame.)
4. Activate the contents frame by clicking in it and split this frame so the links remain at the top of the frame. (Use the Modify>Frameset menu command to split the frame.)
5. Name the new frame blurb.
6. Save the new frame's page as blurb.html and title it Blurb.
7. In the blurb frame, type the following information as shown, breaking each line with a line break <br>:
   We'll see you at
   ExpoPub in
   Chicago!

8. Adjust the blurb frame's width and height to eliminate scroll bars and set the Scroll property to No. Format the frame and its content as desired.
9. Remove borders on all frames.
10. The links in the contents frame's list are already set to the correct pages. Specify the _top frame as the target for each link.
11. You will need to make some changes to links that have already been inserted on home.html:
    - Change the target for the Read Our Mission Statement link to _top.
    - Change the target for the Pearson Web site link to _blank.
12. Save the frameset and each frame you have modified.
13. Preview the index.html frameset page in the browser and test all links. Your frameset should look similar to Illustration A, which shows a portion of the page.

    ✔ *You may need to Allow Blocked Content if you are using Internet Explorer in a Windows XP Pro setup with Service Pack 2.*

14. Close all browser windows.
15. Close any open pages and exit Dreamweaver.

Contact Us

Client Praise

Our People

Services

Our Specialties

We'll see you at
ExpoPub in
Chicago!

CinciTorial Co.
Editorial Services

We build computer books

Read our Mission Statement

Welcome to CinciTorial

CinciTorial is . . .

- Application textbooks
- Practice manuals
- Instructors' notes
- CD- and Web-based support materials

Working with CinciTorial is as easy as 1—2—3:

1. Contact us and set up a consultation.
2. Establish fee and work schedules
3. Sit back and relax!

Let us put the pieces together for you. Contact us today to learn how CinciTorial can computer books to market quickly, efficiently, and affordably.

See books we have produced for Pearson Publishing at the Pearson

ON YOUR OWN

1. Start Dreamweaver and open the gardencenter site.
2. Open the events.html frameset.
3. Adjust the intro frame to fit its contents so that no scroll bars display.
4. Modify the links to the different seasons in the intro material so that they refer to the correct pages and the pages open in the main frame.
5. Modify the links in the intro.html navigation bar so that the pages open in the full window. To do this, you will have to detach the navigation bar library item from the original. Don't forget to adjust the target of the small daylily link.
6. Format the frames as desired by changing page background colors or images, applying border color, and so on. Modify link colors if desired.
7. Preview the page in the browser and check all links. Make any final page adjustments in Dreamweaver.
8. Save all pages and exit Dreamweaver.

Skills Covered

- **About Styles and Style Sheets**
- **Use the Property Inspector to Create Internal CSS Styles**
- **Use the CSS Styles Panel to Create Internal CSS Styles**
- **Apply Internal CSS Styles**
- **Edit Internal CSS Styles**
- **Dreamweaver CSS Reference**

Software Skills   Use styles to create formatting rules that can easily be applied to other pages in the Web site. You can create internal Cascading Style Sheet (CSS) styles using the Property inspector or the CSS Styles panel and use the CSS Styles panel to apply and edit styles.

Application Skills   In this exercise, you will create a new Web site for CinciTorial and then create, apply, and edit CSS styles for the site. You will also redefine a standard HTML tag to change its appearance.

TERMS

Cascading Style Sheets (CSS) HTML 4.0 specifications that permit you to design style properties, save them, and apply them using global formatting at a later time.

Style A rule that specifies how to format an HTML element such as text, an image, or a specific tag.

Style sheet A collection of styles created for a page or Web site.

NOTES

About Styles and Style Sheets

- A **style** is a *rule* that contains instructions on how to format an HTML element. A style may be applied to text (like styles in a word processing program such as Word) or to other HTML elements such as images, AP divs, or frames. You can also create styles that apply to specific HTML tags such as the horizontal rule tag or a heading tag.

- A collection of styles created for a page or a Web site is called a **style sheet**. Using a style sheet, you can format a number of HTML elements quickly and easily. Dreamweaver supports **Cascading Style Sheets (CSS)**, style sheets developed specifically for use in Web design.

- There are several advantages to creating and using styles and style sheets:
  - Working with styles is much more efficient: Style rules need to be created only once but can then be applied multiple times on a page or throughout a Web site. If styles must be edited, they need to be changed in only one location and are then automatically updated throughout the site.
  - Styles offer a great deal more formatting options than HTML: Using styles, you can easily apply borders to any side of a paragraph, position images or blocks of content absolutely, specify space between lines of text, and other options that cannot be achieved with standard HTML coding.

- Styles are not as code-intensive as HTML: Styles take up less room in a document's code than HTML, which means the page's file size is smaller and it will often load more quickly. This is especially true for tags such as <font> which require a number of attributes and values each time a designer wants to adjust text appearance on a page.

- You have several options for creating and applying styles in Dreamweaver:

  - Create *internal (embedded) CSS* styles that are stored in the Head section of a page and can be applied only to text on that page.

  - Create an *external CSS* containing one or more styles that can be linked to all pages in a Web site.

    ✔ *You will work with the first option in this exercise, and you will work with external style sheets in the next exercise.*

  - Create *inline styles* within specific tags in an HTML document. Inline styles are not recommended, and Dreamweaver offers a utility for converting them to style sheets.

    ✔ *You will learn more about inline styles and conversion options in the next exercise.*

- There are several ways to create an internal CSS style. One of the easiest is to use the Style box on the Property inspector. Or you can use the CSS Styles panel in the CSS panel group or the Text>CSS Styles command. These options are discussed in the following sections.

Use the Property Inspector to Create Internal CSS Styles

- By default, Dreamweaver will collect all the formats you apply to text or a paragraph and display them in the Style box on the Property inspector (see the following illustration). Formats are applied to a default style name, such as *style1*.

- For Dreamweaver to display style formats in the Property inspector, you must select *Use CSS instead of HTML tags* in the Preferences dialog box's General settings.

  ✔ *You deselected this option earlier in the course to learn about applying HTML formats.*

- Note in the previous illustration that the font size options differ when you are using CSS tags. Rather than employing the 1 through 7 sizes common in HTML formatting, CSS styles use sizes that look more like those available in a word processing program: 9, 10, 12, 14, 16, 18, 24, and 36. You can also select a unit of measurement for the font size, including pixels, points, inches, centimeters, millimeters, ems, and percentages.

- You also have the option of using descriptive font sizes, such as xx-small, small, medium, and large, or smaller and larger.

  ✔ *Dreamweaver accessibility reports suggest using relative font sizes measured in ems or percentages rather than specific measurements in pixels or points.*

- To save a new style using the Style box, click its list arrow and select Rename from the pop-up menu. Then, in the Rename Style dialog box (see the following illustration), type a new name for the style.

Rename a style

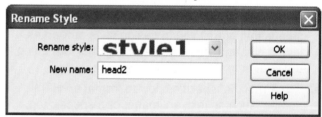

- The Results panel opens with the Search tab active to show you the code of the style and indicate that the style has actually replaced the formats you used to create it.

- The new style information is stored in the Head section of the document enclosed between the <style> </style> tags. The style name displays in the CSS Styles panel.

Formats applied to text

Dreamweaver displays formats that can be saved as styles

Cats

Style box displays default style with formats

Format None | Style **style** | CSS | **B** *I*
Font Verdana, Arial | Size 24 | points | #993300

A style created this way can be used only on the page on which it is created, but it can be used anywhere on that page, as many times as desired. You will learn later in this exercise how to apply internal CSS styles.

Use the CSS Styles Panel to Create Internal CSS Styles

You can also create CSS styles using the CSS Styles panel in the CSS panel group. The CSS Styles panel is designed to help you easily create, apply, and manage CSS styles.

✔ *The CSS Styles panel offers many more options for creating styles than the Property inspector. You are encouraged to use the CSS Styles panel for all but the simplest styles.*

The CSS Styles panel (see the following illustration) lists all CSS styles (also called *rules*) that have been defined for or linked to the current page.

A new CSS style displayed in the CSS Styles panel

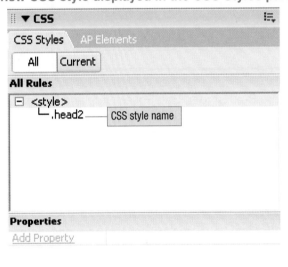

To create a new CSS style using the CSS Styles panel, click the ⬧ New CSS Rule button in the CSS Styles panel to open the New CSS Rule dialog box (see the illustration at the top of the next column).

New CSS Rule dialog box

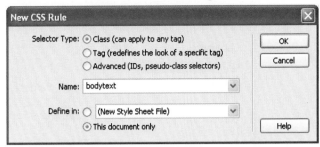

You can also access this dialog box using the Text>CSS Styles>New command, if you are more comfortable working with menus.

First provide a name for the new style. The name must then begin with a letter, and it can consist of only letters and numbers.

Then choose the type of style to create:

- The *Class (can apply to any tag)* option allows you to create a style you can apply to any HTML element. For example, if you define a class style to add 15 pixels of padding, you can apply it to an image as well as a paragraph.

- The *Tag (redefines the look of a specific tag)* option allows you to choose a specific HTML tag (such as h1) and modify the tag with your own formats.

- The *Advanced (IDs, pseudo-class selectors)* option lets you define formats for a specific combination of tags or tags that contain the ID attribute.

✔ *The term selector in the New CSS Rule dialog box refers to the terminology of CSS rules. A rule consists of the selector, which is the name of the styled element, and the declaration, which defines the style's attributes.*

Dreamweaver allows you to define a style for the current document only (that is, the current page only) or create a new style sheet file in which to store new styles.

If you choose the option to define styles in a new style sheet file, Dreamweaver allows you to name and save the style sheet to create an *external style sheet*. You will learn more about external style sheets in the next exercise.

Define a New Class Style

If you chose to create a new class style, clicking OK in the New CSS Rule dialog box opens the CSS Rule definition dialog box for your new style (see the illustration at the top of the next page). You can define formats in eight different categories.

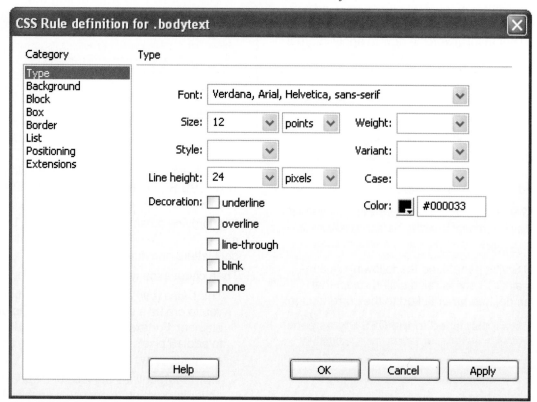

You will use the options in the Type category most often when creating new text formats. You can select the desired font, size, style, weight, and color, as well as "decorations" such as underlines or a blink feature. Note that you can also specify line height to add space between lines that can give text a less crowded look.

Use the Background category to set a background color or image for the style. If you select a background image, you can tile it on the page using the Repeat option in the Repeat list.

Use the Block category to set vertical and horizontal alignment options. You can also create indents in this category.

The Box, Border, List, Positioning, and Extensions categories offer additional settings to fine-tune the style: create box shapes for content, add borders to any or all sides of the style object, create custom list settings (such as bullet characters you specify), position an object absolutely, or apply extensions that insert page breaks or change the look of the cursor.

After you have finished selecting options for the new style rule, the style name displays in the CSS Styles panel. The names of new class styles begin with a period in the styles list. Information about an internal style is stored in the Head area of the document, as shown in the following illustration.

Internal styles stored in the Head section of the page

```
3    <head>
4    <meta http-equiv="Content-Type" content="text/html; charset=utf-8" />
5    <title>New Arrivals</title>
6    <style type="text/css">
7    <!--
8    .head2 {─────────────────────────────────────────────  Style selector (name)
9        font-family: Verdana, Arial, Helvetica, sans-serif;
10       font-weight: bold;
11       font-size: 24pt;─────────────────────  Style declaration enclosed in { }
12       color: #993300;
13   }
14   .bodytext {
15       font-family: Verdana, Arial, Helvetica, sans-serif;
16       font-size: 12pt;
17       line-height: 24px;
18       color: #000033;
19   }
20   h3 {
21       font-family: Verdana, Arial, Helvetica, sans-serif;─────  Redefined HTML tag
22       font-size: 18px;
23       font-weight: bold;
24   }
25   -->
26   </style>
27   </head>
```

Redefine HTML Tags

- You can modify standard HTML tags to format elements uniquely for a page or Web site. To redefine an HTML tag, choose the *Tag (redefines the look of a specific tag)* option in the New CSS Rule dialog box. Instead of supplying a name for a new style, you select the tag you want to redefine from the Tag list (see the following illustration).

Choose HTML tag to redefine

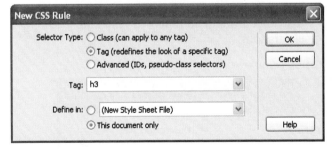

- Choose formats for the HTML tag in the CSS Rule definition dialog box, just as when creating a class CSS style.
- Redefined HTML tags are stored in the Head section of the page along with other internal styles created for that page.
- As with an internal class style, if an HTML tag is redefined for a specific page, it displays its new formats *only* on that page.

Apply Internal CSS Styles

- Internal styles display in the CSS Styles panel. To apply a style to text, click in or select existing text or position the insertion point where you intend to begin typing new text. To apply a style to an object such as an image, select the object. Then:
  - Right-click the style name in the CSS Styles panel and select Apply.
  - Or, click the Style list arrow in the Property inspector and select the style name from the pop-up menu.
- You can also apply a style from within the CSS rule definition dialog box using the `Apply` button.
- If you mistakenly apply a style, click the Style list arrow and select None from the pop-up menu to remove the style.
- After you redefine an HTML tag, apply the new tag just as you would apply the HTML format. Apply paragraph and heading formats from the Property inspector's Format list, for example, or apply a redefined unordered list tag using the Unordered List button on the Property inspector or the Text>List>Unordered List command.

Edit Internal CSS Styles

■ The new CSS Styles panel makes it easy to edit a custom CSS style rule. Select the **All** button to show all styles available for the current document. The following illustration shows that two custom styles have been created, .head2 and .bodytext, and the h3 tag has been redefined.

Edit a style by adding or modifying properties

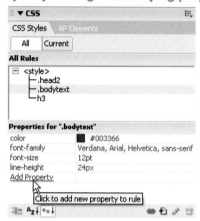

✔ *The <style> heading above these new styles is a default style sheet name used if you do not create a named style sheet.*

■ To see style information for a particular element, click on the element in the document and select the **Current** button. The CSS Styles panel changes to show a summary of the style information for that element and tells you in which rule each attribute is defined.

■ Both the All and the Current versions of the CSS Styles panel display a Properties pane at the bottom of the panel. The Properties pane displays all properties that apply to the currently selected rule or element.

■ In the preceding illustration, for example, the Properties pane shows that the .bodytext rule has four properties: color, font-family, font-size, and line-height.

■ Modify any of these properties by clicking in the box to the right of the property and selecting a new option from those available. Changes to a rule's properties are immediately displayed in the Document window for elements styled with that rule.

■ Add new properties to a rule by clicking the Add Property link as shown in the preceding illustration to display a list of properties that can be applied to the current rule.

■ After selecting a new property, click in the box to the right of the property name to choose an option for the property. This is the same basic procedure you learned for selecting an HTML tag and its attributes using the Tag inspector.

■ You can also edit an internal style by double-clicking the rule in the CSS Styles panel or by clicking the rule and then clicking the ✐ Edit Style button to open the CSS Rule definition dialog box. After you make changes and close the dialog box, all text formatted with that style updates immediately to show the new formats.

Dreamweaver CSS Reference

■ Cascading style sheets are a complex subject. You can get additional help with CSS styles on the Reference panel. Click the Book list arrow and select O'REILLY CSS Reference, and then choose a style you want information on (see the following illustration).

CSS styles Reference panel

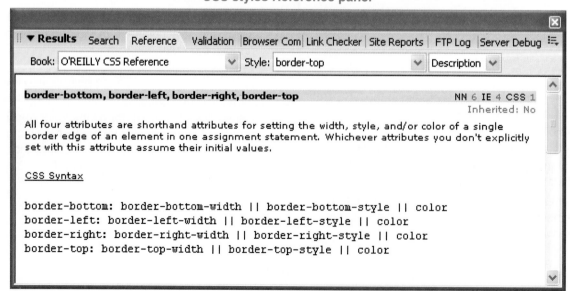

PROCEDURES

Create Internal CSS Styles for Current Page Only (Ctrl + Shift + E)

1. Format text or element as desired to display formats in the Style box on Property inspector.
2. Click the **Style** list arrow and select **Rename**.
3. In the **New name** box, type name for style.
4. Click OK.
   OR
1. Click **Text** . . . . Alt+T
2. Click **CSS Styles** C
3. Click **New** . . . . N, ↵Enter
   OR
- Click **New CSS Rule** button ▣ on the CSS Styles panel.

In the New CSS Rule dialog box:

1. Choose the **Class (can apply to any tag)** option.
2. Type name for style preceded by a period.
3. Choose the **This document only** option.
4. Click OK.
5. Select options from the **Type**, **Background**, **Block** and other categories, as desired.
6. Click OK.

Apply a Style

1. Click in paragraph to style, or select text, or select object.
2. Right-click the style name in the CSS Styles panel.
3. Click **Apply**.
   OR
1. Click in paragraph to style, or select text, or select object.

2. Click the **Style** list arrow on Property inspector.
3. Select the desired style from the pop-up list.

Remove a Style

1. Click in text or object formatted with style.
2. Click the **Style** list arrow on Property inspector.
3. Select **None** from the pop-up list.

Redefine HTML Tags and Apply

1. Click **Text** . . . . Alt+T
2. Click **CSS Styles** C
3. Click **New** . . . . N, ↵Enter
   OR
- Click **New CSS Rule** button ▣ on the CSS Styles panel.

In the New CSS Rule dialog box:

1. Choose the **Tag (redefines the look of a specific tag)** option.
2. Select tag from the **Tag** drop-down list.
3. Click OK.
4. Select options from the categories in the CSS Rule Definition dialog box.
5. Click in paragraph to style.
6. Display Property inspector, if necessary.
7. Click a formatting option (such as Format list or Ordered List) and select redefined HTML style.

Edit CSS Styles

1. Click rule to edit in the CSS Styles panel.
2. Locate property to change in the Properties pane of the CSS Styles panel.
3. Click in box to right of property and select new option for property.
   OR
1. Click rule to edit in the CSS Styles panel.
2. Click the **Add Property** link in the Properties pane of CSS Styles panel.
3. Select new property for current rule.
4. Click in box to right of property and select option for property.
   OR
1. Double-click rule to edit in the CSS Styles panel.
2. Select new options in the CSS Rule definition dialog box.
3. Click OK.

EXERCISE DIRECTIONS

1. Start Dreamweaver and open the Preferences dialog box from the Edit menu. In the General settings, select *Use CSS instead of HTML tags*.

2. CinciTorial is preparing to launch a new Web site that contains online tutorials for popular applications. In this exercise, you will create the new Web site and set up styles for one of its pages. Begin by creating the Web site using the Site Definition wizard in Dreamweaver:
   - Define a new site named tutorials.
   - Do not use a server technology, and choose to edit local copies and upload later.
   - Store the files at the same local location you have used for cincitorial, such as C:\Inetpub\wwwroot.
   - Select None for the remote server option and do not enable check in/check out.

3. In Dreamweaver, open ⊙ products.html and ⊙ index.html from the Lesson 5 Data folder and save them to the new Web site folder.

4. Set index.html as the site's home page.

5. Activate products.html and modify the links in the navigation bar to point to **home.html**, **news.html**, **products.html**, and **support.html**.

   ✔ *There is currently no home.html page. You will fix this link in the last lesson of the book. You will add the other pages to the site in Lesson 6.*

6. Click in the word *Word* in the first column of the table and create a new style using the CSS Styles panel:
   - Name the style tableheads and specify that the style is for this document only.
   - Select Times New Roman font, 12-point size.

   ✔ *Be sure to change the units of measurement for the font size to points, or your text will be very small!*

   - Select the bold weight and color #990033.
   - Choose the center text alignment from the Block category.

7. After you finish defining the style, apply it to the *Word* text.

8. Apply the .tableheads style to the *WordPerfect* text in the first column.

9. Modify the style as follows using the CSS Styles panel. Notice how the new properties are applied immediately to the table text.
   - Select the .tableheads rule in the CSS Styles panel.
   - Change the font-family property to the Arial font.

   - Change the text-align property to Left.
   - Click Add Property in the Properties pane and select the background-color property.
   - Choose the lightest yellow background color (#FFFFCC).

10. Create a second custom style using the Property inspector's Style box. Use the following formats: Arial font and 12-point size. Rename the style tabletext. (Close the Results panel if necessary after creating the style.)

    ✔ *To create this style, select the first table text entry, Working with Word 2007, and apply formats to it.*

11. Apply the .tabletext custom style to all entries in the right column of the table. Close the Results panel.

12. Modify the .tabletext style in the CSS Styles panel to have the lightest blue background (#CCFFFF). Note that the first table text cell will not be fully shaded, because of the <span> tags inserted when you defined the style. You can solve this problem by selecting the table cell again along with the one directly below it and reapplying the style.

13. Redefine the h3 HTML tag to be Arial, 12 point, bold and italic, and the dark blue color #000066.

14. Use the Property inspector to apply the Heading 3 style to the Word Processing head above the table.

15. Note that you have an additional style showing in the <style> list, which was used to format the links on the page. Rename this style to linktext. Close the Results panel after it shows you the renaming information.

16. You want to add an image as a decorative element for the page. Follow these steps to insert the image and create a style for it:
    - Create a new folder in the site with the name images.
    - Click to the right of the heading *Online Tutorials* and insert the ⊙ keyboard.jpg image from the Lesson 5 Data files. Save the image in the **images** folder and supply an appropriate alternate text.
    - Create a new internal class rule named imagestrip and display the Positioning category in the CSS Rule dialog box.

- Choose a Type of absolute, set Width to 379, set Height to 40. In the Placement area of the dialog box, set Top to 45 and Left to 200.
  - Apply the new style to the image.

17. Save changes and preview this page in the browser. It should look similar to Illustration A.

18. Close any open pages and the browser and exit Dreamweaver.

Optional:

For more practice with CSS styles, open the cincitorial site and the praise.html page. Display the CSS Styles panel to see the AP divs listed. For each AP div, open the CSS Rule dialog box just as you would to edit a style and use the Box category to add padding properties for top, left, right, and bottom to insert 6 pixels of padding between the text and the edges of the layer. (Adjust position of AP divs if necessary after adding the padding to avoid overlap.) You may also want to create a style that adds padding to the left or right sides of the pictures on the people.html page to provide more precise spacing adjustments than can be achieved using the H Space HTML tag. These are excellent examples of how you can modify the look of page elements with CSS styles in ways that aren't possible using standard HTML coding.

Illustration A

Home   News   Products   Support

Online Tutorials

You will find complete listings of CinciTorial's online tutorials in the tables below.

Word Processing

Word	Working with Word 2007
	Mastering Word 2007
	Using Word to Create Multipart Documents
WordPerfect	Working with WordPerfect X3
	Mastering WordPerfect X3

ON YOUR OWN

1. Start Dreamweaver and open the gardencenter site.

2. Open the index.html page and create an internal style to add padding to the right side of the daylily image.

3. Open the page that gives information about spring events.

4. Create custom CSS styles for this page; for example:
   - Redefine the *Spring* heading to use formatting other than that currently in use.
   - Create a style to apply to the introductory paragraph below the heading.
   - Create a style that can be applied to the event names. You may want to experiment with a border above or below the heading.
   - Create a style that can be applied to the event descriptions. You may want to experiment with line height and indention for this style.

5. View the page in the browser and then make any changes to the formats you think will improve the page.

6. Close all open pages and exit Dreamweaver.

Exercise | 40

Skills Covered

- **Create External Cascading Style Sheet**
- **Dreamweaver CSS Layouts and Samples**

- **About Inline Styles**
- **Manage Styles**

Software Skills   You can create an external cascading style sheet that can be used throughout the Web site. After you create the external style sheet, attach it to any page in the site to have access to the defined styles. Dreamweaver also offers sample style sheets and CSS layouts you can use as is or customize for your site.

Application Skills   In this exercise, you will create an external style sheet for the CinciTutorial site. You will then create and apply the styles to both pages in the site and adjust styles to change appearance throughout the site.

TERMS

External style sheet A CSS in a separate text file with independent style definitions that can be linked to any HTML file.

NOTES

Create External Cascading Style Sheet

- If you want to apply styles to several Web pages in a site, you need to create an **external style sheet**. An external style sheet is so called because it is a separate, or external, file in a Web site. After you create the external style sheet and link it to the site's pages, any change you make to the external style sheet's styles will immediately be reflected in all pages linked to the style sheet.

- External style sheets have the file extension .css. After the style sheet itself has been saved, you add styles to it just as when creating internal styles or redefining HTML tags.

  ✔ *You cannot simply save a Web page as a .css page. It cannot be linked to a Web page and will generate an error if this is tried.*

Save New External Style Sheet

- As you have seen already, Dreamweaver allows you to create an external style sheet any time you use the New CSS Rule dialog box to define a cus-

tom style or redefine an HTML tag. You can reach this dialog box in a number of ways:

  - In any document, use the Text>CSS Styles>New command.
  - Click the ⊞ New CSS Rule button in the CSS Styles panel.

- In the New CSS Rule dialog box, specify the name of the first style for the style sheet or the tag to be modified and make sure (New Style Sheet File) is selected in the Define in section.

  ✔ *You can create an external style sheet with any page displayed, even one that already contains internal CSS styles. The internal styles, however, will not be included in the external style sheet.*

- Clicking OK opens the Save Style Sheet File As dialog box (see the following illustration) where you can specify a name for the external style sheet and save it in the current site.

Save an external style sheet in the current site

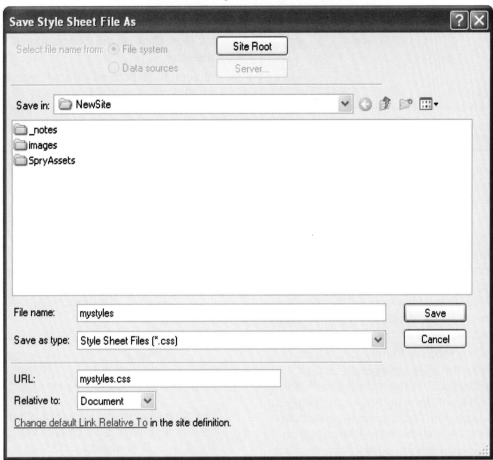

- After you save the style sheet, its name displays in the CSS Styles panel and the CSS Rule Definition dialog box opens so you can define your first style. This process can seem a little backward: You must supply the name of a new style before you have even created the style sheet, and after you save the style sheet, you must go back to defining that first style.

- The external style sheet document displays in the Files panel just like any other page document.

- The next time you define a new style, you have the option in the New CSS Rule dialog box of creating the style for the current document only or for the external style sheet. The style sheet's name is selected by default in this dialog box.

- As you define styles for the external style sheet, they are added to the style sheet document. You must save the external style sheet like any other document after you make changes to it.

- Apply styles from the external style sheet the same way as internal CSS styles. Note that the style information does not appear in a document's Head section after being applied from an external style sheet.

- Edit styles in an external style sheet the same way you edit internal CSS styles: Use the CSS Styles panel's Properties pane to modify current settings or add new properties to any selected style. These changes, once saved, update applicable attributes in any Web page that is linked to the style sheet, which makes for efficient, *global* style revisions.

Attach External Style Sheet to Existing or New Web Document

- After you have created an external style sheet, you can attach it to existing or new documents in the site. This allows you to access the same styles on all pages to ensure consistency throughout a site.

- To attach a style sheet to an existing document, open the page to which you wish to attach the style sheet and click the ● Attach Style Sheet button at the bottom of the CSS Styles panel. Or, use the Text>CSS Styles>Attach Style Sheet command. The Attach External Style Sheet dialog box opens, as shown in the following illustration.

- Type the name of the external style sheet, select it by clicking the File/URL list arrow to display a list of style sheets, or use the Browse... button to locate it in the current site.

- You will normally choose the Link option in the Attach External Style Sheet dialog box. If you select the Import option, the styles are directly imported into the document rather than linked to the external file. This option is suited for Web documents that might be used outside of the Web site in which the .css file resides.

- You can click the Media list arrow to see a list of target media for the style sheet, such as print, handheld, or Braille. This setting tells Dreamweaver to use the styles only for a particular medium, such as if a page is printed. Clicking the Preview button lists the style sheet's styles in the CSS panel so you can see what styles will applied with the style sheet.

- To attach the style sheet to a new document, click the ⊕ Attach Style Sheet button in the New Document dialog box, specify the desired style sheet in the Attach External Style Sheet dialog box, and allow Dreamweaver to create a relative path to the style sheet until you save the new document.

- The linked style sheet is now available to format your document. You can use the styles shown in the CSS Styles panel (or in the Format list on the Property inspector for redefined HTML tags) to apply formats just as when you create internal styles.

- The HTML code that controls the link to an external style sheet is stored in the Head section of a page. If you examine the page's code, you will see code similar to this:

```
<link href="tut_styles.css"
rel="stylesheet" type="text/css">
```

- If you choose to view the Head Content panel at the top of the Document window, you will see the link to an external style sheet represented by a 🔗 link icon. Click on the icon to open a Link Property inspector.

- You can have both an external style sheet and internal styles available for a specific Web page (see the following illustration) or even link more than one style sheet to a page.

CSS Styles panel with internal and external styles

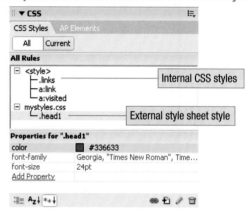

Dreamweaver CSS Layouts and Samples

- The New Document dialog box offers several options for creating documents with CSS formatting. Use a Dreamweaver CSS layout or sample style sheet to quickly create a page that already contains CSS styles.

Use a CSS Layout

- The Layout column of the New Document dialog box offers a number of CSS layouts you can use to start a new page. These layouts are new in Dreamweaver CS3.

- Select a layout to see a preview of the page layout with information on how the sections of the page are formatted (see the illustration at the top of the next page).

CSS layouts in the New Document dialog box

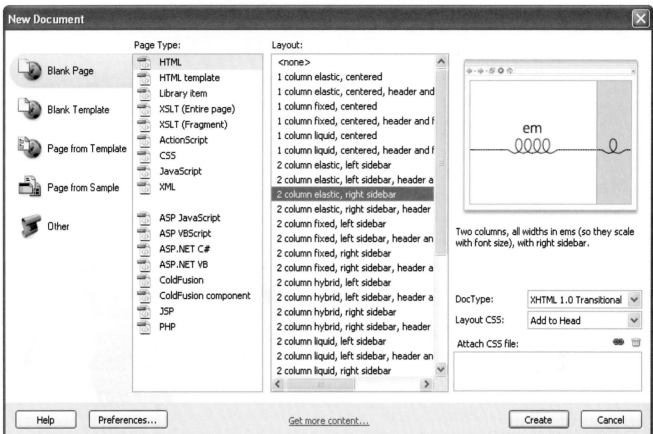

- The columns of these layouts can be fixed, liquid, elastic, or a hybrid of several of these options.

  - *Fixed* columns have a precise measurement in pixels.

  - *Liquid* columns are measured in percentage of browser width, so they can resize according to the size of the browser window.

  - *Elastic* columns are measured in ems, a width measurement that is related to the size of text. If a visitor changes the text size in the browser window, the layout adjusts accordingly.

- A new CSS layout page provides some details on how the page is structured (see the following illustration at the top of the next page) as well as sample text that can be replaced to create the desired page content. The CSS Styles panel contains a list of the styles used to create the page.

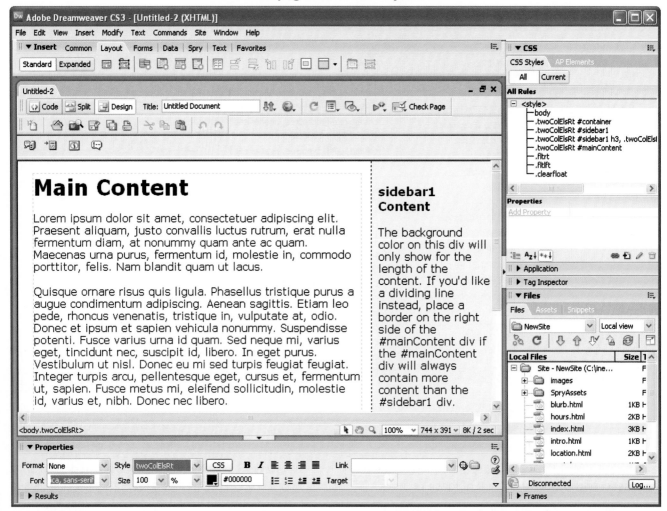

Use a Dreamweaver Sample Style Sheet

▪ Dreamweaver also offers sample style sheets that you can apply to any Web site. These sample style sheets are available in the New Document dialog box (see the illustration at the top of the next page).

▪ These style sheets range from the very simple—style sheets that just apply a specific font—to full designs that offer headings, sidebars, table and link formatting, and so on.

▪ After you select one of these style sheets, you save it in your site with the desired name and then use its styles the same way you use styles you have defined yourself.

About Inline Styles

▪ You have learned the two preferred methods of supplying styles for a Web page: creating internal styles on a single page or external styles that can link to many pages.

▪ It is also possible to create styles within any HTML tag. Such a style is called an *inline style*.

CSS style sheets available in the New Document dialog box

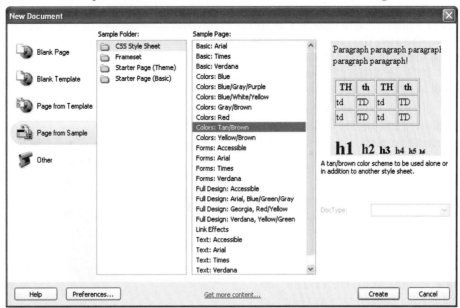

- The first illustration below shows an inline style created within a <p> tag.

- When a browser applies styles, it gives the highest priority to inline styles. This means that you can use inline styles to override other styles.

- However, the use of inline styles is discouraged in most instances. One of the benefits of using CSS is that the styles are located in one place in a page or style sheet, so that a designer can easily make changes to the styles. Having inline code sprinkled throughout a document defeats the real purpose of using CSS.

- Dreamweaver CS3 provides a handy utility for converting inline CSS to a rule. In a code view, right-click the inline style, click CSS Styles, and then click Convert Inline CSS to Rule. (Or, use the Text>CSS Styles>Convert Inline CSS to Rule command.)

- Dreamweaver opens the Convert Inline CSS dialog box, as shown in the second illustration below. Here you can convert the inline CSS to a new class, redefine an HTML tag, or create a new selector. The new CSS can be inserted in an existing external style sheet or added to the Head section of the document to create an internal CSS style.

Inline style that will adjust paragraph size and color

```
8   <body>
9   <p style="font-size: 10pt; color:#FF3300">Here is an inline style</p>
10  </body>
11  </html>
```

Convert Inline CSS dialog box

Manage Styles

- Style sheets supply a great deal of flexibility for formatting pages in a Web site. You can link an external style sheet to a template so that the styles are applied along with other template elements. Or, you can create internal styles for an editable area in a template.

    ✔ *You may need to tweak HTML code in the template to make sure the styles are applied correctly to the editable areas.*

- One of the great benefits of creating an external style sheet is that it can be used in any number of Web sites. You simply link to the style sheet from any site, saving to your current site's root folder when prompted.

- If you have defined internal styles on a page and want to add them to a style sheet, you can easily do so using a new feature, Move CSS Rules. You can move the rule to an existing or new style sheet. You can also duplicate a rule if desired.

- It is possible to apply more than one style to a text element, but doing so can lead to style conflicts. Style conflicts can give unexpected results because of the way browsers read the conflicting style tags.

- Browsers use the following rules to resolve style conflicts:

    - When two different styles are applied to the same text, browsers will display all attributes for both styles, unless the attributes conflict directly (for example, one applies a blue color and the other applies a purple color).

    - In the case of such a conflict, the browser will display the attribute of the style closest to the text in the HTML code.

    - Attributes from CSS styles will override HTML tag styles.

PROCEDURES

Create and Save a New External Style Sheet

To display the New CSS Rule dialog box:

1. Click **Text** . . . . Alt + T
2. Point to **CSS Styles** C
3. Click **New** . . . . N, ↵Enter
   OR
- Click **New CSS Rule** button 🔁 in the CSS Styles panel.

In the New CSS Rule dialog box:

1. Type the name for the first new style.
2. Select **(New Style Sheet File)** in the Define in section of the dialog box.
3. Click ⬓ OK ⬓.
4. Type name for the new external style sheet, including .css extension, in the **File name** text box.
5. Click ⬓ Save ⬓.

Create a New Style for an Existing Style Sheet

1. Click **Text** . . . . Alt + T
2. Point to **CSS Styles** C
3. Click **New** . . . . N, ↵Enter
   OR
- Click **New CSS Rule** button 🔁 in the CSS Styles panel.

In the New CSS Rule dialog box:

1. Type the name for the new style.
2. Click **Define in** and either accept the style sheet name in the Define in box or click list arrow to select another style sheet name.
3. Click ⬓ OK ⬓.
4. Continue the process of defining the new rule, as detailed in the previous exercise.

Attach an External Style Sheet to an Existing Web Document

1. Open page to link to external style sheet.
2. Click **Attach Style Sheet** button ⬛ in the CSS Styles panel.
3. Type the path to the style sheet.
   OR
   a. Click ⬓ Browse... ⬓.
   b. Navigate to the location of the style sheet and select it.
   c. Click ⬓ OK ⬓
4. Click ⬓ OK ⬓.

Attach an External Style Sheet to a New Document

1. Click **File** . . . . Alt + F
2. Click **New** . . . . N
3. Click **Blank Page** or **Blank Template**.
4. Click a page type.

    ✔ *Not all pages types allow style sheets to be attached.*

5. Click **Attach Style Sheet** button ⬚ at lower-right corner of New Document dialog box.
6. Type the path to the style sheet.
   OR
   a. Click [Browse...].
   b. Navigate to the location of the style sheet and select it.
   c. Click [OK]
7. Click [OK] when Dreamweaver suggests making the file:// path.
8. Click [OK].
9. Click [Create].

Move CSS Rules to New or Existing Style Sheet

1. Display the CSS Styles panel on the page that has styles you want to move.
2. Right-click the style to move.
3. Click **Move CSS Rules** on the shortcut menu.
4. Select an existing style sheet to move the rule to, or choose to create a new style sheet.
5. Click [OK].
   OR
   ■ Drag the style from one style sheet to another.

Delete a Style or Style Sheet

To delete a style:
1. Select style in the CSS Styles panel.
2. Click **Delete CSS Rule** button 🗑 on the CSS Styles panel.

To delete a style sheet:
1. Select style sheet name in the CSS Styles panel.
2. Click **Delete CSS Rule** button 🗑 in the CSS Styles panel.

EXERCISE DIRECTIONS

1. Start Dreamweaver and open the tutorials site.
2. Open the products.html page. Create a new external style sheet named tut_styles.css. Add the following styles to the style sheet:
   ■ Create a class style named mainhead that uses Times New Roman, 24 point, bold, and a cranberry color such as #CC0033.
   ■ Redefine the H2 HTML tag to use Times New Roman, 18 point, bold, and a medium blue color such as #3366CC.
   ■ Create a class style named text that uses Arial, 12 point, and a dark blue color such as #000099.
   ■ Create a final class style named firstpar that uses Arial, 18 point, a dark blue color such as #000066, and centered alignment.
3. Save the style sheet.
4. Make sure both pages in the Web site are attached to the tut_styles.css style sheet.
5. Apply styles on the pages as follows:
   ■ On index.html, apply .mainhead to the first heading (*Welcome to …*).
   ■ Apply the .firstpar style to the *CinciTutorial is* paragraph.
   ■ Apply the redefined Heading 2 to the word *Contents* near the bottom of the page.
   ■ Apply the .text style to the three paragraphs that begin with ellipses (. . .), the paragraph below the *Contents* heading, and the paragraph above the form in the blue column at the right.
   ■ On products.html, apply Heading 2 to *Online Tutorials* and .text to the paragraph below the heading.
6. Move the **h3** and **.linktext** rules from the internal style list to the tut_styles.css. Activate index.html and apply the h3 style to the heading *Career Corner* in the blue column.
7. You have decided the blue body text is not effective. Change the .text style's color to black. Note the style changes on both pages.
8. The .firstpar formats are not quite right. Change the size to 14 and alignment to left.
9. Save changes and preview this page in the browser. It should look similar to Illustration A.
10. Close any open pages and exit Dreamweaver.

Welcome to CinciTutorial

CinciTutorial is . . .

. . . A great way to learn the basics of many popular software applications.
. . . An online reference for features and skills.
. . . A useful review tool you can use to polish up skills for certification.

Contents

This site contains the following features:

ON YOUR OWN

1. Start Dreamweaver and open the gardencenter site.
2. Open index.html. Create an external style sheet named garden_styles.css and add the following styles to the style sheet:
   - A class style with a name such as bodytext to be used for paragraph text throughout the site. Define this style as desired.
   - A redefined HTML tag for any unordered lists in the site.
   - Styles for table headings and text for the tables in the site.
3. Attach the garden_styles.css style sheet to all the pages in the site except the form (including the template). Apply the styles you have created to the site pages.
4. Move the internal styles you created for the spring events page in the last exercise to the garden_styles.css style sheet.
5. Attach the new style sheet to the other pages used in the frameset for summer, autumn, and winter events and apply the styles as you did on the spring events page.
6. Preview the site in the browser to check your new styles.
7. Make any final adjustments to styles.
8. Save and close all pages and exit Dreamweaver.

Exercise | 41

Summary Exercise

Application Skills   In this exercise, you will embellish the High Ridge Swim Club site using AP elements and styles. You will redesign the home page using AP divs and create an internal CSS style to format copyright information throughout the site.

DIRECTIONS

1. Start Dreamweaver and open the highridge site.
2. Open index.html. Use AP divs to reorganize this page, as follows:
   - Create an AP div to hold the introductory text below the navigation bar. Cut the text and paste it in the AP div.
   - Create an AP div to hold the Club Features heading and the bulleted list that follows the heading.
   - Create two AP divs to hold the last two paragraphs on the page. Leave the library item as it is at the bottom of the page.
3. Give each AP div an appropriate name.
4. Change the alignment of the picture to Default so it moves to the left margin. Add a drop shadow effect to this picture as follows:
   - First hide all other AP divs so you can concentrate on the picture.
   - Create an AP div the same size as the picture and give it a name such as shadow.
   - In the shadow AP div, insert the ⊙ shadow.jpg file from the Lesson 5 Data folder. The AP div will automatically expand to hold the shadowed rectangle.
   - Nest an AP div inside the shadow AP div that is the same size as the picture, and name it picture.

   - Move the picture into the picture AP div. It will look as if it doesn't fit in the element correctly. You may want to save the page at this point and check how it looks in the browser. Adjust the position of the image slightly if necessary so that it fits completely over the gray shadow rectangle.
5. Move and resize the AP divs on the page to create a pleasing organization. Illustration A shows one possible layout. Check your layout frequently in your browser to make sure AP divs are positioned where you want them.
6. Change the background colors of AP div as desired. If you add color backgrounds to the AP div, consider using CSS padding to create a pleasing margin between the text and the AP div edges. Adjust stacking order as necessary.
7. Change the colors of links on this page if necessary to contrast well with AP div colors.
8. The horizontal rule above the copyright information is not very exciting. Use an internal CSS style to reformat the copyright library item as follows:
   - Open the copyright library item for editing.
   - Delete the horizontal rule above the copyright text.
   - Create a new CSS style that applies a top border to the text. Name the style appropriately and select formats for the border that will add some punch to this item.

- You may want to increase the line height of the text so the border does not sit right on top of the text.
- Apply the new style to the copyright text. Save and update the library item. (You will not see the border on the pages in Dreamweaver.)

9. Preview the site in the browser. You should see the new border on each page of the site.
10. Close all open pages and exit Dreamweaver.

Illustration A

High Ridge Swim & Tennis Club

Home   Information   News   Membership Swimming

Welcome to High Ridge! The High Ridge Swim & Tennis Club has been a part of the High Ridge community for more than 50 years and is one of the oldest clubs in the city. Our heritage is evident in the many mature trees scattered on the club grounds, but our facilities are completely contemporary.

Club Features

Members enjoy the following amenities:

- New clubhouse and changing facilities
- Eight-lane heated lap pool
- Separate diving/family pool
- Children's pool
- Six lighted tennis courts (available for year-round play)
- Sand volleyball court
- Basketball courts
- Shaded picnic area
- Children's playground and plenty of open space for running and jumping

For more information on joining High Ridge, visit our membership page.

In addition, the club offers free swimming lessons and tennis lessons. High Ridge has a silver-medal swim team that competes in weekly meets with other neighborhood clubs, as well as a highly competitive tennis team. Add to this mix a busy social schedule for both children and adults, and you have a great summer resource for family fun.

Exercise | 42

Application Exercise

Application Skills   In this exercise, you will reformat several pages of the Grand Theatre site with framesets.

DIRECTIONS

1. Start Dreamweaver and open the grand Web site.
2. Rename the index.html file as main.html. Do not update pages.
3. Open main.html and delete the navigation bar on this page, as well as the blank paragraph where the navigation bar was.
4. Create a new frameset by splitting this page vertically so the existing text moves into the right frame. Title and name the left frame navigation and the right frame main. Save the new frameset as index.html with an appropriate page title.
5. Save the new left frame page as navigation.html with an appropriate page title. Format the frame as follows:
   - Change the page background of navigation.html to #990000.
   - Create a vertical navigation bar using the ⊙ locationup.gif, ⊙ locationover.gif, ⊙ showup.gif, ⊙ showover.gif, ⊙ findup.gif, and ⊙ findover.gif files from the Lesson 5 Data folder. Link the location buttons to location.html, the show buttons to show.html, and the find buttons to jeffersonmap.html.
   - Insert several blank paragraphs above the navigation bar to move the buttons down, and adjust the frame size so there are no scroll bars in the Document window. Remove frame borders.
6. Preview the index.html page in the browser and check all links from the navigation frame. Your page should look similar to Illustration A.
7. Rename the show.html file as showintro.html. Do not update links. Open the showintro.html page.

8. Create a new frameset by splitting this page vertically so that the existing text moves into the right frame. Name and title the left frame links and the right frame intro. Save the new frameset as show.html.
9. Save the new left frame page as framelinks.html with an appropriate page title. Add content to the frame as follows:
   - Apply an appropriate background color to the frame.
   - Insert four paragraphs that read Screen 1, Screen 2, Screen 3, and Screen 4. Format the text as desired.
   - Cut the text and link (*For external reviews of shows, click here*) from the bottom of the showintro.html page and paste the text and link below the Screen paragraphs.
   - Change the target for the external link so that the browser will open a new window.
10. Now do some work on the showintro.html page:
    - Cut the heading and film listings for each of the four screens and paste the information in new documents with names such as screen1.html, screen2.html, and so on. Don't forget appropriate page titles.
    - On the showintro.html page, remove any extra blank paragraphs and delete the *back to top* link. Remove the named anchor at the top of the page.
11. Insert a new frame in the showintro.html page so that the existing text stays at the top. Name the new frame screens and save the new page as screens.html.

235

> ✔ Do NOT use the Modify>Frameset>Split command, or the links you create from the navigation frame will not work correctly.

12. Set the source of the *screens* frame to `screen1.html` (or the file name you used for the Screen 1 information).

13. Link the *Screen 1, Screen 2, Screen 3,* and *Screen 4* text in the links frame to the four files that contain film listings. Make sure you set the target so the pages open in the screens frame. Change the colors of links on this page if necessary to contrast well with the background color.

14. Save the page and then test the page in the browser and check all links. Make any necessary adjustments to links or frame properties.

15. Save and close all open pages and exit Dreamweaver.

Illustration A

Grand Theatre

Location

Show Times

Find Us

Now Showing at the Grand

Click here to see show times for our current releases.

How to Find Us

The Grand Theatre is located in the historic Madison Village area of Jefferson. Click here to see a selection of maps that will guide you to the general region and show you our exact location and parking options.

Grand Theatre Special Features

- Four screens
- Dolby® surround sound
- Concession stand specialties
- All matinees $6.00
- Bargain Tuesday $5.50 any show
- Senior citizen discounts on all evening shows

Mailing List

Join our weekly movie e-mail list for updated schedules, summaries of new movies, and news on upcoming events. The Grand Theatre Movie List will be sent to you every week. Sign up here!

Exercise | 43

Curriculum Integration

Application Skills   Your Discrete Math class is studying a curriculum that includes Fibonacci numbers and game theory. You have been given the choice of creating some Web material on either Fibonacci (more properly known as Leonardo of Pisa) or John Nash, who won a Nobel Prize for his work with game theory. Before you begin this project, locate:

- One or more Web sites that you can use for background information on Fibonacci numbers or game theory

- Information about Leonardo of Pisa or John Nash, including a picture

You will probably need to use equations in your site. To create superscripts, work in Code view and insert the ^{HTML tag before a superscript number. Close the tag with}. To create subscripts, use . You may then want to change the size of the superscripts and subscripts by selecting them in Design view and adjusting the font size.

DIRECTIONS

Create a new site with an appropriate name. Create a new page with a name appropriate to the subject you have chosen, such as gamehome.html. Then select one of Dreamweaver's external style sheets (you can select one from the New Document dialog box) and save it in the site with an appropriate name. (You may find it easier to use one of the Colors options; the full designs can be difficult for a novice.)

On your first page, insert some biographical information about the subject of your site, including a picture of Leonardo or John Nash. Be sure to indicate why this person is famous in his field. Use the styles from the external style sheet to format elements on the page, and add styles to the style sheet as you need them.

Create a second page that goes into more detail about the chief claim to fame of your subject. If you are working on Fibonacci, explain the concept of Fibonacci numbers and give some examples. If you are working on Nash, explain where game theory stood before he offered his approach to the theory, and explain his theory.

Link the two pages using stand-alone links or a navigation bar.

Test the site in a browser and make sure your equations (if you have used any) display properly.

Close the page and exit Dreamweaver.

Exercise | 44

Critical Thinking

Application Skills   In this exercise, you will continue to work on your personal Web site. Create an external style sheet for the site, attach it to all pages, and apply styles to ensure a consistent format throughout the site.

DIRECTIONS

- Open your personal Web site and display the home page.

- Create an external style sheet for the site and save it with an appropriate name. Add styles to the style sheet to control all the text items in the site. You may create new styles or redefine existing HTML tags.

- Link all pages to the style sheet and apply the styles to text elements. You may need to restore defaults on HTML tags before applying redefined tags to show the style sheet formats.

- Test the site in the browser to make sure all the styles are working correctly and look attractive.

- Close all open pages and exit Dreamweaver.

★ Add frameset to any page.
   name frameset & frames.

Lesson | 6
Create Dynamic and Interactive Pages

Exercise | 45

Skills Covered

- **About the Spry Framework**
- **About Spry Widgets**
- **Insert Spry Validation Widgets**
- **Create a Spry Menu Bar**
- **Create a Spry Collapsible Panel**
- **Create a Spry Accordion**
- **Other Spry Elements**

Software Skills   Use the Spry framework to add interesting interactive features to a Web site. Spry widgets allow you to create objects such as menu bars, validation form fields, collapsible panels, and accordions.

Application Skills   In this exercise, you will explore Spry widgets and add several to your CinciTutorial Web site.

TERMS

Spry A JavaScript library containing a number of interactive elements to place on Web pages.

Validation Process of checking that a form field contains an entry if required or a specific type of data.

Widget Page element that creates a specific kind of interactive content.

NOTES

About the Spry Framework

- **Spry** is a JavaScript library new in Dreamweaver CS3 that allows Web designers to build pages offering interesting interactive options.

- Using the Spry framework, you can add interactive or dynamic tables to a Web page that draw data from XML sources; insert Spry **widgets** such as menu bars, collapsible panels, or form fields with built-in validation; or apply Spry effects such as Appear/Fade or Highlight to give page content extra emphasis.

- Spry uses HTML, CSS, and JavaScript to create a variety of fun-to-use page elements. After creating each Spry object, you can customize it by modifying properties in the Property inspector or the CSS Styles panel.

- In this exercise, you learn about Spry widgets, page elements that allow you to provide a number

of interactive Web page features. You can learn more about creating a Spry table to display XML data in the Dreamweaver in Depth steps at the end of this exercise. Spry effects are covered in Exercise 47.

About Spry Widgets

- Dreamweaver CS3 includes a number of Spry widgets that present specific types of information on a Web page. The four Validation widgets, for example, are used to create four different types of form fields, and the Collapsible Panel widget creates an object that displays a panel of text when you click a heading.

- A widget is composed of HTML code that defines the widget's structure, JavaScript that controls the interaction between a visitor's actions and the object, and CSS coding used to format the widget.

- A widget is identified in Dreamweaver by a blue tabbed outline, as shown in the following illustration. Click the tab to modify or set properties for the widget.

Widget is identified by blue tabbed outline

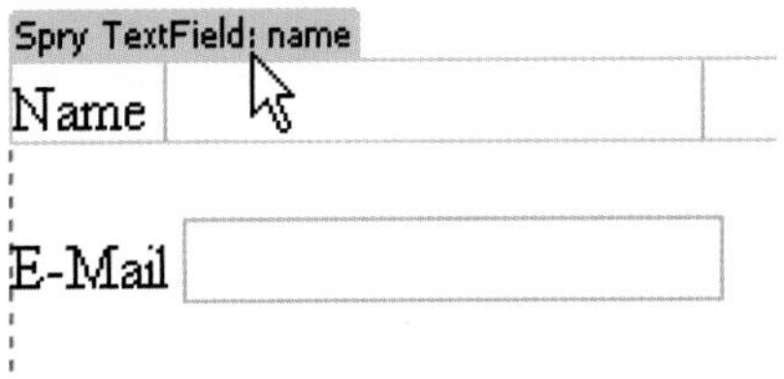

- The first time you save a page after adding a Spry widget (or any other Spry element), Dreamweaver prompts you to copy the files required for the element to your site, as shown at the bottom of the page.

- These files are stored in the SpryAssets folder and, as indicated in the dialog box, must be put on the server along with pages that use Spry elements to enable them to work properly.

- In the following sections, you will learn about several Spry widgets: Validation widgets, the Menu Bar widget, the Collapsible Panel widget, and the Accordion widget.

Insert Spry Validation Widgets

- You can use Spry Validation widgets to create a form that supplies visual interest to visitors as well as indicating clearly if the form data supplied is not correct.

- The following illustration shows a simple form created with Spry Validation widgets. Color coding and messages are used to give visitors feedback.

Form created with Spry form fields

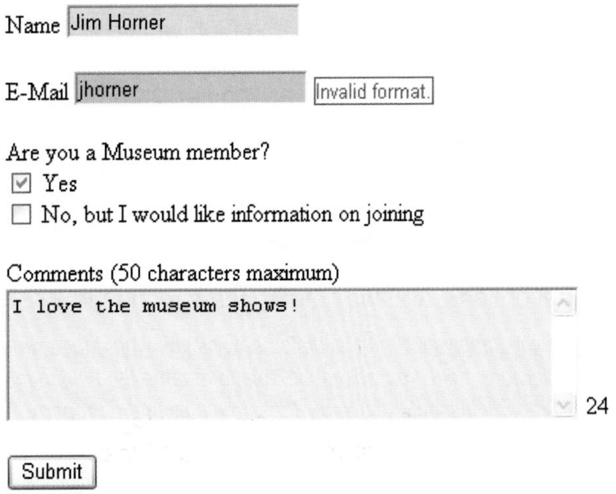

- The green color applied to the Name field indicates the required data has been entered correctly.

- The light orange color applied to the E-Mail field, and the message, indicate that the field does not contain a valid e-mail address.

- The yellow color applied to the Comments field indicates that an entry is being made to the field. Note that this field also has a counter at the lower-right corner to let a visitor know how many characters have been used for this character-limited field.

Dreamweaver prompts you to save Spry files

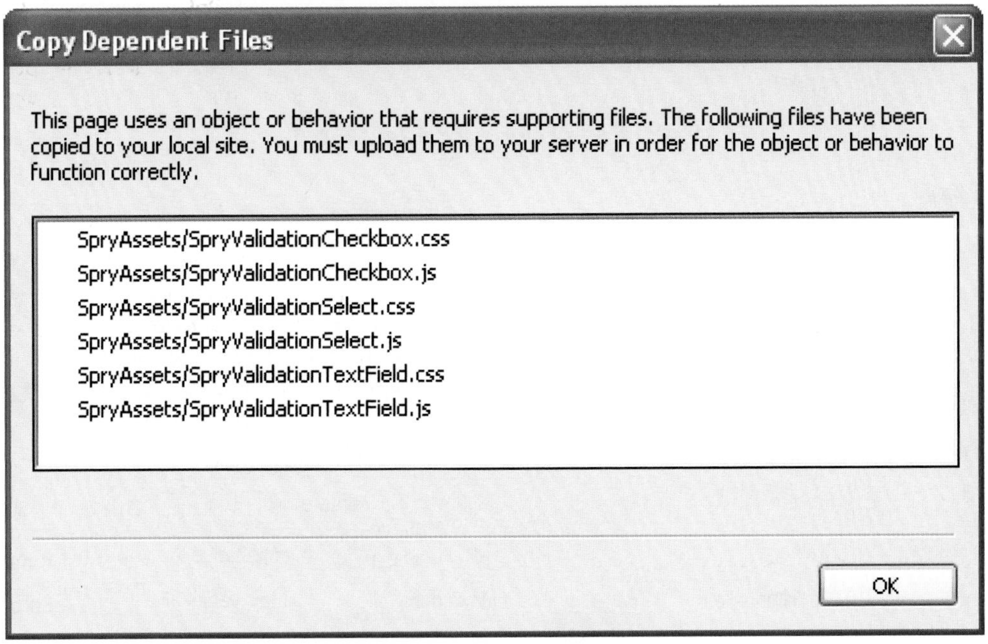

Copy Dependent Files

This page uses an object or behavior that requires supporting files. The following files have been copied to your local site. You must upload them to your server in order for the object or behavior to function correctly.

SpryAssets/SpryValidationCheckbox.css
SpryAssets/SpryValidationCheckbox.js
SpryAssets/SpryValidationSelect.css
SpryAssets/SpryValidationSelect.js
SpryAssets/SpryValidationTextField.css
SpryAssets/SpryValidationTextField.js

OK

Insert Spry Validation Widgets

- You can insert Validation widgets from the Form tab of the Insert bar or the Spry tab of the Insert bar, or use the Insert>Spry command and then select a widget from the submenu.

- Dreamweaver offers four Validation widgets: Text Field, Select, Checkbox, and Textarea. These widgets work in the same way as regular Dreamweaver form fields.

- When you insert one of these widgets, Dreamweaver displays the Input Tag Accessibility Attributes dialog box, just as when inserting a regular form field. Supply a label and any necessary label options, and the field appears in the form.

  ✔ *If you supply an ID in this dialog box, as you would for a regular form field, you will not be able to rename the field in the Property inspector, so apply the name only in the Property inspector.*

Set Properties and Validation

- To set properties for a Validation widget, you click the form field just as you would in any Dreamweaver form. The Property inspector supplies the usual properties for the field.

- When you insert a Spry Validation Select widget, for example, selecting the field gives you the standard List/Menu options so you can supply list items and values.

- When you select a Validation widget's blue tab, options for validating the widget display, as shown in the following illustration. **Validation** is the process of specifying what kind of information a form field should display and determining if an entry is required in the field.

- You can name the field, select the type of data that must appear in the field, choose a format if you have selected a data type such as Date or Time,

provide a pattern to use when inserting data, and supply a hint to help visitors supply the correct information.

- The Preview states list shows you how the field will look for each state that may apply to the field. Initial, for example, shows the field as it will appear when the form loads. If you have specified that the field is required, you can click the Required option in the Preview states list to see what the field will look like if a visitor fails to enter a value in the field. The Valid option shows you how the field will look if the visitor has entered valid data.

- You select the point at which validation occurs: Blur validates the field when the visitor clicks outside the field, and Change validates the field as the visitor is making a change inside the field. The Submit option is also selected by default to validate all fields as the form is submitted.

- Specify a minimum or maximum number of characters to keep entries within a range, and minimum or maximum values if the field requires a numerical entry.

- Select the Required box if visitors must supply an entry in a field. If you have supplied a pattern, such as the way a date must be entered, you can select Enforce pattern to require visitors to enter data according to that pattern.

- Validation options differ depending on the Validation widget you have chosen to enter, but you will always have options to name, preview, and validate the widget.

- After you have inserted Validation widgets, you can adjust text formatting or the formats applied to the fields to show various states by selecting the appropriate style rule in the CSS Styles panel and adjusting formats.

Validation options for a Text Field

Create a Spry Menu Bar

- A Spry Menu Bar widget inserts a navigation bar that displays drop-down and pop-out panels that link to pages in a site. If you have a complex site with many related pages, the Menu Bar widget makes it easy for a visitor to navigate.

- The following illustration shows a simple menu bar created with the Menu Bar widget. There are four main navigation links, Home, Products, News, and Support. Buttons that contain downward pointing triangles link to subordinate pages. The Tutorials subordinate page links to three additional pages.

Spry menu bar

- As shown in the previous illustration, the buttons in the menu bar change color when the mouse pointer hovers over them.

- The navigation buttons themselves are created with a complex arrangement of <ul> and <li> tags, and the text and background colors are controlled by CSS styles.

Insert a Menu Bar Widget

- You can insert a Spry Menu Bar Widget by clicking the 🖼 Spry Menu Bar button on the Spry tab of the Insert bar, or use the Insert>Spry>Spry Menu Bar command.

- The Spry Menu Bar dialog box opens to ask if you want to create a horizontal or vertical menu bar, and then displays the default menu bar on the page. The Property inspector shows the default items in the menu bar, as shown in the illustration at the bottom of the page.

Specify Menu Bar Entries

- You can create the button text and links for the menu bar in the Property inspector. The first column, with entries such as Item 1 and Item 2, represent the main menu buttons. The second column contains submenu options for each item.

- In the illustration below, for example, Item 1.1 in the second column is a page subordinate to the top-level button. It will display below the top-level button.

- To insert button text, replace the Item 1 placeholder in the Text box. Use the Link box to specify the page to link to. You can also supply a ToolTip for the link in the title box and a target for the link.

- Notice the # sign in the Link box in the illustration below. This # sign is called a *dummy link*. Dreamweaver requires an entry in this box, but if you don't want to create a link from a particular button, you can enter the # sign as a placeholder or type javascript:; in the Link box. The button will look like a link, and act like a link, but it won't open a page.

  ✔ *Dummy links can be a great help when creating behaviors, as they allow you to associate events with specific text that you format as a link. You will learn more about behaviors in the next exercise.*

New menu bar and Property inspector

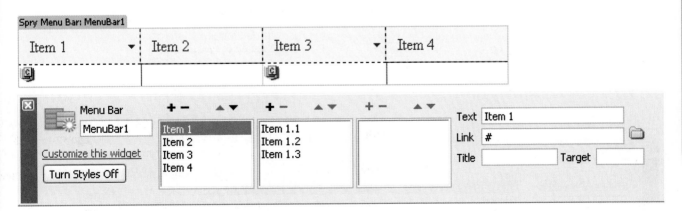

- You repeat the process of creating button names and links for the submenu items. If desired, you can create submenu items for each submenu item too, to create a structure like that shown in the illustration below.

- Use the ✚ Add menu item or ➖ Remove menu item button to insert or delete a menu item. You can reorder a menu item using the ▲ Move item up or ▼ Move item down button.

- If desired, you can click the [Turn Styles Off] button to turn off the CSS button styling and display the menu bar as an outline of links. This can help you better see the structure of your navigation tree.

- The CSS styles required to format a Menu Bar widget can be a forbidding sight, but it is possible with persistence to isolate the rules required to adjust colors and text formats to customize the menu bar for your site.

Create a Spry Collapsible Panel

- A Spry Collapsible Panel widget inserts a tab and a panel that expands or collapses as you click the tab. The illustration at the top of the next column shows the panel open.

- Insert the Collapsible Panel widget using the 🖳 Spry Collapsible Panel button on the Spry tab of the Insert bar or the Insert>Spry>Spry Collapsible Panel command.

Collapsible Panel widget opens and closes a panel in the browser

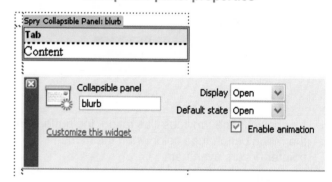

- The new Collapsible Panel will display the full width of the page, so you may want to insert it in a table cell, as shown in the following illustration, or an AP div.

Collapsible panel properties

Menu bar with several levels of submenu items

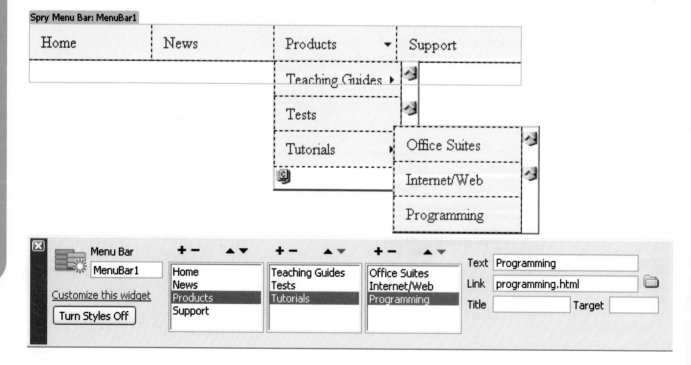

- To create the panel content, replace the word Tab with the content you want to appear as the panel's tab, and then insert the panel's content in the Content area.

- You can choose whether the collapsible panel will be open or closed by default when it displays in the browser. If you enable animation, the text in the panel will appear to scroll down line by line as it appears.

- As for other Spry widgets, you can if desired modify the CSS styles that control tab color and tab and content fonts.

Create a Spry Accordion

- An accordion is an interactive element that shows and hides panels as you click panel labels. In the following illustration, the accordion consists of two labels and two content panels.

Accordion consisting of two labels and panels

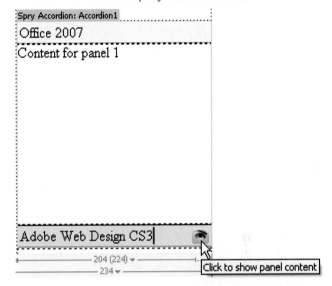

- Clicking a tab hides any other panels to display only the panel below that head. The up and down sliding motion of the panels gives the accordion its name.

- Insert a Spry Accordion widget using the ▦ Spry Accordion button or the Insert>Spry>Spry Accordion command. As for a Collapsible Panel, the Accordion widget will use the full width of the page unless you constrain it in an AP div or table cell.

- You can type new labels and content directly in the widget. When you have completed the first label and its content, move the mouse pointer near the lower-right corner of the next label to display the eye, as shown in the following illustration, and click the eye to display the next panel.

Text displays in status bar

- To add or remove panels, use the **+** or **−** button in the Property inspector. Use the ▲ or ▼ button to change the order of labels and their associated content panels.

Other Spry Elements

- The Spry tab on the Insert bar offers additional Spry objects you can add to a page.

- The Tabbed Panel widget inserts an object with tabs arranged horizontally at the top and panels associated with each tab for content. Click a tab in the browser to see the content panel for that tab. You insert text in the tabs and content panels as for a Collapsible Panel or Accordion widget.

- The Spry data tools offer you a number of ways to work with an existing XML data set:
  - Spry XML Data Set allows you to create a connection to an XML file that you can then use to create a table or interactive region on a page. This process is similar to creating a database connection for a form.

- Use Spry Region to create an area on a page where you can insert another Spry object such as a Spry table or repeat list.

- If you want to insert repetitive data, such as a list of values from a data set, you can use Spry Repeat and Spry Repeat List to format the region and display the list. You can set up a Repeat List as a bulleted, numbered, definition, or drop-down list.

- Use Spry Table to insert a table that displays static or dynamic data. You can add sort functionality to allow a visitor to sort table data by heading in the browser.

  ✔ *You can work with XML data in a Spry table in the Dreamweaver in Depth steps at the end of this exercise.*

PROCEDURES

Insert Spry Validation Widgets

To insert a Validation widget:
1. Click **Insert** . . . . Alt+I
2. Point to **Spry** . . . . S
3. Select the desired Validation widget:
   - **Spry Validation Text Field** . . . . E
   - **Spry Validation Select** . . . . S
   - **Spry Validation Checkbox** C
   - **Spry Validation Textarea** X

   OR

   - Click or drag the desired Validation button from the Spry tab of the Insert bar.

In the Input Tag Accessibility Attributes dialog box:

1. Type a label for the form field and select any label options.
2. Click [OK].

To copy Spry files to the local site:
- Save the page on which you have just inserted a Spry element and click [OK] to copy dependent files to the site.

To set properties for the field:
- Click the form field within the blue tabbed outline and set properties using the Property inspector as for a regular Dreamweaver form field.

To set validation options:
1. Click the blue tabbed outline around the widget to display widget properties.
2. Select validation options from those offered for each field type. For every Validation widget you should:
   a. Insert a name for the Spry field.
   b. Specify whether the field is required.
   c. Indicate the point at which validation occurs.

Insert a Spry Menu Bar Widget

To insert a Menu Bar widget:
1. Click **Insert** . . . . Alt+I
2. Point to **Spry** . . . . S
3. Click **Spry Menu Bar** . . . . . M

   OR

   - Click the **Spry Menu Bar** button 📇 from the Spry tab of the Insert bar.

In the Spry Menu Bar dialog box:

1. Select **Horizontal** or **Vertical**.
2. Click [OK].
3. Name the menu bar in the Property inspector.

To set up links for the menu bar:
1. Click the blue tabbed outline to select the widget.
2. Click **Item 1** in the first column in the Property inspector.

3. Type a name for the button in the **Text** box.
4. Insert a link for the button in the **Link** box if desired.
5. Set up the submenu for the first item, if necessary:
   a. With the first item selected in the first column, click **Item 1.1** in the second column.
   b. Supply a name and a link for the item as directed in steps 3 and 4.
6. Set up a submenu for the submenu item, if necessary:
   a. With the first submenu item selected in the second column, click the **Add menu item** button ✚ above the third column to insert an **Untitled item**.
   b. Supply a name and a link for the item as directed in steps 3 and 4.

To adjust menu items:
- Use the ✚ or ➖ button to add or remove an item.
- Use the ▲ or ▼ button to move an item up or down the list.
- Use the [Turn Styles Off] button to turn off formatting so you can see the navigation outline.

Create a Spry Collapsible Panel

To insert a Collapsible Panel widget:

1. Click **Insert** . . . . ⒜⒧ᵗ+Ⓘ
2. Point to **Spry** . . . . Ⓢ
3. Click **Spry Collapsible Panel** . . . . Ⓒ

   OR

   ▥ Click the **Spry Collapsible Panel** button 🗔 from the Spry tab of the Insert bar.

To add content to the Collapsible Panel widget:

1. Select the **Tab** placeholder text and type new tab content.
2. Select the **Content** placeholder text and type new panel content.

To adjust Collapsible Panel properties:

▥ Type a name for the collapsible panel in the Property inspector.

▥ Change the Display and Default state options from Open to Closed if desired.

▥ Deselect **Enable animation** if you don't want the panel's text to scroll into view.

Create a Spry Accordion

To insert an Accordion widget:

1. Click **Insert** . . . . ⒜⒧ᵗ+Ⓘ
2. Point to **Spry** . . . . Ⓢ
3. Click **Spry Accordion** . . . . Ⓐ

   OR

   Click the **Spry Accordion** button 🖳 from the Spry tab of the Insert bar.

To add content to the Accordion widget:

1. Type a name for the accordion in the Property inspector.

2. Select the **Label 1** placeholder text and type new label content.
3. Select the **Content 1** placeholder text and type new panel content.
4. Select the **Label 2** placeholder text and type new content.
5. Move the mouse pointer over the right side of the Label 2 tab until the eye displays.
6. Click the eye to display the Content 2 panel.
7. Replace the **Content 2** placeholder with new text.

To adjust accordion items:

▥ Use the **+** or **−** button to add or remove a panel.

▥ Use the ▲ or ▼ button to move a panel up or down the list.

EXERCISE DIRECTIONS

1. Start Dreamweaver and open the tutorials site.
2. Add the following pages to the site from the Lesson 6 Data folder: ◎faqs.html, ◎forums.html, ◎news.html, and ◎support.html. Save each page in the site.
3. Set up navigation links as follows:

   ▥ Check links in the navigation tables on products.html, news.html, and support.html to make sure they point to the correct pages. Link the *Home* item in each navigation table to home.html.

   ✔ *There is no home.html page; you are creating broken links so you can fix them in Lesson 7.*

   ▥ Set the *Support Options* links on faqs.html and forums.html to open the support.html page.

   ▥ On the support.html page, update the *FAQs* and *forums* links to point to the correct pages if necessary.

Insert Spry Validation Widgets

1. Open index.html and click in the form in the blue column.
2. Insert a Spry Validation Text Field with the following properties:

   ▥ Type the label Name in the Input Tag Accessibility Attributes dialog box.

   ▥ Select the Wrap with label tag style. (You will need to be able to find this label tag in Exercise 47.)

   ▥ In the Property inspector, replace the default text field name with name.

   ▥ Specify that the field is required and must contain a minimum of 5 characters.

   ▥ Choose to validate on Blur.

3. Preview each state for the field.

4. Click to the left of the Send button and press Enter to create a new line. In the new line, insert another Validation Text Field with the following properties:
   - Type the label **E-Mail** in the Input Tag Accessibility Attributes dialog box.
   - In the Property inspector, replace the default text field name with **email**.
   - Choose the Email Address type.
   - Specify that the field is required and choose to validate on Blur.
5. Click to the left of the Send button and press Enter to create a new line. In the new line, insert a Validation Select field with the following properties:
   - Type the label **I have experience** in the Input Tag Accessibility Attributes dialog box.
   - In the Property inspector, replace the default select field name with **experience**.
   - Click the field to display the field Property inspector. Choose to create a list 3 lines high with the following values:

     | Writing tutorials | writing |
     | Programming | programming |
     | Teaching | teaching |

   - Click the blue tabbed outline to display Spry properties and choose to validate on Blur.
6. Save changes, allowing Dreamweaver to store the Spry files in the site, and then preview the page in the browser. Try entering only a few letters in the Name field and an incomplete address in the E-Mail field to see how you are prompted for required and correct information.

Insert a Spry Menu Bar

1. In Dreamweaver, click in the blank line below the main heading on the **index.html** page.
2. Insert a horizontal Spry Menu Bar widget.
3. Create the menu bar properties as follows in the Property inspector:
   - Name the menu bar **homemenu**.
   - Click **Item 1** and rename the item as **Home**. In the second column, click each submenu item and then click the **−** button to remove the submenu items.
   - Click **Item 2** and rename the item as **News**. Remove the dummy link in the Link box and type **news.html**.
   - Click **Item 3** and rename the item as **Products**, linking to **products.html**. Remove the submenu items in the second and third columns.

- Click **Item 4** and rename the item as **Support**.
- With *Support* still selected in the first column, click the **+** button in the second column to add a submenu item. Name this item **Support Options** and link to **support.html**.
- With *Support Options* selected in the second column, click the **+** button in the third column to add a submenu item. Name this item **FAQs** and link to **faqs.html**.
- Click the **+** button in the third column again to add a second submenu item. Name this item **Forums** and link to **forums.html**.
4. Save the page and preview it in the browser, testing all links. (You will have to use the Back button to return to the home page, because the Home links on the navigation tables are currently incorrect.) Your page should look similar to Illustration A as you select an option from the menu bar.

Insert a Spry Accordion

1. Open the **news.html** page.
2. Click at the top of the light gray table cell and insert a Spry Accordion.
3. Insert content for the accordion as follows:
   - Name the accordion **newsaccord**.
   - Replace Label 1 with the text **Office 2007**. Insert the following text in the Content 1 panel:
     Most versions of Office 2007 ship with all the standard applications: Access, Excel, Outlook, PowerPoint, and Word. Depending on the version you purchase, you may also receive Publisher and InfoPath.
   - Replace Label 2 with the text **Adobe Web Design CS3**. Click the eye to display the content panel and insert the following content:
     The Adobe Web Design CS3 suite includes a powerful array of applications that can help you create dynamite Web content. You receive Illustrator, Photoshop, Fireworks, Dreamweaver, Flash, and supporting programs such as Bridge and Device Central.
4. Save the page, clicking OK to save the supporting Spry files, and preview it in the browser. Click each label to see the color change and the accordion action.
5. Close all open pages and the browser and exit Dreamweaver.

Illustration A

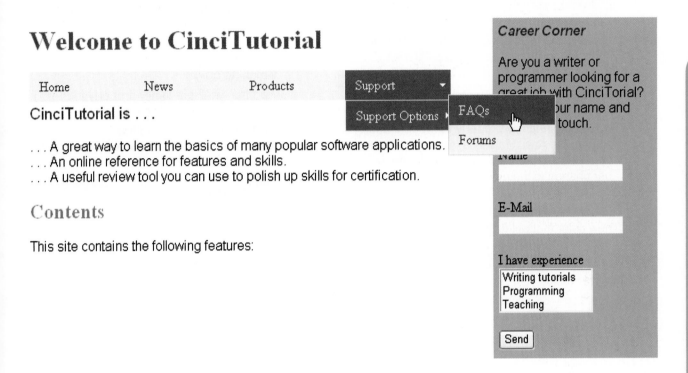

Welcome to CinciTutorial

| Home | News | Products | Support ▾ |

CinciTutorial is . . .

. . . A great way to learn the basics of many popular software applications.
. . . An online reference for features and skills.
. . . A useful review tool you can use to polish up skills for certification.

Contents

This site contains the following features:

Career Corner

Are you a writer or programmer looking for a great job with CinciTorial? ...our name and ... touch.

Name

E-Mail

I have experience
Writing tutorials
Programming
Teaching

Send

Support Options ▸
FAQs
Forums

ON YOUR OWN

As you have learned, Spry widgets are formatted using CSS. To become familiar with the CSS formatting, try adjusting some of the formats of the widgets you have inserted in the tutorials site.

1. Start Dreamweaver and open the tutorials site.

2. Open the index.html page and view the styles in the CSS Styles panel for the Spry horizontal menu bar. Change the font of the menu bar items as follows:

   - Locate the ul.MenuBarHorizontal rule.

   - Add the font-family property to the rule and specify the Arial, Helvetica, sans serif font family. You should see all text in the menu bar change to the new font.

   - Locate the rule that begins ul.MenuBarHorizontal a:hover and choose a new color that will display when you hover the mouse pointer over the buttons.

3. Save changes to all pages and view the page in the browser to see your new styles in effect.

4. Apply the .text CSS style to the form labels, just as you would apply the style to any text: click in the label and apply the style.

5. Open the news.html page and view the styles for the accordion in the CSS Styles panel. Make the following changes:

   - Add a property to the .AccordionPanelTab rule to change the font family to Arial, Helvetica, sans serif.

   - Add another property to change the font weight to bolder.

   - Add the Arial font-family property to the .AccordionPanelContent rule.

   - Add another property to the .AccordionPanelContent rule to change the background color to white.

6. Save changes to the style sheet and view the page in the browser.

7. Close all open pages and the browser and exit Dreamweaver.

DREAMWEAVER IN DEPTH

One of the ways a designer can add dynamic content to a Web site is by using XML data. XML is used for content such as headline news feeds and other kinds of dynamic data that a site visitor can interact with. Spry provides several tools that make displaying XML data easy. You can try your hand at creating an interactive Spry table in the following steps.

1. Start Dreamweaver and create a new site with a name such as spry, using standard settings you have used for other new sites.

2. Create a new blank HTML page and save it in the site as books.html with the page title My Books.

3. Open the ⊙DID45.xml file from the Lesson 6 Data folder and save it in the site as mybooks.xml.

   Take a few moments to look at the XML code on the page. XML coding uses tags similar to those used in HTML coding, but the tags can consist of any words that make sense as a way to organize the data. On the mybooks.xml page, for example, tags have been created to organize a book collection according to genre, title, and author.

4. Activate books.html and insert a heading that reads My Book Collection. In a paragraph below the heading, insert the following text:

   The following table lists a few books from my collection. Click a column heading to sort the collection by that column.

5. Create a Spry data set:
   - Click the ⬒ Spry XML Data Set button on the Spry tab of the Insert bar. The Spry XML Data Set dialog box opens.
   - Replace the default Data Set name with the name books.
   - Click the Browse button and select the mybooks.xml data set.
   - Click the Get Schema button to show the structure of the data set in the Row element box.
   - Click the book element (the < > next to this element shows a small + sign indicating multiple entries for this tag). The Data Set

columns box shows the data types for each column.
   - Click **@bookid** in the Data Set columns area, then click the Data type list arrow and select **number** as the data type.
   - Click OK. The dialog box closes, and the Bindings panel shows the data fields for the XML data set.

6. Create the Spry table that will display the XML data so it can be sorted in the browser:
   - Click below the text paragraph on the books.html page.
   - Click the ▦ Spry Table button on the Spry tab of the Insert bar. The Insert Spry Table dialog box opens.
   - Click the @bookid column and click the ⬆ button three times to move this field to the top of the list of columns.
   - Click on each column in the list and then click the **Sort column when header is clicked** checkbox. Selecting this checkbox for each column allows you to sort by any column in the browser.
   - Click OK, and then click Yes to allow Dreamweaver to add a Spry region for the table.

7. In the resulting table, change the column header @bookid to ID. Apply formats to the header row if desired to make it easier to distinguish column headings from data.

8. Save changes and click OK to allow Spry to copy files to the site.

9. Preview the page in a browser and click on each column head to see how the data sorts.

10. Close the browser and all pages and exit Dreamweaver.

Skills Covered

- About Behaviors
- Use the Behaviors Panel
- Dreamweaver Actions
- Modify or Remove Attached Actions

Software Skills In Dreamweaver, behaviors are JavaScript programs that perform specific tasks when a visitor interacts with a Web page in a browser. This exercise discusses behaviors and describes some actions commonly used with behaviors. You will work with other actions in the next exercise.

Application Skills In this exercise, you will explore behaviors and add several actions to your CinciTorial Web site.

TERMS

Action The task the behavior performs.

Behavior A prewritten JavaScript that performs a specific task in a Dreamweaver site.

Event Operation that triggers an action in a Dreamweaver behavior.

Parameter Settings that control the appearance or actions of an object.

NOTES

About Behaviors

- A Dreamweaver **behavior** is a JavaScript program that performs a specific task when a Web page visitor interacts with the page in some way.

- For example, a behavior can be used to specify that when a visitor moves the mouse pointer over an AP div, another AP div displays in place of the previous one. Behaviors can also be used to validate form fields.

- Because a behavior makes it possible for a visitor to change the HTML coding of a page—for example, to replace one image with another—behaviors are sometimes referred to as *dynamic HTML,* or DHTML.

- For a behavior to work properly, you must specify three things:

  - An **action**—a task that the behavior will perform.

  - An **event**—a specific operation such as a mouse click or the loading of a page.

  - A specific HTML tag to which the action and the event are attached.

- In simple terms, you select a tag to which you want to attach an action, choose the action, and then specify how the action will be triggered. Dreamweaver then adds the necessary JavaScript coding to the page to carry out the behavior.

- You use the Behaviors panel to select actions and events.

- It is important to note that interactive features such as behaviors that use JavaScript are considered to be a potential security threat by many browsers. Behaviors may be blocked by a browser, so that you must give permission for them to run. Some browsers also do not support specific behaviors.

- Before you spend time attaching behaviors to objects in your Web site, consider carefully whether the actions will really contribute to your Web site, whether the information supplied by a behavior will be accessible to all viewers, and whether your target browsers will display the actions correctly (or at all).

Use the Behaviors Panel

- Launch the Behaviors panel using the Window>Behaviors command or click the Behaviors tab in the Tag Inspector panel group.

- The Behaviors panel lists events and actions (see the following illustration) for the currently selected tag. You use this panel to add or remove behaviors.

Behaviors panel

- You use the same general process to attach all Dreamweaver behaviors: Select the tag to attach the behavior to, choose an action, and then specify the event that will trigger the action.

Select Tag

- Behaviors can be attached to an entire page, to links, to images, to table elements, to form fields, and even to specific paragraphs. Before you can attach a behavior to an object, you must select the object's HTML tag.

- Use the tag selector in the status bar to quickly select the desired tag.

- The Tag inspector's title bar displays the currently selected HTML tag. The previous illustration, for example, shows the <a> tag in the title bar, indicating that a link is selected.

Select Action

- Before you begin attaching behaviors, specify a browser version in Dreamweaver by clicking the **+.** Add behavior button, clicking Show Events For, and choosing a browser version from the submenu.

- Setting the browser version saves you from attaching actions that will not work properly in your chosen browser.

  ✔ *Dreamweaver's behaviors are written to work in all Microsoft Internet Explorer and Netscape browser versions later than 4.0 as well as open-source browsers such as Firefox.*

- To select a behavior to attach to the selected object, click the **+.** Add behavior button in the Behaviors panel. Dreamweaver displays a list of actions that can be attached to the currently selected object. Not all actions are available for all kinds of selected objects. For example, some behaviors can be used only with AP elements.

- After you select an action from the list, a dialog box opens to allow you to set **parameters** that control the action. The parameters you set are specific to each action. For the Popup Message action, for example, you type the message that will pop up in a message window (see the illustration below).

- Once parameters have been set, the action displays in the Behaviors panel. You can then specify an event to trigger the action.

- You can set more than one action for a tag and use different events to trigger the actions.

Select Event

- Dreamweaver chooses a default event for some types of selected objects. When an entire page is selected, for example, the default event is onLoad, which means the action will take place when the page is loaded (opened) by a browser.

Popup Message parameter dialog box

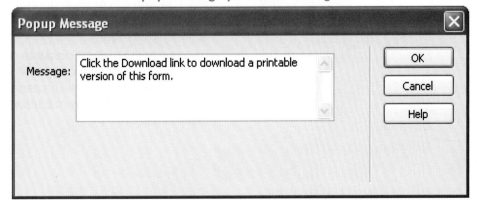

- If you don't want to use the default event, click the event's list arrow to display a drop-down list of available events you can choose among (see the following illustration).

Select event to trigger action

- If more than one action is specified for an event, actions take place in the order in which they are listed in the Behaviors panel. You can change the order in which actions occur by selecting an action and clicking the ▲ or ▼ button.

- Dreamweaver offers over 30 events. Events available at any one time depend on the selected tag, browser version, and action.

  ✔ To see a list of all the Dreamweaver events, consult Dreamweaver's Help files for Behaviors: Click Help>Dreamweaver Help, or, with the Behaviors panel selected, click ⊟ and then click Help in the panel menu.

- Some of the most commonly used events are described in the following table.

Event	Event occurs . . .
onBlur	When selected object stops being the focus of user interaction (for example, when a user clicks outside of an object such as a form field).
onClick	When user clicks specified object.
onDblClick	When user double-clicks specified object.
OnError	When a browser error occurs during a load.
onFocus	When selected object becomes the focus of user interaction (for example, when a user clicks in an object such as a form field).
OnLoad	When a page or image finishes loading.
OnMouseOver	When user moves mouse over top of specified object.
OnMouseOut	When user moves the mouse away from a specified object.
onUnload	When user leaves a page.

Dreamweaver Actions

- Dreamweaver includes more than 20 actions you can use to perform various tasks. Not all actions are available for all tags. Actions unavailable for a specific tag are grayed out on the actions list.

  ✔ To see a list of all the Dreamweaver actions, consult Dreamweaver's Help files for Behaviors.

- Some of Dreamweaver's actions perform advanced tasks beyond the scope of this book. You may also note an entry called Deprecated on the actions list, which gives access to behaviors such as Play Sound that are no longer recommended for use.

- The following sections describe several common actions that you can easily implement in any Web site. Exercise 47 continues this discussion of behaviors and introduces you to some additional common behaviors.

- Because actions are designed to display in a browser, you will not see any evidence of the action in Dreamweaver. Preview the pages to which you have attached behaviors in a browser to see the behaviors in action.

Open Browser Window Action

- If you have spent any time browsing on the Web, you have probably seen behaviors similar to Dreamweaver's Open Browser Window action. This action launches a new browser window containing a specified Web page (document), a common way to display advertising—such as a popup window—or additional information.

- Such content draws the user's attention and forces the user to interact with the Web site by viewing and then closing the second browser window.

- The browser window typically lacks the controls that you normally associate with your Web browser, such as scroll bars, toolbar buttons, and menus (although you can add these controls if you wish). By default, only the Minimize and Close buttons display.

- You can use any type of Web content in the page that will open in the new window: text, an illustration, a feedback form, and so on.

- If you use an illustration for the content of the page that will open in the browser, you might need to adjust the margins of the page to eliminate any white space that appears by default around the image.

- Make this adjustment in the page's Page Properties dialog box. Set the margins to 0 in all four margin boxes to eliminate any default white space in any browser.

- The Open Browser Window action has historically been associated with the opening or closing of a Web page. Because pop-up blockers now tend to suppress new browser windows that open on load or unload, you may have better luck attaching the Open Browser Window action to a link tag. Pop-up blockers usually do not block windows if you initiate the action yourself by clicking a link.

- If you don't want to attach the action to a real link, you can set up a dummy link, formatted so visitors will recognize it as something to click. The # dummy link displays the top of the page after the link is clicked. If you want the focus to stay at the same area of the page where the link appears, use the javascript:; dummy link (the word *javascript* followed by a colon and a semicolon).

- In the parameters dialog box for the action (see the illustration below), specify the address of the page to open in the browser window and the browser window's width and height.

- Typically, this Web page will be contained in your Web's root folder so that the page is available when you publish to a Web server. However, it can be stored in another Internet or intranet server. Include the full path for the file in the *URL to display* text box if it is in another location.

- You can select attributes depending on how much interaction you want to allow your visitors. For example, if visitors need to take further action from the browser window, you can select the Menu bar or Navigation toolbar attribute.

- You can use a number of events for this action, including onClick and all of the onMouse events.

Swap Image Action

- The Swap Image action can be used for creative interactive effects. When an image is set to *swap*, it changes to another image when the specified event occurs.

- This action is very similar to the rollover image feature you learned about in Lesson 3. The Swap Image action, however, gives you greater control over the swapping process because you can specify the event that causes the switch. You can also swap more than one image at a time when an event occurs.

Open Browser Window parameters

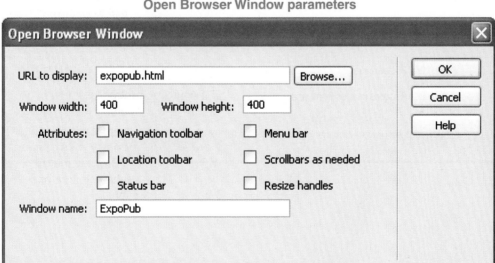

255

- This behavior requires that the page contain the original image that will be swapped. For best results, the image to swap should be the same size as the original image.

- The Swap Image action can *restore* itself after the mouse has passed over it, or it can remain changed to indicate to visitors that they have referenced the image or content associated with the image—which adds user friendliness to an otherwise visual effect.

- Attach the Swap Image action by selecting the tag of the image to swap or the tag of another element such as a link that will control the swap and then choosing Swap Image from the actions list.

  ✔ *Dreamweaver provides a Swap Image Restore action, but this action is added automatically when you select Swap Image. You do not have to choose it unless the Swap Image Restore action is accidentally deleted from the Behaviors panel.*

- In the parameters dialog box, browse to locate the image that will swap with the selected image (see the illustration below). Both images should be stored in your Web site's images folder.

- Note the two checkboxes in the parameter dialog box. Make sure these options are selected to load images with the page and restore the original image after the mouse pointer leaves the swapped image.

- In the Behaviors panel, you will see that two actions have been attached: Swap Image and Swap Image Restore (see the illustration below).

Two actions control the swap

Validate Form Action

- You worked with validation in the previous exercise when you inserted Spry Validation widgets. You can also validate form fields using behaviors.

- You can attach a behavior that generates messages about errors in filling out the form using the Validate Form action.

Set source of image to swap

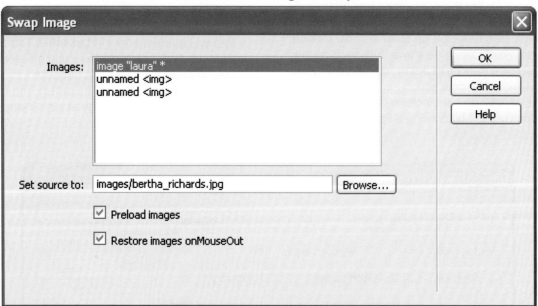

- Click in the field you want to validate and select the Validate Form action from the actions list. The Validate Form parameter dialog box opens with a list of the fields in the current form (see the illustration below).

- Select the Required checkbox to require an entry in a field. After you select this checkbox for a field, the field information displays (R).

- If the field requires a certain type of data entry, specify the required entry type with the Accept options:

  - *Anything* allows any entry, such as names, addresses, and so on.

  - *Email address* allows one e-mail address to be entered in the field. The e-mail address must have the proper SMTP syntax indicated by the @ symbol.

  - *Number* allows numbers, including decimals.

  - *Number from . . . to . . .* allows a specific range of numbers.

- If you choose a specific data entry option, the field name in the Fields list displays an abbreviation of the option, such as (NisNum) for a field with a numerical data entry type. If an entry is required, the *N* is replaced by *R*. A field that requires an e-mail entry will display (RisEmail), as shown below.

- Each time you open the Validate Form parameter dialog box, the first form field in the Fields list is selected by default, even if you have selected another field in the form. You must take care to choose the correct field in the Fields list.

- The default event for a Validate Form action is onBlur. This means that the message will display after the visitor leaves the field that has validation applied.

- Though you can set validation rules for all fields at one time in the parameter box, you should not do so because error messages may display for fields the visitor has not yet visited. Instead, create a separate validate action for each field.

  ✔ *You can create more than one action for each field, however.*

- Test your validation rules by displaying the form page in the browser and leaving out required information or supplying incompatible information. As you leave a field, or when you submit the form, you will see error messages similar to the one shown in the following illustration.

Validation error message

✔ *If you prefer the interactive nature of Spry validation, you can select any form field that has a related Validation widget and apply the widget, even if you used Dreamweaver's standard form tools to insert the field.*

Modify or Remove Attached Actions

- To modify an action, simply double-click the action in the Behaviors panel to launch the parameter dialog box. You can change any of the parameters you originally set.

Validate Form fields

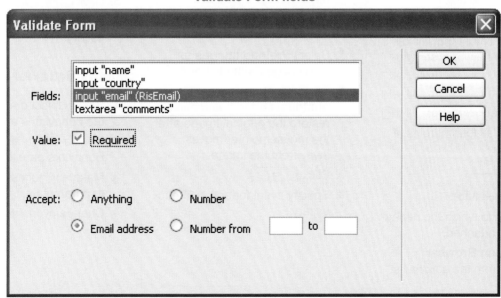

- You can also easily change the event that triggers the action by clicking the current event's list arrow and selecting a different event.

- However, the events that Dreamweaver chooses for you by default are typically the ones that work best with the browser or browsers you have selected for your behavior.

- To remove an attached behavior, select the tag to which the action is attached to see the actions in the Behaviors panel. Then select the action to be removed and click the — Remove event button in the Behaviors panel.

PROCEDURES

Display Behaviors Panel (Shift + F4)

1. Click **Window** . . . . Alt+W
2. Click **Behaviors** . . . . E

Attach Behavior to Tag

1. Select tag to which behavior will be attached.
2. Click **Add behavior** button +, on Behaviors panel.
3. Select action from the actions list.
4. Specify settings in action's parameter dialog box.
5. Accept default event in Behaviors panel, or click the event's list arrow and select new event from the drop-down list.

Open Browser Window Action

Before attaching the behavior:

1. Create Web page that contains the content that will display in the new browser window.
2. Click **Modify** . . . . Alt+M
3. Click **Page Properties** . . . . P
4. Type **0** for all four margins, if necessary.
5. Click OK .

To attach the behavior:

1. Select tag to which the behavior will be attached.
2. Select **Open Browser Window** from the actions list.

3. Type URL of page to open in browser window in the **URL to display** text box.

   OR

   Click Browse... and navigate to page.
4. Set values for **Window width** and **Window height**.
5. Type name for window and select any additional attributes.
6. Click OK .
7. Specify event for action, if necessary.

Swap Image Action

1. Select tag of image or other element to which the behavior will be attached.
2. Select **Swap Image** from the actions list.
3. Select original image.
4. Type source file name in the **Set Source to** text box.

   OR

   Click Browse... and navigate to location of image file.
5. Select **Preload images** to load images with the page.
6. Select **Restore images onMouseOut** to automatically restore the original image after the mouse pointer moves away from the image.
7. Click OK .
8. Specify event for action, if necessary.

Validate Form Action

1. Select form field to validate.

   ✔ *Apply validation actions to each field separately.*
2. Select **Validate Form** from the actions list.
3. Select field from the **Fields** list.
4. Select validation options:
   - Select the **Required** checkbox to make entry required.
   - Select the **Anything** option to allow any entry.
   - Select the **Email address** option to require proper format for e-mail address entry.
   - Select the **Number** option to require an entry in digits (including decimals).
   - Select **Number from** and specify low and high values for range entry.
5. Click OK .
6. Specify event for action, if necessary.

Modify Behavior

1. Select object or page to which the behavior is attached.
2. Double-click action in the Behaviors panel.
3. Make any necessary changes to parameters.
4. Change event, if desired.

Remove Behavior

1. Select object or page to which the behavior is attached.

2. Click action in the Behaviors panel to select it.

3. Click **Remove event** button ━ in the Behaviors panel.

EXERCISE DIRECTIONS

1. Start Dreamweaver and open the cincitorial site.

2. Open ◉ expopub.html from the Lesson 6 Data folder and save it in the cincitorial root folder with the page title See You at ExpoPub!

3. Prepare the page for use:
   - Insert the Logo library item in a blank paragraph below the link on the page.
   - Click the logo and then click the Detach from original button in the Property inspector to detach the image from the library so you can resize it.
   - Resize the logo image to 257 pixels wide by 44 pixels high. Resample the image after resizing.

4. Save and close the page.

5. Open index.html and select the word *ExpoPub* in the blurb frame (the bottom part of the left frame). Type # in the Link box to set up a dummy link.

6. Display the Behaviors panel, click the Add behavior button, and point to Show Events For. Select IE 6.0.

7. Click the *ExpoPub* link and attach the Open Browser Window action to this link as follows:
   - Select expopub.html as the URL to display.
   - Set the Window width and Window height measurements to 400.
   - Type ExpoPub as the Window name.
   - Make sure the onClick event displays in the Events column of the Behaviors panel.

8. Save changes and preview the page. It should look similar to Illustration A. (Your browser window may display in a different location.)

9. Open mission.html. Set up the Swap Image action on this page as follows:
   - Click the image of Laura Brater-Reidel and name the image laura in the Property inspector. Remove the alternate text from this image.
   - In the text below the image, select the words *Bertha Richards* and create a dummy link.
   - Choose the Swap Image action. In the Swap Image dialog box, select image "laura".

   - For Set source to, browse to select ◉ bertha_richards.jpg from the Lesson 6 Data folder. (Save this image in your images folder but do not supply alternate text.)
   - Note that both the Swap Image and Swap Image Restore actions have been added to the Behaviors panel after you close the dialog box.
   - Change the event for Swap Image Restore to onFocusOut. Change the event for Swap Image to onClick.

10. Save the page and preview it. Click the link to swap the image. Click elsewhere on the page to restore the original image.

11. Open contactus.html. Click in the name form field to select it.

12. Use the Validate Form action to specify that this field is required. Verify that the onBlur event is chosen for the action.

13. Use the Validate Form action to require an entry in the country field. (Be sure to select the "country" field in the Fields list.) Use the onBlur event.

14. Require an entry in the email field and specify the Email address option. Use the onBlur event.

15. Save the page and preview it.
    - Insert your name in the Your name field and then press Tab twice to see the message informing you that the Country field requires an entry.
    - Type USA in the Country field.

    ✔ *When you leave the E-mail address field to type the country, an error message will display to tell you an entry is required in the email field. Click OK and proceed.*

    - Type your first name in the E-mail address field and press Tab. You should receive a message telling you to enter an e-mail address in the field.
    - Supply a correct e-mail address in the field.

16. Close the browser and any open pages.

17. Exit Dreamweaver.

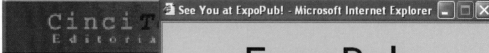

Contact Us

Client Praise

Our People

Services

Our Specialties

Welcome to

CinciTorial is . . .

- Application textbooks
- Practice manuals
- Instructors' notes
- CD- and Web-based sup

Working with CinciTorial is as e

1. Contact us and set up a c
2. Establish fee and work sc
3. Sit back and relax!

Let us put the pieces together for you. Contact us today to learn how CinciTorial can help you get your computer books to market quickly, efficiently, and affordably.

We'll see you at ExpoPub in Chicago!

ExpoPub
March 27-28

ExpoPub is coming to Chicago— and CinciTorial will be there. Make plans to visit our booth!

For more information, click on the link below.

www.expopub.com

CinciTorial Co.
Editorial Services

ON YOUR OWN

1. Start Dreamweaver and open the **gardencenter** site.

2. Create a new page that you can use with the Open Browser Window behavior:
   - Create and save the page as **remind.html** with the page title **Native Plant Seminar**.
   - Insert the following text:

   Native Plant Seminar

   Interested in native plants? Join us at 7:00 p.m. every Tuesday evening for a discussion of plants that not only thrive in our area but are native to the region. Learn how to recognize invasive species that can be eliminated from your garden and what native species give you the best blooms and foliage year round with a minimum of fuss.

   - Format the text as desired (you may want to attach the style sheet you created in the last lesson) and add background color to the document.
   - Save and close the document.

3. Open **favorites.html** and create a link somewhere on the page that launches the **remind.html** document in a new browser window. Test the page in the browser to make sure you have the right size for the new window.

4. Set up required validation in this site's form for the fields you consider to be the most important.

5. View all pages in the browser to test your behaviors.

6. Close all open pages and exit Dreamweaver.

Skills Covered

- ■ **Use Message Actions**
- ■ **Use AP Element Actions**

- ■ **Apply Spry Effects**

Software Skills   Dreamweaver's many behaviors include several that help you transmit important messages to your visitor. Spry effects, new in Dreamweaver CS3, can supply an element of fun by causing objects to change color or move when triggered.

Application Skills   In this exercise, you will explore additional behaviors and add several to your tutorials site.

TERMS

No new terms in this exercise.

NOTES

Use Message Actions

- ■ Dreamweaver offers several actions that relay text content to the visitor, including popup messages and the four Set Text actions.

Popup Message Action

- ■ A popup message is a JavaScript alert that displays a message in a dialog box (see the following illustration). The visitor can read the message and click the OK button to close it.

Popup message in alert box

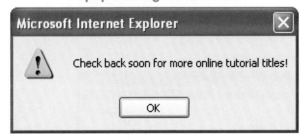

- ■ Popup messages can be used to supply additional information about a button or link or alert the visitor to some aspect of the Web site content.

- ■ Try to be considerate of your visitor when including popup messages. Because they require the visitor to interact with the message to remove it, they can be disruptive. They should be used only for important information.

  - ✔ *When you validate a page with a pop-up message, the Validator suggests that you should warn visitors a pop-up will display.*

- ■ Creating a popup message is easy: After selecting the tag to which the message action will be attached, choose Popup Message on the actions list and type the message in the parameters dialog box (see the illustration at the top of the next page).

- ■ You then need only select the event to trigger the message. Popup messages work well with any Web page event.

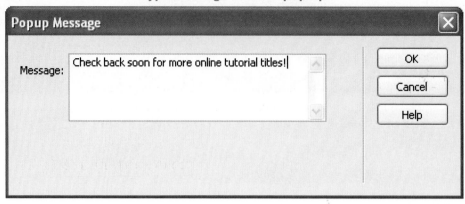

Set Text Actions

- Dreamweaver's Set Text actions offer four options for inserting text in various page elements.

- The Set Text of Container action lets you choose any container on a page, such as a paragraph, table cell, or AP div, and replace its existing text with new text.

- You can type the new HTML content, including tags if you want to format it, directly in the New HTML area, as shown in the first illustration below.

- The Set Text of Frame action allows you to replace the contents of a frame with new HTML content.

- The Set Text of Status Bar action offers a way to use the status bar space to communicate with Web visitors. The status bar can display the destination of a link or information about the content of a Web page.

- You can attach this action to an entire page or to a specific link or button (for example, in a form). Use the Set Text of Status Bar dialog box to insert the message you want to display (see the second illustration below).

- Though this is an easy behavior to configure, you should consider carefully before using it. Some visitors may have turned off the display of the status bar in their browser; many other visitors would never think to look to the status bar for a message.

Set new HTML text to appear in a container

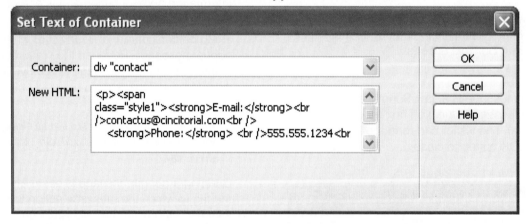

Set text to appear in status bar

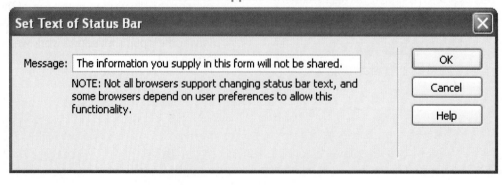

- Most seriously, some newer browsers, such as Firefox and Safari, do not display this behavior. The Set Text of Status Bar dialog box, shown previously, makes note of this situation.

- The Set Text of Text Field action lets you insert text that will appear in a form's text field (see the illustration below). To set the text to appear when a visitor clicks in the field, use the onFocus event. To display the text when the visitor moves to another field, use the onBlur event.

Use AP Element Actions

- Dreamweaver offers several AP element actions that add interesting interactivity to a page: Show-Hide Elements and Drag AP Element.

Show-Hide Elements

- The Show-Hide Elements action uses the visibility property of one or more AP elements to display or hide an AP element when a visitor triggers the action.

- For example, a popular use of Show-Hide Elements is to create an AP div that will pop into

view when a visitor's mouse pointer crosses a particular area of the page. When the mouse pointer moves away, the AP div is hidden again.

- This behavior can be used to swap elements so that one that was initially visible becomes invisible while another element that was initially invisible becomes visible, similar to the way a rollover image or Swap Image action works.

- Setting up this behavior requires you to create the AP elements first and set the correct visibility option for each element you want to control. Then select the tag to which the behavior will be attached and select the Show-Hide Elements action.

- In the Show-Hide Elements dialog box, select which elements to show and which to hide, as shown in the second illustration below.

- Select the desired triggering event. To make an element appear when the mouse pointer moves over it, use onMouseOver.

- You will usually want to repeat the action to rehide elements that were originally hidden.

Set text for a text field

Show-Hide Elements dialog box

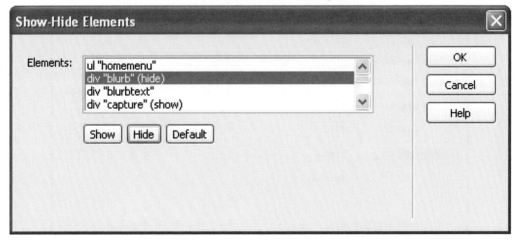

Drag AP Element

- The Drag AP Element behavior allows a visitor to drag an AP element in the browser. Because a visitor would not ordinarily try to move an AP element, you must provide a way of letting the visitor know an element can be repositioned.

- An obvious use for such a behavior would be to allow visitors to assemble a puzzle on a page, each piece of which is a separate AP element. Or, create an interactive learning page in which students can drag definitions next to vocabulary words.

- The Drag AP Element adds an enormous amount of JavaScript to a page, which can impact loading time. If you decide nevertheless that you want to use this behavior, select the <body> tag for a page and then select the Drag AP Element action.

- In the Drag AP Element dialog box, shown in the first illustration below, select the element you want to be able to move.

- You can specify settings such as a specific location that the element will "drop" when it is dragged and a snap setting to grab the element if it is close to the drop target.

Apply Spry Effects

- You worked with Spry data tools and widgets in Exercise 45. Dreamweaver CS3 also includes Spry effects, small programs that apply visual effects to selected tags.

- You can find the Spry effects by pointing to Effects on the Behaviors panel's actions list. Some of these effects require you to specify a target such as a <div> that will receive the action. Other effects can apply directly to the currently selected tag.

- The Highlight effect, for example, will apply a highlight to a tag that changes color over a specified span of time.

- Parameters differ according to the effect chosen. The Highlight dialog box, shown in the second illustration below, allows you to specify the target element, duration of the effect, and colors to display at the start and end of the effect as well as after the effect has finished.

- Select the Toggle effect checkbox to have the effect proceed in reverse order the next time it is triggered.

Drag AP Element dialog box

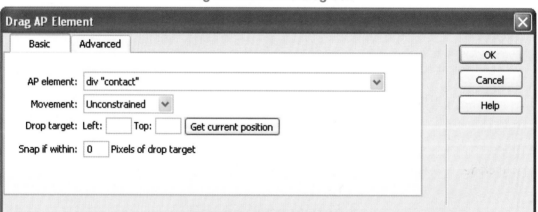

Highlight dialog box

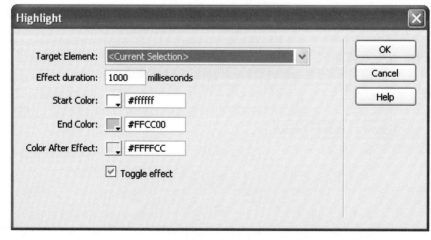

PROCEDURES

Popup Message Behavior

1. Select tag to which the behavior will be attached.
2. Display the **Behaviors** panel.
3. Click **+** to display the actions list.
4. Click **Popup Message**.
5. Type message in the **Message** text box.
6. Click [OK].
7. Specify event for action, if necessary.

Set Text of Container Behavior

1. Select tag of container to which the behavior will be attached.
2. Display the **Behaviors** panel.
3. Click **+** to display the actions list.
4. Point to **Set Text** and click **Set Text of Container**.
5. Click **Container** list arrow and select container that will receive new text.
6. Click in the **New HTML** area and type the new text, along with any desired formatting tags (or paste code that you cut from the Code view of a page).
7. Click [OK].
8. Specify event for action, if necessary.

Set Text of Text Field Behavior

1. Select text field in form to which the behavior will be attached.
2. Display the **Behaviors** panel.
3. Click **+** to display the actions list.
4. Point to **Set Text** and click **Set Text of Text Field**.
5. Select field name from the **Text Field** list, if necessary.
6. Type text to appear in field in the **New text** text box.
7. Click [OK].
8. Specify event for action, if necessary.

Show-Hide Element Behavior

> ✔ Before attaching this behavior, create the elements you want to use and set visibility so that the element that should display when the page loads is visible and any other elements that will be displayed by the action are hidden.

1. Select tag that will perform the action.
2. Display the **Behaviors** panel.
3. Click **+** to display the actions list.
4. Click **Show-Hide Elements**.

5. Click an element that should be hidden when the event occurs and click [Show].
6. Click an element that should be shown when the event occurs and click [Hide].
7. Click [OK].
8. Specify event for action, if necessary.

Apply a Spry Effect

1. Select tag or element to which you will attach the effect.
2. Display the **Behaviors** panel.
3. Click **+** to display the actions list.
4. Point to **Effects** and then click the desired Spry effect.
5. In the parameters dialog box for the chosen effect, select desired settings.
6. Click [OK].
7. Specify event for action, if necessary.

EXERCISE DIRECTIONS

✔ *For best results, point to Show Events For on the actions list and select IE 6.0.*

1. Start Dreamweaver and open the tutorials site.
2. Open products.html and select the <body> tag in the tag selector.
3. Create a popup message that will display the following text when the page closes: **Check back soon for more online tutorial titles!** *On unload.*
4. Save the page and preview it and then click a link to go to a different page in the site. The popup message should display when you exit the page.
5. Open support.html. Use the *Contact us!* link to set the text of the AP div on the page as follows:
   - To make it easy to insert the HTML code in the Set Text of Container dialog box, you will type the text on the page and then cut the code and paste it in the dialog box. Type the following text below the AP anchor point on the page, using line breaks at the end of each line and applying boldface as shown.
   **E-mail:
   cincimail@cincitorial.com
   Phone:
   513.555.4500
   Fax:
   513.555.4501**
   - Apply the .contacttext CSS style to the text you typed.
   - Change to a code view, select the entire paragraph, and then use the Cut command to remove it from the page.
   - Restore Design view and click in the *Contact us!* link.
   - Select the Set Text of Container action.
   - In the Container list, click the div "contact" container. Then paste the text you cut in the New HTML box.
6. Add a Spry effect to the link: With the link still selected, choose the Highlight effect from the Effects list on the action list.
7. Choose an end color and a color to display after the effect. Change the event to onMouseOver.
8. Save your changes and preview the page to text the actions. If desired, adjust the Highlight duration.
9. Open index.html. You want a message to display near the employment form to let visitors know CinciTorial is a good place to work. You can use the Show-Hide Elements behavior to display the message when a visitor starts to fill out the form.

   - First create the AP div that will contain the message. Insert an AP div below the form in the blue column and name it **blurb**. Resize it to 160 W by 85 H. *BY. NOT PX*
   - Insert the ◉divback.gif image from the Lesson 6 Data folder as a background image in the AP div.
   - Open the CSS Rule dialog box for the AP div. In the Background category, set the Repeat to no-repeat. In the Box category, add 6 px of padding on all sides of the AP div. In the Positioning category, set the Top measurement at 425 and the Right measurement at 170.
   - Type the following text in the AP div: **CinciTorial is an Equal Opportunity Employer offering good benefits and great working conditions!**
   - Style the text with the .linktext style. Specify None as the format. Center and boldface the text.
10. Save the page and preview it to make sure the AP div is positioned correctly on the page. The blurb AP div should look similar to Illustration A. (The position of the blurb AP div will vary relative to the form depending how wide your monitor is.)
11. Now adjust visibility and attach the behavior:
    - Hide the blurb AP div by closing the visibility eye in the AP Elements panel.
    - Click in the *Name* label of the form and then use the tag selector to click the <label> tag.
    - Select the Show-Hide Elements action.
    - In the Show-Hide Elements dialog box, click div "blurb" and click the [Hide] button. *Show*
    - Specify the onMouseOver event.
12. Save changes and preview the action. Move the mouse over the first form field to see the blurb appear.
13. Return to the index.html page in Dreamweaver and use the Set Text of Text Field action to insert the following message in the form field: **Type your full name.** Use the onFocusIn event.
14. Save the page and preview again. Click in the first form field to see the text message. Replace the message with your name and press Tab to move to the next field. Continue to fill out the form, then click the Send button. The blurb should close.
15. Close the browser and any open pages.
16. Exit Dreamweaver.

Illustration A

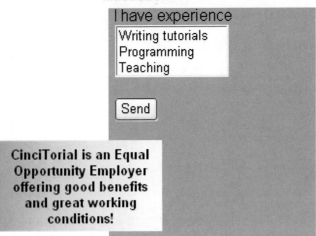

ON YOUR OWN

1. Start Dreamweaver and open the gardencenter site.

2. Add a popup message to the events.html page that lets visitors know the autumn and winter events are coming soon. Display the message when the page unloads.

3. Open the contact.html page. Change the color of the address text to another color used in the site. (You may create either an internal or an external style, if desired, to make it stand out on the page.)

4. Insert an AP div in a blank area of the page that contains the text Coming Soon! Interactive Maps! Name the AP div maps and format the background and the text as desired.

5. Select the paragraph of text that contains the address (select using the tag selector) and attach the Show-Hide Elements behavior to show the maps AP div on mouse over and hide the maps AP div on mouse out.

6. Add another action to the same paragraph of text: Select the Shake Spry effect and apply it to the div "maps". Choose the onMouseOver event

7. Save all pages and view the pages on which you have added behaviors.

8. Close all open pages and exit Dreamweaver.

Exercise | 48

Skills Covered

- **About Multimedia Files**
- **Insert a Flash Movie**
- **Modify and Play a Movie**
- **Insert Flash Buttons and Flash Text**
- **Other Multimedia Plugins**

Software Skills Multimedia files—sound, action, video, and interactive elements such as games—can add new levels of impact, creativity, and interest to a Web site. Flash objects such as movies and buttons, as well as other kinds of multimedia files such as Shockwave movies and Java applets, can easily be added to Web documents.

Application Skills In this exercise, you will work with multimedia objects such as Flash buttons and text and insert a simple Flash movie in the tutorials site.

TERMS

ActiveX Microsoft-developed technology that allows software components to work with other software components regardless of the language used to create them.

Applet Small Java application that can be embedded in a Web page to create interactivity for animations.

Flash Adobe application used to create animation and multimedia programs that can be embedded in Web pages.

Java Programming language that operates on multiple platforms and operating systems.

Multimedia Information presented by video sequences, animation, illustration, and sound.

Plugin Utility programs that extend an application's capabilities.

NOTES

About Multimedia Files

- **Multimedia** files present information in the form of video sequences, animations, illustrations, and sounds. The Media drop-down list on the Common tab of the Insert bar provides buttons for inserting several popular types of multimedia files. These files include Flash movies and objects, Shockwave movies, Java applets, ActiveX controls, and **plugin** files. Plugin files require Netscape Navigator plug-ins for Netscape and Mozilla browsers.

  ✔ *The Shockwave button can also be used to insert QuickTime movies.*

- While multimedia files add an undeniable punch to Web pages, consider carefully before going all out with sound and video embellishments. Multimedia files can add substantially to the size of the site, which may result in slow downloads that turn visitors off.

- Moreover, some multimedia objects, such as Shockwave movies, require a visitor to download a player before the object will display. This can be a time-consuming process that many site visitors will not want to bother with.

- This exercise concentrates on working with Flash, because this application is now so widely used. You will learn in this exercise how to insert Flash movies and how to create Flash buttons and text.

  ✔ *If you have the Adobe Web Creative Suite installed, you can create your own Flash movies.*

Insert a Flash Movie

▪ Adobe **Flash** files are designed to deliver crisp animations and presentations with relatively small file sizes. Flash files are generally called *movies*.

▪ Flash movies can also include sound in the form of MP3. If you want to add sound to your Web site, you can do so by embedding the sound or music in a Flash file.

▪ One caveat about using Flash is that it requires Flash Player to display in the browser, and different versions of Flash Player can vary in the kind of content they can display. If you have built a Flash movie that requires a specific version of Flash Player, you should create a message to that effect and a link to allow visitors to download the required version.

▪ When you insert a Flash file, Dreamweaver uses two sets of HTML tags to provide support for multiple browsers. The <object> tags are supplied for Microsoft browsers and the <embed> tags are supplied for browsers such as Netscape, Opera, and Mozilla.

▪ Flash movies (identified by the .swf extension) can be added to a Web document using menu commands or a button from the Common tab of the Insert bar.

▪ Position the insertion point on the page where the movie is to appear and then use the Insert>Media>Flash command.

▪ Or, click 🎬 Flash on the Media button's list on the Common tab of the Insert bar.

  ✔ *The movie can be inserted directly in the document or in an AP div in the document.*

▪ After you insert the multimedia file and save it in your current Web site, Dreamweaver displays the Object Tag Accessibility Attributes dialog box, as shown in the illustration above right. As for images,

frames, and forms, this dialog box allows you to supply a title for the media object that can be read by a screen reader.

▪ Once you have supplied a title for the object, Dreamweaver inserts a gray placeholder for the object on the page. If you have the Property inspector displayed, it shows properties for the selected multimedia object (see the illustration below).

Object Tag Accessibility Attributes dialog box

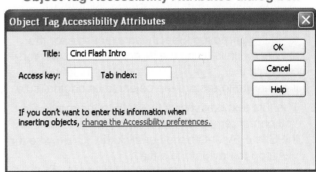

▪ The size of the placeholder is determined by the original size of the multimedia object. You can change the object's size using sizing handles or the Property inspector.

▪ Dreamweaver displays a gray placeholder labeled to identify the media file type. For miscellaneous kinds of plugins, a gray puzzle piece is displayed. More information, specific to the media object or plugin, is also available in its Property inspector.

▪ The first time you save the page after inserting the movie, Dreamweaver copies dependent files to your site to run active content. The file is stored in the Scripts folder and must be uploaded with other files for the Flash movie to run.

Flash file placeholder and properties

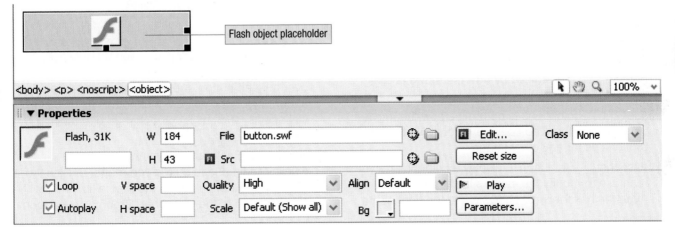

Flash object placeholder

Modify and Play a Movie

- You can use the Flash Property inspector to modify the appearance and performance of the movie in the Web document. Dreamweaver also includes a [▷ Play] button on the Property inspector to allow you to play a movie without previewing the page in a browser.

- The Property inspector displays by default several properties that will look familiar to you from other graphic objects (see the previous illustration).

- Use the Name text box to identify the movie for scripting purposes. Specify an exact size for the movie in pixels using the W and H text boxes. You can click the [Reset size] button after making a sizing change to restore the object to its original size.

- The File text box shows the path to the movie file. You can enter a path in this box, point to the file in the Site or Assets panel, or click the 🗀 Browse for File icon to navigate to a file.

- The [▣ Edit...] button opens Flash so you can edit the movie. Flash will request the original document file, which has the FLA extension. If you know you might need to edit a Flash movie, make sure you have this file as well as the movie file with the SWF extension.

  ✔ When you insert an SWF Flash file, you are inserting a file exported from Flash with properties suitable for embedding in a Web page, not the original Flash file.

- Select the Loop checkbox if you want the movie to play over and over when displayed in the browser. This option is selected by default.

- Select the Autoplay checkbox to play the movie automatically when the page loads. This option is selected by default.

- Use the V space and H space text boxes in the Property inspector to set an amount of white space in pixels above, below, and on both sides of the movie.

- The default Quality setting of High is adequate for most browsers. The other settings (for example, Low) can be used depending on how the movie was made.

- The Scale property sets the scale parameter for the <object> and <embed> tags. This is an advanced setting also determined by how the movie is created in Flash.

- Use the Align options to determine how the movie is aligned in the Web document. You have the same options as for any other image.

- Use the 🔲 Bg button to display a color palette you can use to modify the movie's background color (or type the hexadecimal equivalent to the right of the button). The background color appears when the movie is active.

- Click the [Parameters...] button to launch a dialog box that allows you to enter additional movie parameters. These advanced settings are beyond the scope of this book, but you can consult Dreamweaver Help for more information.

  ✔ The param button on the Media drop-down list inserts a <param> tag using the Tag Editor dialog box. It is used for applying parameters in Code view.

- Click the [▷ Play] button in the Property inspector to preview the appearance and function of the movie in Dreamweaver. Using this button saves time because you do not have to switch back and forth from the page to the browser to see results of modifications.

- Click the [■ Stop] button to turn off the movie. You must click this button even after the movie stops playing to restore the gray placeholder and make further modifications.

Insert Flash Buttons and Flash Text

- Dreamweaver includes two features that can add visual interest as well as functionality to Web pages: Flash buttons and Flash text. When you use these features, you create your own Flash objects without having to leave Dreamweaver.

Insert Flash Button

- Dreamweaver includes a set of predesigned Flash buttons that you can customize and insert on your Web pages. These buttons (see the following illustration) are not only graphically interesting, they also provide functional ways to navigate a site. Because you do not have to create the various up, over, and down states in another application, Flash buttons can save you a great deal of time.

Flash button on a Web page

- Flash buttons have additional appeal because of their interactive effects. When the mouse pointer is over a Flash button, most buttons change their appearance. Each type of button has its own special effects, such as a color change or a moving part.

- To insert a Flash button, use the Insert>Media>Flash button command, or click the 🔏 Flash Button button on the Media list on the Common tab of the Insert bar. Dreamweaver opens

- the Insert Flash Button dialog box shown in the illustration below.
- Choose a button style from the Style list, which offers over 40 different Flash buttons. (Some buttons have the same appearance except for color.) You can then type the text that will appear on the button and choose the font and size for the text.

  ✔ *The buttons can fit only a limited amount of text—typically one or two words. Keep your labels short.*

- Dreamweaver suggests a font and size for each button style. If your system does not have the default font for a particular button, Dreamweaver displays a message at the bottom of the dialog box to let you know you do not have the font. You can then choose a different font from the Font list.
- You can also change the font and size as desired even if your system has the default font. Choose a new font from the Font list and type a new size in the Size box.

  ✔ *The Sample button in the dialog box will not change as you make changes in the dialog box.*

- Flash buttons are designed to work like links, so you can type in the Link box or browse to locate the page that will open when the button is clicked. You can also specify a target for the linked page.
- If you want to surround the button with a background color other than the default white, use the ⬚. Bg color box to choose a new color. The background color displays as a rectangle of color behind the Flash button.
- Dreamweaver suggests a default file name for the Flash button. You can change the default name in the Save as text box if desired.
- If you have specified accessibility for media objects, you will be prompted to create a title for the Flash button (and for Flash text as well) before the button is actually inserted in the page.
- To modify a Flash button, double-click it to open the Insert Flash Button dialog box again or click the [✎ Edit...] button in the Property inspector. As you make changes, you can click the [Apply] button in the dialog box to see the result of your changes on the button on the Web page.

Insert Flash Button dialog box

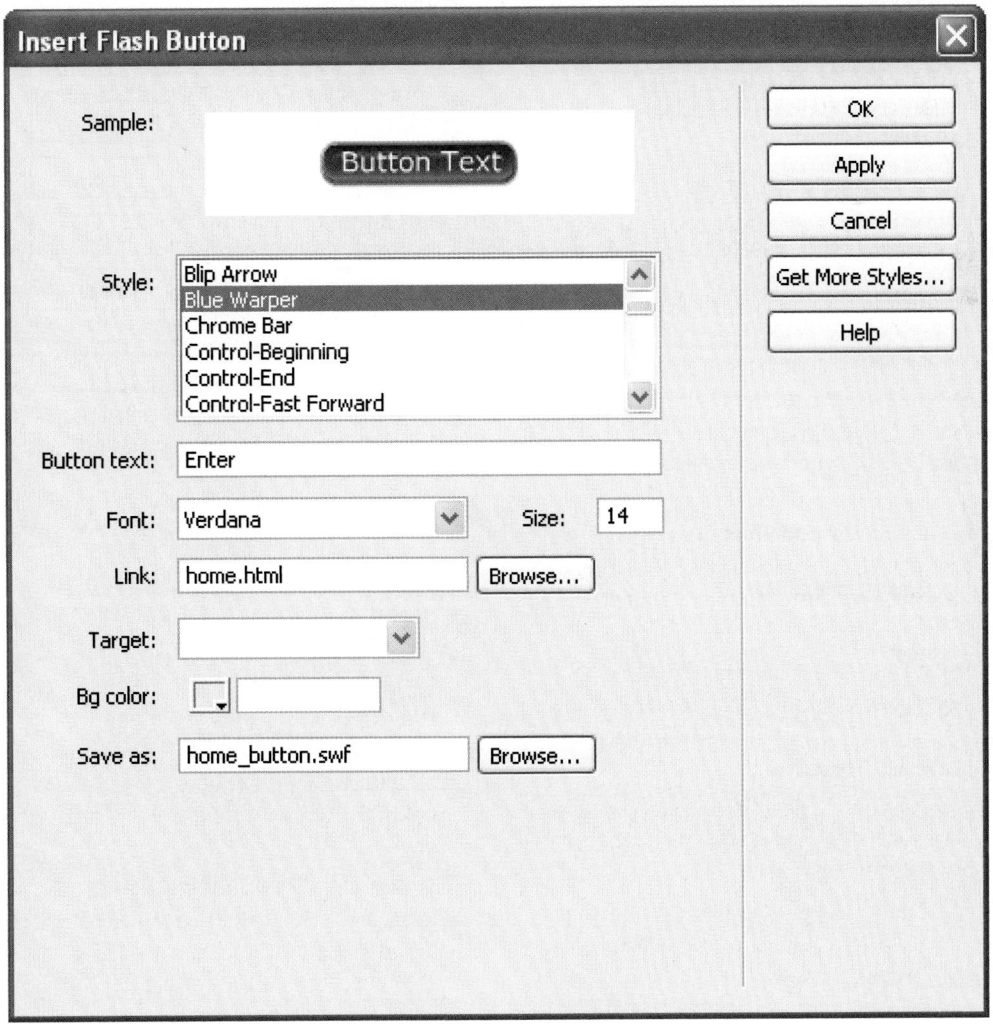

- You can also make some modifications in the Flash button's Property inspector. Because a Flash button is actually a Flash movie, the Property inspector shows some of the same settings as for any Flash movie.

- To see a button's special effects, for example, click the ▶ Play button in the Property inspector and then move the mouse pointer over the button to activate the special effects. This saves you the step of previewing in the browser. Press the ■ Stop button when you are finished previewing the effects to be able to make further modifications to the button's properties.

Insert Flash Text

- Dreamweaver's Flash text feature allows you to create a short Flash movie that consists of text only. As for a Flash button, you can use this text as a link to another page or Web site, or you can use it simply to create a special text effect on a page.

- Flash text changes color when the mouse pointer rests on it. This effect occurs whether or not the text is linked to another page. Such an effect is called a *rollover* effect, because it occurs when the mouse "rolls over" the object.

- To create a Flash text movie, use the Insert>Media>Flash Text command, or click the 🗛 Flash Text button on the Media list on the Common tab of the Insert bar. Dreamweaver opens the Insert Flash Text dialog box shown in the illustration below.

- Choose a font, font size, font style, and alignment for the Flash text object. Use the Color box to select the initial color for the text in the object and the Rollover color box to choose the color that displays when the mouse pointer rests on the text.

- Type the Flash text itself in the Text box. As you can see by the dimensions of this box, you can create a word, phrase, or entire paragraph if desired. Note that the Text box does not have a wrap feature. If you want text in a paragraph to wrap, you must press Enter to start new lines.

- With the Show font checkbox selected, text in the Text box displays in the font you have chosen. Using this feature can help you judge how your Flash text will look on the page.

Insert Flash Text dialog box

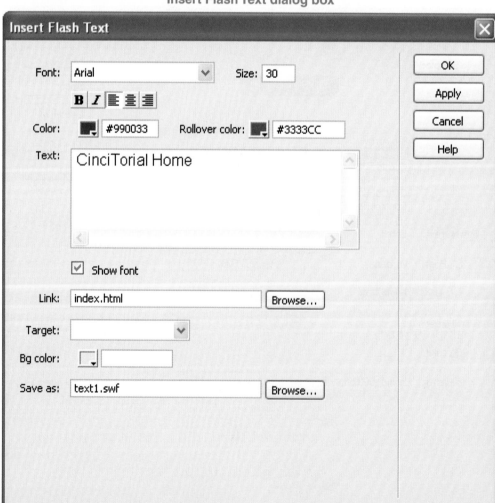

■ As for a Flash button, you can create a link for the Flash text to open, specify a target, and select a background color. You can also save the Flash text object with a file name other than the default shown in the Save as text box.

■ Double-click a Flash text object to make further changes in the Insert Flash Text dialog box—or click the [Edit...] button in the Property inspector. As for a Flash button, you can use the [Apply] button to see how your changes look on the page and the Property inspector to "play" the movie.

■ Roll the mouse over the text to see the color change take effect after clicking the [▶ Play] button, and click [■ Stop] when you have finished.

Other Multimedia Plugins

■ You can employ the same techniques used to insert Flash movies to insert Shockwave movies and other plugin types from the Media drop-down list. Click the appropriate button, navigate to the location of the file, insert it, and adjust properties as necessary.

■ Use the 🍵 ▾ Applet button on the Media drop-down list to insert **Java** applets. An **applet** is a small application that can be embedded in a Web page.

✔ You can work with a simple applet in the Dreamweaver in Depth steps at the end of this exercise.

■ For example, an applet can be used to insert Web site counters that tabulate the number of "hits" or visits your site receives, visual effects, games, Web site tools, and so on.

■ Use the 🔲 ▾ ActiveX button to insert **ActiveX** components. Formerly known as OLE controls, ActiveX components function like browser plugins to perform specific tasks. They are typically used for buttons, forms, and the like.

■ ActiveX components run only in Windows-based Internet Explorer. They will not work in a Macintosh environment or in Netscape and Mozilla browsers.

■ If you need to insert a file that requires a Netscape plugin to play properly, use the 🧩 ▾ Plugin button.

■ All of these objects are created in other programs—some of which require programming skills—and are beyond the scope of this course. Your instructor can, however, provide you with, or help you locate, files that you can use.

✔ You can also use a Web browser search engine and type in keywords such as "free Java applets," "free ActiveX controls," and so on to obtain such files to insert in your Web pages.

PROCEDURES

Insert Flash Movie (Ctrl + Alt + F)

1. Position insertion point where movie should appear on the page.
2. Click **I**nsert . . . . (Alt)+(I)
3. Point to **Media** . . . . (M)
4. Click **F**lash . . . . (F)
   OR
■ Click **Flash** button 🎬 from the Media drop-down list on the Common tab of the Insert bar.

In the Select File dialog box:

1. Navigate to file location.
2. Click file.
3. Click [OK].

In Dreamweaver:

1. Store file in current Web site when prompted.
2. Supply a title for the file.

3. Click [OK].

✔ You can use these steps to insert any media plugin—Java applet, ActiveX, Netscape plugin—on the Media drop-down list.

To copy script files to the local site:

■ Save the page on which you have just inserted media file and click [OK] to copy dependent files to the site.

Play Movie

1. Click movie to select placeholder, if necessary.
2. Click [▶ Play] in expanded Property inspector to play movie in Web page.
3. Click [■ Stop] in expanded Property inspector to stop playing movie.

Modify Movie

1. Click movie to select placeholder, if necessary.
2. Change properties as follows:
   ■ Type name for movie in the Name text box.
   ■ Set exact width and height in the **W** and **H** text boxes.
   ■ Specify or locate media file in the **File** text box.
   ■ Set vertical alignment for movie in the **Align** list box.
   ■ Change background color using the **Bg** button 🔲 (or type hexadecimal value).
   ■ Set space above and below and on each side of movie using the **V space** and **H space** text boxes.
   ■ Set quality in the **Quality** list box.

- Specify continuous play by selecting the **Loop** check-box.
- Set the movie to play when the page loads by selecting the **Autoplay** checkbox.

Insert Flash Button

1. Click **Insert** . . . . Alt+I
2. Point to **Media** . . . . M
3. Click **Flash Button** . . . . . . B

   OR

- Click **Flash Button** button 🔳 on the Media drop-down list on the Common tab of the Insert bar.

In the Insert Flash Button dialog box:

1. Customize the button:
   - Choose a button style.
   - Enter text to label button.
   - Select new font and size, if desired.
   - Type or browse to page to link to button.
   - Specify target, if necessary.
   - Select background color for button.
   - Save button with default or other file name.
2. Click [OK].

In Dreamweaver:

1. Supply a title for the media object.
2. Click [OK].

Insert Flash Text

1. Click **Insert** . . . . Alt+I
2. Point to **Media** . . . . M
3. Click **Flash Text** . . . . T

   OR

- Click **Flash Text** button 🔳 on the Media drop-down list on the Common tab of the Insert bar.

In the Insert Flash Text dialog box:

1. Create Flash text:
   - Choose a font and size.
   - Choose font style and alignment, if desired.
   - Choose color for initial text and rollover color.
   - Type text for object.
   - Type or browse to page to link to text.
   - Specify target, if necessary.
   - Select background color for text.

- Save text with default or other file name.
2. Click [OK].

In Dreamweaver:

1. Supply a title for the media object.
2. Click [OK].

Modify Flash Button or Flash Text

1. Double-click the Flash button or Flash text.

   OR

   a. Click the Flash button or Flash text.
   b. Click [🖉 Edit...] in the Property inspector.
2. Change properties in the dialog box and click [OK].
3. Change other properties in the Property inspector.

EXERCISE DIRECTIONS

1. Start Dreamweaver and open the **tutorials** site.
2. Open ⦿**intro.html** from the Lesson 6 Data folder and save the page in the current site with the same name.
3. With the insertion point in the blank paragraph above the main head, insert the ⦿**cinci_flash.swf** Flash file from the Lesson 6 Data folder. Save the file in your images folder and supply the title **Flash intro**.
4. Name the object **intro** in the Property inspector. Deselect the Loop checkbox.
5. Click [▶ Play] to play the movie.
6. Click [■ Stop] to stop the movie and display the placeholder again.

7. Save changes, allowing Dreamweaver to copy dependent files to the site, and preview the page in the browser to see the Flash movie play once as the page is loaded.
8. On the **intro.html** page in Dreamweaver, insert a new paragraph below the last paragraph. Insert a Flash button and customize it as follows:
   - Choose the Glass-Turquoise style.
   - Type the button text **Home**.
   - Change the font to Arial and the size to 12, if necessary.
   - Type a link to the **index.html** page in your **cincitorial** folder on your hard drive, such as C:\Inetpub\wwwroot\cincitorial\index.html.

   ✔ *Be sure to type the link. You cannot browse to this location and have the text link correctly.*

- Save the button as home.swf.

9. Close the dialog box and supply the title home. Use the Property inspector to name the button **home**.

10. "Play" the button: Rest the mouse pointer over the button to see its color change.

11. The button's text is a bit small. Change the size of the label to 14.

12. Click to the right of the Flash button, then press Ctrl + Shift + spacebar twice to insert two non-breaking spaces.

13. Insert another Flash button with the same format as the previous one.

- Type Tutorials as the button label, and change the font to Arial and the size to 14.

- Link the button to the index.html file in the tutorials site.

- Save the Flash button as tutorials.swf.

14. Supply the title tutorials and, in the Property inspector, name the button tutorials.

15. Preview the page in the browser. It should look similar to Illustration A.

16. Test the link to the CinciTorial site to make sure you entered the link properly. Use the Back button to return to the intro page and then test the link to the CinciTutorials site.

17. Close any open pages and the browser and exit Dreamweaver.

Illustration A

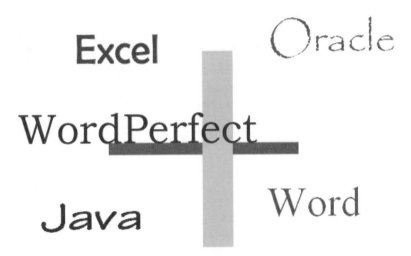

Welcome to CinciTorial

If you work with applications such as those shown above, or if you publish courseware on these applications, CinciTorial can help you. CinciTorial offers a full range of editorial services as well as comprehensive instruction options.

For more information on our company, click the Home button. For more information on our online tutorials, click the Tutorials button.

Home   Tutorials

ON YOUR OWN

1. Start Dreamweaver and open the gardencenter site.

2. Open index.html. You should create a link on this page to the mailing list form—you can use a Flash button for this purpose.
   - Insert the button below the current text with accompanying text to let visitors know they can click the button to open the mailing list form.
   - Choose any Flash button that goes well with the page. Be sure to give the button an appropriate name.

3. Open contact.html. Below the table, insert a new paragraph and type the text Other Links. Format the text as Heading 3 in a style and color that matches other headings in the site.

4. Below the heading, insert the following Flash text object:
   - The text should read Ohio State Extension Services.
   - Format the text with your choice of font, font size, color, and rollover color.
   - Create the link to http://extension.osu.edu.
   - Give the text an appropriate title and name.

5. Open info.html. Insert a Flash movie on this page as follows:
   - Add a new AP div to the page and name it movie.
   - Insert in the AP div the Flash movie ⊙gardenmovie.swf from the Lesson 6 Data folder. Resize the AP div if necessary to fit closely around the movie.
   - Deselect the Loop option for the Flash movie and play it to preview it.
   - Move the AP div to fit under the picture at the right side of the window.
   - Save the page and preview. You may need to adjust the position of the copyright notice or the AP div for your browser.

6. Preview the entire site, checking your new multi-media enhancements on the index.html, contact.html, and info.html pages.

   ✔ *If you receive a message about Flash stopping a potentially unsafe operation, see your instructor for information on how to change settings to allow the Flash text to work.*

7. Close any open pages and exit Dreamweaver.

DREAMWEAVER IN DEPTH

Java applets can perform useful tasks on a Web page or simply add interesting effects. The Web is a rich source of Java applets that you can download and customize for your site. To see how to add an applet to a Web page, follow these steps.

1. Create a new site named java with settings you have used for other sites.

2. Open the ⊙DID48.html file from the Lesson 6 Data folder and save it in the java site as java.html with the page title My Java Applet.

3. Copy into the site the ⊙vInferno.class file from the Lesson 6 Data folder.

4. Now insert the code that will control the applet file:
   - Switch to Code view.
   - Locate the blank paragraph below the *Interactive and Dynamic* heading and click after the opening tag.
   - Type the following code:
     ```
     <applet code=vInferno.class name=vInferno
     width=360 height=150 class="applet">

         <param name=message
     value="Java^1Applets^3Are^4Smokin!^2">

         <param name=ferocity value=90>

         <param name=fontname value="Arial">

         <param name=fontsize value="30">

     </applet>
     ```

5. Switch to Design view and save changes. Preview the page in a browser and watch the animation. To see another effect, move the mouse pointer over the applet when type displays and move the pointer to control the position of the text in the applet.

6. Close the browser and any open pages and exit Dreamweaver.

Summary Exercise

Application Skills In this exercise, you will attach behaviors to some pages of the High Ridge site. You will also create Flash text to link the site to the USA Swimming site.

DIRECTIONS

1. Start Dreamweaver and open the highridge site.
2. Create a new page to use with the Open Browser Window behavior. Name the page meetresults.html with the page title Flying Fish Meet Results. Insert the following text:

   Swim Meet Results

   At the most recent meet, the High Ridge Flying Fish posted the following scores:

   Diving: 85 points
   Swimming: 255 points

   The combined score of 340 points was enough to beat Valley View by 35 points. Go Fish!

3. Format the text as desired.
4. Open the swimdive.html page and detach the page from the template. Insert a heading that reads Meet Results above the table with formats that match the page and create a dummy link from the heading.
5. Attach the Open Browser Window behavior to the dummy link to open the meetresults.html page in a new browser window when the link is clicked.

6. Open the membership.html page. Create the following popup message that will display when the page unloads:

   High Ridge is currently accepting new members. If you have any further questions about membership, please contact us! We'd love to have you!

7. Activate or open the swimdive.html page and insert the following text as Flash text below the calendar table:

   For more swimming news and information, visit USA Swimming!

8. Format the text as desired and set the link to **http://www.usaswimming.org**. Give the text an appropriate name and title.
9. Preview the site in the browser to test your behaviors and other multimedia effects.
10. Close all open pages and exit Dreamweaver.

Exercise | 50
Application Exercise

Application Skills   In this exercise, you will add a Flash movie to the Grand site and use Show-Hide Elements to swap AP divs.

DIRECTIONS

1. Start Dreamweaver and open the grand Web site.

2. Open main.html. A colleague has created a Flash movie for this page using the same artwork as the *Grand Theatre* image. The movie simulates a neon sign flickering to life.

3. Delete the grand.gif image from the page. Replace it with ⊙ grandmovie.swf from the Lesson 6 Data folder. Save the movie in your images folder and supply an appropriate title.

4. Play the movie from the Property inspector. After you stop the movie, deselect the Loop option so it will play only once in the browser.

5. Open showintro.html. Cut the boldfaced information near the top of the page and insert it in an AP div named rates.

6. Format the AP div and text as desired, inserting padding if desired.

7. Position the AP div so it is centered below the navigation bar and above the last heading on the page. Preview the page in the browser to make sure there is enough space below the AP div and above the last heading.

8. Create another AP div the same size and insert the following text:

   Anniversary Celebration!

   Bargain Tuesday Rates

   $5.50

   for All Shows, All Week!

9. Format the text and AP div as desired. Name the new AP div anniversary.

10. Position the anniversary AP div at the same position as the rates AP div. Hide the anniversary AP div.

11. Use the Show-Hide Elements behavior to show the anniversary AP div and hide the rates AP div when the rates AP div is clicked. Add another behavior to redisplay rates and hide anniversary when the mouse moves away from the AP div.

12. Open the frame page that contains the links for the page and add text such as Click rates to see our Anniversary Special!

13. Save all pages and test the Web site, viewing each of your multimedia elements and behaviors.

14. Save and close all open pages and exit Dreamweaver.

Curriculum Integration

Application Skills   For your Modern British Literature class, you have been assigned the task of creating a Web page on James Joyce. You will use the Show-Hide Elements behavior to create a timeline of his birth, major works, and death. Prepare for this task by locating the following information:

- Biographical information on James Joyce, including a picture of the author

- Information on when each of his four major works—*Dubliners, Finnegans Wake, Portrait of the Artist as a Young Man,* and *Ulysses*—was published

DIRECTIONS

Create a new site with an appropriate name. Create a new page with a name such as **joycetimeline.html** and an appropriate page title. You may want to use a table or layers to organize the page.

On your page, insert the picture you found and an appropriate heading. Provide a brief introduction that tells where and when Joyce was born, summarizes his education, and explains where he lived after he left Ireland.

Create small, book-shaped AP divs for each of the four major works and insert in the AP div the book title. Format each AP div in a different color. Position the AP divs in a vertical column, in alphabetical order, so that you begin with *Dubliners* and end with *Ulysses.*

Prepare a paragraph summary for each work and position the paragraphs in AP divs to the right of their book AP divs. You may want to include the first few lines of each book (you can copy this information from books you have on hand or from an online version of the book). At the end of each summary, insert the sentence *When was it published?* Format each of these sentences as a dummy link. (To prevent the browser from jumping to the top of the page each time you click a dummy link, create the dummy by typing javascript:; in the Link box.)

At the bottom of the page, create a table to be used for the timeline itself. Include in the timeline the dates of Joyce's birth, death, and years each major work was published. Illustration A shows one possible layout for the timeline.

Create a copy of each book AP div and position it in the correct location on the timeline. Specify the exact location for each AP div above its year date using the Property inspector.

Attach the Show-Hide Elements behavior to each *When was it published?* link so that when you click the link, the book "disappears" from its original location and displays on the timeline.

Test the site in a browser and make sure your behavior works properly.

Close the page and exit Dreamweaver.

Illustration A

Born in Dublin   *Died in Zurich*

| | | | | | |
| 1882 | 1914 | 1916 | 1922 | 1939 | 1941 |

Exercise | 52

Critical Thinking

Application Skills In this exercise, you will replace the navigation bar on all pages with a Spry menu bar. You will also add behaviors to improve the site.

DIRECTIONS

- Open your personal Web site. Open the Library and delete the navigation bar item.

- Open the home page and remove the existing navigation bar. Replace it with a Spry navigation bar that links to all pages in your site. Illustration A shows a sample menu bar on a home page.

- If desired, adjust formats of the Widget to use fonts and colors from your site.

- Copy the menu bar.

- Open each page, including the template page, remove the original navigation bar, and replace it with a copy of the Spry menu bar.

- Test the site in the browser to make sure the menu bars are working correctly and look attractive.

- Display the page that has a form on it. Use actions to validate form fields and add text messages in fields to help visitors fill out the form. (If desired, you may apply Spry Validation widgets to the form's text fields to validate them.) Test the form in the browser to make sure your validation works correctly.

- Close all open pages and exit Dreamweaver.

★ Add spry accordian
★ Add show/hide element
★ Add flash text
★ Add flash button

Clifton Drama Club

| Home | Join | Outings | Seminars |

Welcome to the Drama Club!

The Clifton Drama Club is a group of people who love everything about the theater, including:

- o Acting
- o Writing drama
- o Production design
- o Costume design
- o Makeup design
- o Stage management
- o Lighting and other technical support

If you're interested in any of these areas, the Drama Club is for you. Like more information? Fill out the form on the Join the Club page and we'll be in touch.

What We Do

The Clifton Drama Club sponsors four plays a year and contributes expertise and support for the school's musical production. When we're not working on school dramatics, we schedule visits to local and regional theater productions to see how the pros do it. The Drama Club also arranges for seminars and workshops with local theater groups to learn the nuts and bolts of production design, costumes and makeup, and the behind-the-scenes technical skills without which the show would never be able to go on.

For more information on the Drama Club, contact studentname@website.net.

Lesson | 7

Manage and Publish a Web Site

Skills Covered

■ **Use Browser Compatibility Check**   ■ **Check and Modify Links**

Software Skills   After creating your Web site, you can use Dreamweaver tools and features to manage the site and publish it to a server. Dreamweaver allows you to check pages for compatibility in a number of browsers and check and modify links to prevent broken links or unlinked pages.

Application Skills   In this exercise, you will begin some final cleanup on the CinciTutorial site. You will check links throughout the site and check pages in the site against your specified target browser and make some corrections required by the browser.

TERMS

No new terms in this exercise.

NOTES

Use Browser Compatibility Check

■ As you create your Web sites in Dreamweaver, you have some options for tailoring content to specific browsers. The Behaviors panel, for example, allows you to select behaviors that will perform correctly in a target browser version.

■ A feature new in Dreamweaver CS3, the Browser Compatibility Check, allows you to check a page to find potential CSS problems that might affect how a page displays across a variety of browsers. Checking compatibility both during and at the end of the site-creation process prevents you from designing pages that cannot be viewed correctly in browsers you wish to support.

■ Launch this feature using the File>Check Page>Browser Compatibility command, or click the ▦ Check Page Check Page button and then click Check Browser Compatibility.

■ You can also access to the Check Browser Compatibility command by clicking the ▶ Check Browser Compatibility button in the Browser Compatibility Check panel of the Results panel group.

■ The Browser Compatibility Check feature automatically checks for compatibility with Internet Explorer 6.0 and 7.0 for Windows and 5.2 for Macintosh, Firefox 1.5, Netscape Navigator 8.0, Opera 8.0 and 9.0, and Safari 2.0.

■ You can select which browsers to check by clicking Settings on the Check Page menu. In the Target Browsers dialog box, shown in the following illustration, you can select browsers to check your pages against. For browsers that have a number of versions, such as Internet Explorer and Netscape Navigator, click the version number to see a drop-down menu on which you can select a specific browser version.

Choose target browsers to check

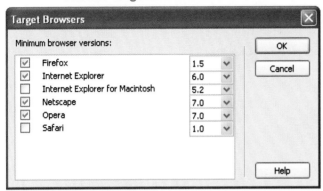

✔ *Many dynamic features such as behaviors and movies require the most recent browser versions. Keep this in mind when designing pages.*

▪ If Dreamweaver finds errors or problems during a browser compatibility check, the Browser Compatibility Check panel of the Results panel group opens (see the illustration below) with an explanation of the issue.

▪ The left pane in the Browser Compatibility Check panel lists the line of code of the reported issue and the name of the issue. The circle to the left of the line number indicates visually how likely the problem is to occur: The more filled the circle is, the more likely the problem.

▪ The issue is described in the right pane, along with a listing of what browser is affected and likelihood. A link at the bottom of the pane takes you to the Adobe CSS Advisor, where you can read more about the problem and how to solve it.

▪ The Browser Compatibility Check feature can report three levels of issues:

▪ Errors that might cause serious visible problems in a browser.

▪ Warnings about code that isn't supported in one of the target browsers but will cause no serious visible problem.

▪ Messages about code that isn't supported but will have no visible effect.

▪ To select the object affected by a reported issue, double-click the issue in the left pane. You can then determine how the problem might affect that element and make adjustments if necessary.

▪ If you know the error is related to a specific browser that you don't need to support, you can right-click the issue and select Ignore Issue.

▪ After you make suggested changes, you can check the page or pages again to make sure the browser errors have disappeared.

▪ The Browser Compatibility Check feature does not offer a sitewide check. Open each page you want to check and run the check.

▪ The Browser Compatibility Check panel has a toolbar with buttons that help you manage your results report.

▪ In some cases, you may need to stop the browser check before it is completed. To do this, click the ⊗ Stop Report button.

▪ Click the ⓘ More Info button to go to the Adobe CSS Advisor for more information on the issue.

▪ Because the report you see in the Browser Compatibility Check panel is a temporary file, you may want to save it for you or others to reference in the future. Click the 🖫 Save Report button to save an .XML text file of the report in your Web site folder.

Results of browser check

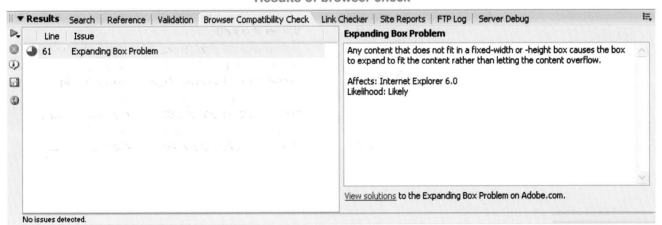

Browser Compatibility Check results report in Web browser document

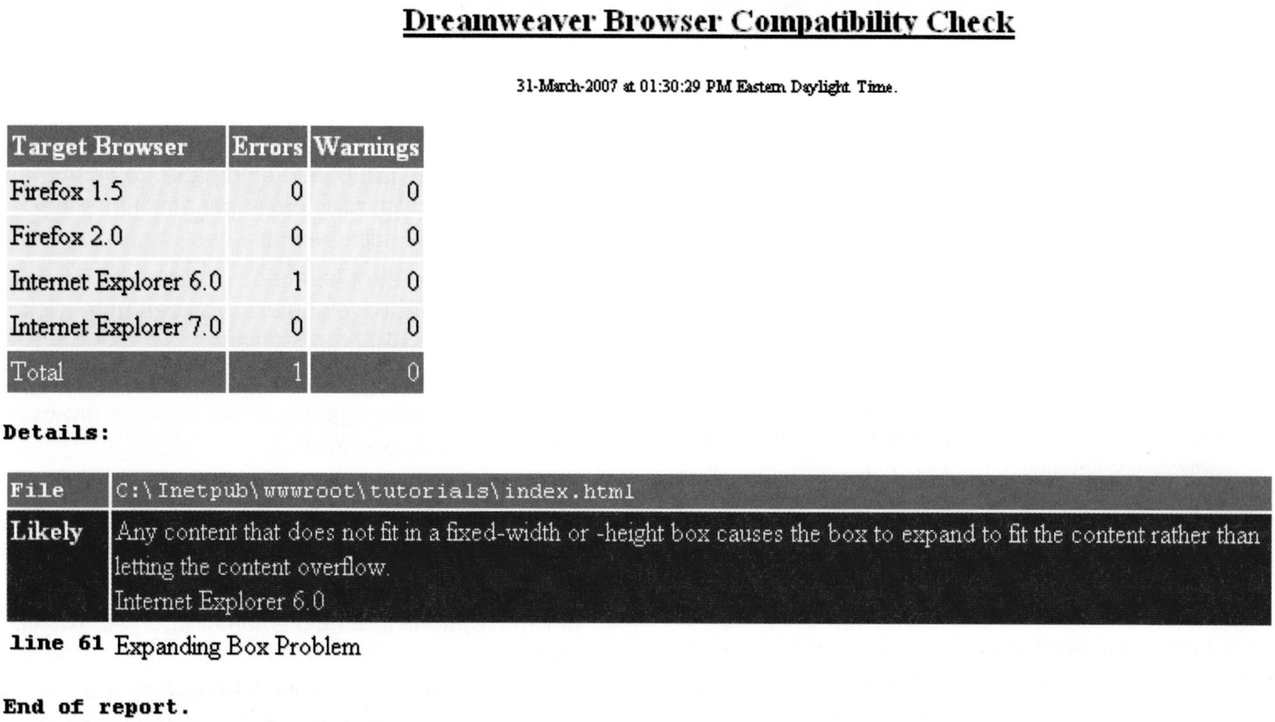

Dreamweaver Browser Compatibility Check

31-March-2007 at 01:30:29 PM Eastern Daylight Time.

Target Browser	Errors	Warnings
Firefox 1.5	0	0
Firefox 2.0	0	0
Internet Explorer 6.0	1	0
Internet Explorer 7.0	0	0
Total	1	0

Details:

File	C:\Inetpub\wwwroot\tutorials\index.html
Likely	Any content that does not fit in a fixed-width or -height box causes the box to expand to fit the content rather than letting the content overflow. Internet Explorer 6.0

line 61 Expanding Box Problem

End of report.

- An HTML document of the report can be created by clicking the Browse Report button. The report opens in your Web browser (see the illustration above) and it provides the same information the Results panel shows in an easy-to-read format that you can also print.
- To clear the report in the Browser Compatibility Check panel, right-click anywhere in its report pane and select Clear Results.

Check and Modify Links

- As pages are added to and removed from Web sites, it is all too easy to forget to update or remove links. Maintaining and fine-tuning your Web site's navigation structure are important parts of Web site upkeep.
- Clicking each link on a number of pages to check its source can take a considerable amount of time. Instead, use Dreamweaver commands to speed the process.

Check Links

- Dreamweaver gives you a great deal of flexibility when checking links in a Web site. You can check links from either the Document window or the Files panel—either in its collapsed or expanded form.
- To check links in the current document only, use the File>Check Page> Links command in the Document window. In the collapsed or expanded Files panel, right-click the site name or any file and select Check Links, and then choose Selected Files or Entire Local Site. In the expanded Files panel, use the File>Check Links command.
- To check links throughout the site, you can also use the Site>Check Links Sitewide command in Design view or in the expanded Files panel.
- When you issue a command to check links, Dreamweaver examines the current open document or Web site and lists any link problems in the Link Checker panel of the Results panel group (see the following illustration).

Link Checker panel displays link problems

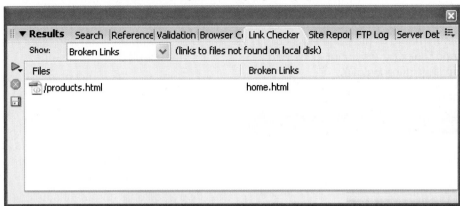

- Dreamweaver displays broken links by default in the Link Checker panel, but you can click the Show list arrow to see lists of external links (links outside the site that Dreamweaver cannot check) and orphaned files (files that are not linked to other files).

  ✔ *Don't be alarmed if the Link Checker shows orphaned files. Files such as style sheets are included in this list.*

- The Link Checker panel features a toolbar from which you can click the ▶ Check Links button and from the drop-down menu select Check Links in Current Document, Check Links for Entire Current Local Site, or Check Links for Selected Files in Site.

- In some cases, you may need to stop the Link Checker before it is completed. To do this, click the ⊗ Stop Report button.

- Because the report you see in the Link Checker panel is a temporary file, you may want to save it for you or others to reference. Click the 🔲 Save Report button to save a .TXT text file of the report in your Web site folder.

Repair Links

- Identifying link problems is just the first step to maintaining links. After you have identified problems, you have a number of options for fixing links.

- To repair a link identified as a problem in the Link Checker panel, click the file name to select it and then click on the link in the Broken Link column to select it. Dreamweaver highlights the link and also displays a 📁 browse folder icon (see the following illustration).

- You can either type the correct file name for the link or click the folder and navigate to the correct file in the Select File dialog box. When you click OK, you will be prompted to fix any other instances of the same broken link, which Dreamweaver does automatically.

- If your site contains a number of links to a specific file that you want to change to another file, you can use the Change Link Sitewide command to substitute one link for another throughout the site.

Repair a link identified as a problem

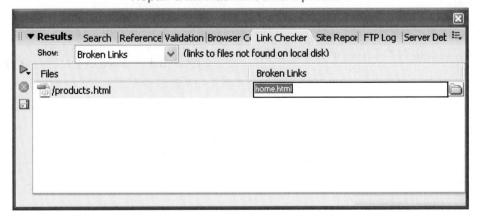

- Issue the Site>Change Link Sitewide command in the Document window or expanded Files window. Dreamweaver displays the Change Link Sitewide dialog box. Type the name of the page links currently point to and the page they should instead point to (see the illustration below).

Change a link sitewide

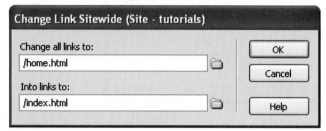

Modify Links in Site Map Pane

- The Site Map in the expanded Files panel window gives you a number of other ways to view and modify links. You can select a page in the Site Map and modify its links using commands on the Files panel menu (or right-click the page and select commands from the shortcut menu).
  - Link to New File lets you insert a link to a new Web document. This allows you to create the document and the link to it at the same time. You supply a file name and page title along with the text of the link.
  - Link to Existing File launches the Select Internet File dialog box in which an existing file can be linked to the selected Web document.

- Change Link launches the Select HTML File dialog box in which a new file can be selected to replace a link. When you change a link, you may be prompted to update other links in the site that are affected by the change.
- Remove Link removes a link and also launches a dialog box that gives you the option of updating links throughout the site that might be affected by the modification.
- Open to Source of Link opens the source file of the link in the Document window with the link text selected for editing.

- Two additional commands help you control the display of linked pages in the Site Map:
  - Use View>Site Map Options>Show/Hide Link to view a portion of the Site Map. You can, for example, hide e-mail links or dependent files by choosing this command to hide them. To display a hidden file again, use the View>Show Map Options>Show Files Marked as Hidden command.

    ✔ *The file name of a hidden file is italicized. Unmark a hidden file by right-clicking it and selecting Show/Hide Link again.*

  - Use View>Site Map Options>View as Root to place a subordinate—or child—Web document at the top of the site map, rather than the designated home page. This allows you to concentrate on links to and from a specific page.

    ✔ *The Site Navigation field above the site map displays the original path from the home page to the page chosen to view as the root. Click once on the home page in the Site Navigation field to return the site map to the original layout.*

E-Commerce Connection

Web Site Maintenance

Web sites can expand to use hundreds of pages with content that must be kept current. It can be a challenge for a Web master to deal with new content, errors, and attacks from outside the site. A regular maintenance schedule can help.

Web Site Maintenance Issues

Use the Internet to search for information about what tasks are required for regular Web site maintenance. Write a report in which you summarize tasks and propose a maintenance strategy for an e-commerce Web site.

PROCEDURES

Select Browsers to Check for Compatibility

1. Click the **Check Page** button ▦ Check Page in the Document toolbar to display the drop-down list.
2. Click **Settings**.
3. Click in checkbox for desired browser(s).
4. Click version number to display the drop-down list and select the version number, if desired.
5. Click [OK].

Run Browser Compatibility Check

1. Open a page to check.
2. Click **File** . . . . Alt+F
3. Point to **Check Page** . . . . . H
4. Click **Browser Compatibility** . . . . B

   OR

1. Click **Check Page** button ▦ Check Page on Document toolbar.
2. Click **Check Browser Compatibility**.

   OR

In the Results panel group:

1. Click the Browser Compatibility Check tab.
2. Click the **Check Browser Compatibility** button ▶.
3. Click **Check Browser Compatibility**.

In the Browser Compatibility Check panel of Results panel group:

- View report of errors and warnings and read information about making necessary corrections:
  - Click ✖ to stop the report.
  - Double-click a problem in the report pane to select the problem element.

- Select a problem in the report pane and click ⓘ to read the expanded description.
- Click ▦ to save the report.
- Click ⊕ to view or print the report in the Web browser.

Check Links (Shift + F8, Ctrl + F8)

To check links on the current page:

1. With desired Web page open, click **File** . . . . Alt+F
2. Point to **Check Page** . . . . . H
3. Click **Links** L

   OR

1. Right-click page in **Files** list.
2. Point to **Check Links**.
3. Click **Selected File**.

In Link Checker panel of Results panel group:

- View report in the Link Checker panel:
  - Click ✖ to stop Link Checker.
  - Click ▦ to save the report.
  - Repair link if desired.

To check links throughout the site:

1. Click **Site** . . . . Alt+S
2. Click **Check Links Sitewide** . . . . W

   OR

1. Right-click page in **Files** list.
2. Point to **Check Links**.
3. Click **Entire Local Site**.

   OR

1. Click **Window** . . . . Alt+W
2. Click **Results** . . . . R
3. Click the **Link Checker** panel.
4. Click ▶ in the Link Checker panel and select from the menu:

- **Check Links in Current Document**
- **Check Links For Entire Current Local Site**
- **Check Links For Selected Files in Site**

In Link Checker panel of Results panel group:

- View report in the Link Checker panel:
  - Click ✖ to stop Link Checker.
  - Click ▦ to save the report.
  - Repair link(s) if desired.

Repair Links

In the Link Checker panel:

1. Select **Broken Links** from the **Show** drop-down list, if necessary.
2. Click file name to select it.
3. Click link in **Broken Links** column to select it.
4. Type correct link.

   OR

- Click 🗀 and select correct file in the Select File dialog box.

Change Links Sitewide

1. Click **Site** . . . . Alt+S
2. Click **Change Link Sitewide** . . . . K
3. In Change all links to box, type **/** and then type file name of existing link.
4. In Into links to box, type **/** and then type file name of new link target.
5. Click [OK].

Modify Links in Site Panel Map Pane

With the site map displayed in the expanded or collapsed Files panel:

1. Right-click on a page in the site map that displays links.

2. Click one of the options below:

   - Click **Link to New File** to create new document and link at the same time.
   - Click **Link to Existing File** to choose file to link to.
   - Click **Change Link** to replace link with link to another page.
   - Click **Remove Link** to remove link from page (or remove page from site map).
   - Click **Open to Source of Link** to open a page with the link itself highlighted.

EXERCISE DIRECTIONS

1. Start Dreamweaver and open the *tutorials* site.
2. Check links throughout the site. Note that several pages have a link to the home.html page, which does not exist in the site.
3. Change the home.html links to link to index.html.
4. Change the target browser settings to check only Internet Explorer 6.0 and Firefox 1.5. Run the Browser Compatibility Check to check for any compatibility problems.
5. Dreamweaver may flag a portion of the Spry menu bar that might be affected by the Expanding Box Problem. If so, correct the problem as follows:

   - Open index.html and select the menu bar by clicking its blue tab. In the Item list in the Property inspector, click *Support* in the first column, click *Support Options* in the second column, and then click *FAQs* in the third column. The div that contains the *FAQs* and *Forums* entries should be displaying in the Document window.
   - Select the div and then, in the expanded portion of the Property inspector, click the Overflow list and select **auto**.

6. Run the Browser Compatibility Check again and note that there are no problems listed.
7. Save and close all pages and exit Dreamweaver.

ON YOUR OWN

1. Start Dreamweaver and open the *gardencenter* site.
2. Check links throughout the site. If you find any broken links, repair them.
3. Specify the Internet Explorer 6.0 browser and another browser such as Mozilla or Firefox.
4. Check the entire site for the specified browsers. You may receive warnings about the following items:

   - The Flash button on index.html. You can ignore this warning, as there is no easy fix for it.
   - The Expanding Box Problem for the Flash movie on info.html. Set the overflow to Visible for the AP div that contains the movie.

5. Save and close all pages and exit Dreamweaver.

Skills Covered

- **Run Dreamweaver Reports**
- **Validating Web Pages**

Software Skills   View reports to help you identify problems in a site and check accessibility for all types of site visitors. Validate your code to help you locate errors in syntax for a number of languages, including HTML and XHTML.

Application Skills   In this exercise, you will continue fine-tuning the CinciTutorial site in preparation for publishing it. You will view several reports on the site and run the Validator to see if you have any critical errors in coding on the site pages.

TERMS

No new terms in this exercise.

NOTES

Run Dreamweaver Reports

- Dreamweaver's Site>Reports command in either the Document window or the expanded Files panel menu bar displays the Reports dialog box (see the illustration at right). From this dialog box, you can run a number of workflow and HTML reports to check your site before publishing it.

- To run a report, first choose what you want to report on by clicking the Report on list arrow. You can run a report on the current document, the entire current site, selected files, or a folder. Then select the checkbox of the report you want to run and click the Run button.

  ✓ *Click the ▷ Reports button in the Site Reports panel in the Results panel group to open the Reports dialog box. You can then select other reports to run.*

- Use the Workflow reports to show what pages a team member has checked out and to find information stored in Design Notes. Selecting one of these reports displays the [Report Settings...] button that allows you to specify further settings.

Reports dialog box

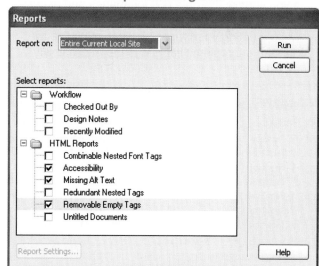

- For example, to find out what files a team member has checked out, click the Report Settings button and type the team member's name in the Checked Out By dialog box. When you run the report, Dreamweaver displays a list of all files checked out by the team member you specified.

  ✔ *You will learn more about checking files in and out in the next exercise.*

- The HTML reports help you locate HTML code problems and oversights such as pages that have no page titles. These reports can help you to locate errors in code you import from other sources.

  ✔ *Several of the HTML reports search for the same kinds of code problems identified in the Clean Up XHTML dialog box.*

- The Accessibility report locates problems that might affect your Web pages when people access them using text-only browsers and browsers designed for the hearing or visually challenged.

  ✔ *You can also check accessibility using the File>Check Page>Accessibility command.*

- One of the primary issues it will alert you to is how images, colors, and sounds and other multimedia files will be interpreted by text-only browsers—including the browsers used in cell phones and PDAs—or browsers that actually "read" the content text to a visually challenged person. The report will tell you, for example, that colors you have applied to text are not essential in a site designed to be read.

- If you supply alternate text for images and accessibility tags for forms, frames, and media objects while creating your pages, you can minimize the number of problems flagged in the Accessibility report.

- The Accessibility report will also analyze your text and warn you if sentences are not in natural English or have other issues that might be a disservice to the physically—and cognitively—challenged.

- You can run reports one at a time to isolate results, or you can select all reports and click Run to check all categories. Dreamweaver displays the report results in the Site Reports panel in the Results panel group (see the illustration below).

- Selecting a file in the report pane and clicking the ⓘ More Info button opens the Reference panel with a discussion of the issues that might occur and suggested ways to fix it. For example, if the information you convey depends on an image file, you will want to add a text description in the Alt text box of the Properties panel.

- To open a page identified in a report, right-click its file name in the File column and then click Open File.

- As in other Results group panels, you can stop running a report by clicking the ⊗ Stop Report button. Click the 🖫 Save Report button to save an .XML text file of the report in your Web site folder.

Validating Web Pages

- Use Dreamweaver's Validator feature to locate tag and syntax errors in your code.

- Validator is used much like the other report tools in the Results panel group. You can check one Web page, selected pages or files, or an entire Web site.

- To check the page that is in the Document window, use the File> Validate>Markup command.

Results of Accessibility report

	File	Line	Description
?	faqs.html	6	Style sheets should not be necessary [5508 d/WCAG 6.1 P1] -- MANUAL -- The page uses style sheets to present its cont.
?	faqs.html	9	Use clear language for site's content [WCAG 14.1 P1] -- MANUAL --
?	faqs.html	9	Clarify natural language usage [WCAG 4.1 P1] -- MANUAL --
?	faqs.html	2	Ensure sufficient contrast between foreground and background colors [WCAG 2.2 P2] -- MANUAL --
?	faqs.html	2	Document should be valid with respect to published grammars [WCAG 3.2 P2] -- MANUAL -- Use the Markup Validator to c..
?	faqs.html	2	Document should be valid with respect to published grammars [WCAG 3.2 P2] -- MANUAL -- Use a CSS validator to check t.
✕	faqs.html	6	Use relative units in CSS [WCAG 3.4 P2] -- FAILED --

Results ▾   Search | Reference | Validation | Browser Compatibility Check | Link Checker | Site Reports | FTP Log | Server Debug

Complete.

✔ *If you are validating an .XML page, you use the Validate As XML command.*

▦ The report that is created appears in the Validation panel of the Results panel group, as shown in the illustration below. As with checking links and target browsers, the Validation panel has a ▶ button on its toolbar that allows you to validate single Web pages, selected pages and folders, and the entire site.

▦ There are also buttons to stop running a report, to read more information, to save the report, and to open the report in your browser.

▦ Dreamweaver's Validator feature can report errors and warnings that may not require immediate editing or correction. When a problem occurs after you publish your Web site to a remote server, the Validator may provide you with the information that you, your Web server administrator, or your ISP may need to use to repair your Web stie so that it looks and functions as expected.

▦ Before you use the Validator, you must use the Edit>Preferences command and click the Validator category in the Preferences dialog box. The default setting for Dreamweaver is to validate against HTML version 4.0. You can select and deselect other codes and browsers to validate against.

✔ *See Appendix A: Dreamweaver Preferences to learn more about setting up preferences.*

▦ The Options button in the Preferences dialog box opens the Validator Options dialog box, in which the different levels of warnings and error messages can be selected or deselected.

▦ It is beyond the scope of this book to cover this advanced trouble-shooting feature at length. In many instances, the reports that the Validator creates will alert you more often to possible or potential problems rather than to anything that you will notice in your site whether locally or published on a remote Web server and accessed by most version 4 or later browsers.

Validation issues to check and correct for an entire site

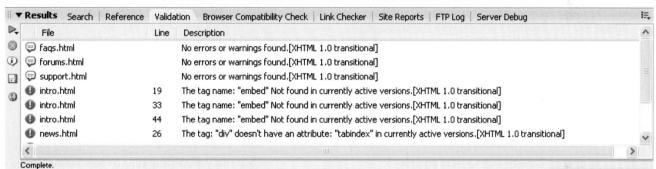

PROCEDURES

Run Dreamweaver Reports

In the Document window or Site panel menu:

1. Click **Site** . . . . Alt + S
2. Click **Reports** . . . . T
3. Click the **Report on** list arrow and select subject for the report.
4. Select checkbox for desired report.
5. Click Report Settings... if necessary (for Workflow reports) and supply additional settings for report.
6. Click Run .

7. View report in the Site Reports panel:
   ▪ Click ⊗ to stop the site report.
   ▪ Select a problem in the report pane and click ⓘ to read the expanded description.
   ▪ Double-click a problem in the report pane to open the page in Code and Design views.
   ▪ Click ⊟ to save the report.

Validate a Web Page (Shift + F6)

To validate the current page:

1. Click **Edit** . . . . Alt + E
2. Click **Preferences** . . . . . . P
3. Click **Validator** in the Category list.
4. Choose Validator options and click OK .
5. With desired Web page open, click **File** . . . . Alt + F
6. Point to **Validate**.
7. Click **Markup** . . . . M

8. View report in the Validation panel:

- Click ⊗ to stop the Validator.
- Click 🔲 to save the report.
- Click 🌐 to view or print the report in the Web browser.

To validate the entire site:

1. Click **Window** . . . . Alt+W
2. Click **Results** . . . . R
3. Click the **Validation** tab.
4. Click ▶ in the Validation panel.
5. Choose **Settings**.

---

6. Choose Validator options and click ⬜ OK .

7. Click ▶ in the Validation panel and select from the menu:

- Validate Current Document
- Validate Current Document as XML
- Validate Entire Current Local Site
- Validate Selected Files in Site

---

8. View report in the Validation panel:

- Click ⊗ to stop the Validator.
- Click 🔲 to save the report.
- Click 🌐 to view or print the report in the Web browser.

EXERCISE DIRECTIONS

1. Start Dreamweaver and open the *tutorials* site.
2. Run a report on accessibility for the entire site.
3. In the report pane of the Site Reports panel, select the first problem shown with a red X and read more information on the problem. You will find that the Accessibility report prefers using relative units in the CSS style sheet; this is flagged for every page of the site that is linked to the style sheet.
   - In the style sheet, change the size of the .mainhead style to **xx-large**.
   - Change the size of the .text style to **medium**.
   - Change the size of the .firstpar style to **large**.
   - Change the size of the .linktext style to **small**.
   - Change the size of the h2 style to **x-large**.
   - Change the size of the h3 style to **large**.
4. Save changes to the style sheet and run the Accessibility report again. You should not see any problems with CSS styles.
5. There are other accessibility issues you may be able to fix with some study of accessibility guidelines. For now, save the report in your site so you can refer to it later with the name **AccessibilityResultsReport.xml**.
6. Run the Missing Alt Text report and fix any missing Alt attributes using the <empty> attribute.

7. Just for fun, use the Validator to check your code as follows:
   - Open the Preferences dialog box and choose to validate code against HTML 4.0 and Internet Explorer 4.0 extensions.
   - Run the Validator for all pages in the current site.
   - Note the reference to the <table> tag's height attribute. On any page where this problem appears, display code and remove the height attribute and its value.
   - Run the Validator again to make sure you have taken care of the code problem.
   - You can ignore all references to the <embed> tag; this tag is supported by all browsers (even though it is not a standard HTML tag) and is used because the <object> tag does not always work correctly in some browsers.
   - Correct any additional problems you feel comfortable tackling, such as removing quotation marks around font names in the **tut_styles.css** page.
8. Save and close the pages and exit Dreamweaver.

ON YOUR OWN

1. Start Dreamweaver and open the *gardencenter* site.

2. Run an accessibility report for the entire local site.

3. Correct as many of the red X problems as you feel comfortable modifying. For example, you may want to:

   ▪ Supply content for the <object> tags on all pages. To do this, double-click the entry to display the code and read the code until you find the closing </embed> tag at the end of the code selection. Click in the code just after </embed> and before </object> and type a brief description of the object.

   ▪ Adjust style sheet font sizes using relative measurements such as small, medium, and large.

   ✔ *Read the information for each problem even if you decide not to fix it.*

4. Run some of the other Dreamweaver reports, such as Untitled Documents and Removable Empty Tags, and fix any problems you find.

5. Run the Validator for the entire current local site, validating against HTML 4.0 and Internet Explorer 4.0 extensions. Read information on some of the tag cautions and warnings.

6. Save all pages and close Dreamweaver.

Exercise | 55

Skills Covered

- **Publish a Web Site on a Server**
- **Check Files In and Out**
- **Copy Files from a Remote Server**

Software Skills You can put files on an FTP, WebDAV, or local server to make them available to visitors. When you configure the site for remote access, you can also enable check out/in to prevent more than one team member at a time from working on a site file. If you need to work on a published file, you can copy it from the remote server to your local server.

Application Skills In this exercise, you will complete your work on the CinciTutorial site by publishing it to a server. When you set up the remote access for the site, you will enable file check out/in and check out one of the site files.

TERMS

Publishing Copying Web site files from a local computer to a server.

FTP (File Transfer Protocol) A method for copying files to and from servers on a network.

HTTP (Hypertext Transfer Protocol) Fixed set of messages and replies between a browser and server on the Web.

NOTES

Publish a Web Site on a Server

- **Publishing** is the process of copying Web site files from a local computer to the server that *hosts* the site and where visitors can access it. The server to which you copy, publish, or "put" files can be an **FTP** (file transfer protocol) server; a local/network server that can be on your computer or on your network; or a WebDAV **HTTP** (hypertext transfer protocol) server on the Internet.

- Dreamweaver also makes it easy for you to publish your Web site on remote RDS (Remote Development Services) and Microsoft Visual SourceSafe servers. It is beyond the scope of this book to discuss how to configure a connection to these specialized servers. Consult Dreamweaver Help and your Web server administrator or ISP for more information.

- When you created your site as described in Exercise 2, you had the option of selecting and configuring your remote server using the Site

Definition wizard. In the following section, you will learn how to use settings in the site Definition dialog box to set up an FTP, WebDav, or local/network server—three of the most common ways to publish a Web site so that it can be accessed on the Internet or on an intranet.

Associating an FTP Server with a Web Site

- Use the Remote Info category on the Advanced tab of the Site Definition dialog box to enter the appropriate settings to publish on an FTP server. You specify the same settings whether you create a site using the Site Definition wizard or create the site using the Site Definition dialog box's Advanced tab, so the procedure discussed here can be used when you first set up your site—or if you need to edit an existing site to specify settings.

- Use the Site>Manage Sites command to open the Manage Sites dialog box and select the desired Web site. Then click the [Edit...] button.

- Select the Advanced tab's Remote Info category in the Site Definition dialog box and choose FTP on the Access list. You must then supply the following information:

  - Enter the FTP server's address in the FTP host text box. The following illustration shows the proper syntax. You do not need to enter "ftp://" before the address because it is already incorporated.

  - In the Host directory text box, enter the name of the folder on the server that contains the site files.

  - Most servers require a login name to connect to the server. Enter that name in the Login text box. If you do not enter a login name, a dialog box will request it—and the password—when you attempt to connect to the FTP server.

- Most servers, for security reasons and to prevent hackers from tampering with the Web site, also require a password. If you do not supply a password and click the Save option, a dialog box will request it when you attempt to connect to the server.

- The options for Use passive FTP, Use IPv6 transfer mode, Use firewall, and Use Secure FTP (SFTP) may need to be selected. Consult with the Web administrator of the FTP server to find out if you need to select these settings.

- To make sure that your FTP settings work, use the Test button to test them. Dreamweaver will then attempt to connect to the FTP server and tell you if the test is successful—or unsuccessful (see the illustrations at the top of the next page).

Set up FTP connection in Dreamweaver

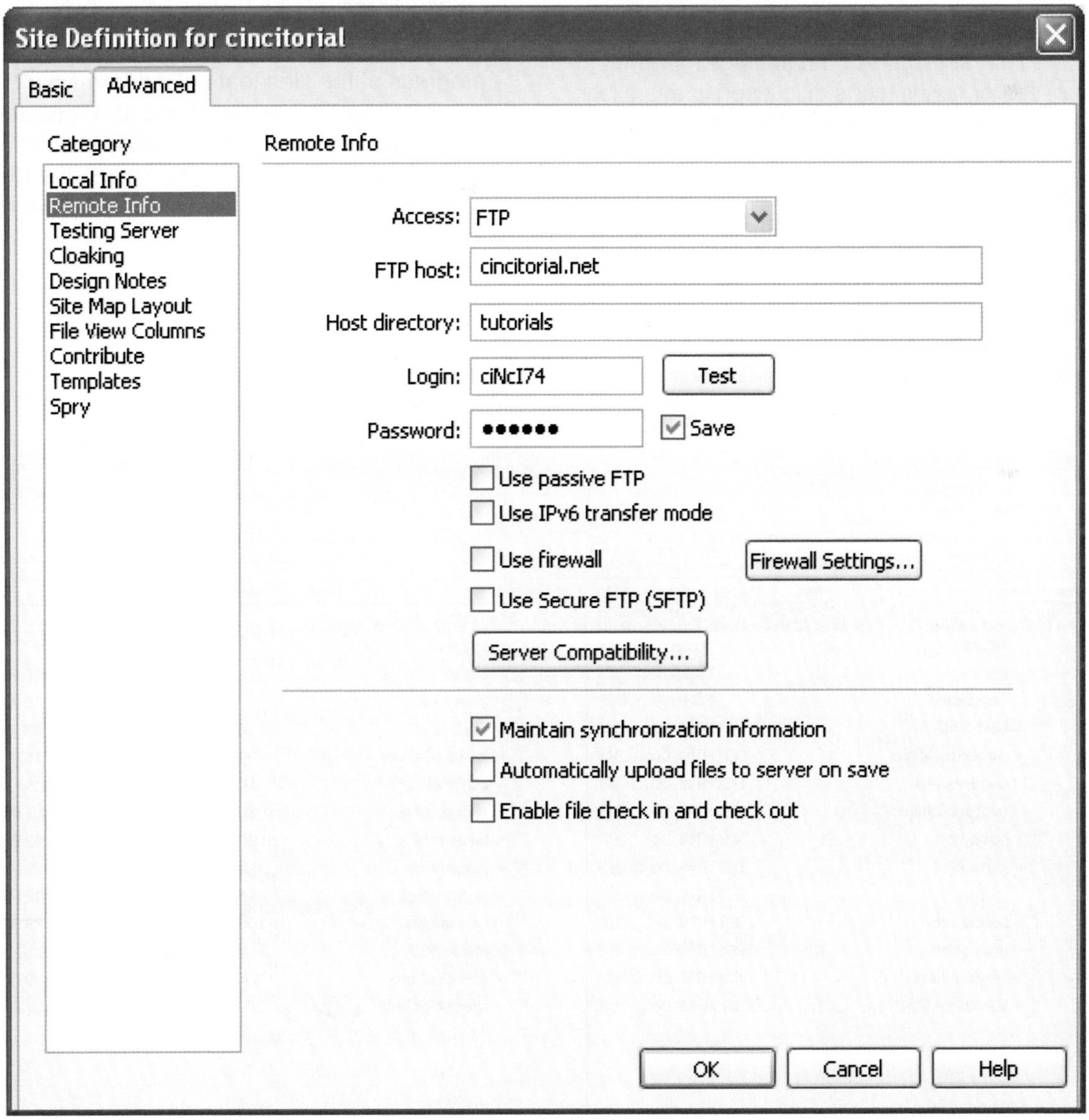

Site Definition for cincitorial ☒

| Basic | Advanced |

Category

Local Info
Remote Info
Testing Server
Cloaking
Design Notes
Site Map Layout
File View Columns
Contribute
Templates
Spry

Remote Info

Access: FTP ⌄

FTP host: cincitorial.net

Host directory: tutorials

Login: ciNcI74 [Test]

Password: ●●●●●● ☑ Save

☐ Use passive FTP
☐ Use IPv6 transfer mode
☐ Use firewall [Firewall Settings...]
☐ Use Secure FTP (SFTP)

[Server Compatibility...]

☑ Maintain synchronization information
☐ Automatically upload files to server on save
☐ Enable file check in and check out

[OK] [Cancel] [Help]

- The Remote Info category also allows you to enable file check out/in. File check out/in is discussed in a later section of this exercise.

Putting the Web Site on the FTP Server

- Once the FTP settings—or the settings for other kinds of server connections discussed in this exercise—have been specified, the Web site is ready to be copied to the server.

- You can publish your site—or *put* the files on the server, to use Dreamweaver's term—using the Files panel in either its collapsed or expanded form. Using the expanded form, however, gives you the best view of the process because it clearly shows both the local and remote site files in one window at the same time.

- In the expanded Files panel window toolbar, click the ⬛ Site Files button to display the Remote Site pane and then click the 🔌 Connects to remote host button to establish the connection to the FTP server.

- A message box informs you when you have made a connection with a server. If you cannot connect, you will receive messages explaining why. A live connection will be indicated by the 🔌 button.

- In the Local Files pane, select the desired files to be published on the FTP server and drag them onto the host directory folder in the Remote Site pane. Or, you can select the desired files in the Local Files pane and click the ⬆ Put File(s) button in the Files panel toolbar.

  ✔ *Typically, you will want to publish all of the contents of the local folder. You can simply select the local Web site's folder at the top of the file tree rather than select files individually. You may need to click Yes to put all of the files.*

- The Background File Activity dialog box records the progress of the files that upload from your local server to the FTP server. If you have enabled check out/in, Dreamweaver automatically checks out the files. The process is completed when the files appear in the Remote Site pane as shown in the following illustration.

Files "put" on FTP server

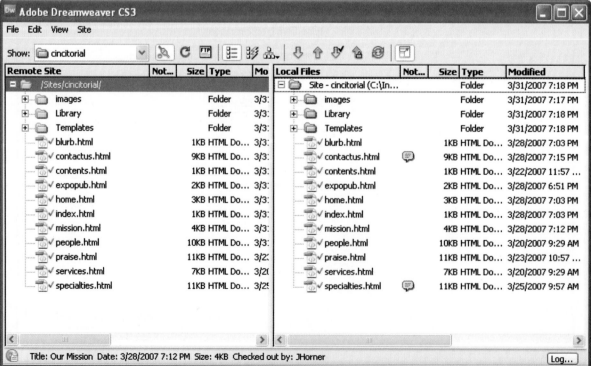

✔ *Dreamweaver may ask during this process if you want to include dependent files. Be sure to click Yes, or files such as images will not be transferred to the server.*

■ You can put an open document on the server from the Document window. Click the File Management button on the Document toolbar and select Put from the menu. You can also use the Site>Put command.

■ Click the ↻ Refresh button if necessary to arrange the folders and files in the Remote Site pane in the same order as the Local Files pane. When you have finished the process of copying files, click to disconnect from the server.

■ The View Site FTP Log button in the expanded Files panel window opens the FTP Log panel in the Results panel group, which displays a log report of all the activity experienced by the FTP server. It can be used for a number of administrative purposes, including security.

■ The FTP server administrator or your instructor can supply you with the URL for the Web so that you can see the published Web in a browser.

■ You will need to enter the URL in the HTTP address box in the Site Definition dialog box's Local Info pane (see the following illustration).

Associating a WebDAV Connection (HTTP server) with a Web Site

■ If you are going to publish directly to an HTTP site, you can use the WebDAV standard. WebDAV, or Web-based Distributed Authoring and Versioning, uses the Microsoft Internet Information Server (IIS) 5.0 that comes with Windows 2000, Windows 2000 Server, Windows XP Professional, and the like.

■ To configure a WebDAV site, you must have its URL and any login and password information that you will need.

■ As with configuring an FTP site, you must set up a remote HTTP server by selecting the Remote Info category in the Site Definition dialog box and choosing WebDAV on the Access list. You must then supply the following information in the appropriate text box: the site URL, Login, and Password (see the illustration at the top of the next page.).

■ If you want Dreamweaver to remember your password, select the Save checkbox.

■ To publish to a WebDAV server connection, use the same procedures for putting files on an FTP site in the Files panel window. (You may encounter different message boxes.)

Specify URL for published Web site

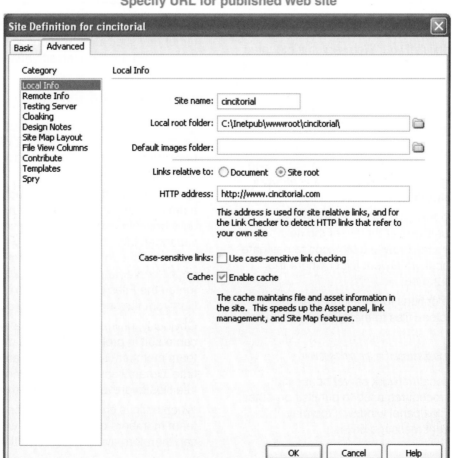

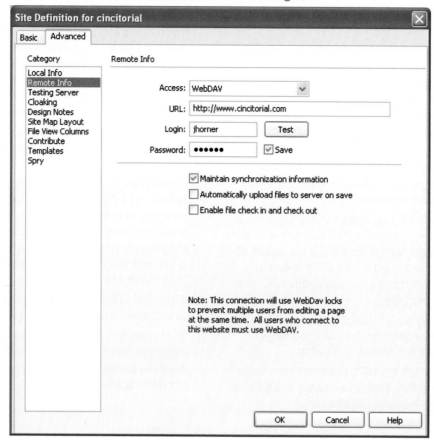

Associating a Local or Network Server with a Web Site

- You can also publish if your Web server is mounted as a network drive (Windows) or as an AppleTalk or NFS server (Macintosh), or if you are running a personal Web server on your local computer such as Microsoft Personal Web Server (PWS) or Microsoft Internet Information Service (IIS).

- Just as when specifying FTP and WebDAV settings, you specify local/network settings in the Site Definition dialog box. In the Remote Info category, select Local/Network from the Access list.

- Type the path to the local network's folder, as shown in the illustration at the top of the next page. You can also use the browse folder icon to navigate directly to the local or network folder where the Web site will be stored.

- You can choose options to refresh files on the server and to upload files to the server when they are saved.

  ✔ *File checkout/in is discussed in the next section.*

- To publish to a local/network server connection, use the same procedures used to put files on other servers in the Files panel window. (You may encounter different message boxes.)

- Consult with your instructor or Web site administrator for any special instructions and obtaining the correct URL for the Web site after it is published.

Check Files In and Out

- When you define a remote server site in the Site Definition dialog box for an FTP, WebDAV, Local/Network, or RDS connection, you have the option of enabling the file check out/in feature.

- Established Web sites are frequently managed by teams of several members. Team members typically drag files from the remote server in the expanded Files panel window to their local computer to work on the files. Or, they may select files on the server and then use the ⇩ Get File(s) button on the Files panel toolbar to copy the selected files from the server to the local computer.

- Obviously, unlimited access to a Web site's files can result in problems, such as more than one team member working on the same file at the same time. Dreamweaver's check out/in feature can regulate files to prevent such problems.

- When a file is checked out on the remote server, all team members can see who is working on it and can therefore avoid working on that file.

Set up local network connection

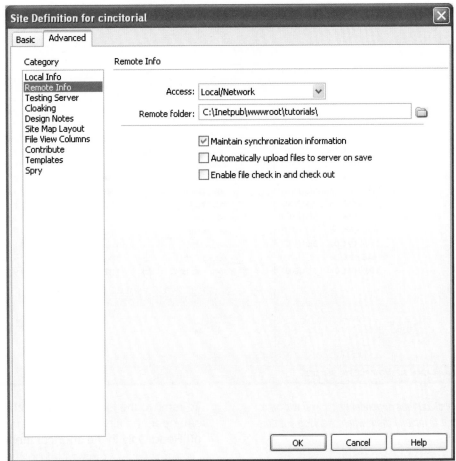

Enable check out/in
options in Remote Info category

- You enable check out/in in the Remote Info category of the Site Definition dialog box for the FTP, WebDAV, Local/Network, and RDS server connections (see the following illustration). Note that this feature is not active unless a remote server location has been established for the Web site.

- If you have enabled check out/in, files you put on a remote server are automatically checked out to you at the time you publish them.

- Select the *Check out files when opening* option to automatically check out files when you double-click to open them from the Files panel.

- You can also supply your e-mail address so that team members can send e-mail to you while you are working on checked-out files.

- When you enable check out/in, the Check Out File(s) and Check In buttons are activated on the Files panel's toolbar in both the collapsed and expanded form.

- To check out a file on your computer, select the file (or select more than one file) in either the Remote Site or Local Files pane and use the Site>Check Out command on the menu bar, or click the Check Out File(s) button on the Files panel toolbar.

  ✔ *You can undo the check-out process using the Site>Undo Check Out command, or right-click the checked-out file and select Undo Check Out on the shortcut menu.*

- Checking out a file tells others that you are working on the file now. If they open the file, it will be a read-only version.

- When a file is checked out, a check mark displays next to the file's icon in both the Remote Site and Local Files panes (see the following illustration).

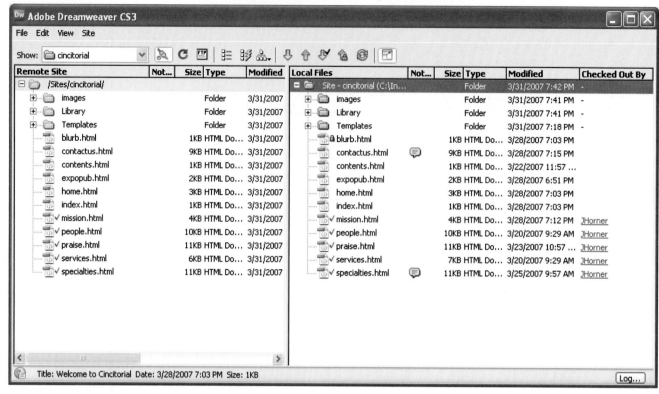

✔ *If the file you check out has dependent files, you will be asked if you want to include them when checking out the file.*

▣ Check mark colors give you additional information about who has checked out a file. You will see a green check mark when you have checked out a file on your computer. A red check mark means the file is checked out by another person on another computer.

▣ The name of the person who checked out the file displays in the Checked Out By column of the Files panel and also displays in the status bar of the Files window when the mouse button hovers over the file name.

▣ When you have finished working on a file, you check it in by selecting the file in either the Local Files or Remote Site pane and using the Site>Check In command. Or, click the 🔒 Check In button in the Files panel toolbar.

▣ Checking in a file makes the file available to other team members. The green check mark in the Remote Site pane is removed and a lock icon displays next to the checked-in file in the Local Files pane.

▣ While the lock icon displays, other team members will see a message box informing them that the file is a read-only file that can be viewed but not changed.

▣ To remove the lock symbol so other team members can open the file, right-click the file and select Turn off Read Only in the shortcut menu.

Copy Files from a Remote Server

▣ You can reverse the publishing process if you need to "get" files from a remote server and copy them to your local site. Select the files you want to copy in the Remote Site pane of the expanded Files panel window and drag them into the Local Files pane. Or click the ⬇ Get File(s) button in the Files panel toolbar.

✔ *You can get files while working in the Document window by clicking the File Management button on the Document toolbar and selecting Get from the menu.*

▣ If the Check In/Out feature is active, dragging a file or files—or using the Get File(s) button—results in a read-only local copy of the file. The file remains available on the remote site for others to check out. If the Check In/Out feature is deselected in the Site Definition dialog box, then copying/getting a file transfers a copy that has read and write privileges.

E-Commerce Connection

Hosting an E-Commerce Site

An e-commerce business must consider a number of issues when setting up a Web site, such as server technology and hardware specifications. Moreover, an e-business must consider whether to host the site themselves—requiring an in-house Web staff—or put the site on an external host run by a third party.

Investigate Hosting Issues

Use the Internet to search for information about how to choose hardware and software for an e-commerce Web site and the pros and cons of hosting internally versus externally. Write a report in which you compare several hardware and software options for an e-commerce site and give your opinion on how to host the site

PROCEDURES

Display Site Definition Dialog Box

1. Click **Site** . . . . `Alt`+`S`
2. Click **Manage Sites** . . . . . `M`
3. Click name of site to modify.
4. Click `Edit...`.
5. Click the **Advanced** tab.
6. When finished modifying the site, click `Done`.

Set Up FTP Connection

In the Site Definition dialog box (Advanced tab):

1. Click the **Remote Info** category.
2. Click the **Access** list arrow . . . . `Alt`+`A`
3. Click **FTP**.
4. Enter FTP settings:
   a. Click in **FTP host** box . . . . `Alt`+`H` and type FTP server address.
   b. Click in **Host directory** box . . . . `Alt`+`D` and type name of folder that holds files.
   c. Click in **Login** box. . . . . `Alt`+`L` and type name or code necessary to log in to server.

   d. Click in **Password** box. . . . . `Alt`+`P` and type password necessary to log in to server.
   e. Click `Test` to test the connection.
   f. Select firewall options, if desired.

   ✔ *Select the Save checkbox to avoid having to enter this information each time you log on.*

5. Click `OK`.

Set Up WebDAV HTTP Server

In the Site Definition dialog box (Advanced tab):

1. Click the **Remote Info** category.
2. Click the **Access** list arrow . . . . `Alt`+`A`
3. Click **WebDAV**.
4. Enter the following information in the proper text boxes:
   a. Click in **URL** box. . . . . `Alt`+`U` and type URL for Web site.
   b. Click in **Login** box. . . . . `Alt`+`L` and type name or code necessary to log in to server.
   c. Click in **Password** box. . . . . `Alt`+`P` and type password necessary to log in to server.

   d. Click the **Save** checkbox . . . . `Alt`+`V` to save password if desired.
5. Test the connection if desired.
6. Click `OK`.

Set Up Local/Network Server

In the Site Definition dialog box (Advanced tab):

1. Click the **Remote Info** category.
2. Click the **Access** list arrow . . . . `Alt`+`A`
3. Click **Local/Network**.
4. Click in **Remote folder** box. . . . . `Alt`+`R` and type path to local/network folder.

   OR

   ▪ Click 📁 and navigate to folder.

Enable File Check Out/In

In the Site Definition dialog box of FTP, WebDav, Local/Host, and RDS servers:

1. Click the **Remote Info** category.
2. Click the **Enable file check in and check out** checkbox . . . . `Alt`+`E`
3. Click **Check out files when opening** . . . . `Alt`+`C` if desired.

4. Click the **Check out name** box . . . . Alt+N and type name to be used to identify you.

5. Click the **Email address** box . . . . Alt+M and type e-mail address.

Put Files on Server

In the expanded Files panel window:

1. Click **Site Files** button ≣ on the Files panel window toolbar to display the Remote Site pane.

2. Click 🌐 on the Files panel window toolbar.

3. Select file, files, or entire root folder in the Local Files pane.

4. Click ⬆ on the Files panel window toolbar.

5. Click [OK] if necessary to include dependent files.

6. Click 🔌 to disconnect from remote server.

Check File Out
(Ctrl + Alt + Shift + D)

1. Select file in the Remote Site or Local Files pane of the Files panel (expanded or collapsed).

2. Click **Site** . . . . Alt+S

3. Click **Check Out** C
OR

Click 🔽 in the Files panel toolbar.

Check File In
(Ctrl + Alt + Shift + U)

1. Select file in the Remote Site or Local Files pane of the Files panel (expanded or collapsed).

2. Click **Site** . . . . Alt+S

3. Click **Check In** I
OR

Click 🔼 in the Files panel toolbar.

✔ *To remove the Read Only lock icon from the file, right-click the file in the Site panel and click Turn Off Read Only.*

Copy Files from Remote Server

1. Select file or files in the Remote Site or Local Files pane of the Files panel (expanded or collapsed).

2. Click ⬇ in the Files panel toolbar.

EXERCISE DIRECTIONS

1. Start Dreamweaver and open the *tutorials* site.

2. Publish your Web site to a server or to a local folder. Put all the files on the remote site.

   ✔ *If you have not yet selected a remote server, your instructor will supply information for putting your Web site files on an FTP, WebDAV HTTP server, or a local network server. If no server is available, create a folder on your hard drive. In the Site Definition dialog box, use the Local/Network server access option and make sure the path to the folder you created appears in the Remote Folder box on the Web Server Info or Remote Info category. Then publish your Web site files to this folder.*

3. Use the Site Definition dialog box to make sure the check out/in feature is enabled for the current site. (Be sure to insert your name where indicated so it will display when you check files out.)

4. Check out the *index.html* file, if necessary, and rest the mouse pointer on the file name to see your name in the Files window's status bar.

5. Run the Checked Out By report to see what files you have checked out.

6. Check in the *index.html* file. Click in the file and then remove the lock symbol from the local version of the file and any dependent files.

7. Disconnect from the server, if necessary.

8. Close any open pages and exit Dreamweaver.

ON YOUR OWN

1. Start Dreamweaver and open the *gardencenter* site.

2. Publish the Web site to a server or local folder, as indicated by your instructor. When you set up remote access, enable the check out/in feature.

3. If possible, ask a classmate to access the site and check out a page so you can see how the site files look when someone other than you has checked out a file.

4. Make a change to at least one file that you have checked out and put it again on the server to update your site.

5. Disconnect from the server, if necessary.

6. Close any open pages and exit Dreamweaver.

Exercise | 56

Summary Exercise

Application Skills   In this exercise, you will do some final work on the High Ridge site and then publish the site on a server or at a network location.

DIRECTIONS

1. Start Dreamweaver and open the *highridge* site.

2. Open each page in the site and check browser compatibility using Internet Explorer 6.0 and Firefox 1.5. If you receive the Expanding Box Problem on index.html, change the Overflow of the shadow AP div to visible.

3. Check links throughout the site.

4. Run the Missing Alt Text report for the entire site. Because you have been supplying alternate text while adding images to the page, you should not have any results from this report. (If you have missed adding alternate text to any of the site's images, insert it now where indicated by the report.)

5. Run the Untitled Documents report to make sure all pages have titles.

6. Publish the site on the network your instructor indicates. Enable the check out/in feature.

7. Put all files on the remote site.

8. Check out several pages, and then check them back in.

9. Close all open pages and exit Dreamweaver.

Exercise | 57

Application Exercise

Application Skills In this exercise, you will finish your work on the Grand Theatre site by running reports and the Validator. You will then put the files on a server or network to be available for site visitors.

DIRECTIONS

1. Start Dreamweaver and open the *grand* Web site.
2. Specify several target browsers and run the browser compatibility check on each page in the site. Read any information you receive about browser incompatibilities.
3. Check links throughout the site and fix any broken links you find.
4. Check for missing Alt attributes throughout the site and supply appropriate attributes where needed.
5. Specify that the Validator will check HTML 4.0 and Internet Explorer 4.0 extensions, and then validate markup sitewide.
6. Review the markup problems and fix any that you feel comfortable changing.
7. Publish the site as directed by your instructor and then visit the site using your Web browser.
8. Close the browser.
9. Save and close all open pages and exit Dreamweaver.

Exercise | 58

Curriculum Integration

Application Skills Your Physical Sciences class is studying natural disasters such as earthquakes, volcanoes, and hurricanes. Choose one type of disaster and create several pages on the subject that you can publish on a Web site. Do the following research:

- Locate general information on your natural disaster; for example, what causes a hurricane? What kinds of faults lead to damaging earthquakes? How do volcanoes provide a vent for the magma below the earth's crust?

- Locate graphic files if possible to illustrate your site.

- Locate information on the social impact of your type of disaster, such as the ten costliest hurricanes in terms of lives lost or property damage or the destruction caused by a volcanic eruption.

DIRECTIONS

Create a new site with an appropriate name for your disaster. As you define the site, specify both a local server and a remote server, using information provided by your instructor.

Create a home page for the site with an appropriate name and page title. You may want to use one of Dreamweaver's Starter (Theme) pages to save layout and formatting time.

Insert general information about your natural disaster on the home page, including one or more images you found.

Create a second page for the site that discusses a particular example of your disaster or general information about the destructive impact of the type of disaster. You may want to include additional images or a table of data. Link the pages by inserting or modifying existing links.

Specify Internet Explorer 6.0 and Netscape 8.0 as target browsers. Check each page for browser compatibility.

Run an Accessibility report on the current site. (You may discover, if you used Dreamweaver Starter pages, that even professionally designed sites don't meet every accessibility standard required.)

Validate the markup sitewide.

Put your files on the remote server you identified when you defined the site.

Close any open pages and exit Dreamweaver.

Exercise | 59

Critical Thinking

Application Skills In this exercise, you will complete your work on your personal Web site by running reports and validating code. Then you will publish the site for others to visit.

DIRECTIONS

- Open the personal Web site you have been working on throughout this course.

- Select one or more target browsers for the site and check all pages to see if there are any browser problems you need to fix.

- Check links sitewide and make any necessary changes.

- Run any reports you think necessary to locate problems on the pages.

- Validate the markup throughout the site.

- Specify remote access information for the Web site, using a server or network connection.

- Put all local files on the remote server. Invite several of your classmates to visit your site, if possible, and ask them for feedback on the site.

- Close all open pages and exit Dreamweaver.

Capstone Project: Deep Creek Inn Web Site

Application Skills   In this Capstone Project, you will begin work on a Web site for the Deep Creek Inn, a lodge and conference center in a scenic rural area. You will create pages using Dreamweaver's Starter Theme pages and customize them for your new site, add images and a movie, insert a form and a Spry element, create a table and an AP div, attach behaviors, and finally run reports and put the site on a remote server.

DIRECTIONS

Create the Site and Add Starter Pages

1. Create a new site on your local server with the name *deepcreek*. Do not set up a remote server at this time or use a server technology. Do not enable check out/in.

2. In the Welcome Screen or the New Document dialog box, click Starter Page (Theme). Create three pages from the Sample pages list as follows:
   - Select the Lodging – Home Page sample page, click Create, and save the page as *index.html* in the *deepcreek* site. Copy dependent files when prompted. Change the page title to *Deep Creek Home Page*.
   - Open the New Document dialog box and select the Lodging – Product Page sample page. Save the page as *directions.html* in the site and copy dependent files. Change the page title to *Getting Here*.
   - Open the New Document dialog box and select Lodging – Text Page. Save the page as *reservations.html* in the site and copy dependent files. Change the page title to *Reservation Request*.

3. Create a folder in the site named *images* to hold all site images. Move the GIF and JPG files into the images folder and update links.

4. With *index.html* displayed, add the following keywords to the site: Deep Creek Inn, Deep Creek Conference Center, Oxford lodging, Oak Ridge Lake.

5. Display the CSS Styles panel and make the following CSS changes to apply to all pages in the site:
   - Click the body rule. Add the background-color property to this rule and change background color to #006633.
   - Locate the .logo rule. Change the text color to white.

6. Display the *reservations.html* page. You know you will need several more pages in this format for the site, so create a template as follows:
   - Change the *WEBSITE NAME HERE* placeholder to *DEEP CREEK INN*.
   - Set the HOME link to open the *index.html* page.
   - Save the page as a template with the name *deep_text.dwt*.
   - Remove the page title from the template.
   - Select the table cell that contains the navigation link (<td.navText#navigation>) and create an editable region named *navigation*.
   - Click the second <table> tag in the tag selector to select the Page Name Here heading and the text below it and create an editable region named *text*.

   ✔ You are now ready to work on the individual pages of the site.

Modify the Home Page

1. Activate the index.html page. Change the site name in the top table cell to *DEEP CREEK INN*.

2. Adjust table cell colors on this page as follows:
   - Select the entire table row that contains the navigation links (currently a light blue-green).
   - Change the background color to #ededde by typing this value in the box to the right of the ⬜ Bg box. (This is a color used on other pages of this theme.)
   - Apply the same background color to the three-cell table below the sample image at the left side of the page.

3. Change the links in the navigation bar as follows:
   - You are not yet ready to create a page showing lodge rooms, so delete the *OUR ROOMS* link and the spaces following the link.
   - Change the *ABOUT US* link to *GETTING HERE* and link the text to directions.html.
   - Link *MAKE A RESERVATION* to reservations.html.
   - Change the *THINGS TO DO* link to *THINGS TO SEE*. You will link this text later after creating another new page.
   - Remove the *CONTACT* link for now.

4. Insert an image on the page as follows:
   - Select the placeholder image and delete it.
   - With the insertion point still in the same place, insert the ◉ waterfall.jpg image from the Capstone Data folder.
   - Save the image to your images folder and supply the alternate text *Deep Creek waterfall*.
   - Delete the placeholder image from the images folder.

5. Replace the text in the caption area below the image with the following text:
   Deep Creek plunges over many waterfalls and rushes through winding gorges in an area known for its wild beauty.

6. Change the *Welcome Message Here* placeholder text to *Welcome to Deep Creek Inn*.

7. Delete the placeholder text below the header. Import the Word text in the ◉ welcome.doc.

8. Apply bullet list formatting to the paragraph that reads *Meeting rooms that accommodate up to 300 people* and to the next three paragraphs.

9. Click below the last paragraph of text and insert the following copyright notice:
   © Deep Creek Inn. All rights reserved. Questions or comments: mail@deepcreek.com

10. Create an e-mail link to the e-mail address in the copyright notice.

11. Insert a Spry Collapsible Panel widget as follows:
    - Click the outside border of the caption table below the image to select all three cells. Press the right arrow key to move the insertion point to the right of this table.
    - Insert the Spry Collapsible Panel widget. It should position just below the caption table.

12. The text in the tab and the content panel will be very small. Adjust styles as follows:
    - Display the Assets panel and show the colors for the current site.
    - Select the .CollapsiblePanelTab style rule and change the background-color property to #cc3300 by clicking the color box and then using the eyedropper to select that color in the Assets panel.
    - Change the font property to bold 1em sans-serif.
    - If desired, choose different colors for the tab background when the mouse hovers and when the mouse focuses. Use colors from the Assets panel.

13. Change the *Tab* placeholder text to *News*.

14. Change the *Content* placeholder text to the following paragraph:
    Deep Creek Inn is proud to announce that it has been selected as one of Ohio's top five conference centers in the recent Ohio Magazine's survey of statewide lodging.

15. Set properties for the collapsible panel: name it *news* and change display and default state to Closed.

16. Save your changes to the page and preview it in your browser. It should look similar to Illustration A after you open the collapsible panel.

Illustration A

DEEP CREEK INN

GETTING HERE   MAKE A RESERVATION   THINGS TO SEE

Deep Creek plunges over many waterfalls and rushes through winding gorges in an area known for its wild beauty.

News

Deep Creek Inn is proud to announce that it has been selected as one of Ohio's top five conference centers in the recent Ohio Magazine's survey of statewide lodging.

Welcome to Deep Creek Inn

Located on the pacific shores of beautiful Oak Ridge Lake, the Deep Creek Inn is a refuge for those looking to get away from the daily grind. Come by yourself or bring your family along and enjoy our comfortable accommodations and unique natural surroundings.

The Inn has 60 spacious guest rooms, many with a view of the lake, and two suites with three bedrooms and kitchen facilities. We have recently refurbished the housekeeping cottages in the Oak Grove to include microwaves and VCRs. Dining facilities include the full-service Creek Rock Cafe and the Waterfall Lounge.

The Deep Creek Inn also offers outstanding conference facilities for both large and small groups. We can provide:

- Meeting rooms that accommodate up to 300 people
- State-of-the-art audiovisual support
- Fax and online services
- Full-service banquet facilities

The Deep Creek Inn has recreation options for visitors of all ages. Hike our trails, enjoy a vigorous set of tennis, swim in the indoor or outdoor pool, try your hand at fishing in the lake, or just bask in the sauna.

For more information on getting here and what you'll see when you arrive, click the links at the top of this page.

© Deep Creek Inn. All rights reserved. Questions or comments: mail@deepcreek.com

Modify the Directions Page

✔ *This page contains driving directions to the Deep Creek Inn. You will add a map and text to the page. Fortunately you have HTML text you can use for the driving directions.*

1. Activate the directions.html page. Change the Web site name in the top table cell to **DEEP CREEK INN**.

2. Change the HOME link to open index.html.

3. Change the *Page Name Here* placeholder text to *Getting Here*. Change the *Product Name* placeholder to *Driving Directions*.

4. Delete the placeholder paragraph below the second heading.

5. Open the ⊙ driving.html file from the Capstone Data folder in Dreamweaver. Copy the driving directions (not the heading) and paste the text on the directions.html page.

6. Delete the PayPal button placeholder.

7. Delete the Large Product Image placeholder and insert the ⊙ map.gif image from the Capstone Data folder. Save the image in your images folder and supply the alternate text *Map to Deep Creek*.

   ✔ *Click in the Driving Directions cell if necessary to readjust spacing on the page after inserting the image.*

8. Save your changes and preview the page. It should look similar to Illustration B.

Create the Things to See Page

✔ *On this page, you will use the Swap Image behavior to create an interactive page on which visitors can click a link to see an image.*

1. Save the directions.html page as naturalwonders.html. Change the page title to *Things to See*.

2. Change the main heading to *The Deep Creek Environment* and the subheading to *Natural Wonders*.

3. Delete the driving directions and insert the following text. The last five lines should be created with line breaks rather than new paragraphs.

Deep Creek Inn is located in an area of unique natural beauty. A system of trails and roads links three communities—lakeshore, wetland, and forest—to give visitors breathtaking views of unspoiled wildlife.

Click a link to see our natural wonders.

Flyers

Flowers

Wildlife

Gorges

Lake

4. Check spelling on the page.

5. Delete the map and insert the ⊙ butterfly.psd image from the Capstone Data folder. On the File tab of the Image Preview dialog box, change the width of the image to 250 pixels. (The height will change automatically.) Save the image in your images folder and supply the alternate text *Natural wonders*.

6. Name the image *butterfly*.

7. Use the Files panel to copy these files from the Capstone Data folder to your site's images folder: ⊙ flower.jpg, ⊙ deer.jpg, ⊙ gorge.jpg, and ⊙ lake.jpg.

8. Set up the five single-word lines of text as dummy links using the javascript:; entry in the Link box.

Illustration B

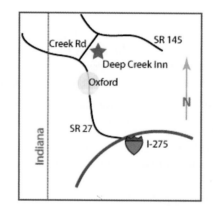

9. Use this procedure to set up the Swap Image behavior:

- Click the *Flyers* link, choose the Swap Image behavior, select image "butterfly" in the top box of the dialog box, and set the source to butterfly.jpg. Deselect the Restore images onMouseOut checkbox, and change the event to onClick.

- Click the *Flowers* link, choose the Swap Image behavior, select image "butterfly" in the top box of the dialog box, and set the source to flower.jpg. Deselect the Restore images onMouseOut checkbox, and change the event to onClick.

- Follow the procedure above to swap images for Wildlife (deer.jpg), Gorges (gorge.jpg), and Lake (lake.jpg), choosing the image "butterfly" each time as the image to replace.

✔ *Be sure to deselect the Restore image checkbox each time, or you will see the butterfly image each time you move off a link.*

10. Save your changes and preview the page in the browser to test your behaviors. Your page should look similar to Illustration C.

Illustration C

DEEP CREEK INN

HOME

The Deep Creek Environment
Natural Wonders

Deep Creek Inn is located in an area of unique natural beauty. A system of trails and roads link three communities—lakeshore, wetland, and forest—to give visitors breathtaking views of unspoiled wildlife.

Click a link to see our natural wonders.

Flyers

Flowers
Wildlife

Gorges

Lake

Modify the Reservations Page

✔ *You will add a reservation request form to this page to allow visitors to request information on availability.*

1. Open reservations.html.
2. Change the placeholder heading to *Reservation Request*.
3. Type the following text in place of the placeholder text:

   To request information on reservations at the Deep Creek Inn, fill out the following form. We will contact you within 24 hours. For information on room types, click here.

4. Insert a form on the page and then add the form fields shown in the following illustration. Use this information to create the fields:

   - You may use either Dreamweaver form fields or Spry form fields.
   - Make sure each field has a name and a label.
   - Select appropriate character widths for fields.
   - For the *Number of rooms* field, offer a selection of 1, 2, or 3.
   - For the *Number of adults* field, offer a selection of 1, 2, or 3.
   - For the *Number of children* field, offer a selection of 0, 1, 2, or 3.

Create the form

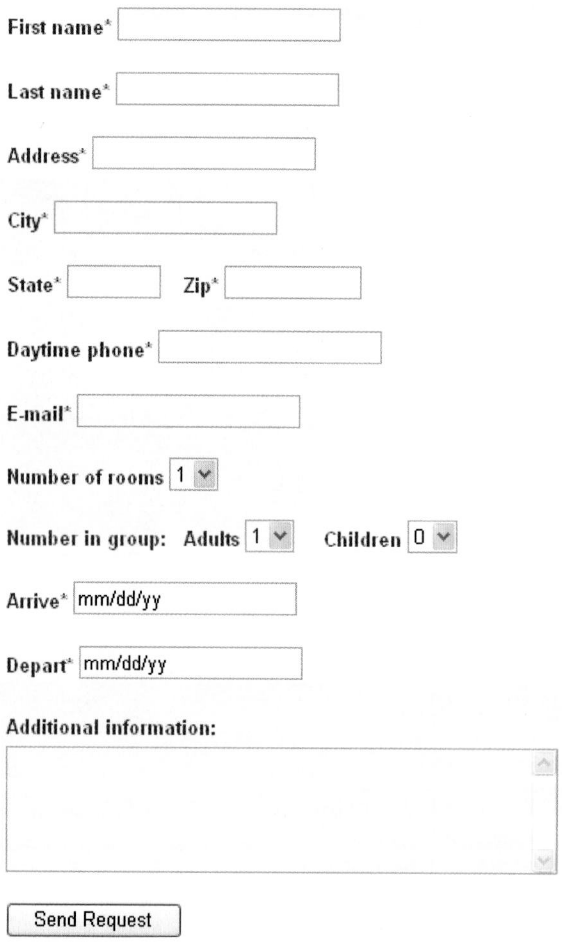

First name* [   ]

Last name* [   ]

Address* [   ]

City* [   ]

State* [   ]   Zip* [   ]

Daytime phone* [   ]

E-mail* [   ]

Number of rooms [1 ▾]

Number in group: Adults [1 ▾]   Children [0 ▾]

Arrive* [mm/dd/yy   ]

Depart* [mm/dd/yy   ]

Additional information:

[   ]

[Send Request]

5. The text is quite small and may be difficult to read. Create a new CSS rule named .formtext that you add to the current style sheet and specify Arial as the font, small font size, and bold weight.

6. Apply the new style to the form labels.

7. Validate the form fields using Spry validation or behaviors.

8. Click in the table cell furthest to the right of the form. (The insertion point will display about halfway down the cell.)

9. Set vertical alignment in this cell to Top.

10. Insert in this cell the ⊙**deepanimation.swf** file from the Capstone Data folder. Save the movie in your images folder and title it *Deep Creek movie*.

11. Change the width of the Flash placeholder to 200, deselect the Loop option, then play the movie in Dreamweaver.

12. Save your changes and preview the page in the browser. The top of the page should look similar to Illustration D after the movie plays. Test the form by filling out all fields.

Illustration D

DEEP CREEK INN

HOME

Reservation Request

To request information on reservations at the Deep Creek Inn, fill out the following form.

We will contact you within 24 hours. For information on room types, click here.

First name*

Last name*

Address*

City*

State* Zip*

Daytime phone*

E-mail*

Number of rooms 1

Number in group: Adults 1   Children 0

Arrive* mm/dd/yy

Seasonal Packages
Available

Open All Year

Create the Rates Page

✔ *The final page you will create will include a table that gives rates of different types of inn rooms according to season.*

1. Create a new page from the template and save it as **rates.html** with the page title *Room Rates*.

   ✔ *If you find the page will not accept a new page title, open the template page and in Code view insert the following code in the header area above the first meta tag:*

   <!— TemplateBeginEditable name="doctitle" —><title></title><!— TemplateEndEditable —>

   Then save the template.

2. Change the *HOME* link text to *RESERVATIONS* and make the link to the **reservations.html** page.

3. Change the page heading placeholder to *Rates by Room Type*.

4. Delete the placeholder text and insert the following paragraph:

   The Deep Creek Inn offers four types of rooms and cottages. Rates vary according to season, as shown below.

5. Insert the following table below the paragraph.

	Winter	Spring	Summer	Fall
Queen lake view	$105	$115	$125	$130
Queen court view	$99	$109	$119	$125
King court view	$120	$125	$130	$135
King suite	$135	$145	$160	$145
Cottage/week	$600	$725	$750	$725

6. Create a new CSS style for table text and save it in the current style sheet. Apply the new style to all table text.

7. Format the table as desired with borders and cell colors. You can use colors from the current site or colors that reflect the seasons to make it easy to understand the rate structure.

8. Insert an AP div on the page and position it in the empty column to the left of the table. Add padding on all sides of the AP div.

9. Name the AP div *info* and resize it to fit in the column. Add a background color of your choice and insert the following text:

   All Deep Creek Inn rooms are nonsmoking and include coffee facilities and refrigerators.

10. Apply one of the text styles from the current style sheet to the text, such as .sidebarText.

11. Hide the info AP div. Select the rate table using the <table> tag in the tag selector and attach the Show-Hide Elements behavior to show the info AP div onMouseOver. Attach the Show-Hide Elements behavior to the info AP div to hide the AP div onMouseOut.

12. Save your changes and preview the page in the browser. It should look similar to Illustration E.

13. Open the **reservations.html** page if necessary and select the words *click here* at the end of the first paragraph. Create a link to **rates.html**.

14. Save and close all pages except the **index.html** page.

Illustration E

DEEP CREEK INN

RESERVATIONS

Rates by Room Type

The Deep Creek Inn offers four types of rooms and cottages. Rates vary according to season, as shown below.

	Winter	Spring	Summer	Fall
Queen lake view	$105	$115	$125	$130
Queen court view	$99	$109	$119	$125
King court view	$120	$125	$130	$135
King suite	$135	$145	$160	$145
Cottage/week	$600	$725	$750	$725

All Deep Creek Inn rooms are nonsmoking and include coffee facilities and refrigerators.

Check and Publish the Site

1. Run reports to check for missing Alt tags and untitled documents.

2. Check links sitewide.

3. Expand the Files panel and display the site map. Notice that you still have a javascript:; link from the index.html page.

4. On the index.html page, create the link from *THINGS TO SEE* to naturalwonders.html.

5. Choose to check compatibility for Internet Explorer 6.0 and any other browser of your choice. Open each page and run the browser compatibility check for the page. You should not find any errors.

6. Validate the entire site and read descriptions of any problems flagged.

7. Set up a remote site to put the files on, using information your instructor supplies.

8. Put all files on the site.

9. Navigate to the location where you put the files and view each page, testing all links.

10. Close the browser and any open files, and exit Dreamweaver.

Appendix A: Dreamweaver Preferences

Use the Preferences Dialog Box

- As you become familiar with Dreamweaver features, you can consider changing default configurations to make the program more responsive to your particular needs.

- You change default settings in the Preferences dialog box. Display this dialog box using the Edit>Preferences command on the menu bar, or use the Ctrl + U keystroke combination as a shortcut.

- The Preferences dialog box (see the following illustration) contains a list of categories at the left of the dialog box. Settings for the selected category display in the main portion of the dialog box. These categories are discussed in detail in the following sections.

General

- The General category provides settings for startup and general editing operations. Concentrate on the following items:

  - By default, Dreamweaver opens with the Welcome Screen page. If you prefer not to see the Welcome Screen options, clear the *Show Welcome Screen* checkbox.

Dreamweaver CS3 Preferences dialog box

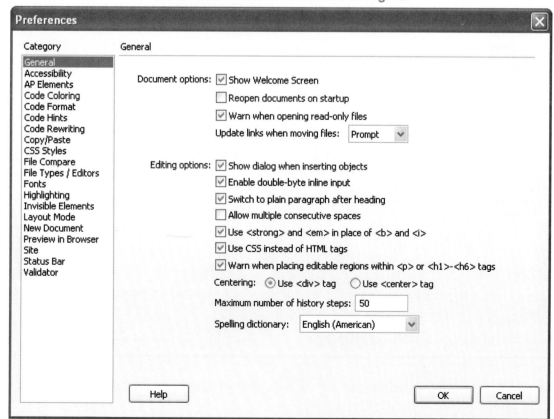

- By default, Dreamweaver prompts you to update links when you move or rename a file. You can change this preference to have Dreamweaver always update links or never update links automatically.

- By default, Dreamweaver will use CSS for formatting rather than HTML tags. If you prefer to work in HTML, clear the *Use CSS instead of HTML tags* checkbox.

- If you routinely work with large, complex Web sites, consider increasing the maximum number of History steps. Remember, you can use the History panel to repeat steps on any page, so the more steps you track, the less work you might need to do to copy text and formatting.

Accessibility

- This category allows you to decide whether you want Dreamweaver to prompt you for accessibility information for forms, frames, media objects, and images. You have worked with these accessibility attributes throughout this course.

- These options are selected by default. If you decide you do not need to supply accessibility attributes for your site, clear some or all of these checkboxes.

AP Elements

- Use the AP Elements category (see the following illustration) to make a number of changes to default AP element properties. You can specify default visibility settings and width, height, background color, and background image settings.

- If you always want to create a nested AP div when you draw an AP div within another AP div, select the *Nest when created within an AP div* checkbox. If you want to leave your options open, clear this checkbox. You can hold down the Alt key while drawing an AP div to nest it within an existing AP div.

- The Netscape 4 browser has a known bug that causes AP elements to lose their positioning if a visitor resizes the browser window. You can choose to add a fix for this bug if you are targeting your site for older Netscape browsers.

AP Elements category

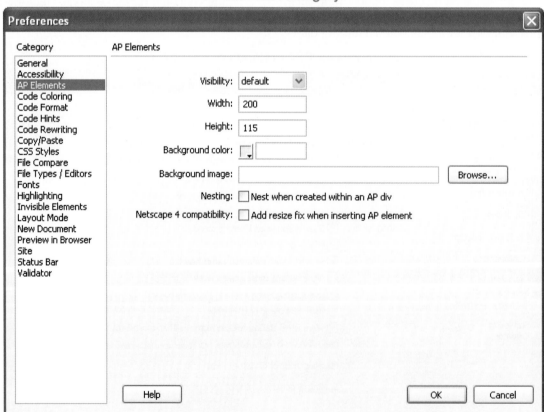

Code Coloring

- The Code Coloring category allows you to select default colors for various features such as text, tags, and so on in the different types of documents that Dreamweaver creates. For example, you can select HTML as the document type and click the [Edit Coloring Scheme] button. In the Edit Coloring Scheme dialog box, you can apply different colors to the various kinds of tags and attributes that appear in HTML pages. Besides changing background, text, and tag colors, you can select colors for script objects such as keywords and strings.

Code Format

- Use the Code Format category (see the following illustration) to change default HTML settings such as items to indent in displayed code.

- To control the indention of code, use the Indent setting. The default setting is two spaces. You can also specify that the indent use tabs.

- If you prefer to see HTML tags and attributes in all capital letters when viewing a page's code, you can select uppercase in the Default tag case and Default attribute case lists.

  ✔ *To make it easy to differentiate between tags and attributes, you may find it helpful to use different case options for the two items.*

Code Format category

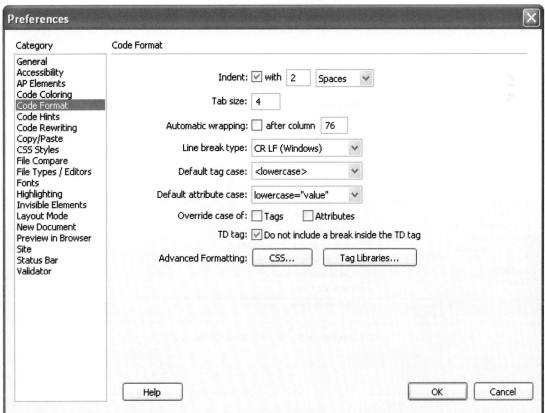

Code Hints

- The Code Hints category allows you to insert tag names, attributes, and values as you enter code in Code view (see the following illustration).

- You can choose how close tags display. The default is to complete the open tag after you type </, but you can also choose to display the close tag immediately after completing the opening tag's final wicket, or choose never to display a close tag automatically.

- The *Enable code hints* checkbox is selected by default. You can adjust the Delay slider control to control when the hint menu appears. You can also select and deselect the kinds of code hint menus you want to see.

- More advanced Web page designers can add or remove tags and attributes by clicking *Tag library editor* to open the Tag Library Editor dialog box.

Code Rewriting

- If you plan to use previously created or imported documents coded in HTML, ColdFusion, and the like in your site, take time to set up the Code Rewriting category. Settings in this category will clean up nested or overlapped tags, insert proper quotation marks or closing brackets, and protect the layout.

Code Hints category

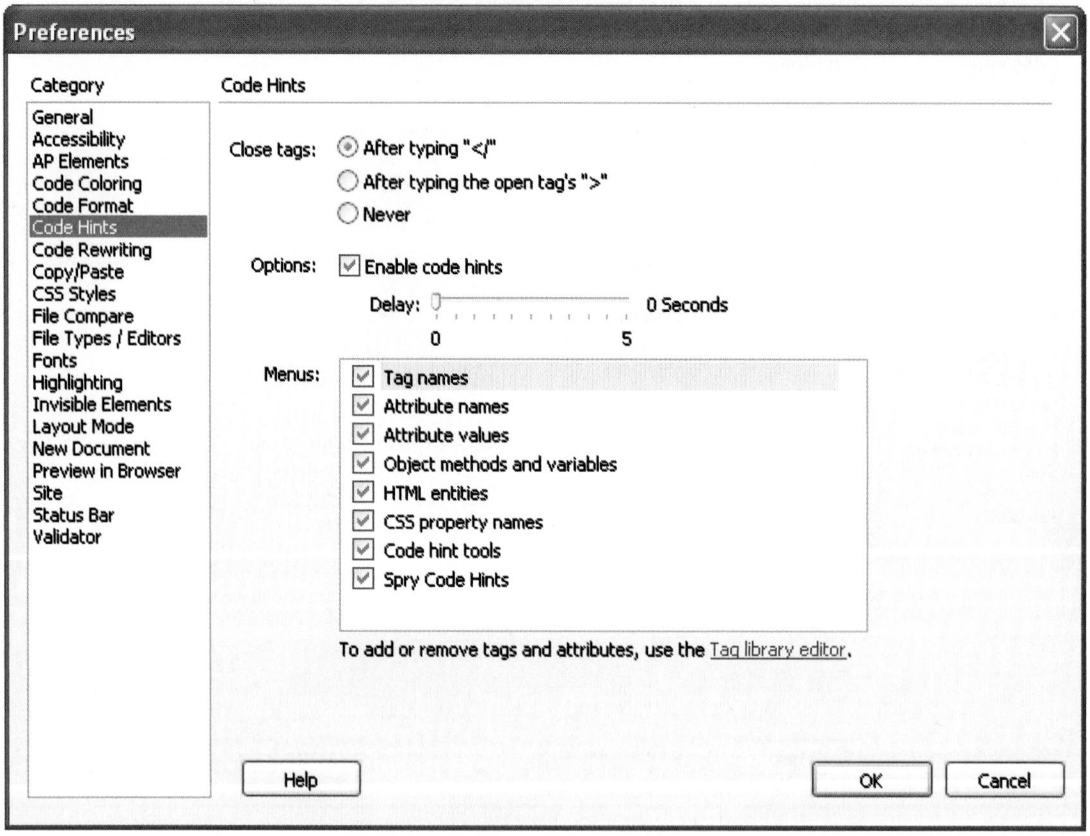

- The Code Rewriting options are applied when Dreamweaver opens the document. It does not rewrite when you actually create or work with a Web page after it has opened.

- If you're comfortable coding in HTML or other kinds of Web page coding, you may wish to deselect some of the options in this category. Dreamweaver automatically writes associated code based on internal features and will modify them only if you indicate these choices in the Code Rewriting category.

Copy/Paste

- Use the Copy/Paste category options to control how material from other applications pastes into Dreamweaver. As shown in the following illustration, you can paste material as text only, text with structure, text with structure plus basic formatting, and text with structure plus full formatting.

- If you have selected a paste option other than Text only, you can choose whether to retain the text's line breaks. If you have selected the *Text with structure* or *Text with structure plus basic formatting* option to paste Word text, you can choose to eliminate extra space between paragraphs.

Copy/Paste category

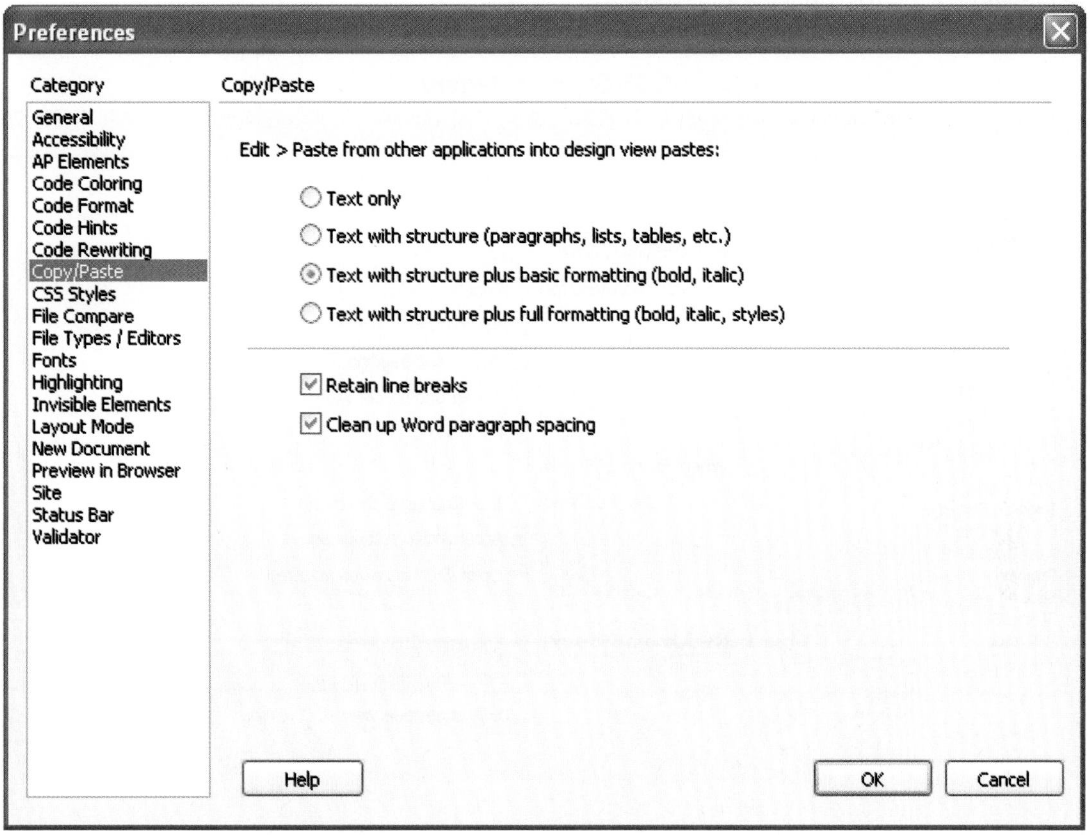

Preferences

Category

Copy/Paste

General
Accessibility
AP Elements
Code Coloring
Code Format
Code Hints
Code Rewriting
Copy/Paste
CSS Styles
File Compare
File Types / Editors
Fonts
Highlighting
Invisible Elements
Layout Mode
New Document
Preview in Browser
Site
Status Bar
Validator

Edit > Paste from other applications into design view pastes:

○ Text only

○ Text with structure (paragraphs, lists, tables, etc.)

◉ Text with structure plus basic formatting (bold, italic)

○ Text with structure plus full formatting (bold, italic, styles)

☑ Retain line breaks

☑ Clean up Word paragraph spacing

Help   OK   Cancel

CSS Styles

- CSS (cascading style sheets) information can be written in a shorthand form that some people prefer. Older browsers, however, cannot interpret CSS shorthand correctly.

- By default, Dreamweaver does not use this shorthand notation to write CSS code. If you wish to use shorthand, you can specify when to use shorthand in the CSS Styles category (see the following illustration). You may also need to adjust these settings if you are using code from another source that contains CSS shorthand.

- You can also specify where to edit a CSS style that you double-click in the CSS panel: in a CSS dialog box, in the panel's Properties pane, or in Code view.

File Compare

- Use the File Compare category to specify an application designed to compare files. You use this feature when determining which files to publish to a remote site. The file comparison application can help you determine the most recent file.

- Dreamweaver installs a comparison tool automatically, but you can specify a different application if desired. Use the Browse... button to navigate to the location of the application you wish to use.

CSS Styles category

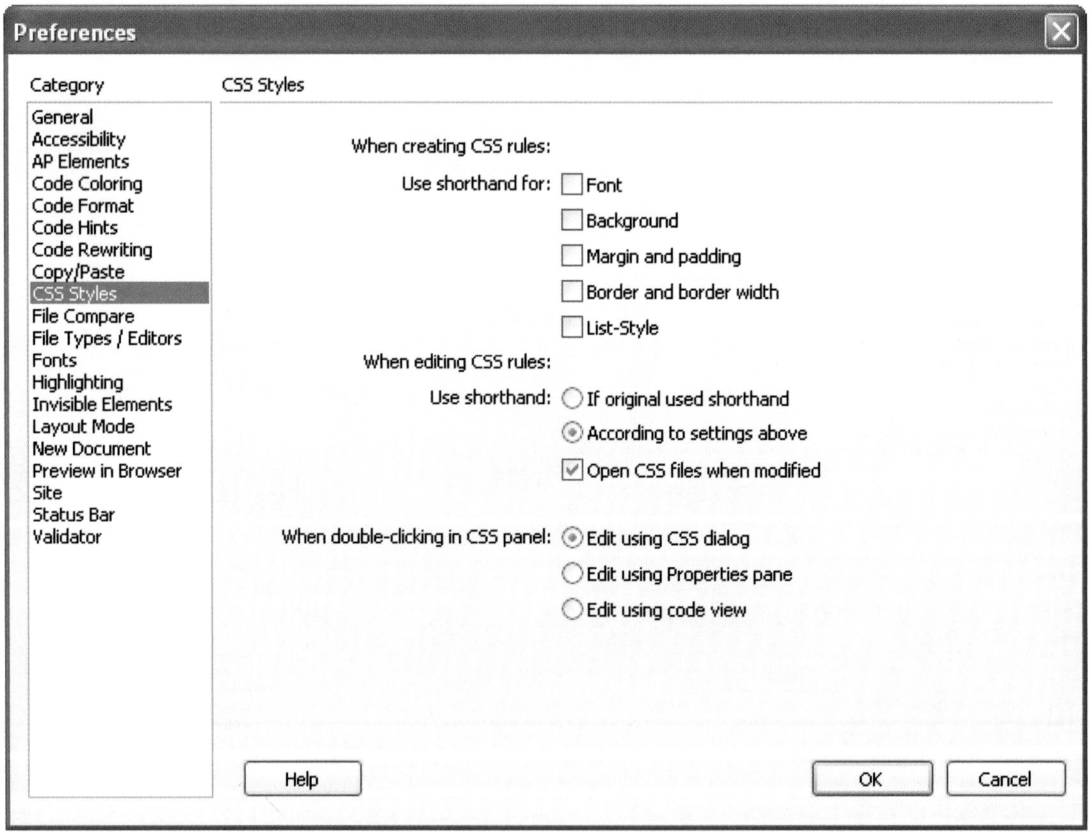

File Types / Editors

■ You can specify different kinds of code editors to supplement Dreamweaver by associating a file type with another code editor or program.

■ Similarly, you can change the association of a file type such as .gif, .jpg, and the like with another external program in which they can be edited (see the illustration below).

File Types / Editors category

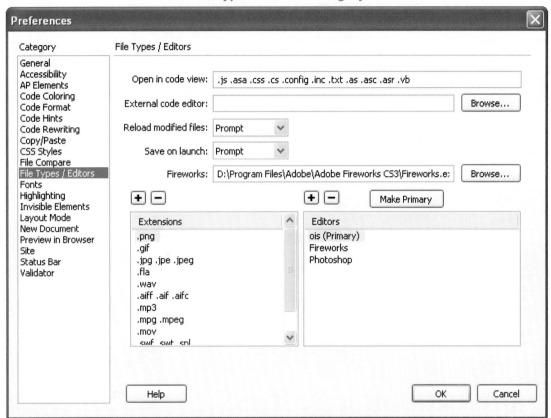

Fonts

- Use the Fonts category (see the following illustration) to select default fonts and sizes for Web pages and HTML code. Settings selected in this category will be applied to each new document you create.

- This category allows you to work in the font and size you prefer while maintaining the default encoding that will display in the browser.

- For example, you can choose a sans serif font such as Arial as the default proportional font and create your Web pages using this font. When the page is displayed in the browser, however, the browser will use Western European, which is a serif font similar to Times New Roman.

Fonts category

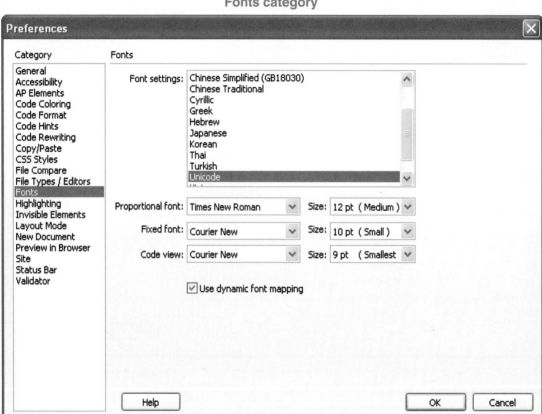

Highlighting

- Use the Highlighting category (see the following illustration) to select colors used to highlight editable and noneditable regions in templates and library items. You can also select a highlight color for third-party tags supplied by external editors.

Highlighting category

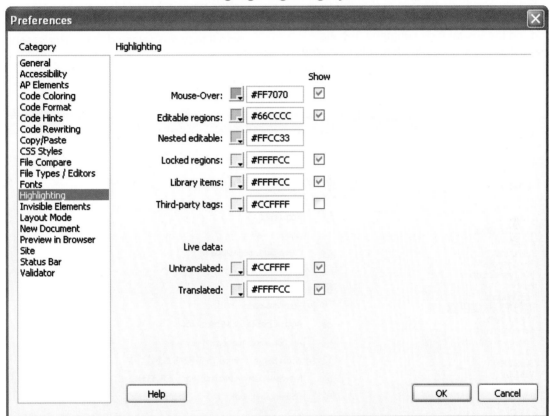

Invisible Elements

- The Invisible Elements category (see the following illustration) works in conjunction with the View>Visual Aids>Invisible Elements menu command (or the 👁 button on the Document toolbar) to display nontext items on your Web pages. Remember, for example, that a named anchor is designated on a page by an anchor marker.

- When the Invisible Elements command is selected (checked) on the Visual Aids submenu, the elements selected in the Invisible Elements category display on your page. If you do not want to see one or more of these elements on your page, deselect their checkboxes in the Invisible Elements category.

- For example, you might deselect the *Form delimiter* checkbox to prevent the red dashed form delimiter from appearing on your page.

- If the Invisible Elements command is *not* selected on the View>Visual Aids submenu, none of the items in the Invisible Elements category will display, even if they are selected in the Preferences dialog box.

Invisible Elements category

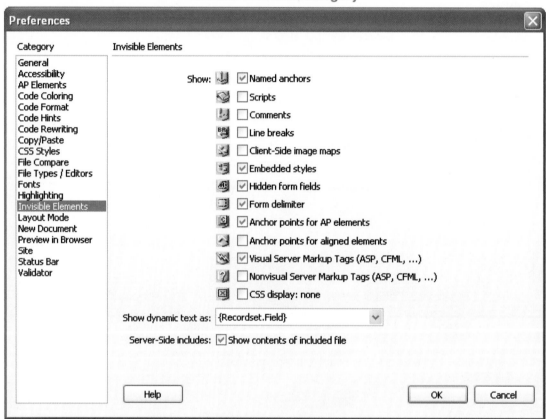

Layout Mode

- The Layout Mode category (see the illustration below) allows you to specify settings for Layout mode. You can specify whether a spacer image is used to autostretch tables and if so, the name and location of the spacer image.

- You can also select the colors used for layout table and layout cell outlines (the outlines that display when a table or cell is selected or highlighted) and the background color of the layout table.

Layout Mode category

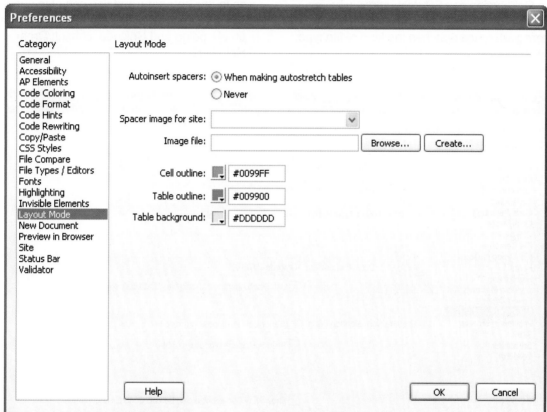

New Document

- The New Document category allows you to change which document type Dreamweaver opens as a default document for a site (see the following illustration). The default option is an HTML document with the .html extension.

- If most pages in your site are a different file type such as ColdFusion or ASP documents, you can reset your document preferences so that your new document preference matches the kind of file type.

- Note that the default new document type is XHTML 1.0 Transitional, the most current version of HTML. You can choose from a number of other document types, however, including HTML 4.0 Strict and XHTML Mobile 1.0.

- If you need to change default encoding, you can do so in this category, and you can also specify a Unicode normalization option. For more information on encoding and Unicode, consult Dreamweaver's Help files.

New Document category

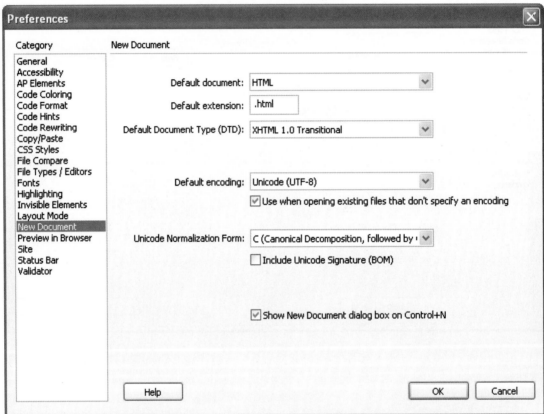

Preview in Browser

▪ To make it simple to preview your pages in one or more browsers, set up browsers in the Preview in Browser category (see the following illustration). Your default browser will be selected by default and will have the F12 shortcut key.

▪ Use the ➕ button to open the Add Browser dialog box, in which you can specify the name and location of another browser. (You will find the executable files for browsers in the Program Files folder on your hard drive.) You designate this (and subsequent browsers) as secondary browsers that use other keystroke shortcuts to start.

Preview in Browser category

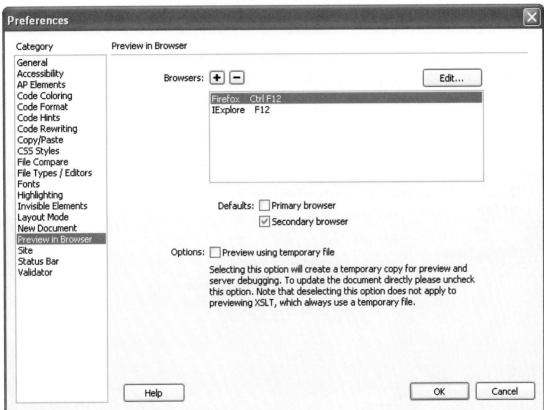

Site

■ The Site category (see the following illustration) lets you manage the Files panel window in its expanded form as well as FTP settings for a Web site. (Some settings will also apply to the Files panel in its collapsed form.) You can choose where to display local files, for example, and activate options to prompt for dependent files.

■ If you use a firewall to safeguard your server, you can supply the firewall host name and port in this category.

■ If you use another kind of remote server setting, such as WebDAV, you can still use the FTP connection settings to control how long a connection is maintained, and so on.

Site category

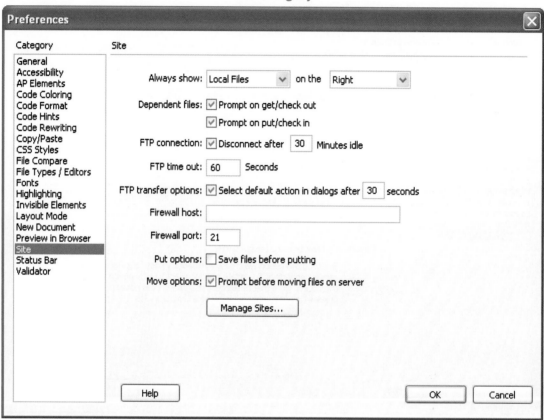

Status Bar

- Use the Status Bar category (see the following illustration below) to customize status bar elements.

- The Document window status bar contains a pop-up menu (see the illustration at right) that allows you to choose a specific size at which to display the Document window, such as 592 pixels wide or 600 pixels wide by 300 pixels high. This list will be grayed out if the Document window is already maximized.

- You can edit the default window sizes or add new sizes of your own that will display on the pop-up menu.

Status bar window size menu

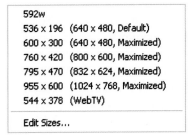

- One setting on the status bar you should always pay attention to is the download time for the current page. The connection speed used to calculate the download time is selected in the Status Bar category (56.0, by default).

- You can choose a new default connection speed that more closely reflects the hardware capabilities of your intended audience. If your Web site will be published on a corporate intranet, for example, you can choose 1500.

Status Bar category

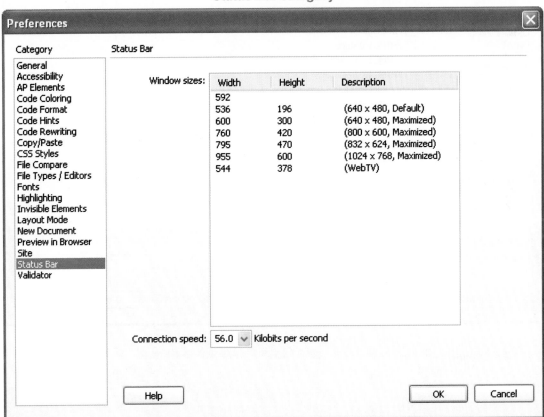

Validator

Validator Options dialog box

- The Validator category (see the illustration below) allows you to control the types of code tags that the Validator reports against in the Validation panel of the Results panel group when running its reports.

- Click the ⬚ Options... button to choose the kinds of errors that you want reported (see the illustration at right).

- See the discussion of the Validator in Exercise 54 and Dreamweaver Help for more information about using Validator preferences.

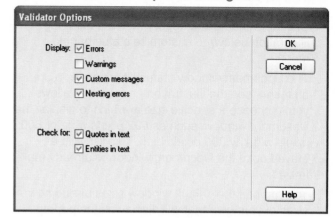

Validator Options dialog box

Validator category

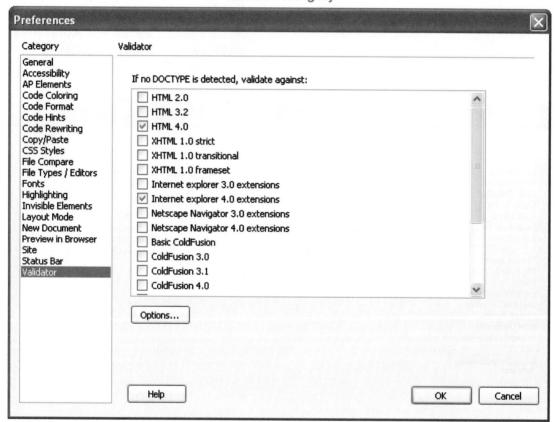

Index

SINGLE PC LICENSE AGREEMENT AND LIMITED WARRANTY

READ THIS LICENSE CAREFULLY BEFORE OPENING THIS PACKAGE. BY OPENING THIS PACKAGE, YOU ARE AGREEING TO THE TERMS AND CONDITIONS OF THIS LICENSE. IF YOU DO NOT AGREE, DO NOT OPEN THE PACKAGE. PROMPTLY RETURN THE UNOPENED PACKAGE AND ALL ACCOMPANYING ITEMS TO THE PLACE YOU OBTAINED THEM. THESE TERMS APPLY TO ALL LICENSED SOFTWARE ON THE DISK EXCEPT THAT THE TERMS FOR USE OF ANY SHAREWARE OR FREEWARE ON THE DISKETTES ARE AS SET FORTH IN THE ELECTRONIC LICENSE LOCATED ON THE DISK:

1. GRANT OF LICENSE and OWNERSHIP: The enclosed computer programs and data ("Software") are licensed, not sold, to you by Pearson Education, Inc. ("We" or the "Company") and in consideration of your purchase or adoption of the accompanying Company textbooks and/or other materials, and your agreement to these terms. We reserve any rights not granted to you. You own only the disk(s) but we and/or our licensors own the Software itself. This license allows you to use and display your copy of the Software on a single computer (i.e., with a single CPU) at a single location for academic use only, so long as you comply with the terms of this Agreement.

2. RESTRICTIONS: You may not transfer or distribute the Software or documentation to anyone else. Except for backup, you may not copy the documentation or the Software. You may not network the Software or otherwise use it on more than one computer or computer terminal at the same time. You may not reverse engineer, disassemble, decompile, modify, adapt, translate, or create derivative works based on the Software or the Documentation. You may be held legally responsible for any copying or copyright infringement which is caused by your failure to abide by the terms of these restrictions.

3. TERMINATION: This license is effective until terminated. This license will terminate automatically without notice from the Company if you fail to comply with any provisions or limitations of this license. Upon termination, you shall destroy the Documentation and all copies of the Software. All provisions of this Agreement as to limitation and disclaimer of warranties, limitation of liability, remedies or damages, and our ownership rights shall survive termination.

4. LIMITED WARRANTY AND DISCLAIMER OF WARRANTY: Company warrants that for a period of 60 days from the date you purchase this SOFTWARE (or purchase or adopt the accompanying textbook), the Software, when properly installed and used in accordance with the Documentation, will operate in substantial conformity with the description of the Software set forth in the Documentation, and that for a period of 30 days the disk(s) on which the Software is delivered shall be free from defects in materials and workmanship under normal use. The Company does not warrant that the Software will meet your requirements or that the operation of the Software will be uninterrupted or error-free. Your only remedy and the Company's only obligation under these limited warranties is, at the Company's option, return of the disk for a refund of any amounts paid for it by you or replacement of the disk. THIS LIMITED WARRANTY IS THE ONLY WARRANTY PROVIDED BY THE COMPANY AND ITS LICENSORS, AND THE COMPANY AND ITS LICENSORS DISCLAIM ALL OTHER WARRANTIES, EXPRESS OR IMPLIED, INCLUDING WITHOUT LIMITATION, THE IMPLIED WARRANTIES OF MERCHANTABILITY AND FITNESS FOR A PARTICULAR PURPOSE. THE COMPANY DOES NOT WARRANT, GUARANTEE OR MAKE ANY REPRESENTATION REGARDING THE ACCURACY, RELIABILITY, CURRENTNESS, USE, OR RESULTS OF USE, OF THE SOFTWARE.

5. LIMITATION OF REMEDIES AND DAMAGES: IN NO EVENT, SHALL THE COMPANY OR ITS EMPLOYEES, AGENTS, LICENSORS, OR CONTRACTORS BE LIABLE FOR ANY INCIDENTAL, INDIRECT, SPECIAL, OR CONSEQUENTIAL DAMAGES ARISING OUT OF OR IN CONNECTION WITH THIS LICENSE OR THE SOFTWARE, INCLUDING FOR LOSS OF USE, LOSS OF DATA, LOSS OF INCOME OR PROFIT, OR OTHER LOSSES, SUSTAINED AS A RESULT OF INJURY TO ANY PERSON, OR LOSS OF OR DAMAGE TO PROPERTY, OR CLAIMS OF THIRD PARTIES, EVEN IF THE COMPANY OR AN AUTHORIZED REPRESENTATIVE OF THE COMPANY HAS BEEN ADVISED OF THE POSSIBILITY OF SUCH DAMAGES. IN NO EVENT SHALL THE LIABILITY OF THE COMPANY FOR DAMAGES WITH RESPECT TO THE SOFTWARE EXCEED THE AMOUNTS ACTUALLY PAID BY YOU, IF ANY, FOR THE SOFTWARE OR THE ACCOMPANYING TEXTBOOK. BECAUSE SOME JURISDICTIONS DO NOT ALLOW THE LIMITATION OF LIABILITY IN CERTAIN CIRCUMSTANCES, THE ABOVE LIMITATIONS MAY NOT ALWAYS APPLY TO YOU.

6. GENERAL: THIS AGREEMENT SHALL BE CONSTRUED IN ACCORDANCE WITH THE LAWS OF THE UNITED STATES OF AMERICA AND THE STATE OF NEW YORK, APPLICABLE TO CONTRACTS MADE IN NEW YORK, AND SHALL BENEFIT THE COMPANY, ITS AFFILIATES AND ASSIGNEES. HIS AGREEMENT IS THE COMPLETE AND EXCLUSIVE STATEMENT OF THE AGREEMENT BETWEEN YOU AND THE COMPANY AND SUPERSEDES ALL PROPOSALS OR PRIOR AGREEMENTS, ORAL, OR WRITTEN, AND ANY OTHER COMMUNICATIONS BETWEEN YOU AND THE COMPANY OR ANY REPRESENTATIVE OF THE COMPANY RELATING TO THE SUBJECT MATTER OF THIS AGREEMENT. If you are a U.S. Government user, this Software is licensed with "restricted rights" as set forth in subparagraphs (a)-(d) of the Commercial Computer-Restricted Rights clause at FAR 52.227-19 or in subparagraphs (c)(1)(ii) of the Rights in Technical Data and Computer Software clause at DFARS 252.227-7013, and similar clauses, as applicable.